ASHRAE GreenGuide

The Design, Construction, and Operation of Sustainable Buildings

This publication was developed under the auspices of TC 2.8, Building Environmental Impacts and Sustainability. TC 2.8 is concerned with the impacts of buildings on the local, regional, and global environment; means for identifying and reducing these impacts; and enhancing ASHRAE member awareness of the impacts.

John M. Swift, Jr., RE, CEM, LEED, is coeditor of the *ASHRAE GreenGuide, Third Edition*, and is a principal at Cannon Design in Boston. He serves as chair of the proposed ASHRAE Standard for Water Efficiency in Buildings and is vice-chair of ASHRAE Technical Committee 2.8. Mr. Swift recently served on Massachusetts Governor Patrick's Zero Net Energy Buildings Task Force and was an original contributor to the development of the U.S. Environmental Protection Agency's Labs 21 Environmental Performance Criteria guidelines.

Tom Lawrence, PhD, PE, LEED-AP, is also coeditor of the *ASHRAE GreenGuide, Third Edition*, and is a public service associate with the University of Georgia with 30 years of experience in engineering and related fields. He is chair of ASHRAE Technical Committee 2.8 and is a member of the committee that wrote *ANSI/ASHRAE/USGBC/IES Standard 189.1-2009, Standard for the Design of High-Performance Green Buildings*. Dr. Lawrence is also a member of ASHRAE's Handbook and Technical Activities Committees. As an ASHRAE Distinguished Lecturer, he gives seminars on green building design at venues around the world.

Amelia Pavlik, assistant editor in ASHRAE Special Publications, served as staff editor for the *ASHRAE GreenGuide, Third Edition*.

ASHRAE STAFF

SPECIAL PUBLICATIONS
Mark S. Owen
*Editor/Group Manager
of Handbook and
Special Publications*
Cindy Sheffield Michaels
Managing Editor
James Madison Walker
Associate Editor
Amelia Pavlik
Assistant Editor
Elisabeth Parrish
Assistant Editor
Michshell Phillips
Editorial Coordinator

PUBLISHING SERVICES
David Soltis
*Group Manager
of Publishing Services
and Electronic Communications*
Tracy Becker
Graphic Applications Specialist
Jayne Jackson
Publication Traffic Administrator
PUBLISHER
W. Stephen Comstock

Updates/errata for this publication will be posted on the ASHRAE Web site at www.ashrae.org/publicationupdates.

ASHRAE GreenGuide

The Design, Construction, and Operation of Sustainable Buildings

Third Edition

American Society of Heating, Refrigerating and Air-Conditioning Engineers, Inc.

ISBN 978-1-933742-85-4

Cover design by Tracy Becker

Library of Congress Cataloging-in-Publication Data

ASHRAE greenguide : the design, construction, and operation of sustainable buildings. -- 3rd ed.

p. cm.

Includes bibliographical references and index.

Summary: "The third edition of the ASHRAE GreenGuide features information for anyone charged with designing a sustainable building on a variety of
green-design issues that should be considered when tasked with this type of
project"-- Provided by publisher.

ISBN 978-1-933742-85-4 (hardcover)

1. Sustainable buildings--Design and construction. 2. Sustainable architecture. 3. Buildings--Environmental engineering. 4. Sustainable construction.
I. American Society of Heating, Refrigerating and Air-Conditioning Engineers.

TH880.A83 2010

720'.47--dc22

2010038430

Tomorrow's Child

Without a name, an unseen face,
And knowing not the time or place,
Tomorrow's Child, though yet unborn,
I saw you first last Tuesday morn.
A wise friend introduced us two,
And through his shining point of view
I saw a day, which you would see,
A day for you, and not for me.
Knowing you has changed my thinking,
Never having had an inkling
That perhaps the things I do
Might someday threaten you.
Tomorrow's Child, my daughter-son,
I'm afraid I've just begun
To think of you and of your good,
Though always having known I should.
Begin I will to weigh the cost
Of what I squander, what is lost,
If ever I forget that you
Will someday come to live here too.

by Glenn Thomas, ©1996

Reprinted from
*Mid-Course Correction:
Toward a
Sustainable Enterprise:
The Interface Model*
by Ray Anderson.
Chelsea Green
Publishing Company, 1999.

CONTENTS

SECTION I: BASICS

SECTION 2: THE DESIGN PROCESS

SECTION 3: POSTDESIGN—
CONSTRUCTION AND BEYOND

Add: *• Greenroofs*

GREENTIPS

Building-Type GreenTips

DIGGING DEEPER SIDEBARS

FOREWORD
by William Coad

Mechanical engineering has been defined as "the applied science of energy conversion." ASHRAE is the preeminent technical society that represents engineers practicing in the fields of heating, refrigeration, and air conditioning—the technology that utilizes approximately one-third of the global nonrenewable energy consumed annually.

ASHRAE membership has actively pursued more effective means of utilizing these precious nonrenewable resources for many decades from the standpoints of source availability, efficiency of utilization, and technology of substituting with renewable sources. One significant publication in *ASHRAE Transactions* is a paper authored in 1951 by G.W. Gleason, Dean of Engineering at Oregon State University, titled "Energy—Choose it Wisely Today for Safety Tomorrow." The flip side of the energy coin is the environment and, again, ASHRAE has historically dealt with the impact that the practice of the HVAC&R sciences have had upon both the indoor and the global environment.

However, the engineering community, to a great extent, serves the needs and desires of accepted economic norms and the consuming public, a large majority of whom have not embraced the energy/environmental ethic. As a result, much of the technology in energy effectiveness and environmental sensitivity that ASHRAE members have developed over this past century has had limited impact upon society.

In 1975, when ASHRAE published *ASHRAE Standard 90-75, Energy Conservation in New Building Design* (ASHRAE 1975), that standard served as our initial outreach effort to develop an awareness of the energy ethic and to extend our capabilities throughout society as a whole. Since that time, updated revisions of Standard 90 have moved the science ahead. In 1993, the chapter on "Energy Resources" was added to the 1993 *ASHRAE Handbook—Fundamentals*. In 2002, ASHRAE entered into a partnering agreement with the U.S. Green Building Council, and it is intended that this and future editions of this design guide will continue to assist ASHRAE in its efforts at promoting sustainable design, as well as the many other organizations that have advocated for high-performance building design.

The consuming public and other representative groups of building professionals continue to become more and more aware of the societal need to provide buildings that are more energy resource effective and environmentally compatible. This publication, authored and edited by ASHRAE volunteers, is intended to complement those efforts.

ASHRAE will continue to advance its leadership through initiatives such as "The Sustainability Roadmap." Information on this effort can be found on ASHRAE's Engineering for Sustainability Web site, www.engineeringfor sustainability.org/.

PREFACE

by John Swift and David Grumman

When the *ASHRAE GreenGuide* was first developed in 2003, it was intended that the Guide would be a continuous work in progress. The second and now this third edition fulfill that intent and represent ASHRAE's continued commitment to leadership in the areas of high-performance building design and operation.

The third edition features new information on guidelines on sustainable energy master planning, updates on teaming strategies, information on how issues related to carbon emissions affect building design and operational decisions, building information modeling, strategies for greening existing buildings, updates on newly developed green building rating systems and standards, additional information on building energy modeling and follow-up measurement and verification, compliance strategies for key ASHRAE standards. This edition also includes new chapters on water efficiency and indoor environmental quality, and new GreenTips including those with green strategies for chilled-water plant and boiler plant design.

WHO SHOULD USE THE *ASHRAE GREENGUIDE*

The *ASHRAE GreenGuide* is primarily for HVAC&R designers, but it is also a useful reference for architects, owners, building managers, operators, contractors, and others in the building industry who want to understand some of the technical issues regarding high-performance design from an integrated, building systems perspective. Considerable emphasis is placed on teamwork and close coordination between parties.

This is intended to be a publication that a design engineer, about to embark on a green building design project as part of a team, could read for immediate ideas and guidance on what to do, where to turn, what to advise, and how to interact with other team members in a productive way. This Guide is intended to be a key reference for engineers to find information about any green-design subject that may arise. A comprehensive index is provided to facilitate rapid access to reference material on a given subject.

THE PURPOSE OF THE *ASHRAE GREENGUIDE*

When the original subcommittee first started its work, it set forth some characteristics of what the guide was to be. One was that it have a well-defined purpose. That purpose was to provide guidance on how to apply green design techniques, not necessarily to motivate the use of them. Much has been written on the need for green building design, and this aspect is covered herein. The reader should assume that when the HVAC&R designer finds himself or herself in a situation where a green design is to be done, this Guide will help answer the following question: "What do I do now?"

Other characteristics sought were that it be relevant to the target audience, useful and practical, concise and succinct, well organized and logical. Furthermore, the Guide is intended to be used as a tool to encourage team effort and to stimulate innovative ideas and independent thought. Finally, we wanted the reader to be able to find information easily.

HOW TO USE THE *ASHRAE GREENGUIDE*

This document is intended to be used more as a reference than as something one would read in sequence from beginning to end. The table of contents is the best place for any reader to get an overall view of what is covered in this publication. Throughout the Guide, numerous techniques, processes, measures, or special systems are described succinctly in a modified outline or bullet form. These are called ASHRAE GreenTips. Each GreenTip concludes with a listing of other sources that may be referenced for greater detail. (A list of GreenTips and Digging Deeper sidebars can be found in the Table of Contents.)

All readers should take the time to read Chapter 1, "Green/Sustainable High-Performance Design," which provides some essential definitions and meanings of key terms. Chapter 2, "Background and Fundamentals," might well be skipped by the more experienced readers. This chapter covers the background of the green design movement and what other organizations have done, and it reviews some engineering fundamentals that govern the technical aspects of green design.

Chapter 3 provides an overview of project strategies. Chapter 4 covers the early stages of the design process, and Chapter 5 highlights architectural design and planning impacts. These chapters are essential reading for all who are interested in how the green design process works. Building-Type GreenTips are included at the end of Chapter 5. Chapter 6 provides an overview of the commissioning process, a critical component that needs to be addressed from the beginning on all truly successful high-performance building projects. Chapter 7 describes green rating systems and the relevant standards and paths to compliance, as they relate to the work of the mechanical engineers. GreenTips focused on compliance with ASHRAE Standards are provided at the end of Chapter 7.

The next nine chapters deal with virtually all of the practical suggestions for possible strategies and concepts to be appropriately incorporated into a green building design. Chapters 17–18 cover what happens after the design documents for the project have been completed—that is, during construction, final commissioning, and the post occupancy phases of a building project. There is some sound advice and helpful tips in these chapters. So, even though they cover a postdesign time frame, reading them should not be put off until construction begins.

At the end of the Guide there is a comprehensive "References and Resources" section, which compiles all the sources mentioned throughout the guide, and an index for rapid location of a particular subject of interest.

BACKGROUND ON THE *ASHRAE GREENGUIDE*

The *GreenGuide* Subcommittee of ASHRAE Technical Committee (TC) 1.10, Energy Resources, was responsible for creating this guide. (Just prior to completion of the first edition, TC 1.10 merged with Task Group [TG] Buildings' Impact on the Environment [BIE] to form TC 2.8, Building Environmental Impact and Sustainability.) Members of that first subcommittee were David L. Grumman, Fellow ASHRAE, chair and editor; Jordan L. Heiman, Fellow ASHRAE; and Sheila Hayter, chair of TC 1.10.

The idea for the publication was initiated by 1999–2000 ASHRAE President Jim Wolf and carried forward by then President Elect (and subsequently President) William J. Coad.

The *GreenGuide* Subcommittee responsible for the second and third editions consisted of John Swift, Tom Lawrence, and the people noted in the Acknowledgments section.

All work performed—by the authors, editors, developing subcommittees, other reviewers, and TC participants—was voluntary.

ACKNOWLEDGMENTS

The following individuals served as coeditors on this edition of the *ASHRAE GreenGuide,* provided written materials and editorial content, and formed the Senior Editorial Group of the ASHRAE TC 2.8 *GreenGuide* Subcommittee for the second and third editions:

John M. Swift, Jr.
Cannon Design, Boston, MA

Thomas Lawrence
University of Georgia, Athens, GA

The following individuals contributed written materials on various topics for one or all of the first three editions of the *ASHRAE GreenGuide.* All or portions of these contributions were incorporated, with editing.

David L. Grumman
Editor of the first edition of the
GreenGuide
Grumman/Butkus Associates,
Evanston, IL

H. Jay Enck
Senior Editor of the second edition
Commissioning & Green Building
Solutions, Buford, GA

Malcolm Lewis
Senior Editor of the second edition
CTG Energetics, Irvine, CA

Rand Ekman, Stu Brodsky
OWP/P- Cannon Design, Chicago, IL

Mark Loeffler
Altier Ten, New Haven, CT

B. Andrew Price
Stanley Consultants, Inc.
Muscatine, IA

Steven Baumgartner
Buro Happold
Consulting Engineers, PC
New York, NY

Dimitri Contoyannis
Integrated Environmental
Solutions Limited
San Francisco, CA

Dunstan Macauley
Encon Group, Inc., Kensington, MD

Kevin Cross
Honeywell, Ft. Collins, CO

Jason Perry
University of Georgia, Athens, GA

Neil Moiseev
Shen Milsom & Wilke, Inc.,
New York, NY

John Lane and Daryn Cline
Evapco, Inc., Taneytown, MD

John Andrepont
The Cool Solutions Company, Lisle, IL

Paul Torcellini and Michael Deru
*National Renewable Energy
Laboratory, Golden, CO*

Wladyslaw Jan Kowalski
*Pennsylvania State University,
University Park, PA*

Steven Rosen
Autodesk, Boston, MA

Jerry Ackerman
*Clearwater Systems Corporation,
Essex, CT*

Jordan L. Heiman
St. Louis, MO

**Mark Mendell, Sara Schonour,
Michael Forth, and James Bones**
Cannon Design, Boston, MA

Len Damiano
*Green Building Controls Subcommittee
Chair, ASHRAE TC 1.4, and Ebtron*

Kimberly Barker
ASHRAE TC 1.4, and Siemens

Bill Becker
*Chicago ITT and Urban Wind Design,
Chicago, IL*

Bion Howard
*Building Environmental Science
and Technology, Hilton Head, SC*

Mark Hertel
ASHRAE TC 6.7, and SunEarth, Inc.

Constantinos A. Balaras
*Institute for Environmental Research
& Sustainable Development,
National Observatory of Athens (NOA)*

E. Mitchell Swann
MDC Systems Corp., LLC

Ainul Abedin
*Past President,
ASHRAE Pakistan Chapter*

Brian A. Rock
*School of Architecture
and Urban Design,
The University of Kansas,
Lawrence, KS*

Amy Butterfield
*Georgia Institute of Technology,
Atlanta, GA*

Michael Gallivan
Turner Construction Co., Inc.

Mark Hydemann and Glenn Friedman
Taylor Engineering, Alameda, CA

Ron Perkins
Supersymmetry USA, Navasota, TX

Vikas Patnaik and Mick Schwedler
Trane, Co., LaCrosse, WI

Hal Levin
*Building Ecology Research Group,
Santa Cruz, CA*

Krishnan Gowri
*Pacific Northwest Laboratory,
Richland, WA*

Gail S. Brager
University of California, Berkely, CA

Dean Borges
University of Nevada, Reno, NV

Paul McGregor
*McGregor & Associates,
Lake Cove, Australia*

Brad Jones
Sebesta Blomberg, Boston, MA

David Bearg
Life Energy Associates, Newton, MA

Karl Stum
*Summit Building Engineering, LLC,
Vancouver, WA*

Guy S. Frankenfield
Natgun Corporation

James Benya
Benya Lighting Design, West Linn, OR

Stephen Carpenter
*Enermodal Engineering, Ltd.,
Kitchener, ON CAN*

Michael Deru
*National Renewable Energy
Laboratory, Golden, CO*

Kevin Dickens
Jacobs Facilities, Inc., St. Louis, MO

**Michael Haggans and Garrick
Maine**
Flad & Associates, Madison, WI

Jordan L. Heiman
St. Louis, MO

Mark Hydemann
Taylor Engineering, Alameda, CA

James Keller
Gausman & Moore, St. Paul, MN

John Kokko
*Enermodal Engineering, Ltd.,
Kitchener, ON CAN*

Nils L. Larsson
*CETC, National Resources Canada,
Ottawa, ON CAN*

Blair McCarry
*Keen Engineering Co., Ltd., North
Vancouver, BC, CAN*

Ron Perkins
Supersymmetry USA, Navasota, TX

Douglas T. Reindl
*University of Wisconsin-Madison,
Madison, WI*

Wayne Robertson
Energy Ace, Inc., Decatur, GA

Marc Rosenbaum
Energysmiths, Meriden, NH

Mick Schwedler
Trane, La Crosse, WI

Eddie Leonardi
*School of Mechanical
and Manufacturing Engineering,
The University of New South Wales,
Sydney, Australia*

Eugene Stamper
*New Jersey Institute of Technology
(retired), Newark, NJ*

Stephen Turner
Stephen Turner, Inc., Providence, RI

Charles Wilkin
*Hanson Professional Services, Inc.,
Springfield, IL*

Lastly, we want to express our thanks to Megan Firko, a mechanical engineer at Cannon Design, Boston, Massachusetts, for her help with organizing the graphics that were used in the third edition and obtaining the necessary permissions to use them.

Section 1: Basics

CHAPTER ONE

GREEN/SUSTAINABLE HIGH-PERFORMANCE DESIGN

INTRODUCTION

Global discussions have escalated regarding concerns about carbon and other pollutant emissions due to the use of fossil fuels, as well as issues relating to access to energy and water resources. In conjunction with these global concerns, there continues to be a growing awareness of the impact of the built environment on the natural environment. This information has been both written and spoken about, and there have been many conferences and seminars on the subject. In addition, many countries in the world now have green building rating systems (voluntary) and/or codes (mandatory in some form or the other). Organizations devoted specifically to this issue are now in existence in most countries. Not only have the messages contained in this outpouring of information attempted simply to explain what this issue is, they have promoted the concept of green design, exhorted to action, strived to motivate, warned of consequences from ignoring it, and instructed how to do it.

While this vast amount of promotion has been helpful, much has not been directly useful to the practicing designer of HVAC systems and equipment for buildings (i.e., to the ASHRAE member involved on a day-to-day basis in the mechanical/electrical building system design process). ASHRAE identified a need for guidance on the green-building concept specifically directed toward such practitioners. One key element of the development of this Guide is that it contains information that has direct practical use. This Guide is ASHRAE's way to provide information and guidance to the industry and practicing professionals.

Green is one of those words that can have more than a half-dozen meanings, depending on the circumstances. One of these is the greenery of nature (e.g., grass, trees, and leaves). This symbolic reference to nature is the meaning this term relates to in this publication. The difference between a green and sustainable design is the degree to which the design helps to minimize the building impact on the environment while simultaneously providing a healthy, comfortable indoor environment. This Guide is not intended to cover the full breadth of sustainability. For key characteristics and more detailed discussion of sustainability, refer to Chapter 35 in the 2009 *ASHRAE Handbook—Fundamentals* (ASHRAE 2009).

Our definition of *green buildings* inevitably extends beyond the concerns of HVAC&R designers alone, since the very concept places an emphasis on integrated design of mechanical, electrical, architectural, and other systems.

Specifically, the viewpoint held by many is that a green/sustainable building design is one that achieves high performance, over the full life cycle, in the following areas:

- Minimizing natural resource consumption through more efficient utilization of nonrenewable energy and other natural resources, land, water, and construction materials, including utilization of renewable energy resources to strive to achieve net zero energy consumption.
- Minimizing emissions that negatively impact our global atmosphere and ultimately the indoor environment, especially those related to indoor air quality (IAQ), greenhouse gases, global warming, particulates, or acid rain.
- Minimizing discharge of solid waste and liquid effluents, including demolition and occupant waste, sewer, and stormwater, and the associated infrastructure required to accommodate removal.
- Minimizing negative impacts on site ecosystems.
- Optimizing the quality of the indoor environment, including air quality, thermal regime, illumination, acoustics/noise, and visual aspects to provide comfortable human physiological and psychological perceptions.

Ultimately, even if a project does not have overtly stated green/sustainable goals, the overall approaches, processes, and concepts presented in this Guide provide a design philosophy useful for any project. Using the principles of this Guide, an owner or a member of his or her team can document the objectives and criteria to include in a project, forming the foundation for a collaborative integrated project delivery approach. This can lower design, construction, and operational costs, resulting in a lower total cost for the life of the project.

RELATIONSHIP TO SUSTAINABILITY

The related term *sustainable design* is very commonly used, almost to the point of losing any consistent meaning. While there have been some rather varied and complex definitions put forth (see the sidebar titled "Some Definitions and Views of Sustainability from Other Sources"), we prefer a simple one (very similar to the third one in the sidebar). Sustainability is providing for the needs of the present without detracting from the ability to fulfill the needs of the future.

The preceding discussion suggests that the concepts of green design and sustainable design have no absolutes—that is, they cannot be defined in black-and-white terms. These terms are more useful when thought of as a mindset: a goal to be sought and a process to follow. This Guide is a means of: (1) encouraging designers of the built environment to employ strategies that can be utilized in developing a green/sustainable design, and (2) setting forth some practical techniques to help practitioners achieve the goal of green design, thus making a significant contribution to the sustainability of the planet.

Another method for assessing sustainability is through the concept of The Triple Bottom Line (Savitz and Weber 2006). This concept advances the idea that monetary cost is not the only way to value project design options. The Triple Bottom Line concept advocates for the criteria to include economic, social, and environmental impacts of building design and operations decisions.

GOOD DESIGN

Good design might be said to be the process that results in a well-designed building. The broad characteristics of good building design, encompassing both the engineering and nonengineering disciplines, might be briefly defined as meeting the defined objectives and criteria of the owner. As owners expand their criteria to include green and sustainable objectives, good designs can transition to green and sustainable designs. Does good design intrinsically mean that green design has been achieved as well? More significantly, does green design automatically incorporate the characteristics of good design? It is important to clarify this question for users of this Guide, because many definitions of green design do assume that it includes at least some, if not all, of the characteristics of good design (Grondzik 2001).

COMMITMENT TO GREEN/SUSTAINABLE
HIGH-PERFORMANCE PROJECTS

Green projects require more than a project team with good intentions; they require commitment from the owner, early documentation of sustainable/green goals documented by the Owner's Project Requirement document, and the designer's documented basis of design. The most successful projects incorporating green design are ones with dedicated, proactive owners who are willing to examine (or give the design team the freedom to examine) the entire spectrum of ownership—from design to construction to long-term operation of their facilities. These owners understand that green buildings require more planning, better execution, and better operational procedures, requiring a firm commitment to changing how building projects are designed, constructed, operated, and maintained to achieve a lower total cost of ownership and lower long-term environmental impacts.

Implementing green/sustainable practices could indeed raise the initial design soft costs associated with a project, particularly compared to the code minimum building design. Implementing the commissioning process early in the predesign phase of a project adds an initial budget line item but, in most cases, actually reduces overall total design/construction costs.

In addition, significant savings and improved productivity of the building occupants can be realized for the life of the building, lowering the total cost of ownership. To achieve lifelong benefits also requires operating procedures for monitoring performance, making adjustments (continuing commissioning) when needed, and appropriate maintenance.

WHAT DRIVES GREEN PROJECTS

Green building advocates can cite plenty of reasons why buildings should be designed utilizing integrated green concepts. The fact that these reasons exist does not make it happen, nor does the existence of designers—or design firms—with green design experience. The main driver of green building design is the motivation of the owner—the one who initiates the creation of a project, the one who pays for it (or who carries the burden of its financing), and the one who has (or has identified) the need to be met by the project in question. If the owner does not believe that green design is needed, thinks it is unimportant, or thinks it is of secondary importance to other needs, then it will not happen.

Some owners of new and existing buildings have already discovered the benefits of commissioning without any intent to green their new or existing buildings. Owners with no commissioning experience often believe that their design and construction teams will provide a quality project without the commissioning process. What these owners often receive is a project where most of the materials and equipment were installed and have the appearance of operating as intended. However, they later discover, after the end of the warranty period, that the systems do not perform as expected, leaving the owner with the impacts of poor building performance due to higher operation and maintenance costs and reduced occupant satisfaction and productivity, all of which significantly increase the total cost of ownership and environmental impacts.

The commissioning process plays a key role in assisting a project delivery team and owner in reducing project risk, lowering design and construction costs, and reducing the total cost of ownership. Beginning in the predesign stage, documenting the objectives, criteria, and basis of design places the delivery team on a solid foundation for success, providing clear direction and a benchmark for success against which the design, construction, and operation efforts will be judged. This is particularly important in green projects when clear objectives and criteria are needed to alert the design team of the owner's commitment to sustainability and a green building.

In the very early stages of a building's development—perhaps during the designer interview process or before a designer has even been engaged—an owner may become informed on the latest trends in building design. This may occur through an owner doing research, conferring with others in the field, or discussing the merits of green design with the designer/design firm the owner intends to hire.

This initial interaction between the owner and the design professional is where the design firm with green design experience can be very effective in turning a project not initially so destined into one that's a candidate for green design. When an owner engages a designer, it is because the owner has faith in the professional ability of that designer and is inclined to listen to that designer's ideas on what the building's design direction and themes should be. As the designer works with the owner to meet his or her defined objectives and criteria for the project, the designer has the opportunity to identify approaches that can meet those objectives and criteria in a green/sustainable way. Thus, designers should regard the very early contacts with a potential owner as a golden opportunity to steer the project in a green direction.

THE IMPACT OF CARBON CONSIDERATIONS

The attention paid to concerns about greenhouse gas emissions has certainly increased. During the first decade of the twenty-first century, two organizations issued challenges to the industry to design and implement buildings that had a significantly lower energy consumption compared to current typical designs. The Architecture 2030 Challenge (see the "References and Resources" section at the end of the chapter for more information) is one of these. Architecture 2030 was initiated by Edward Mazria in 2003, and has a chief goal of net zero energy and net zero carbon buildings by the year 2030. This goal is realized by achieving substantially better energy results on a sliding scale from 2010 through 2030. The near-term focus of the challenge has been adopted by the American Institute of Architects (AIA). The Architecture 2010 Imperative sets a goal of having buildings routinely built by the year 2010 that would show a 50% improvement in energy efficiency compared to the 1999 version of *ANSI/ASHRAE/IESNA Standard 90.1-1999, Energy Standard for Buildings Except Low-Rise Residential Buildings* (ASHRAE 1999).

ASHRAE has taken the lead in meeting these challenges in several ways. To address the Architecture 2010 Imperative, significant effort was put into modifying Standard 90.1 (ASHRAE 1999) to drastically improve energy efficiency. The 2010 version of Standard 90.1, in essence, meets the AIA challenge for 2010 by introducing requirement changes. Although the specific requirements may differ in some cases, the initial version of the new *ANSI/ASHRAE/USGBC/IES Standard 189.1-2009, Standard for the Design of High-Performance Green Buildings* (ASHRAE 2009) has energy efficiency levels comparable to the 90.1.

To meet the Architecture 2030 Challenge, Standard 90.1 (ASHRAE 2010) and Standard 189.1 (ASHRAE 2009) will be continually updated to raise the bar for building energy performance. One way this is being accomplished is through the production of the ASHRAE *Advanced Energy Design Guide* series. The series covers prescriptive measures that result in significant energy efficiency improvements, with the first series dealing with measures that should achieve a 30% savings over Standard 90.1 (ASHRAE 1999). A continuation of that series is in process that will lead to a 50% energy improvement (to be completed between

2011–2013). Guidance on achieving net zero energy performance is planned to be completed by the end of this decade.

THE ENGINEERING/ENERGY CONSERVATION ETHIC

Since the 1973 oil embargo, the HVAC&R industry has continued to improve the efficiency of air-conditioning systems and equipment, promulgated energy conservation standards, developed energy-efficient designs, experimented with a wide variety of design approaches, strived for good IAQ, and shared the lessons learned with industry colleagues. As in the past, efforts must continue to find new and better solutions to improve energy efficiency, further reduce dependence on nonrenewable energy sources, and increase the comfort of people in the buildings they occupy. In addition, concerns about the human impact on climate makes the need to work toward greater energy efficient even more imperative.

Most designers have guided owners through life-cycle analyses of various options, identified approaches to improve building efficiency, and developed strategies to meet the stated goals of owners. Owners have often rejected their ideas because payback periods are too long. Despite those setbacks, progress toward green/sustainable design is becoming more prevalent, and is becoming an industry standard practice. It is incumbent on our industry to recognize the impact its work has on the environment, which goes beyond matters of first cost, recurring costs, and even life-cycle cost. The ethics of the industry requires practitioners to strive to identify these environmental costs and assign values to them—values that represent the total cost to society rather than just conventional measurements of capital.

Digging Deeper

INTERNATIONAL PERSPECTIVE: REGULATIONS AND COMMENTARY

Society has recognized that previous industrial and developmental actions caused long-term damage to our environment, resulting in loss of food sources and plant and animal species, and changes to the Earth's climate. As a result of learning from past mistakes and studying the environment, the international community identified certain actions that threaten the ecosystem's biodiversity, and, consequently, it developed several governmental regulations designed to protect our environment. Thus, in this sense, the green design initiative began with the implementation of building regulations. An example is the regulated phasing out of fully halogenated chlorofluorocarbons (CFCs) and partially halogenated refrigerant hydrochlorofluorocarbons (HCFCs).

In Europe, the Directive on the Energy Performance of Buildings (EPBD) (European Commission 2002) has been in effect since January 4, 2006, throughout the European Union. All EU member states are obligated to bring into force national laws, regulations, and administrative provisions for setting minimum requirements on the energy performance of new and existing buildings that are subject to major renovations and for energy performance certification of buildings. Additional requirements include regular inspection of building systems and installations, an assessment of the existing facilities, and provision of advice on possible improvements and alternative solutions. The objective is to properly design new buildings and renovate existing buildings in a manner that will use the minimum nonrenewable energy, produce minimum air pollution as a result of the building operating systems, and minimize construction waste. All of this will be achieved with acceptable investment and operating costs, while improving the indoor environment for comfort, health, and safety.

An energy performance certificate (EPC) will be issued when buildings are constructed, sold, or rented out (see Figures 1-1a through 1-1d for examples). The EPC will document the energy performance of the building and will be expressed as a numeric indicator that allows benchmarking. The certificate will also include recommendations for cost-effective improvement of the energy performance, and will be valid for up to ten years.

According to the EPBD, minimum energy performance requirements are set for new buildings and for the major renovation of large existing buildings in each EU member state. Energy performance will have to be upgraded in order to meet minimum requirements that are technically, functionally, and economically feasible. In the case of large new buildings, alternative energy supply systems should be considered (e.g., decentralized energy supply systems based on renewable energy, combined heat and power, district or block heating or cooling, heat pumps, etc.). The inspection of boilers and air-conditioning units on a regular base is compulsory. To further promote the efforts, public buildings will have to display the EPC to the public. The Concerted Action EPBD that was launched by the European Commission provides updated information on the implementation status in the various European countries (www.epbd-ca.org).

It is not just in the developed countries that green building design and energy efficiency concerns are taking hold. The later part of the past decade has seen an explosion of green building design programs and standards. For example, India was the first expansion of the Leadership in Energy and Environmental Design programs outside of the United States, with the establishment of the India Green Building Council in 2003.

Digging Deeper

Digging Deeper

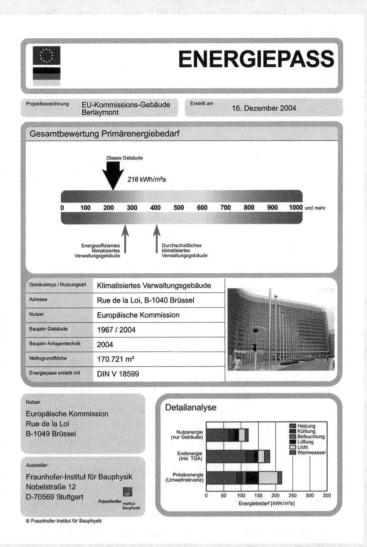

Image courtesy of Dr. Gerd Hauser

Figure 1-1a Example of Belgium's EPC.

Energy Performance Certificate

S$\hat{A}$P

17 Any Street,
Any Town,
County,
YY3 5XX

Dwelling type: Detached house
Date of assessment: 02 February 2007
Date of certificate: [dd mmmm yyyy]
Reference number: 0000-0000-0000-0000-0000
Total floor area: 166 m²

This home's performance is rated in terms of the energy use per square metre of floor area, energy efficiency based on fuel costs and environmental impact based on carbon dioxide (CO_2) emissions.

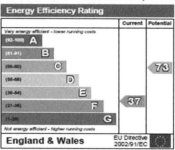

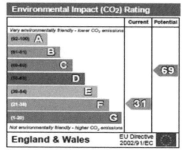

The energy efficiency rating is a measure of the overall efficiency of a home. The higher the rating the more energy efficient the home is and the lower the fuel bills will be.

The environmental impact rating is a measure of a home's impact on the environment in terms of carbon dioxide (CO_2) emissions. The higher the rating the less impact it has on the environment.

Estimated energy use, carbon dioxide (CO_2) emissions and fuel costs of this home

	Current	Potential
Energy Use	453 kWh/m² per year	178 kWh/m² per year
Carbon dioxide emissions	13 tonnes per year	4.9 tonnes per year
Lighting	£81 per year	£65 per year
Heating	£1173 per year	£457 per year
Hot water	£219 per year	£104 per year

Based on standardised assumptions about occupancy, heating patterns and geographical location, the above table provides an indication of how much it will cost to provide lighting, heating and hot water to this home. The fuel costs only take into account the cost of fuel and not any associated service, maintenance or safety inspection. This certificate has been provided for comparative purposes only and enables one home to be compared with another. Always check the date the certificate was issued, because fuel prices can increase over time and energy saving recommendations will evolve.

To see how this home can achieve its potential rating please see the recommended measures.

 Remember to look for the energy saving recommended logo when buying energy-efficient products. It's a quick and easy way to identify the most energy-efficient products on the market.

For advice on how to take action and to find out about offers available to help make your home more energy efficient, call 0800 512 012 or visit www.energysavingtrust.org.uk/myhome

Image courtesy of Communities and Local Government (2010)

Figure 1-1b Example of England and Wales' EPC.

Digging Deeper

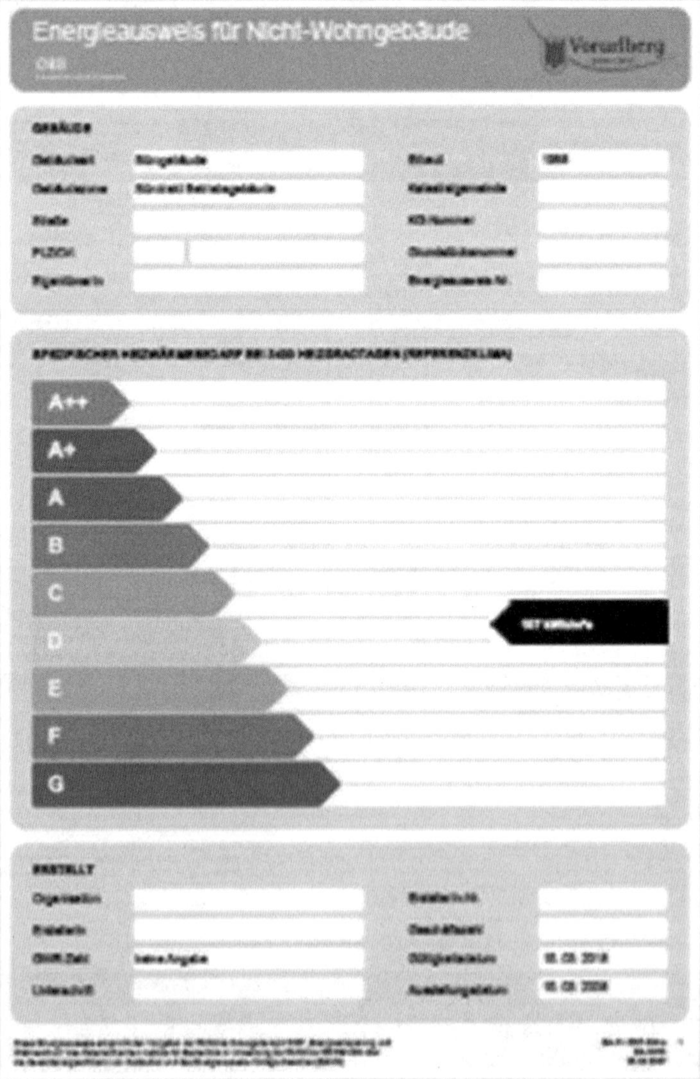

Image courtesy of Amt der Vorarlberger Landesregierung/Energieinstitut Vorarlberg

Figure 1-1c Example of Austria's EPC.

Image courtesy of NINN Studio MILANO - Arch. Nicola Ingenuo, Arch. Antonella Puopolo

Figure 1-1d Example of Italy's EPC.

Digging Deeper

At the beginning of 2010, a total of over 60 buildings have been certified, with several hundred more registered and in process of certification.

Green buildings programs already exist or are in development in many countries across the world, thus establishing that the green building movement is not just a fad, but truly is transforming the marketplace worldwide.

Digging Deeper

SOME DEFINITIONS AND VIEWS OF SUSTAINABILITY FROM OTHER SOURCES

- "The best chance we have of addressing the combined challenges of energy supply and demand, climate change and energy security is to accelerate the introduction of new technologies for energy supply and use and deploy them on a very large scale." *(Thomas Friedman, Hot, Flat and Crowded.)*
- "Humanity must rediscover its ancient ability to recognize and live within the cycles of the natural world." *(The Natural Step for Business)*
- Development is sustainable "if it meets the needs of the present without compromising the ability of future generations to meet their own needs." *(Brundtland Commission of the United Nations)*
- To be sustainable, "a society needs to meet three conditions: Its rates of use of renewable resources should not exceed their rates of regeneration; its rates of use of nonrenewable resources should not exceed the rate at which sustainable renewable substitutes are developed; and its rates of pollution emissions should not exceed the assimilative capacity of the environment." *(Herman Daly)*
- "Sustainability is a state or process that can be maintained indefinitely. The principles of sustainability integrate three closely intertwined elements – the environment, the economy, and the social system – into a system that can be maintained in a healthy state indefinitely." *(Design Ecology Project)*
- "In this disorganized, fast-paced world, we have reached a critical point. Now is the time to rethink the way we work, to balance our most important assets." *(Paola Antonelli, Curator, Department of Architecture and Design, New York City Museum of Modern Art)*

REFERENCES AND RESOURCES

Published

ASHRAE. 1999. *ANSI/ASHRAE/IESNA Standard 90.1-1999, Energy Standard for Buildings Except Low-Rise Residential Buildings.* Atlanta: American Society of Heating, Refrigerating and Air-Conditioning Engineers, Inc.

ASHRAE. 2009. *ASHRAE Handbook—Fundamentals,* Ch. 35. Atlanta: American Society of Heating, Refrigerating and Air-Conditioning Engineers, Inc.

ASHRAE. 2009. *ANSI/ASHRAE/USGBC/IES Standard 189.1-2009, Standard for the Design of High-Performance Green Buildings.* Atlanta: American Society of Heating, Refrigerating and Air-Conditioning Engineers, Inc.

ASHRAE. 2010. *ANSI/ASHRAE/IES Standard 90.1-2010, Energy Standard for Buildings Except Low-Rise Residential Buildings.* Atlanta: American Society of Heating, Refrigerating and Air-Conditioning Engineers, Inc.

European Commission. 2002. Energy Performance of Buildings, Directive 2002/91/EC of the European Parliament and of the Council. Official Journal of the European Communities, Brussels.

Grondzik, W.T. 2001. The (mechanical) engineer's role in sustainable design: Indoor environmental quality issues in sustainable design. HTML presentation available at www.polaris.net/~gzik/ieq/ieq.htm.

Savitz, A.W., and K. Weber. 2006. *The Triple Bottom Line.* San Francisco: John Wiley & Sons, Inc.

Online

Architecture 2030 Challenge
www.architecture2030.org/
European Commission, Concerted Action Energy Performance of Buildings Directive
www.epbd-ca.org

CHAPTER TWO

BACKGROUND
AND FUNDAMENTALS

Blend into Chapter 1 (handwritten annotation)

The use of green engineering concepts has evolved quite rapidly in recent years and is now a legitimate and spreading movement in the HVAC&R and related engineering professions. Much of this recent work has been driven by the emergence of green architecture, also commonly referred to as *sustainable* or *environmentally conscious* architecture. This, in turn, is being encouraged by increased client demand for more sustainable buildings.

The emergence of green building engineering is best understood in the context of the movement in architecture toward sustainable buildings and communities. Detailed reviews of this movement appear elsewhere and fall outside the scope of this document. A brief review of the history and background of the green design movement is provided, followed by a discussion of its applicability. Several leading methodologies for performing and evaluating green building design efforts are reviewed.

SUSTAINABILITY IN ARCHITECTURE

Prior to the industrial revolution, building efforts were often directed throughout design and construction by a single architect—the so-called Master Builder Model. The master builder alone bore full responsibility for the design and construction of the building, including any engineering required. This model lent itself to a building designed as one system, with the means of providing heat, light, water, and other building services often closely integrated into the architectural elements. Sustainability, semantically if not conceptually, predates these eras, and some modern unsustainable practices had yet to arise. Sustainability in itself was not the goal of yesteryear's master builders. Yet some of the resulting structures appear to have achieved an admirable combination of great longevity and sustainability in construction, operation, and maintenance. It would be interesting to compare the ecological footprint (a concept discussed later in this book) of, say, Roman structures from two millennia ago heated by radiant floors to a twentieth century structure of comparable size, site, and use.

In the nineteenth century, as ever more complicated technologies and the scientific method developed, the discipline of engineering emerged separate from architecture. This change was not arbitrary or willful but rather was due to the increasing complexity of design tools and construction technologies and a burgeoning range of available materials and techniques. This complexity continued to grow throughout the twentieth century and continues today. With the architect transformed from master builder to lead design consultant, most HVAC&R engineering practices performed work predominantly as a subcontract to the architect, whose firm, in turn, was retained by the client. Hand-in-hand with these trends emerged the twentieth century doctrine of Buildings Over Nature, an approach still widely demanded by clients and supplied by architectural and engineering firms.

Under this approach (buildings are designed under the architect, who is prime consultant, following the Buildings Over Nature paradigm) the architect conceives the shell and interior design concepts first. Only then does the architect turn to structural engineers, then HVAC&R engineers, then electrical engineers, etc. (Not coincidentally, this hierarchy and sequence of engineering involvement mirrors the relative expense of the subsystems being designed.)

With notable exceptions, this sequence has reinforced the trend toward Buildings Over Nature: relying on the brute force of sizable HVAC systems that are resource-intensive—and energy-intensive to operate—to build and maintain conditions acceptable for human occupancy. In this approach to the design process, many opportunities to integrate architectural elements with engineered systems are missed—often because it's too late. Even with an integrated design team to bridge back over the gaps in the traditional design process, a sustainable building with optimally engineered subsystems will not result if not done by professionals with appropriate knowledge and insight.

When Green Design is Applicable

One leading trend in architecture, especially in the design of smaller buildings, is to invite nature in as an alternative to walling it off with a shell and then providing sufficiently powerful mechanical/electrical systems to perpetuate this isolation. This situation presents a significant opportunity for engineers today. Architects and clients who take this approach require fresh and complementary engineering approaches, not tradition-bound engineering that incorporates extra capacity to overcome the natural forces a design team may have invited into a building. Natural ventilation and hybrid mechanical/natural ventilation, radiant heating, and radiant cooling are examples of the tools with which today's engineers are increasingly required to acquire fluency. One example of a building designed with this in mind is the GAP, Inc. building in San Bruno, California. (See Chapter 8 for GreenTips relating to alternative ventilation techniques and see Watson and Chapman [2002] for radiant heating/cooling design guidance.)

Fortunately, there is a great deal of information available about green building design. Further, new tools for understanding and defending engineering decisions in such projects are emerging, including a revised ASHRAE thermal comfort standard, *ANSI/ASHRAE Standard 55-2010, Thermal Environmental Conditions for Human Occupancy* (ASHRAE 2010), that includes an adaptive design method that is more applicable to buildings that interact more freely with the outdoor environment. ASHRAE Standard 55 also accomodates an increasing variety of design solutions intended both to provide comfort and to respect the imperative for sustainable buildings.

Another more widely demanded approach to green HVAC engineering presents a significant opportunity for engineers. This approach applies to projects ranging from flagship green building projects to more conventional ones where the client has only some appetite for green. The demand for environmentally conscious engineering is evidenced by the expansion of engineering groups, either within or outside architectural practices, that have built a reputation for a green approach to building design.

Work done by others on such projects can inform engineers' building designs. In addition, many informative resources are available to help engineers better understand the principles, techniques, and details of green building design, and to raise environmental consciousness in their engineering practices. By learning and acquiring appropriate resources, obtaining project-based experience, and finding like-minded professionals, engineers can reorient their thinking to deliver better services to their clients.

Green HVAC engineering can be provided, for its own sake, independent of any client or architect demand. The appetite for environmentally conscious engineering must be carefully gauged, and opportunities to educate the design team carefully seized. In this way, engineers can bring greater value to their projects and distinguish themselves from competing individuals and firms.

Embodied Energy and Life-Cycle Assessment

Building materials used in the construction and operation of buildings have energy embodied in them due to the manufacturing, transportation, and installation processes of converting raw materials to final products. The material selection process should consider the environmental impact of demolition and disposal after the service life of the products. Life-cycle assessment (LCA) databases and tools are used to calculate and compare the embodied energy of common building materials and products. Designers should give preference to resource-efficient materials and reduce waste by recycling and reusing whenever possible.

The HVAC&R designer has a variety of options to consider if conducting an LCA analysis. The International Organization for Standardization 14000 series of standards on environmental management serves as a method to govern the development of these tools. LCA tools are available from both private commercial as well as governmental or public domain sources. The Building for Environmental and Economic Sustainability (BEES) tool was developed by the National Institute for Standards and

Technology in the United States, with support from the U.S. Environmental Protection Agency. The Tools for the Reduction and Assessment of Chemical and Other Environmental Impacts (TRACI) from the EPA focuses on chemical releases and raw materials usage in products. Some commercial firms also offer tools.

The Carbon Economy

Depending on whom you talk with, the controversy either continues or has been settled regarding the extent of concern about anthropogenic (human-caused) emissions of greenhouse gases and the consequent impact these emissions have on the environment and society. Some think that the issue needs further study before significant investments and changes are mandated, while others, such as the Intergovernmental Panel on Climate Change (IPCC), think a consensus has been reached (reports supporting this stance can be found at www.ipcc.ch.) One thing that cannot be argued is the documented fact that CO_2 levels in the atmosphere have been steadily rising (definitive records have been kept since at least early in the twentieth century), as seen in Figure 2-1.

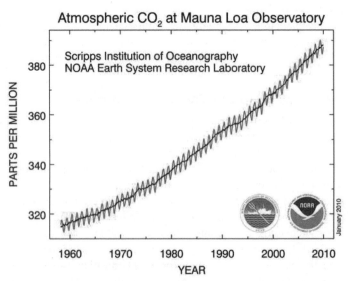

Image courtesy of C.D. Keeling of the Scripps Institute of Oceanography, La Jolla, California, and Pieter Tans of NOAA's Earth System Research Laboratory in Boulder, CO.

Figure 2-1 Historical trends in atmospheric CO_2 levels.

There is bad news and good news when we look at how buildings are involved with greenhouse gas emissions. First the bad news: buildings (commercial and residential) are responsible for approximately 30% of the greenhouse gas emissions in the United States and most developed countries, and the trend is also holding up in key developing nations. The good news is that buildings have also been identified as the economic sector with the best potential for cost-effective mitigation of greenhouse gas emissions, as highlighted in Figure 2-2. Therefore, the building industry can and should take responsibility for reducing greenhouse gas emissions, primarily through a reduction in energy consumption.

Past experience shows that is it unrealistic to expect voluntary reduction in greenhouse gas emissions to occur in large enough quantities to stem the documented rise in CO_2 levels. The reason for moving beyond voluntary control can be attributed to the following public policy measures: (1) a tax on emissions of carbon (directly for a source or indirectly through the purchase of fuels, etc.) or (2) a cap and trade program.

The concept of a tax on carbon is relatively simple to grasp, although implementation would require a lot of concern for details. Many economists and business leaders prefer a carbon tax over a cap and trade system, because it is a known measure that can be planned for within a business model. However, politicians tend to prefer a cap and trade system, since that provides a more politically safe approach.

In the past, a cap and trade system has been implemented in the United States. It addressed air pollution concerns and involved major polluters such as electric utilities. However, at the time there were fewer emissions sources. Initially, the cap and trade programs in the European Union have stumbled, as implementation problems were worked out. Currently, a cap and trade system is again being considered in the United States, and this too will focus on major emissions sources such as electrical utilities.

The HVAC&R engineer can provide a significant benefit to society (as well as to the building project's owners) via CO_2 emissions reduction associated with energy use. All new building projects should estimate the CO_2 equivalent emissions footprint of the building (of which a large part is through energy consumption). For existing buildings, compute the reduction in emissions associated with energy conservation measures being proposed. In both cases, the greenhouse gas emissions factor used should be based on source energy and not on energy consumed on site alone. A good reference source for emissions factors is contained in a National Renewable Energy Laboratory (NREL) report released in 2007 (Deru and Torcellini).

Green Building Rating Systems, Standards, and Environmental Performance Improvement Programs

There are two general types of programs that exist to encourage green building design. One type might be termed a rating system (per se) and the other a guide or

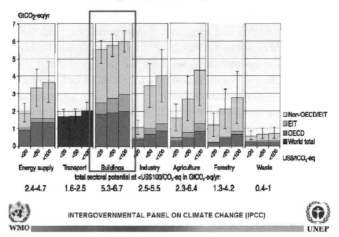

Economic mitigation potential by sector in 2030

Source: Climate Change 2007: Synthesis Report. Contribution of Working Groups I, II, and III to the Fourth Assessment Report of the IPCC, Figure 4.2. IPCC, Geneva, Switzerland.

Figure 2-2 Buildings have the best potential for economical mitigation of greenhouse gas emissions.

program to encourage and assist designers in achieving green building design. (This book is in the latter category.)

Green Building Rating Systems. Various rating systems that have been developed by reputable organizations in both the United States and internationally that attempt to indicate how well a building meets prescribed requirements and to determine whether a building design is green or the degree of greenness it has. They all provide useful tools to identify and prioritize key environmental issues. These tools incorporate a coordinated method for accomplishing, validating, and benchmarking sustainably designed projects.

As with any generalized method, each has its own limitations and may not apply directly to every project's regional and other specific aspects, such as indoor environmental quality (IEQ) (Grondzik 2001).

It should not be implied that this Guide advocates the exclusion of these elements. By advocating both green and good design in any building design endeavor, this is avoided. Yet, this Guide does not intend to discourage use of the mentioned rating systems or other programs by ASHRAE members or by the design teams in which its members participate. Thus, while this Guide does not endorse or recommend use of any one rating system or program, it is also not opposed to the use of one if it is perceived that such will be of help in achieving a green design. Each method may play a valuable role in increasing an engineer's ability to help deliver sustainably designed projects.

The leading rating method in the United States is the Leadership in Energy and Environmental Design (LEED®) program, created by the U.S. Green Building Council (USGBC). The USGBC started offering this system in 1998 and describes it as a voluntary, consensus-based, market-driven green building certification system. It evaluates environmental performance from a "whole building" perspective over a building's life cycle, providing a numerical standard for what constitutes a "green building." USGBC's goal has been to raise awareness of the benefits of building green, and it has transformed the marketplace. LEED has been applied to numerous projects over a range of project certification levels, and its use has grown rapidly over the past several years. The LEED rating system started out with a basic LEED for new construction. Because a large majority of buildings already exist, a LEED for existing buildings was released in 2004 and updated in 2005. LEED rating systems have also been developed, or are in the development process, for a variety of building project types. These include, for example, building core and shell and commercial interiors for project developers and tenants (respectively), as well as schools, health care, and homes. LEED also qualifies individuals as LEED consultants, although it does not require such consultants on projects seeking LEED ratings. The LEED program and registered building projects have already been, or are being, established in other countries including India, Australia, Canada, and China. Other countries are developing their own green building rating systems based on the criteria in LEED and other rating systems (e.g., Indonesia and Malaysia).

Another rating method that was originally developed in Canada and is being introduced in the United States is the Green Globes program. Green Globes is an online auditing tool that includes many of the same concepts as LEED. While both aim to help a building owner or designer develop a sustainable design, Green Globes is primarily a self-assessment tool (although third-party assessment is an option) and also provides recommendations for the project team to follow for improving the sustainability of the design. In the UK, Green Globes is known as the Global Environmental Method program.

The Building Research Establishment Environmental Assessment Method (BREEAM®) rating program was established in the United Kingdom in 1990. This is a voluntary, consensus-based, market-oriented assessment program. With one mandatory and two optional assessment areas, BREEAM® encourages and benchmarks sustainably designed office buildings. The mandatory assessment area is the potential environmental impact of the building; the two optional areas are design process and operation/maintenance. Several other countries and regions have developed or are developing related spinoffs inspired by BREEAM®.

Standards or Building Code Implementation. Since 2005, there has been a movement to make green building more mandatory. Several cities in the United States now require LEED certification for building projects above a certain size or classification (such as a government building). In addition, ASHRAE has initiated a process to create a series of new standards for high-performance green buildings, releasing in early 2010 *ANSI/ASHRAE/USGBC/IES Standard 189.1-2009, Standard for the Design of High-Performance Green Buildings* (ASHRAE 2009). Also in 2010, California became the first state to issue a green building code (known as *CALGreen*).

Environmental Performance Improvement Programs. Several other programs exist or have been conducted in the past with the purpose of guiding or encouraging green building design but without assigning a specific rating (see the "References and Resources" section at the end of this chapter for more information), including the following:

- *C-2000, Integrated Design Process.* Natural Resources Canada initiated the C-2000 program in 1993 as a way to achieve very high levels of building performance. It was assumed that some level of financial incentive would be required at various stages of the building process to make the program a success. Its technical requirements cover energy performance, environmental impacts, indoor environment, functionality, and a range of other parameters. Experience with the program in the first group of projects to which it was applied yielded the fact that the program's guidance in producing integrated design was the main reason high-performance levels were achieved. The program was then called the *Integrated Design Process*, and it now focuses its project interventions on design advice in the very early stages.

- *GBC, the Green Building Challenge (later became: Sustainable Building Challenge).* Canada began a process in 1998 called the *Green Building Challenge*, which involved about 20 countries developing and testing a second-generation environmental performance assessment system. That system was designed to reflect the very different priorities, technologies, building traditions, and even cultural values that exist in various regions and countries.

- CBIP, Commercial Buildings Incentive Program. An offshoot of the C-2000 Program, CBIP was an effort to create a larger national program to move the Canadian building industry toward energy efficiency. Its financial incentives provide incremental costs for the design process. Because it attempts to address a larger audience, it is simpler than the C-2000 program. A computer tool, EE4 CBIP, is offered by Natural Resources Canada's Office of Energy Efficiency to building owners and developers to help them design buildings that use 25% less energy than the Canadian Model National Energy Code for Buildings.

- *Other Resources.* (Further information regarding these resources can be found in the "References and Resources" section at the end of the chapter.) Other guides and methods include:

  - *The Whole Building Design Guide*
  - The Living Building Challenge V2.0
  - *Green Building Advisor*
  - California Collaborative for High Performance Schools
  - *Minnesota Sustainable Design Guide*
  - *New York High Performance Building Guidelines*

  Work referred to by architects includes:
  - *The Hannover Principles*
  - *GreenSpec*® Product Guide
  - Information from the The Natural Step (a nonprofit organization)
  - International Organization for Standardization family of 14000 standards,
  - BEES 4.0
  - TRACI

FUNDAMENTALS OF RELATED ENGINEERING TOPICS

Understanding the basic tenets that define the engineer's profession is imperative for thoughtful design. While this Guide is not intended to serve as an engineering textbook, we will review some key fundamentals of engineering that influence the design of sustainable buildings (from the perspective of the HVAC&R engineer). These include the first and second laws of thermodynamics, heat transfer, and fluid systems. This will provide the reader with insights into the opportunities available for energy conservation as well as other green building design opportunities.

The fundamental engineering concepts are presented first in this section. (Applications of these principals to HVAC systems are discussed in the following section.) The purpose of this section is to identify key relationships and dependencies using the language of the engineer: the fundamental laws and formulae. It is assumed that the reader is a practicing engineer with some experience rather than a neophyte, so this section is not meant to be a primer on the science behind HVAC&R. However, before delving into the greener aspects of the topic, it is good to review the basics.

Merriam-Webster defines *formula* as "a general fact, rule or principle expressed in mathematical symbols." In HVAC&R, the facts, rules, or principles we are most concerned with are the laws of thermodynamics. It has been said that if you can write an equation for a problem, you have the solution. But we must not confuse a plug-and-chug approach using formulae with engineering. The successful engineer must be able to both write the formula and understand its underlying principles.

A formula is composed of constants and variables. Constants are defined (given) and cannot be influenced. Therefore, we can only resolve a problem (influence an outcome) by manipulating its variables. When this simple premise is understood, key relationships and dependencies manifest themselves and the solution becomes obvious.

Thermodynamic Laws

The laws of thermodynamics are at the core of the analysis and design of HVAC systems. This section briefly summarizes the first and second laws and their implications in green design.

The first law in its basic form is

$$Q - (W_{flow} + W_{shaft}) = \Delta U + \Delta E_{potential} + \Delta E_{kinetic}.$$

For a system in steady state, and substituting in for the internal, potential, and kinetic energy terms, leads to the following rate equation (a dot over a symbol means *the rate of*):

$$\dot{Q} - \dot{W} = \dot{m}[(u_2 - u_1) + (p_2 v_2 - p_1 v_1) + (V_2^2 - V_1^2)/2 + g(z_2 - z_1)]$$

where

$\dot{Q}$	=	heat transferred to or from the system; the dotted symbol refers to the rate of heat being transferred
E	=	energy contained in the system (potential or kinetic)
$\dot{W}$	=	work produced or required by the system; the dotted symbol refers to the rate of work being done
u	=	internal energy of the fluid (i.e., water, steam, air, refrigerant) per unit mass
m	=	mass of fluid
pv	=	product of the pressure and specific volume of the fluid
V	=	velocity of the fluid in the system
h	=	enthalpy of the fluid per unit mass, expressed as $(u + pv)$
z	=	height or potential energy of the fluid
1 and 2	=	subscripts denoting before and after states of the parameter

The internal energy (u) and flow energy (pv) terms can be combined into the fluid enthalpy equation, given by

$$h = u + pv.$$

In psychrometrics, the enthalpy of air represents the total energy content of the air that includes both the sensible energy (the temperature) and the latent energy (corresponding to the moisture content).

The second law is represented by several equations involving the change in entropy of the fluid. But for the purposes of making decisions on energy and green design, studying the Carnot cycle, as represented on temperature-entropy coordinates, is particularly useful.

One common application of the first-law equation to a building HVAC system is combustion generating heat to raise the temperature of a fluid for providing heat to a building. When looking at the heating means, be it a boiler, hot-water generator, or warm-air furnace, the terms for work (W), changes in kinetic energy $(V_2^2 - V_1^2)/2$, and potential energy $z_2 - z_1$ are small in comparison to enthalpy difference. So, the first law becomes

$$\dot{Q} \cong \dot{m}(h_2 - h_1).$$

Exergy Analysis as an Aid to Green Design

Exergy is in essence the availability of energy to do work. Many industry engineers may have memories (good or bad) of their engineering school days and their course(s) in thermodynamics. The concept of exergy analysis has grown in importance as the push to maximize energy efficiency in a sustainable society continues. Actual application of exergy analysis can be complex, or at least appear to be daunting and reserved for the world of a PhD.

Application of exergy principles to green design can be expressed in some simple concepts. Energy at a high temperature has a higher value than the same equivalent amount of energy at a lower temperature. Green design calls for using an energy source appropriate for the application. For example, using electricity to heat domestic hot water is a poor use of a valuable energy resource compared to using a low-grade thermal energy source such as water heat. Electricity can be used to run your laptop computer, while a low-grade heat source cannot.

Another example of the application of exergy is a combined heat and power system, where energy (such as that contained in natural gas) is first used to generate high-value energy such as steam or electricity, and then the waste heat is used for other needs such as domestic hot water and/or chilled water in a heat-powered chiller.

Green Design Implications of Thermodynamic Laws

There are two types of energy: stored (potential) energy and the energy of motion, called *kinetic energy*. Regardless of its form, however, the first law of thermodynamics always applies. For a closed system, in essence, it states:

Energy cannot be created or destroyed.

A closed system is one in which energy and materials do not flow across the system boundary. The first law is why energy efficiency and green design are a necessity. If we could create energy, there would be no reason to conserve it. We must be aware that we are largely dependent on sources of energy that are in finite supply. Therefore, it is logical to use less energy of this type as a rule and to move toward renewable, more efficient energy sources in general.

If energy is the ability to do work, then what happens when we tap that potential? The result is threefold: work, heat, and entropy. Work is the transfer of energy by mechanical means, such as a fan or pump. Heat refers to a transfer of energy from one object to another because of a temperature difference. And entropy, simply stated, is an indicator of the state of disorder of a system.

The second law of thermodynamics helps us to appreciate the relevance of sustainable design even more:

All processes irreversibly increase the entropy of a system and its environment.

If you understand that the Earth is our system, then you realize that the limited amount of usable energy we have been granted (first law) will eventually and irreversibly be converted into unusable energy (second law), which brings us full circle. Of course, the earth is not a completely closed system, meaning that energy is entering (via solar radiation) and leaving (such as through Earth radiating energy out into space). Regardless, our dependence on energy in a useful form, and the immutable laws of nature, set the tone for proper (green) design. Energy should be used judiciously and effectively.

Fundamentals of Heat Transfer

Heat travels in three ways: conduction, convection, and radiation. Note the following general correlations:

- Conduction $\approx$ heat transfer by molecular motion within a material or between materials in direct contact
- Convection $\approx$ energy exchange via contact between a fluid in motion and a solid
- Radiation $\approx$ no contact required; heat transfer by electromagnetic waves

In real-world situations, heat transfer occurs via all three modes at the same time. Depending on the problem type, one or two of these modes generally dominates the rate of heat transfer at any given moment. But to keep things simple, we will discuss each mode of heat transfer separately.

Conduction. Consider heat transfer through a portion of the building shell (e.g., wall, window, door, floor, or roof). The process can be expressed as follows:

$$\dot{Q} = UA\Delta T$$

where $\dot{Q}$ is the rate of heat being transferred, A is the exposed surface area, and the temperature delta (ΔT) is the difference between the two boundaries of the wall (outdoor air and indoor air).

The rate at which heat is transferred by conduction is controlled by the overall heat transfer coefficient U:

$$U = 1/\Sigma R$$

where ΣR is the overall thermal resistance for the material layers of the system in question. The overall thermal resistance typically includes terms for convective heat transfer resistances, in effect, on both the inside and outside surfaces (see the discussion regarding convection that follows).

In the equation for conduction through a portion of the building shell, there are no fixed variables other than the fact that the outdoor air temperature is dictated by the project's location. The design team does have the ability to minimize $\dot{Q}$ by minimizing the U-factor, area, and temperature difference. Therefore, steps that can be taken include:

- Limit conduction heat gains or losses by providing an envelope with a low over-all U-factor. This can be accomplished through the use of insulating materials, air spaces in glass and walls, thermal breaks in construction, etc. Table 5.5 of *ANSI/ASHRAE/IES Standard 90.1-2010, Energy Standard for Buildings Except Low-Rise Residential Buildings* (ASHRAE 2010) contains minimum requirements for building envelope materials based on climate zones.
- Create an indoor environment wherein the space dry bulb can be higher or lower than traditional design norms in the summer and winter, respectively. This can be done using dehumidification and/or humidification, as long as you stay within acceptable ranges (see ANSI/ASHRAE Standard 55 [ASHRAE 2010]).
- Limit the surface area exposed to large temperature differentials by increasing shading, both on the building and what occurs naturally through the use of land-scaping. Considering low-profile, semiburied buildings is another option.

Convection. There are numerous formulas describing energy transfer through con-vection. The 2009 *ASHRAE Handbook—Fundamentals* (ASHRAE 2009) gives at least 12 factors used in determining convective heat transfer coefficients, and it lists no fewer than 25 equations for calculating heat transfer through forced convection. We will limit this discussion to the comparison of natural versus forced convection.

Natural convection is often called free convection and is primarily due to differ-ences in density and the action of gravity. To see convection in action, consider the LAVA® lamp that was so popular a number of years ago. The so-called lava gains heat from the lightbulb and rises; as it cools, it falls again. Replace the lightbulb with a hot-water-filled finned tube and swap the lava for air, and you get a fair idea of how convection works in a heating application. The lesson from this fairly obvious example is that natural convection is a simple law of nature that can be used to the designer's benefit in a number of ways. Forced convection occurs when the fluid (air, water, etc.) movement is done via an external mover, such as a fan or pump.

Recommendations for HVAC design related to convective heat transfer include the following:

- Consider the use of displacement ventilation when appropriate. In a displacement ventilation design, cool air is supplied at a low level and returned at the higher levels of a room. The design relies on the natural increase in buoyancy as air is warmed by heat generation sources such as people or equipment. This has the benefit of better IAQ since the upward flow of air naturally lifts pollutants out of the occupied space.
- Locate returns or exhaust directly over heat-generating equipment such as copiers and refrigerators, which removes heat from the space at the source, thus lowering the imposed space sensible cooling load.
- Provide baseboard heat to warm the exterior envelope surfaces to reduce radiant heat loss from occupants to walls and windows. (Note: While this may increase comfort, it can increase heat loss through the surface by action of the natural convective flow, reducing the surface heat transfer coefficient.)
- Use perimeter radiant ceiling panels to counteract perimeter heating loss (as an alternative to the last recommendation).
- Apply passive ventilation or hybrid ventilation, provided extreme outside conditions do not preclude its successful application.

By supplying low and returning high, you reduce the need for mixing that accompanies traditional overhead supply and return systems. By removing sensible load at the source, you reduce the sensible load in the space and, in turn, the supply air required to handle it. By allowing ventilation air to enter and exit a building naturally, the need for forced ventilation through air-handling systems and ductwork is eliminated. All of these steps decrease the amount of work required to address loads within a space, which leads to our next section.

Radiation. Heat transfer via radiation presents a unique challenge and opportunity for the designer. We have all stood next to a cold window and felt chilled even though the ambient temperature was at a comfortable level. The same holds true for sunny days when one can get too warm even though the thermostat says all is well. The simplified form of the equation describing radiant heat transfer is

$$\dot{Q} = \varepsilon\sigma A(T_1^4 - T_2^4),$$

where ε is emissivity, σ is the Stefan-Boltzmann constant, A is surface area, and the temperature (T) terms are the absolute temperature difference between the radiant object (subscript 1, with emissivity of ε) and its surroundings (subscript 2, a blackbody, which the surrounding ambient conditions could be considered as being).

Emissivity is a property that reflects the ability of that material to emit thermal radiation energy relative to the maximum amount that is theoretically possible at the material's temperature. Emissivity is a function of both the material itself and surface conditions. A dull black surface such as charcoal has an emissivity close to 1 (that of a blackbody), while shiny metallic surfaces have lower values, more in the range of 0.05 to 0.4. A related property for thermal radiation is the material absorptivity, which reflects that material's ability to absorb incident thermal radiation. A material with absorptivity of 0.8 will absorb 80% of the incoming thermal radiation. In general, one can consider the material's absorptivity and emissivity to be the same value. Surfaces with higher emissivity will absorb and emit more thermal energy. But notice the dramatic difference changing the temperature difference can make; the rate at which an object radiates or absorbs heat is proportional to the difference in the fourth powers of the absolute temperatures involved.

When the designer is faced with the challenge of minimizing the heat transferred by radiant means, the following steps can be taken for situations where cooling loads dominate:

- Explore the possibility of eliminating or drastically reducing the area (A) directly exposed to the radiant source through shading or other means. For most building applications, the radiant source is the sun, which can be treated as an object emitting energy at 5800 K, or 10,000°F.
- Recommend the use of cool-roof technologies that balance the emissivity and absorptivity of the surface to minimize the net solar heat gain to the roof.
- With glazing, the designer should evaluate the trade-off of using a low-emissivity material with other selective (reflective) coatings.
- Avoid dark colors on the building exterior, since they typically have a higher emissivity and absorb more heat.
- Limit east and west exposures, especially those with a large amount of glass.
- Offset the radiant load. For example, in a large atrium with a large glazing exposure and/or exterior walls, offsetting the radiant gains from the envelope with radiant cooling in the floor will produce a net effect that is significantly more comfortable for the occupant.

For situations where heating loads are significant and you are looking to maximize the heat gained ($\dot{Q}$), as with solar collection or passive heating, do just the opposite of the above. Increase exposure, maximize surface area, and use dark colors and high emissivity materials (AIA 1996).

When heating or cooling with radiant panels, remember the power of the temperature difference in maximizing thermal efficiency. You may be able to accommodate the architect's aesthetic sense by minimizing the need for excessive radiant surface area of high emissivity materials. For example, refer to Chapter 6, Figure 1, "Radiation Heat Transfer from Heated Ceiling, Floor, or Wall Panel," in 2008 *ASHRAE Handbook—Systems and Equipment* (ASHRAE 2008). Note that, assuming a 70°F (21°C) room temperature and other factors being equal, raising the effective panel temperature from 100°F to 200°F (38°C to 93°C) would raise the radiant heat transfer by a factor of 5.7. In turn, significantly less panel surface area would be required to accomplish the same amount of heating. Standing under a higher temperature panel may result in a warmer head relative to the other body areas and, consequently, may cause discomfort.

Fundamentals of Fluid Flow

The analysis of fluid flow and systems is also a fundamental concept for HVAC&R designers. For an incompressible, steady-flowing fluid, the Bernoulli equation governs. This equation is based on the conservation of energy principle and states that between Points 1 and 2 within a system, the following relationship holds:

$$0 = \frac{P_2 - P_1}{\rho g} + \frac{V_2^2 - V_1^2}{2g} + (z_2 - z_1)$$

where P is the fluid pressure, V is the fluid velocity, and z is the elevation at Points 1 and 2. This equation can generally be thought of as being applicable to most HVAC&R fluid applications.

When a fluid passes through a fan or pump, additional energy is input into the system in the form of an increase in pressure and perhaps fluid velocity. The power required to move a fluid involves, in essence, a modification of the Bernoulli equation with the left-hand side not being zero but reflecting the additional energy input to the fluid.

APPLICATIONS TO HVAC SYSTEMS AND PROCESSES

Power Generation

For steam boilers, with the water undergoing phase change, the enthalpy change through the boiler is much larger than it is for either the water in hot-water generators or the air in warm-air furnaces, where the enthalpy change is proportional to the temperature rise of the fluid.

Combustion of the fuel/air mixture results in the flue gases being discharged to the chimney or vent having high temperatures. Green design requires examining the recovery of the energy in the flue gases for possible reuse—as in preheating outside air, heating hot water for domestic use, or serving as a heat source for other building heating purposes such as snow-melting systems. Be mindful of the potential of condensing water vapor in the exhaust gases.

When looking at the generation of power for on-site power production (e.g., with cogeneration systems) or at vapor-compression refrigeration systems in building air conditioning (where the work produced or required is a major energy concern), looking at the first and second laws together is necessary.

Theoretically, the most efficient power generation system is given by the Carnot cycle. This can be represented as a rectangle on temperature-entropy coordinates (see Figure 2-3). The area of the rectangle represents the total energy (both work and thermal) involved in the case of a power plant generating power or of vapor compression refrigeration air-conditioning or heat-pump systems. For example, in Figure 2-3 the shaded area represents the heat load transported by a vapor-compression refrigeration cycle (Q_{load}), and the cross-hatched area represents the amount of work output necessary by the compressor to move the heat (W). The total of the two represents the heat rejected to the environment at the condenser ($Q_{rejected}$).

For power generation, the upper temperature, representing the high temperature in the Carnot cycle (T_h) should be as high as possible to maximize work output. Similarly, the lower temperature in the Carnot cycle (T_c) should be as

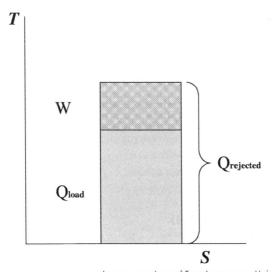

Image courtesy of Tom Lawrence, University of Georgia

Figure 2-3 Carnot cycle for refrigeration.

low as possible. While real power generation systems do not operate precisely on the Carnot cycle, the principle is still valid.

In real cycles, the work produced by the turbines (gas or steam) is the enthalpy difference across the turbine multiplied by the mass flow rate. The net power generated is the difference between this enthalpy difference and that required for the compression of combustion air, plus the work to pump the water in the steam part of the cycle.

Similarly, for refrigeration, where one wants to minimize the work input (power required), T_h should be as low as possible and T_c as high as possible.

Power Production or Combined Heat and Power

Many buildings or building groups use on-site electric power generation plants that, when combined with some sort of heat recovery, are termed *cogeneration plants*.

A common modern generation plant may employ a gas turbine, which requires compressing air before combustion of fuel in a combustion chamber. This, in turn, yields high-temperature combustion gases at high pressure, which expand through the turbine, generating power. The work required to compress a fluid is a function of the fluid density and compressibility, with low-density fluids (i.e., air) requiring more work to achieve a given pressure increase than higher-density fluids (i.e., liquids like water). This results in relatively low-pressure gases entering the turbine and high-temperature exhaust leaving the turbine at the lower atmospheric pressure obtained after expansion.

Modern combined-cycle power plants use high-temperature turbine exhaust as the heating medium for heat recovery steam generators. These steam generators operate at much higher pressures than gas turbines, since water must first be pumped to the high pressures entering the steam generators, and this high-density fluid requires much less energy to achieve the high pressure than the air in the gas turbine cycle. The steam expands through a steam turbine to low condensing temperatures (T_c) for heat rejection in a condenser. For on-site power generation without combined cycles, the gas turbine exhaust is used as a heat source for other building energy needs, achieving the lower T_c in that manner. This wasted heat could also be used in an absorption cooling to produce chilled water, resulting in a process known as trigeneration (power, heat, and chilled water).

Air Conditioning (Cooling)

In a refrigeration system, where the end-purpose is the cooling of air for building cooling purposes, the chiller or direct expansion refrigerant should have the cooling fluid at as high a temperature (T_c) as possible to minimize work input. Of course, this temperature is limited by the temperature to which the air must be cooled. The closer T_c is to that air temperature, however, the more heat transfer surface area will be required in the heat exchanger used to cool the air in both the cooling coils in the direct expansion systems or in chilled-water coils.

The high temperature (T_h) at which heat is rejected is limited by the temperature of the heat sink (the ambient air in an air-cooled condenser) or by the approach to the air wet-bulb temperature with water-cooled condensers used in conjunction with cooling towers. Again, the closer the refrigerant (T_h) is to the coolant temperature, the larger and more expensive the heat exchanger (condenser) required will be.

For the refrigeration cycle using expansion valves, the work input is the enthalpy difference across the compressor. A sample refrigeration cycle is plotted on a pressure-enthalpy diagram and is given in Figure 2-4. On the diagram, the refrigerant vapor leaving the evaporator (Point 1) enters the compressor and leaves at Point 2. After going through the condenser, the refrigerant is at Point 3 and leaves the expansion valve at Point 4.

Hydraulic Machine (Pumps or Fans) Similarity Analysis

The performance of a pump or fan at one operating point can be used to predict the performance of the same (or similar) equipment at a different operating condition.

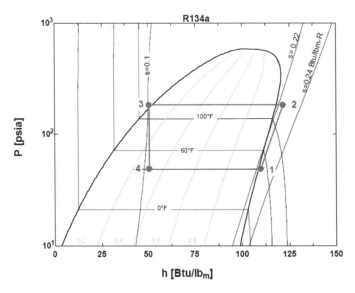

Image courtesy of Tom Lawrence, University of Georgia

Figure 2-4 Carnot cycle shown on pressure-enthalpy diagram.

This is done using similarity relations. Since the energy required in pumping water needed in chilled-water systems—and that needed to power the fans used in air-distribution systems—can be quite substantial, a closer look at these relations can be useful in analyzing possibilities for saving energy. Similarity relations, at the point of maximum efficiency, yield

$$\left.\frac{Pv}{N^3 D^5}\right|_{\text{Maximum Efficiency}} = \text{Constant},$$

and

$$\left.\frac{Q}{ND^3}\right|_{\text{Maximum Efficiency}} = \text{Constant},$$

where

Q = volumetric flow rate,

N = impeller rotative speed,

D = impeller diameter,

P = power input to the pump or fan, and

v = specific volume of the fluid.

When considering performance of the same pump or fan at different operating conditions, the impeller diameter is the same. The first similarity relation listed then reduces to

$$\left.\frac{Pv}{N^3}\right|_{\text{Maximum Efficiency}} = \text{Constant}.$$

The power input needed to run the pump or fan is therefore proportional to N^3—or to the cube of the rotating speed. This gives rise to the use of variable-speed drives, where part loads on the system result in decreased flow requirements. The reduction in flow is accomplished by lowering the pump or fan rotating speed (N). Input power to the fan or pump will therefore decrease as the cube of N.

The use of variable-speed (or variable-frequency) drives does involve additional controls and engineering design analysis of operating conditions to ensure that the system will perform. This will add to the initial cost of the system. However, the cost of equipment and controls needed to implement a variable-speed drive has decreased over the past decade or so and has reached the point that even relatively small power equipment (1 to 2 hp) can economically be controlled with a variable-speed system.

Forced Convection and Mass Transfer

In HVAC&R, mass transfer by forced convection is used to facilitate a thermodynamic transfer of energy. Though all types of fluids and gases are moved in HVAC applications, the discussion here is limited to water and air. Note in the following the key relationship between mass flow rates, the fluid's thermal properties, and the load. Additional technical information on fluid transport is provided in Chapter 10, "Energy Distribution Systems."

Water. The amount of energy required to address a sensible load ($\dot{Q}_s$) within a system is found to be proportional to the fluid mass flow rate (m) into the system and to the temperature difference (ΔT) between the system and the fluid. This can be expressed as

$$\dot{Q}_s = \dot{m}c_p\Delta T,$$

where c_p is the specific heat at constant pressure p of the medium. For temperature changes that are not too great, c_p can be considered a constant. The sensible heat formula for water in I-P and SI, respectively, are

$$\dot{Q}_s = (\text{gpm})(500)\Delta T \ [\text{Btu/h}] \quad \text{and} \quad \dot{Q}_s = (\text{L/s})(4.187)\Delta T \ [\text{kW}].$$

The key relationships are clear. If $\dot{Q}$ is a given, then the only variables are flow and temperature difference. The greater the temperature difference (ΔT), the less flow will be required, and vice versa. If the load ($\dot{Q}$) is variable, then one can react by varying flow (ΔT) or both. Recommended strategies include:

- Use high ΔT designs whenever feasible, barring any negative efficiency impacts that may result from a lowered chiller coefficient of performance (COP). The greater the temperature difference, the less flow that will be required.
- Maintain a constant ΔT and vary the flow in response to load. The value of this strategy becomes clearer when considered with the fan/pump affinity laws discussed later in this chapter.

Moist Air. When working with air, we are rarely dealing with a dry gas. Instead, air is usually a mixture of water and air. In turn, air-side energy calculations not only involve the temperature difference (sensible heat) but also must factor in the changes of state (latent heat). The sensible load in standard air is similar to that discussed above for water and can be quantified (in I-P and SI, respectively) as follows:

$$\dot{Q}_s = (\text{cfm})(1.08)\Delta T \ [\text{Btu/h}] \quad \text{and} \quad \dot{Q}_s = (\text{L/s})(1.21)\Delta T \ [\text{W}]$$

The amount of energy required to address a latent load ($\dot{Q}$) within a system is found to be proportional to the fluid mass flow rate (m) into the system and to the humidity ratio difference $\Delta\omega$ between the air in the system and the air entering the system, which can be expressed as

$$\dot{Q}_L = \dot{m} h_{fg} \Delta\omega,$$

where h_{fg} is the latent heat of vaporization for water. For temperature changes that are not too great, h_{fg} can be considered a constant. Here are the latent heat equations in I-P for standard air:

$$\dot{Q}_L = (\text{cfm})(0.68)\Delta\omega_{\text{grains/lb}}$$

$$\dot{Q}_L = (\text{cfm})(4840)\Delta\omega_{\text{lb/lb}}$$

The latent heat equation in SI for standard air is

$$\dot{Q}_L = (\text{L/s})(2.97)\Delta\omega,$$

where the units for $\Delta\omega$ are g/kg.

The key relationships again are obvious. If $\dot{Q}$ is a given, then the only variables are flow and moisture content of the air delivered. The greater the humidity ratio difference (i.e., the dryer the supply air), the less flow will be required.

Last, addressing total heat in a space leads us to the following:

$$\dot{Q}_T = \dot{Q}_s + \dot{Q}_L = \dot{m}\Delta h$$

where Δh is the difference in enthalpy between the air/water vapor in the space and the supply air/water vapor. For standard air, the process (in I-P) is

$$\dot{Q}_T = (\text{cfm})(4.45)\Delta h.$$

In all of the air formulas, the relationship remains. The only actions at our disposal are varying flow rates and altering thermal properties. To minimize the flow rate and energy required in air systems, consider the following possible steps:

- Move less air by supplying colder air and increasing the temperature difference when possible. The designer will need to account for any negative chiller efficiency impacts due to lowered COP. High-induction diffusers or fan terminal units can be used to temper the supply air at the point of distribution to avoid drafts and discomfort.

- Maintain a constant (ΔT) and vary the airflow in response to load.
- Use energy recovery to pretreat outdoor air to minimize mixed-air differentials and, in turn, reduce the load associated with the dictated ventilation quantity.
- Consider passive preheating strategies, such as buried duct or solar walls, when introducing outdoor air in the winter, again to minimize the mixed-air differentials and the associated load.
- Create an indoor environment wherein the space dry bulb can be higher than traditional design norms in the summer. Lowering relative humidity levels by means of passive dehumidification via return air bypass can allow a higher space temperature, which equates to a higher ΔT in reference to the supply air.
- Create an indoor environment wherein the space dry bulb can be lower than traditional design norms in the winter (see ANSI/ASHRAE Standard 55 [ASHRAE 2004]). Utilize radiant task heating for comfort in lower ambient air temperatures (Chapman et al. 2001).
- Use hybrid radiant/convective systems where conditions, artifacts, or special needs of individuals conflict with comfort of viewers, visitors, or personnel.
- Capture sensible load at the source and remove it from the space. In turn, less supply air is required to handle the space load.
- Use stratification strategies such as displacement ventilation and remove the ceiling load from the space comfort equation. Note that the central equipment still sees this load, but we do not have to move as much air in the space.

Work and Power

We know that it takes energy to change the thermal properties of our heating and cooling medium (i.e., temperature and enthalpy). When possible, we want to take advantage of natural forces such as free convection and thermal radiation heat transfer. For the remainder of the load, we will need to transfer energy using forced convection and mass transfer. To move all of that mass, we need to do work. Work is quantified in terms of input power, and we want to use as little power as possible.

Power Requirements

If moving a fluid, the efficiency (E) of the device and the motor/drive combination, combined with the specific gravity (sg) of the fluid, will determine the amount of power required. For a pump, the equation for motor horsepower (mhp) is

$$\text{mhp} = \frac{(\text{gpm})(\Delta P \text{ ft} - \text{hd})(\text{sg})}{(3960)E_{pump}E_{motordrive}} \quad \text{or} \quad \text{mkW} = \frac{(\text{L/s})(\Delta P \text{ kPa})(\text{sg})}{(1000)E_{pump}E_{motordrive}},$$

and, for a fan,

$$\text{mhp} = \frac{(\text{cfm})(\Delta P \text{ in. w.g.})(\text{sg})}{(6356)E_{fan}E_{motordrive}} \quad \text{or} \quad \text{mkW} = \frac{(\text{L/s})(\Delta P \text{ kPa})(\text{sg})}{(1000)E_{fan}E_{motordrive}}.$$

In most instances, the specific gravity is fixed, because the fluid is determined by the design (i.e., air at sea level, water, water with glycol, etc.). So the key actions that can be taken are to minimize flow and pressure drop and to maximize equipment and drive efficiencies. We have discussed flow already, but regarding pressure drop and efficiency, consider these steps:

- Minimize pressure drop by increasing conduit size (i.e., duct or pipe size) and limiting the number of fittings. Obviously, there is a breakeven point where increased size becomes unworkable or not cost-effective, but that is a matter of judgment and/or technical evaluation.
- Keep fluid specific gravity in check. For example, adding glycol not only decreases thermodynamic performance, but it also increases the amount of pumping energy required to move the fluid.
- Select equipment based on judicial review of the efficiency curves. Maximize efficiency, but avoid unsteady locations or fringe selections on the operating curves.
- Specify premium efficiency motors, not just high-efficiency motors. The difference is usually worth the added cost, which can be confirmed through a life-cycle cost analysis.
- Consider different pump speeds and types to maximize efficiency and performance (e.g., end suction-vertical in-line, 1750 to 3600 rpm).
- Evaluate the right fan for the right need (e.g., forward-curved versus backward-inclined, prop versus centrifugal, plenum versus housed).

Pump or Fan Affinity Laws

The affinity laws are often called the fan laws or the pump laws depending on the equipment you are using. The fact is that, regardless of the medium—be it air, water, or maple syrup—the affinity laws present a series of powerful relationships that can make or break a design. Here are the laws:

$$\frac{\text{rpm}_2}{\text{rpm}_1} = \frac{Flow_2}{Flow_1}$$

$$\frac{\Delta P_2}{\Delta P_1} = \left(\frac{Flow_2}{Flow_1}\right)^2$$

$$\frac{\text{mhp}_2}{\text{mhp}_1} = \left(\frac{Flow_2}{Flow_1}\right)^3$$

The relationships are simple. Flow and speed are directly proportional. But the static pressure in a system varies by the square of the flow, and the required motor horsepower varies by the cube of the flow. What does this mean in terms of energy required? See the following example.

Consider a typical office building at 10,000 ft² (929 m²) with a varying load. Peak load is 200 ft²/ton (5.28 m²/kW), which translates to 600,000 Btu/h (176 kW). The original design utilized a constant-flow, variable-temperature, multizone air-handling system. Design airflow is based on a 55°F (12.8°C) supply temperature and 75°F (23.9°C) zone temperature for a 20°F (11.1 K) ΔT. Fans were selected for 28,000 cfm (13,215 L/s) at 4 in. (0.996 kPa) total static pressure (1.0 kPa), with a fan efficiency of 75% and motor efficiency equal to 95%.

$$\text{mhp} = \frac{(\text{cfm})(\Delta P \text{ in. w.g.})(\text{sg})}{(6356)\varepsilon_{Fan}\varepsilon_{Motor}} = \frac{(28,000)(4 \text{ in. w.g.})(1)}{(6356)(0.75)(0.95)} \approx 25 \text{ hp} \qquad \text{(I-P)}$$

$$\text{mkW} = \frac{(\text{L/s})(\Delta P \text{ kPa})(\text{sg})}{(1000)\varepsilon_{Fan}\varepsilon_{Motor-Drive}} = \frac{(13,215)(0.996 \text{ kPa})(1)}{(1000)(0.75)(0.95)} \approx 18.5 \text{ kW} \qquad \text{(SI)}$$

The owner is considering replacing the aging system with a constant-temperature, variable-volume system. The average load diversity within the building is 75%, which means that the fan at any given time will have to deliver, on average, no more than 21,000 cfm (9910 L/s). Based on fan energy alone, what kind of energy savings can we expect? In I-P:

$$\frac{\text{mhp}_2}{\text{mhp}_1} = \left(\frac{\text{Flow}_2}{\text{Flow}_1}\right)^3 = \frac{\text{mhp}_2}{25 \text{ hp}} = \left(\frac{21,000}{28,000}\right)^3$$

$$\text{mhp}_2 = 10.5 \text{ hp}$$

$$\Delta\text{mhp} = 25 - 10.5 = 14.5 \text{ hp}$$

$$1 \text{ hp} = 2545 \text{ Btu/h}$$

$$(14.5 \text{ hp})(2545 \text{ Btu/h} - \text{hp}) = 36,903 \text{ Btu/h}$$

In SI:

$$\frac{\text{mkW}_2}{\text{mkW}_1} = \left(\frac{\text{Flow}_2}{\text{Flow}_1}\right)^3 = \frac{\text{mkW}_2}{18.5 \text{ kW}} = \left(\frac{9910}{13,215}\right)^3$$

$$\text{mkW}_2 = 7.8 \text{ kW}$$

$$\Delta kW = 18.5 - 7.8 = 10.7 \text{ kW}$$

Note that a 25% decrease in flow equates to a 58% decrease in required power, and these principles apply to variable-flow water systems as well. Clearly, there is an incentive to minimize flow and pressure drop whenever possible.

SUMMARY OF ENGINEERING APPLICATION FUNDAMENTALS

- Understanding a formula's key relationships and dependencies will often make green-oriented measures obvious.
- Because we have a limited supply of energy and cannot create it, a good sustainable design will work to conserve energy.
- When designing building envelopes, heat transfer by conduction and solar radiation should be optimized for the energy transfer process (i.e., heating or cooling) involved.
- When designing heating and cooling systems, the use of heat transfer and ventilation through natural means (e.g., natural convection or radiation) should be considered from the beginning of the design process and utilized fully when possible.
- When forced convection and mass transfer are necessary, minimize flow and pressure drop, maximize the effect of thermal characteristic (temperature, enthalpy, or humidity ratio) differences, and specify equipment with the highest efficiencies.

REFERENCES AND RESOURCES

Published

AIA. 1996. *Environmental Resource Guide*. Edited by Joseph Demkin. New York: John Wiley & Sons.

ASHRAE. 2010. *ANSI/ASHRAE Standard 55-2010, Thermal Environmental Conditions for Human Occupancy*. Atlanta: American Society of Heating, Refrigerating and Air-Conditioning Engineers, Inc.

ASHRAE. 2008. *ASHRAE Handbook—Systems and Equipment*, Ch. 6. Atlanta: American Society of Heating, Refrigerating and Air-Conditioning Engineers, Inc.

ASHRAE. 2009. *ASHRAE Handbook—Fundamentals*. Atlanta: American Society of Heating, Refrigerating and Air-Conditioning Engineers, Inc.

ASHRAE. 2009. *ANSI/ASHRAE/USGBC/IES Standard 189.1-2009, Standard for the Design of High-Performance Green Buildings*. Atlanta: American Society of Heating, Refrigerating and Air-Conditioning Engineers, Inc.

ASHRAE. 2010. *ANSI/ASHRAE/IES Standard 90.1-2010, Energy Standard for Buildings Except Low-Rise Residential Buildings*. Atlanta: American Society of Heating, Refrigerating and Air-Conditioning Engineers, Inc.

Chapman, K.S., J.E. Howell, and R.D. Watson. 2001. Radiant panel surface temperature over a range of ambient temperatures. *ASHRAE Transactions* 107(1):383–89.

Deru, M., and P. Torcellini. 2007. *Source Energy and Emissions Factors for Energy Use in Buidlings.* Technical Report NREL/TP_550-38617, National Renewable Energy Laboratory, Golden, CO.

Grondzik, W.T. 2001. The (mechanical) engineer's role in sustainable design: Indoor environmental quality issues in sustainable design. HTML presentation available at www.polaris.net/~gzik/ieq/ieq.htm.

Watson, R.D., and K.S. Chapman. 2002. *Radiant Heating and Cooling Handbook.* McGraw-Hill.

Online

The American Institute of Architects
   www.aia.org
Building for Environmental and Economic Sustainability (BEES)
   www.bfrl.nist.gov/oae/software/bees.html
BuildingGreen (for purchase)
   www.greenbuildingadvisor.com
Building Research Establishment Environmental Assessment Method (BREEAM®) rating program
   www.breeam.org
Center of Excellence for Sustainable Development, Smart Communities Network
   www.smartcommunities.ncat.org
Green Building Advisor
   www.greenbuildingadvisor.com
Green Globes
   www.greenglobes.com
GreenSpec® Product Guide
   www.buildinggreen.com/menus/index.cfm
The Hannover Principles
   www.mindfully.org/Sustainability/Hannover-Principles.htm
International Living Building Institute, The Living Building Challenge V2.0
   http://ilbi.org/the-standard/version-2-0
International Organization for Standardization family of 14000 standards,
   www.iso.org/iso/en/iso9000-14000/index.html
Intergovernmental Panel on Climate Change
   www.ipcc.ch
Lawrence Berkeley National Laboratories,
   Environmental Energy Technologies Division
   http://eetd.lbl.gov/

Minnesota Sustainable Design Guide
www.sustainabledesignguide.umn.edu
National Renewable Energy Laboratory, Buildings Research
www.nrel.gov/buildings/
Natural Resources Canada, Commercial Buildings Incentive Program
http://nrcan.gc.ca/evaluation/reprap/2001/cbip-pebc-eng.php
Natural Resources Canada, EE4 Commercial Buildings Incentive Program
http://canmetenergy-canmetenergie.nrcan-rncan.gc.ca/eng/software_
tools/ee4.html
The Natural Step
www.naturalstep.org
New Buildings Institute
www.newbuildings.org/
Oikos: Green Building Source
www.oikos.com
Rocky Mountain Institute
www.rmi.org
Sustainable Building Challenge
www.iisbe.org/
Sustainable Buildings Industry Council
www.sbicouncil.org
Tools for the Reduction and Assessment of Chemical and Other Environmental
Impacts (TRACI)
www.epa.gov/nrmrl/std/sab/traci/
U.S. Green Building Council, Leadership in Energy and Environmental Design,
Green Building Certification System
www.usgbc.org/DisplayPage.aspx?CategoryID=19
The Whole Building Design Guide
www.wbdg.org

Section 2:
The Design Process

CHAPTER THREE

PROJECT
STRATEGIES

INGREDIENTS OF A SUCCESSFUL GREEN PROJECT ENDEAVOR

The following ingredients are essential in delivering a successful green design:

- Commitment from the entire project team, starting with the owner.
- Establishing Owner's Project Requirements (OPR), including green design goals, early in the design process.
- Integration of team ideas.
- Effective execution throughout the project's phases—from predesign through the end of its useful service life.

Establishing Green Design Goals Early

Establishing goals early in the project planning stages is key to developing a successful green design and minimizing costs. It is easy to say that goals need to be established, but many designers and owners struggle with what green design is and what green/sustainable goals should be established. Some typical questions to ask are:

- What does it cost to design and construct a green project?
- Where do you get the best return for the investment?
- How far should the team go to accomplish a green design?

Today there are many guides a team can use with ideas on which green/sustainable principles should be considered. Chapter 7 of this Guide presents several rating systems and references on environmental performance improvement. The essence of these documents is to provide guidance on how to reduce the impact the building will have on the environment. While the approaches and goals contained in each differ, all suggest common principles that designers may find helpful to apply to their projects.

Integration of Team Ideas

No green project will be successful if the various project stakeholders are not included in the process. These stakeholders include the owner, the owner's operations staff, the commissioning authority, design disciplines, contractors, and users. These stakeholders, if known, should work in close coordination, beginning in the earliest stages. Use the commissioning process, as discussed in Chapter 6, to obtain input from the various stakeholders and develop the OPR document that defines the owner's objectives and criteria (which includes the green/sustainable project goals that set the foundation for what the team is tasked with delivering and benchmarks for success). Based on the owner's stated objectives and criteria, the integrated team works together with a clear direction and focus to deliver the project. Gone are the days when the mechanical, electrical, and plumbing engineers and landscape architects become involved only after the building's form and space arrangements are set (i.e., end of schematic design). That is far too late for the necessary "cross-pollenization" of ideas between engineering and architectural disciplines that must occur for green design to be effective.

Effective Execution

Still, all the good intentions an owner and project team may have during the early stages are meaningless without follow-through both during the construction process and over the entire life of the facility. Ideally, success requires a committed owner, use of the commissioning process, the owner's defined objectives and criteria, including green/sustainable project goals established in predesign, knowledgeable design practitioners working in concert to develop a green/sustainable design, competent contractors who buy into the green concept, and, finally, operators armed with the necessary tools and who are properly trained and dedicated to keeping the facility operating at peak performance for its life.

INCENTIVES FOR GREEN DESIGN

For both individuals and firms in the design and construction profession, many incentives exist to develop green/sustainable projects. As with any aspect of business practice that adds value to a project, fees and client expectations must be carefully managed. While some clients may balk at added fees charged for the commissioning, additional coordination, and studies necessary to meet green/sustainable goals for systems that are part of a traditional project scope, others welcome these services. First, the appetite of the project client and full project team for a green/sustainable project must be gaged. Then, the commensurate level of commissioning, design, construction, and operational services can be provided. The OPR, defined early and documented in writing, facilitate such understandings and provide a more defined initial fee proposal and acceptance.

Individuals and firms are finding that green project capabilities can positively impact building professionals' careers and the firms that employ them. Firms can enhance these capabilities by providing leadership on green issues, building individual competencies, providing ongoing support for professional development in relevant areas, rewarding accomplishments, marketing or promoting green success stories, and building their clientele's interest in green/sustainable design.

When properly delivered, green design/construction/operation capabilities can lead to enhanced service to clients, repeat business, increased public relations and marketing value, and increased demand for these green design services, especially among the architects or owners that represent a substantial proportion of many firms' billings. In addition, green capabilities can also improve employee retention and employee satisfaction. Finally, green/sustainable project competency can reduce risks in practice, meaning that knowledge of green issues is necessary to manage risk when participating in aggressively green projects.

Human Productivity. While difficult to measure, the benefits of improving the learning, living, and workplace environment (all aspects of indoor environmental quality [IEQ]) and feelings of well-being can yield big gains in human productivity. Figure 3-1 shows the typical relationship among the various categories of the costs of operating a business with human costs outstripping all other costs several times over.

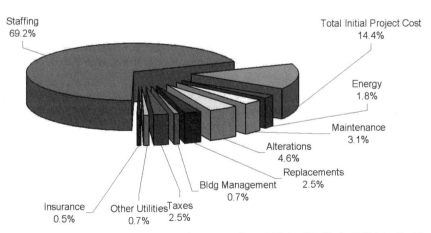

Image courtesy of Michael Dell'Isola, Faithful + Gould

Figure 3-1 People cost vs. other costs in business operation.

Below are some examples of some data generated by private commercial organizations that support the concept that green design increases productivity:

Lockheed
- 15% rise in production
- 15% drop in absenteeism

West Bend Mutual Insurance
- 16% increase in claims processes

NG Bank
- 15% drop in absenteeism

Verifone
- 5% increase in productivity
- 40% drop in absenteeism

Similar results have been shown in learning and living environments. Some projects may lend themselves to the incorporation of green concepts without incurring additional costs beyond the business's own investment in the knowledge of, and experience with, green projects. Other sustainable design projects may require additional services for a greater number of design considerations not customarily included in ordinary design fees, such as extended energy analysis, daylighting penetration, and solar load analysis, or extended review (of materials and components, environmental impacts such as embodied energy, transportation, construction, composition, and indoor air quality [IAQ] performance). Other categories of additional services may include project-specific research or training of the engineering team (where required) and client education and communication.

Financial Incentives. Two broad categories of incentives, external and internal, can each encompass both direct and indirect financial benefits and nonfinancial advantages.

The familiar range of energy incentives offered by many utility-administered, state-mandated, demand-side management programs represents one obvious form of external financial incentive—the rebate check available to owners or utility ratepayers who pursue energy conservation measures in buildings and mechanical/electrical systems. Of course, the availability of these and other financial incentives varies from place to place and project to project. But many other external financial incentives can reduce project costs where applicable, such as:

- sustainable design tax credits
- marketable emissions credits
- tax rebates
- brownfield funds

- historic preservation funds
- community redevelopment funds
- economic development funds
- charitable foundation funds

In addition, future public policy initiatives associated with climate concerns may direct attention toward low-carbon or net zero carbon designs, as discussed later in this Guide.

The European Union's support programs have, in the past and currently under the Intelligent Energy-Europe program, provided additional funding sources for projects that support the promotion of energy efficiency and the use of alternative energy sources in buildings. For example, the eco-buildings projects utilize a new approach when it comes to the design, construction, and operation of new and/or refurbished buildings. This approach is based on the best combination of the double approach: to reduce substantially, and, if possible, to avoid, the demand for heating, cooling, and lighting and to supply the necessary heating, cooling, and lighting in the most efficient way, based as much as possible on renewable energy sources and polygeneration. Information on eco-building demonstration projects throughout Europe, supported by the European Commission (DG TREN), is available at www.sara-project.net.

In 2009, the European Commission launched its BUILD UP initiative to increase the awareness of all parties in the building chain of the savings potential, which remains untapped. BUILD UP will promote better and smarter buildings across Europe by connecting building professionals, local authorities, and citizens. Its interactive Web portal will catalyze and release Europe's collective intelligence for an effective implementation of energy-saving measures in buildings. The BUILD UP Web portal (www.buildup.eu/) shares and promotes existing knowledge, guidelines, tools, and best practices for energy-saving measures, while it also informs and updates the market about the legislative framework in terms of goals, practical implications, and future revisions.

Dena—the German Energy Agency's (www.dena.de/en/) Subsidy Overview EU-27 offers the latest information on grant programs and regulatory frameworks in the EU member states. At this site, the information on technologies that generate heat from renewable energies is presented in concise table form.

Incentives that are internal to a project can be created through contractual arrangements. The simplest example is an added fee for added scope in doing the work needed to evaluate green design alternatives. At the other end of the spectrum, some proactive firms offer design review and commissioning services on a performance basis. Construction project insurance offerings have included rebates if no IAQ claims are made a predetermined number of years after construction is completed. If both client and firm are willing, there are many ways to create internal incentives for green engineering design on a project-specific basis. Many individuals and groups have done valuable work in exploring various incentives for green design. *ASHRAE Journal* and many other industry periodicals carry case studies with green engineering elements. Assembling and familiarizing oneself with the many successfully completed green projects is useful when you must sell and deliver green engineering services.

BUILDING TEAM SPIRIT

Sustainable development requires buy-in from all parties: the owner initiating the project, the computer-aided design operator in the office, the installing subcontractors, and the maintenance person keeping the facility functioning—each plays an indispensable role. Ultimately, the owner is the most important member of the team. It is important to understand that within the owner's organization there are often different departments or staff that focus on user activities, design and construction, or operation and maintenance and do not necessarily communicate (or are invited to communicate) their objectives and criteria to the design and construction team. Success of the project and the long-term benefits of established green/sustainable goals can be easily lost if all of the owner's staff is not included. For example, operators with insufficient training and understanding of the project's intended operation can inadvertently negate the benefits through improper operation.

SUCCESSFUL APPROACHES TO DESIGN

Sustainable Design with System Commissioning

Institutions and real estate managers throughout the country, recognizing the long-term cost benefits of sustainable design with system commissioning, are successfully implementing changes in how their projects are designed, constructed, and operated. Emory University's Whitehead Biomedical Research Building, for example, uses enthalpy wheels that recover 83% of the energy exhausted by the general exhaust system, captures air-conditioning condensate to displace potable water otherwise used for cooling tower makeup, and captures all the rainwater from the roof for site irrigation, displacing more than 3 million gal of potable water usage per year. Refer to Chapter 6 for a more extensive discussion on the benefits of the commissioning process and how it can be successfully implemented on a project.

The following sections describe other approaches to the green building design process that have been successful.

Zero Energy Design

A net zero energy building (NZEB) (also known as a *zero energy building*) is a general term applied to a building with zero net energy consumption and zero annual carbon emissions. NZEBs are autonomous from the energy grid supply—

Pg 53 updates
pg 53 add NREL ZEB RSF
to the examples.

Sheraton

energy is produced on site. This design principle is gaining considerable interest as renewable energy becomes a means to cut greenhouse gas emissions (http://zeb.buildinggreen.com).

An example of a NZEB is the Aldo Leopold Legacy Center in Baraboo, Wisconsin. The building is a carbon-neutral NZEB that uses 39.6 kW rooftop photovoltaic (PV) array to produce about 10% more electricity than that needed annually to operate the building. Specifically, the Legacy Center qualifies as a:

- Site NZEB: The building produces at least as much energy as it uses in a year, when accounted for at the site (on-site PV). It burns locally harvested, renewable wood in the winter for heat.

- Source NZEB: The building produces at least as much energy as it uses in a year, when accounted for at the source. It is the source of its own energy, which is generated on site through PV and wood.

- Emissions (carbon) NZEB: The building produces or purchases at least as much emission-free renewable energy as it uses from emission-producing energy sources annually. The excess renewable energy the building produces, combined with on-site carbon sequestration through its forested land, offset the carbon emissions from the building operations.

(The source for this information is http://zeb.buildinggreen.com/.)

[handwritten marginalia: Ref NREL design papers]

[handwritten note: update from Paul T.]

Low-Energy Design Process: National Renewable Energy Laboratory's Experience

This process was used to design and construct the visitor's center at Zion National Park. The visitor's center was targeted to use 70% less energy than a comparable visitor's center built to Federal Energy Code 10 CFR 435 (CFR 1995). The authors used an integrated design process, including extensive simulations, to minimize the building's energy consumption. The result was a passive solar commercial building that makes good use of the thermal envelope, daylighting, and natural ventilation. Passive, downdraft cooltowers provide all the cooling. Two trombe walls provide a significant amount of heat for the building. After two years of metering, the results show a net energy use intensity of 24.7 kBtu/ft^2·yr (281 MJ/m^2·yr) and a 67% energy cost saving. Low energy use and aggressive demand management result in an energy cost intensity of $0.43/ft^2 ($4.63/m^2). For more information, Torcellini et al. (2006) discusses lessons learned related to the design process, the daylighting, the PV system, and the HVAC system.

Early Identification of Funding Sources

The economic benefits of green design strategies as discussed earlier in this chapter are enhanced by identifying funding sources for the high-performance design concepts that are being considered for a building design project. Having the knowledge of where the opportunities can be found and assisting the team in obtaining the funding enhances the engineer's role and importance in the green design process, and significantly improves the owner's return on investment (ROI). Funding sources include utility company rebates, state and federal grant programs for energy efficiency and renewable energy measures, and private foundation grants for design enhancements and green rating system implementation.

For example, a 26-story, 960-bed residence hall project completed in 2009 at Boston University utilized the NSTAR Comprehensive Design Rebate Program (NSTAR is a Massachusetts-based electric and gas utility). The program provides incentives for purchasing and installing high-efficiency equipment for use in commercial and industrial operations. NSTAR offers incentives of 90% of the incremental cost differential for comprehensive design or up to 75% of the incremental cost differential between standard base line and high-efficiency equipment. In addition, customers are eligible to receive cost sharing for engineering services and design and commissioning services.

On the BU Housing project, NSTAR and the design team held an energy conservation measure charrette during the schematic design phase. Measures incorporated into the design included energy recovery for the 100% outside air ventilation units, chilled-water system energy enhancements, energy conservation measure motors and variable-speed control logic for the fan coil units, upgraded glazing performance, and variable-speed drives on all pump motors (with integrated system control logic) on the project. The net result was that for an investment of just over $500,000 on a $130 million project, BU received a rebate from NSTAR for $240,000. In addition, the estimated energy savings from incorporation of these measures is estimated to be $210,000, annually. The result is an annual ROI of greater than 70%.

The following link provides information on incentive programs for all 50 states: www.dsireusa.org/.

Integrated Design Process

Recent building design experiences in North America and Europe have led to the recognition of key factors that are relevant to acheiving very high levels of environmental performance. These include use of an integrated design process, which incorporates passive and bioclimatic approaches and also includes an iterative process. Originally established in the early 1990s by Canada's C-2000 program, the process has been incorporated on many projects in North America and beyond.

JUSTIFICATIONS FOR GREEN DESIGN

Doing the Right Thing

The motivation and reasons for implementing green buildings are diverse but can be condensed into essentially wanting to do the right thing to protect the Earth's resources. For some, a wake-up call occurred in 1973 with the oil embargo—with the embargo came a realization that there may be a need to manage our planet's finite resources.

Regulations

Society has recognized that previous industrial and developmental actions caused long-term damage to our environment, resulting in loss of food sources and plant and animal species, and changes to the Earth's climate. As a result of learning from past mistakes and studying the environment, the international community identified certain actions that threaten our ecosystem's biodiversity. Consequently, it developed several governmental regulations designed to protect our environment. Thus, in this sense, the green design initiative began with the implementation of building regulations. An example is the regulated phasing out of chlorofluorocarbons.

Lowering Ownership Costs

A third driver for green design is lowering the total cost of ownership in terms of construction costs, resource management and energy efficiency, and operational costs, including marketing and public relations. Ways to lower costs include providing a better set of construction documents that reduce or eliminate change orders, controlling site stormwater for use in irrigation, incorporating energy-efficiency measures in HVAC&R design, developing maintenance strategies to ensure continued high-level building performance and higher occupant satisfaction, and reducing marketing and administrative costs.

Case studies on commissioning show that construction and operating costs can be reduced from 1 to 70 times the initial cost of commissioning. A recent study by an international engineering firm indicated that treating stormwater on site cost one-third as much as having the state or local government treat stormwater at a central facility, significantly lowering the burden to the tax base.

A 123,000 ft^2 (11,427 m^2) higher education building constructed in 1997 in Atlanta, Georgia—a building that already had many sustainable principles applied during its design—provides an example of how commissioning, measurement, and verification play a critical role in ensuring that the

Digging Deeper

sustainable attributes designed into the building are actually realized at $1.00/square foot ($10.80/square meter) savings when recommissioned, lowering the total cost of ownership. Recommissioning identified several seemingly inconspicuous operational practices that were causing higher-than-needed consumption in the following areas: chilled-water cooling, by 40%; steam, by 59%; and electricity, by 15%. Implementing continuing measurement and verification ensures that the building will continue to perform as designed, again, lowering the total cost of ownership.

More esoteric is the cost of unhappy occupants, which includes administrative costs, marketing costs due to more frequent tenant turnover, or increased business cost due to absenteeism or reduced productivity, as well as the impact on marketplace image. Marketplace image is a significant driving force in promoting green/sustainable design. Green/sustainable projects provide owners an opportunity to distinguish themselves in public as well as promote their business or project in order to obtain the desired result. Promotion of green/sustainable attributes of a project can help with public relations and help overcome community resistance to a new project.

Increased Productivity

Another driver for green design is the recognition of increased productivity from a building that is comfortable and enjoyable and provides healthy indoor conditions. Comfortable occupants are less distracted, able to focus better on their tasks/activities, and appreciate the physiological benefits good green design provides.

A case study conducted by Pacific Northwest Laboratory points out many interesting observations about human response to daylight harvesting, outside views, and thermal comfort. The study, which compares worker productivity in two buildings owned by the same manufacturer, illustrates both the positive and negative impact the application of green design principles can have on human productivity. (Heerwagen et al. 1995)

The first building is an older, smaller industrial facility, divided into offices, and a manufacturing area. It has high-ribbon windows around the perimeter walls in both office and manufacturing areas, providing only limited daylight harvesting. It has an employee lounge, a small outdoor seating area with picnic tables, and conference rooms.

The newer facility is 50% larger with energy-efficient features, such as large-scale use of daylight harvesting, energy-efficient florescent lamps, daylight harvesting controls, direct digital HVAC controls, environmentally sensitive building materials, and a fitness center at each end of the manufacturing area.

The study focuses on individual quality-of-work issues and the manufacturer's own production performance parameters. The study provides a mixed review of green design and gives insight on what conditions need to be avoided. While occupants perceived satisfaction and comfort stemming from daylighting and outside views, they also expressed complaints regarding glare and lack of thermal comfort. The green building studied did not appear to have controlled the quality of daylight through proper glazing selection, which may be the cause of the complaints about glare and thermal comfort.

Subsequent chapters discuss specific design parameters relative to building envelope design, including daylight harvesting, energy efficiency, and thermal comfort.

Filling A Design Need

There are increasing numbers of building owners and developers asking for green design services. As a result, there is considerable business for design professionals who can master the principles of green design and provide leadership in this arena.

Some publications that demonstrate the drivers of green design include *Economic Renewal Guide* (Kinsley 1997), *Natural Capitalism* (Hawken, Lovins, and Lovins 1999), and the *Earth From Above* books (Arthus-Bertrand 2002), and *Green to Gold: How Smart Companies Use Environmental Strategy to Innovate, Create Value, and Build Competitive Advantage* (Esty, Winston 2006).

Digging Deeper

REFERENCES AND RESOURCES

Published

Arthus-Bertrand, Y. 2002. *Earth From Above*. New York: Harry N. Abrams.

CFR. 1995. Energy conservation voluntary performance standards for commercial and multi-family high rise residential buildings; mandatory for new federal buildings. Code of Federal Regulations 10 CFR 435, Office of the Federal Register, National Archives and Records Administration, Washington, DC.

Esty, D.C., and A.S. Winston. 2006. *Green to Gold: How Smart Companies Use Environmental Strategy to Innovate, Create Value, and Build Competitive Advantage*. New Haven, CT: Yale University Press.

Hawkin, P., A. Lovins, and L.H. Lovins. 1999. *Natural Capitalism*. Little Brown.

Heerwagen, J.H., J.C. Montgomery, W.C. Weimer, and J.G. Heubach. 1995. Assessing the human and organizational impacts of green buildings. Pacific Northwest Laboratory, Richland, WA.

Kinsley, M. 1997. *Economic Renewal Guide*. Colorado: Rocky Mountain Institute.

Torcellini, P., S. Pless, M. Deru, B. Griffith, N. Long, and R. Judkoff. 2006. Lessons learned from case studies of six high-performance buildings. Technical report, NREL/ TP-550-37542. National Renewable Energy Laboratory, Golden, CO.

Online

Dena
www.dena.de/en/
Euporean Commission, BUILD UP program
www.buildup.eu/
European Commission (DG TREN), SARA Project
www.sara-project.net
North Carolina Solar Center, DSIRE
www.dsireusa.org/
U.S. Department of Energy, Energy Efficiency and Renewable Energy, Zero Energy Buildings
http://zeb.buildinggreen.com

CHAPTER FOUR

THE DESIGN PROCESS—
EARLY STAGES

OVERVIEW

The design process is the first crucial element in producing a green building. For design efficiency, it is necessary to define the owner's objectives and criteria, including sustainable/green goals, before beginning the design in order to minimize the potential of increased design costs. Once designed, the building must be constructed, its performance verified, and it must be operated in a way that supports the green concept. If it is not designed with the intent to make it green, the desired results will never be achieved.

Figure 4-1 conceptually shows the impact of providing design input at succeeding stages of a project, relative to the cost and effort required. The solid curve shows that it is much easier to have a major impact on the performance (potential energy savings, water efficiency, maintenance costs, etc.) of a building if you start at the very earliest stages of the design process. The available impacts diminish thereafter as you proceed through the subsequent design and construction phases. A corollary to this is that the cost of implementing changes to improve building performance rises at each successive stage of the project (cost is shown as the dotted curve of this graph).

Designers are often challenged and sometimes affronted by the idea of green design, for many feel they have been producing good designs for years. The experience of many is that they have been forced to design with low construction costs in mind, and when they offer opportunities to improve a building's design, they are often blocked by the owner due to budget constraints. The typical experience is that owners will not accept cost increases that do not show a return in potential savings in five years or less, and many demand 18 months or less. Many owners, especially owners who own the project for life, allow longer return on investments and use life-cycle cost parameters to lower the total cost of ownership.

Achieving green or sustainable design goals requires a different approach than has been customarily applied. Engineers and other designers are asked to become advocates, not just objective designers. Some have expressed the view that significant reductions in energy usage and greenhouse gas emissions will never occur by simply tweaking current practice. In other words, simply installing high-efficiency systems or equipment will not reduce energy usage sufficiently. Sustainable design requires designers to take a holistic approach and go beyond designing for just the owner and building occupants. They need to look at the long-term environmental impacts the development of a building will create. This may make many uncomfortable, because it seemingly asks them to go beyond their area of expertise.

Both first cost and operating costs can be reduced by applying sustainable/green principles. Correct orientation and correct selection of glazing can reduce HVAC equipment size and cost, as can the use of recycled materials such as crushed concrete (in place of virgin stone) for soil stabilization and structural fill.

Using the commissioning process, the CxA (Commissioning Agent) can assist the design team with agreeing upon the objectives, the criteria, and the sustainable/green goals for the project through the development of the Owner's Project Requirements (OPR). The OPR forms the basis from which all design, construction, acceptance, and operational decisions are made (see Chapter 6 for more information). The OPR document provides the foundation of understanding for the designers to efficiently accomplish the task of designing a sustainable/green project

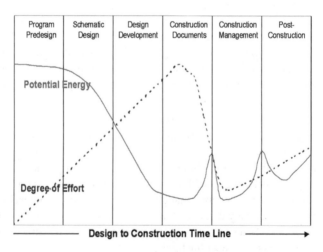

Image courtesy of Malcolm Lewis, CTG Energetics, Inc.

Figure 4-1 Impact of early design input on building performance.

within the owner's business model and the constraints and limitations of the project. This process allows improved design efficiency and better team integration, because there are clear objectives and criteria established before design begins. While sustainable/green principles can lower first cost as well as operational costs, the soft costs of design do increase slightly, due to the additional design and coordination efforts required of the team.

Starting in predesign and carrying through to postoccupancy is essential for the success of a sustainable/green design. It starts with examining every aspect of the process (e.g., the owner's site selection, building configuration, architectural elements, and efficient construction and operation) and can only occur with an integrated approach. Defining the OPR document containing the project goals, even before site selection if possible, is the suggested starting point.

At the very start of the project, green design goals have to be discussed, correlated to the owner's objectives and criteria, agreed to, and in fact, embraced by the extended project team. This is often done in a charette format or simply a session spent discussing the issues. As these goals are defined, they are included in the OPR document.

Goals for a project traditionally include the functional program, leasable or usable area, capital cost, schedule, project image, and similar issues. The charette simply puts environmental goals on a plane with the capital cost and other traditional goals.

One of the goals may be to achieve the environmental goals at the same or similar capital cost. (As with any goals, the environmental goals should be measurable and verifiable.) Another one of the goals may be a specific green-building rating system target and an energy target, or perhaps an energy target alone.

A typical set of goals for a green design project might be as follows:

1. Achieve a level of energy use at least 50% lower than the U.S. Department of Energy (DOE)-compiled average levels for the same building type and region, both projected and in actual operation. (Actual energy numbers may be adjusted for actual versus assumed climatic conditions and hours of usage.)
2. Achieve an actual peak aggregate electrical demand level not exceeding 4.5 kW/ft^2 (50 kW/m^2) of building gross area.
3. Provide at least 15% of the building's annual energy use (in operation) from renewable energy sources. (Such energy usage may be discounted from the aggregate energy use determined under the above-mentioned Goal 1.)
4. Taking into account the determinations of Goals 1, 2, and 3, assess the impact of the lesser net energy use on raw energy resource use (including off-site energy use) compared to that of a comparable but conventional building, including the changed environmental impacts from that resource use, and verify that the aggregate energy and environmental impacts are no greater.

5. Achieve a per capita (city) water usage that is 40% lower than the documented average for this building type and region.
6. Achieve an aggregate up-front capital cost for the project that does not exceed x dollars/ft^2 (m^2) of building gross area, which has been deemed by the project team to be no higher than 102% of what a conventional building would cost.
7. Recycle (or arrange for the recycling of) at least 60% of the aggregate waste materials generated by the building.
8. By means of postoccupancy surveys of building users conducted periodically over a five-year period, achieve an aggregate satisfaction level of 85% or better. Survey shall solicit occupant satisfaction with the indoor environment as to the following dimensions: thermal comfort, air quality, acoustical quality, and visual/general comfort.
9. Obtain a gold-level U.S. Green Building Council (USGBC) LEED certification for the building.

(For an example of what one major firm has done, see the Digging Deeper sidebar, "One Firm's Green Building Design Process Checklist," featured later in this chapter.)

THE OWNER'S ROLE

Of all of the participants, it is the owner who is the most crucial when it comes to making a green building happen. With the owner's commitment, the design, construction, and operating teams will receive the motivation and empowerment needed to create a green design.

Key design team members can—and should—attempt to educate the owner on the long-term benefits of a sustainable/green design, particularly if the owner is unfamiliar with the concept. After all, experienced design team members are in the best position to sell the merits of green design. However, to be effective, such a commitment on the part of the owner must be made early in the design process.

Specific roles that an owner can fill in making a sustainable/green design effort successful include the following:

- Expressing commitment and enthusiasm for the green endeavor.
- Establishing a basic value system (i.e., what is important, what is not).
- Selecting a CxA.
- Participating in selection of design team members.
- Setting schedules and budgets.
- Participating in the design process, especially the early stages.
- Maintaining interest, commitment, and enthusiasm throughout the project.

The owner on a project could be a corporation or small business, hospital, university or college, office building developer, nonprofit organization, or an individual. In any case, that owner will have a designated representative on the building project team, presumably one who is very familiar with the owner's views and philosophy and can speak for that owner with authority.

THE DESIGN TEAM

Setting It Up

One of the first tasks in a sustainable/green design project is forming the design team and the commissioning team. This team should include the design team leader (often the architect), the owner, the CxA, the design engineers, and operations staff. Much of the design team's successful functioning depends not just on having ideas about what should go into the project but on being able to analyze the impact of the ideas quickly and accurately. It's likely that a large part of this analysis will be completed by one of the engineers on the project.

A traditional project team includes the following members:

- Owner
- Project manager
- Architect
- HVAC&R engineer
- Plumbing/fire protection engineer
- Electrical engineer
- Lighting designer
- Structural engineer
- Landscaping/site specialist
- Civil engineer
- Code enforcement official

An expanded project team for a sustainable/green design with commissioning would also include:

- Energy analyst
- Daylighting consultant
- Environmental design consultant
- CxA
- Construction manager/contractor
- Cost estimator
- Building operator
- Building users/occupants

The preceding lists the possible roles that might need to be filled on a reasonably large design project. Some roles may not be applicable or even needed on certain types of projects (e.g., civil engineer or landscaping/site specialist), and other roles may not be feasible in the early stages of project (e.g., building operator, building users, or code enforcement official). Further, the variety of roles does not mean that there needs to be an equal number of distinct individuals to fill them; one individual may fill several roles (e.g., the architect often serves as project manager, the HVAC&R engineer as plumbing engineer or energy analyst, the electrical engineer as lighting designer, and a contractor on the team as cost estimator). Likewise, depending on the type of project, there could be other specialists as well.

There are a few roles that are particularly important in green design including energy analyst, environmental design consultant, and CxA, which are discussed below.

Energy Analyst. Although this role has existed for some time, it assumes a much more intense and timely function in sustainable/green design, as there is a need to quickly evaluate various ideas (and interactions between them) in terms of impact on energy. These can range from different building forms and architectural features to different mechanical and electrical systems. The person in this role must be intimately familiar with energy and daylight analysis modeling tools and able to provide feedback on ideas expressed reasonably quickly. In short, he or she is a much more integral part of a sustainable/green design team than in a traditional design effort. In this respect, for a sizable project, it might be difficult for a single person to fill this role plus another.

Environmental Design Consultant (EDC). As owners begin to request sustainable/green buildings from the design professions, a new discipline has emerged: the EDC. The role of this person is to help teams recognize design synergies and opportunities to implement sustainable and green features without increasing construction costs. When the CxA is also the EDC, the owner and designers benefit from an improved integration of the design process across disciplines, with the intent of creating an outcome with much lower environmental impact and higher user satisfaction. Leading projects show that this can often be accomplished without adding cost. The EDC has input in areas such as site, water, waste, materials, Indoor Environmental Quality [IEQ], energy, durability, envelope design, renewable energy, and transportation. The CxA documents these objectives and criteria into the OPR document. Although this Guide will focus primarily on those areas pertinent to the HVAC&R design professional, it is becoming evident that this profession must broaden its sphere of concern in order to contribute meaningfully to the creation of sustainable/green buildings.

The CxA already has a collaborative relationship with the designers and, as an EDC, works with the HVAC&R team and others throughout the process to meet the owner's objectives and criteria. For example, a design reviewer may raise questions for the team to consider, such as:

• Is the building orientation optimized for minimum energy use?

- Is the combined system of building envelope, including glazing choices and the HVAC system, optimized for minimum energy use and lowest life-cycle cost?
- Have passive, active and renewable strategies for optimizing building energy usage been optimized?
- Are the loads, occupancy, and design conditions properly described?
- Are the proposed analytical tools adequate for the task of computing life-cycle costs and guiding design decisions?
- Is the proposed integrated design approach going to deliver excellent air quality to occupants under all conditions?
- Is the proposed integrated design approach going to deliver thermal comfort to occupants under all conditions?
- Is the proposed integrated design approach going to be easy to maintain? Is there enough space for mechanical equipment and adequate access to service and perhaps to eventually replace it?
- Is the proposed mechanical approach going to give appropriate control of the system to users?
- Is the proposed integrated design approach going to consume a minimum amount of parasitic energy to run pumps and fans?
- Are there site or other conditions likely to impact the mechanical system in unusual ways?
- Has the impact of the building on the site and surroundings been identified and taken into account?
- Are the proposed systems properly sized for the loads?

While it may seem that the role of the EDC is very similar to that of the energy analyst, the roles differ in that the EDC is more of a question-asker or issue-raiser, similar to the CxA asking questions and suggesting strategies or solutions for the team to consider. The EDC's brief is broader and more comprehensive in scope; his or her role is to take a step back from the project and ask the broader questions regarding the environmental impact of the project.

CxA. (Please refer also to Chapter 6.) The CxA has the very important role of documenting the OPR as early as possible, starting in the predesign phase of the project. This function is beneficial to both the owner and project team in that it condenses the mass of information into a single, cogent document. It records the owner's objectives, criteria, and goals and benchmarks for gauging success in achieving the defined requirements. The OPR forms the basis from which all design, construction, acceptance, and operational decisions are made. Changes to the OPR document, for various reasons, are made by the owner and generally provide clarification of an objective or goal or tradeoffs due to budget constraints. In response to an OPR, designers develop design concepts, having the benefit of well-defined requirements, and document their assumptions, studies, and accompanying calculations into the basis of design. The designer creates the basis of design to clearly convey the assumptions made in developing a design solution that fulfills the intent and criteria in the OPR. The OPR records the various changes in design direction, why they occurred, and the assumptions made by the design team. The document is updated as changes occur throughout the project and tracks why these changes were necessary.

Successful cost-effective application of green design principles must start early and be defined in predesign; this allows the team to look for synergies that help control hard and soft costs by more accurately defining design direction. The CxA helps the design team define what the owner is communicating and can help draw out how the owner expects the building to function and perform.

The CxA incorporates the information into the OPR, which is used during the project as a benchmark for judging how well the project team meets the project requirements. It also serves as a written reminder of the goals and decisions that resulted in the final deliverable to the owner. The final version of the OPR should be refined to approximately 20 to 30 pages in length and delivered along with the commissioning report as a reminder of the designer's original charge and the assumptions that were made with the owner's knowledge and direction.

The OPR document also serves as a guide to the building operating staff on how the facility was intended to operate and the features designed into the project. Development guidelines for OPR are contained in *ASHRAE Guideline 0-2005, The Commissioning Process* (ASHRAE 2005).

The Team's Role

Green design requires owners to make decisions sooner, design documents to be more complete and comprehensive, the construction process to be better coordinated, and operators to be better trained in maintaining facilities. All of this will impact the viability and success of a green project endeavor. Contractors not familiar with this project model may sound the cost and schedule alarm due to their inexperience in the new procedure. First-time application of sustainable development principles can result in slightly higher first cost, but this phenomenon will reverse itself as teams gain experience and improve their learning curve. As the building industry becomes more familiar with applying these principles, lower costs of ownership will result.

In addition to the standard tasks associated with a design project, the design team is responsible for developing and implementing new concepts that will create a green project. For most, this will require learning on their own time, becoming familiar with new advances in software tools, green materials, and alternative systems. There is an abundance of information; advances are occurring daily in the development of green products and materials as well as processes. The speed of these changes requires designers to continuously add to their knowledge base.

The greatest challenge to accomplishing green design is creating a team organizational structure that provides the following:

- Criteria for assessing how green the project should be.
- Strong leadership through the green design process to integrate team members.
- Clearly defined objectives that result from careful examination of design alternatives, costs, and schedule impacts.
- Documentation of success.
- Strong leadership by experienced green building practitioners leading the team through the decision process.
- Definition of what tasks are required to accomplish green design.
- Identification of who is responsible for each of the tasks.
- Identification of when tasks must be completed, so as not to impede the design process or the project schedule.
- Establishment of criteria for the selection of green design features considered for incorporation into a project.
- Assistance with integrating selected green design goals into the construction documents.
- Definition of the level of effort required for each of the green project goals.
- Help to enable contractors overcome psychological and physical constraints.
- Establishment of how to track, measure, and document the success of accomplished project goals.

The designers must also help inform their clients that there are costs for the depletion of resources to be consumed beyond the cost of extraction. The practice of looking only at simple payback when analyzing alternatives based on extraction cost has never been realistic because there is no way to replace many resources at any cost.

Currently, most design teams are eager to develop green designs but lack the experience of actually integrating green design into their projects. The addition of an experienced EDC will shorten the learning curve by helping them integrate their extensive knowledge, which will result in a cost-effective practical green design that meets the owner's requirements. In addition, most teams struggle with what makes a design green, how to incorporate green design principles, and the logistics of incorporating these principles into the design. Green design creates a need for a broader involvement of disciplines and a wider range of experience to ensure that a wider range of input and participation gets factored into the decision-making process.

The project team—from the initial concept to the construction documents, construction, and building operations—must work as an integrated unit to achieve the goals set by the owner's objectives and criteria, creating better project performance, which is a basic principle of green design. This model will require the project team to investigate new approaches and process more information than ever before, as they strive to increase performance and lower the total cost of ownership. The decision-making process must change from the traditional hierarchical method, with an emphasis on lowest first cost, to an integrated method focused on life-cycle cost. To achieve this requires close collaboration of the project team combined with innovative thinking among all disciplines.

The design team's responsibility as part of the project team is to assist the owner with setting sustainability/green goals that often include

- Life-cycle cost optimization of energy-consuming systems, materials, and maintenance;
- Systems integration and maintainability;
- Minimization of environmental impact;
- Documenting basis of design; and
- Assisting with training of building operations and management staff during commissioning.

Team Leadership

The integrated building design process requires the team members to explore the various opportunities to incorporate sustainable principles into the project. For example, the architect, mechanical engineers, and electrical engineers must interact closely to develop a high-performance building that will provide an improved work environment, lower operating costs, and will consume minimal natural resources. Strong leadership is essential to meeting these objectives.

Designers should provide input to the OPR to help establish sustainable/green project criteria. Designers can suggest criteria for sustainable/green goals or take the easier route by using one of the established rating systems developed through a balanced consensus process and add goals not contained in the established rating system.

THE ENGINEER'S ROLE

The HVAC&R engineer is a crucial player in the design of a green building. In fact, it is virtually impossible (and certainly not cost-effective) to design a green building without major involvement from that discipline. The HVAC&R engineer must get outside the normal box in which he or she lives and become more involved in the why of a design, as well as the how. This means moving beyond responding to questions asked by others and participating in the decision making regarding how project goals will be achieved.

Engineers help analyze the various options to be considered, create mathematical computer models that are used to judge alternatives, provide creative input, and assist with development of new techniques and solutions. The HVAC&R engineer can be invaluable in helping the architect with building orientation considerations, floor plate form and dimension, and deciding which type of glazing will provide the maximum quantity of natural light, while at the same time analyzing the heat transfer characteristics of the glazing options. The HVAC&R engineer can also help the architect select structural systems and exterior walls to utilize thermal mass features to reduce equipment needs. Working with the electrical engineer and architect, the HVAC&R engineer can offer ideas and various options, such as incorporating daylighting and lighting controls to reduce artificial light when natural light is available, which, in turn, can result in lower cooling requirements and lowered HVAC requirements to meet peak load. Smaller equipment size translates into reduced structural and electrical requirements, lower operating and maintenance costs, and lower construction costs, all of which lower the total cost of ownership.

The plumbing engineer, working with the structural and civil engineers, and the landscape architect can reduce the facility's potable water, sewer, and stormwater conveyance requirements. Some examples are waterless urinals or use of stormwater or graywater for irrigation of vegetation or for flushing toilets. Depending on the type of building, water from condensate can be used for graywater applications or for cooling tower makeup. The design engineer must weigh the benefits of water-cooled versus air-cooled condensers and the water versus electrical energy consumed by each. The engineer must examine the site climate, determine what alternatives and strategies can best be applied, and develop life-cycle analyses to guide the owner through the decision process posed by the maze of complex issues surrounding green design.

PROJECT DELIVERY METHODS AND CONTRACTOR SELECTION

Successful projects depend upon the entire team of players involved: architect, engineers, program managers, construction managers, owner's representatives, facilities personnel, building users, and contractors. It is assumed that all parties will be ethical, reliable, diligent, and experienced. There are a number of project delivery methods that could be used to deliver the design and construction of a project. The major methods, to be briefly discussed here, are the construction manager approach, the design/bid/build approach (D/B/B), the design/build (D/B) approach, and the public-private partnership (P3) approach. It is important that the project delivery method be chosen early in the project for the same reasons that it is important when considering green design options. The discussion of the three methods below is intended only to relate to the effect this decision will have on the success of the optimized design and operation of the building.

Construction Manager Method

The construction manager method is the process undertaken by public and private owners in which a firm with extensive experience in construction management and general contracting is hired during the design phase of the project to assess project capital costs and constructibility issues. This is especially important when considering design alternatives that are being considered in an effort to deliver a high-performance building to the client. The initial design process often includes a project definition stage, or programming, in which the owner works with the design professionals, the CxA, and the construction manager to define the specific scope of the project. The design professional uses this information to prepare a set of bidding documents that the construction manager uses to obtain bids from qualified subcontractors. The lowest responsible price is usually selected and the contractor then constructs the project.

- *Advantages:* Budget control, buy-in of green concepts by contractors.
- *Disadvantages:* Perceived lack of competitive general contractor and subcontractor pricing, innovative systems could be shelved due to overly conservative first-cost estimates.

D/B/B Method

D/B/B construction is the traditional process undertaken by public and private owners. The initial design process often includes a project definition stage, or programming, in which the owner works with the design professionals to define the specific scope of the project. The design professional uses this information to prepare a set of bidding documents. The bid documents are then available for qualified contractors and subcontractors to prepare pricing. The lowest responsible price is usually selected and the contractor then constructs the project.

- *Advantages:* Usually results in the lowest first cost at the outset of the construction of a project.
- *Disadvantages:* No contractor buy-in to green process and concepts, prequalification of contractors is difficult to do well.

D/B Method

D/B construction is typically a response to a request-for-proposal (RFP) developed by an owner. The RFP is usually a document that defines the general scope of the project and then solicits price proposals to accomplish this work. The work effort to prepare the specific design of the project is to be included in the D/B offering. The D/B team usually consists of an architect, engineers for the various disciplines involved, a general contractor, and the trade subcontractors. This entire team should be in place until the project is turned over to the owner.

As the D/B team develops the design, it must respond to the premises defined in the original scope of work.

- *Advantages:* Can result in lowest first cost, agreement by design/construction team with regard to design and building operation concepts.
- *Disadvantages:* Can result in uneven distribution of risk among team members, can result in loss of design team members as owner advisors.

P3

The use of P3 is well established in Canada, and is beginning to gain favor in the United States and other countries. P3 are playing a bigger role in building and capital projects across all areas of government, including power generation, energy delivery, water and wastewater facilities, waste disposal, transportation, communications, education and health facilities, and public service buildings. Recently, its popularity has led to P3 being used more frequently in smaller-scale developments across Canada, such as schools, courthouses, and hospitals.

Bridging documents are provided to guide an integrated and facilitated P3 process by

- Providing narratives that describe, in conceptual terms, the requirements for the new facility;
- Outlining general performance and prescriptive requirements, operations requirements, programmatic space requirements and room data sheets, space standards, adjacency requirements, conceptual blocking and stacking;
- Defining business terms; and
- Proposing criteria for evaluation of submitted proposals.

The P3 process allows market forces to play out, with the opportunity for the government entity to decide later on funding options. Projects are delivered quickly. Competition on a wide variety of services is balanced by an integrated approach, while risk transfer from the public to private sector in the areas of pricing, compliance, and operations benefits the stakeholders of the government entity.

Information from this section was taken from the Mondaq Web site (www.mondaq.com/canada/article.asp?articleid=23737) and from a document published by the California Debt & Investment Advisory Commission (www.treasurer.ca.gov/cdiac/publications/p3.pdf.)

Factors in Choosing an Approach

In all of the above scenarios, the team or contractors should be prequalified to perform the work prior to a request for pricing. It's important to confirm that the team or contractors fulfill the following requirements:

- They have experience in similar work.
- They possess a record of past performance by responsible references.
- They have financial capability to complete the project.
- They have the experienced staff available to work on the project.

A record of exemplary performance and fiscal capability may be more important than experience in similar work. In any case, it is valuable to preselect the teams or contractors from whom you request pricing. Successful projects occur due to careful planning and implementation.

What Does *Integrated Design* Mean?

One of the key attributes of a well-designed, cost-effective green building is that it is designed in an integrated fashion, wherein all systems and components work together to produce overall functionality and environmental performance. This has a major impact on the design process for HVAC-related systems, as conceptual development must begin with HVAC system integration into the building form and into the approaches being taken to meet other green building aspects. For example, consider the following:

- HVAC systems that use natural ventilation and underfloor air distribution, often used in green buildings, can have major impacts on building form.
- Other building energy innovations, such as daylighting, passive solar, exterior shading devices, and active double wall systems, often have significant impacts on the design of the HVAC system.
- On-site energy systems that produce waste heat, such as fuel cells, engine-driven generators, or microturbines, affect the design of HVAC systems so that waste heat can be used most effectively.

Beyond these form-giving elements, there are many other specific features of a green building that affect (or are affected by) HVAC systems to achieve the best overall performance. Some of these strongly impact HVAC system conceptual design, and some require only minor adjustments to HVAC specifications. Such features might include the following:

- Using the commissioning process to document the owner's defined sustainable/green objectives and criteria and assist the project team to deliver.
- Effective use of ventilation (and indoor air quality [IAQ] sensors linked to the ventilation system) to improve IAQ.
- Provision of user controls for temperature and humidity control.
- Reduced system capacities to reflect lower internal loads and building envelope loads.
- Utilization of thermal energy storage systems to reduce the overall size of the chiller plant equipment, such as chillers, cooling towers, and pumps. Reduction in chiller plant equipment size will save capital costs, ongoing energy, and operational costs, and can reduce outdoor noise levels during the daytime.
- Selection of non-ozone-depleting refrigerants.
- Reduction and optimization of building energy usage below the levels of *ANSI/ASHRAE/IES Standard 90.1-2010, Energy Standard for Buildings Except Low-Rise Residential Buildings*-based (ASHRAE 2010) codes or other applicable

state and local energy codes. (Levels of reduction of as much as 40% to 50% below Standard 90.1 are becoming more common and are encouraged.)
- Use of reclaimed water for cooling tower makeup, and minimization of cooling tower blowdown discharge to the sanitary sewer system.
- Testing of the key systems, especially the HVAC systems.

Key Steps

The integrated design process (IDP) includes the following elements:

- Ensuring that as many of the interested parties as possible are represented on the design team as early as possible—including not only architects, engineers, and the owner (client), but also CxA, construction specialist (contractor), cost estimator, operations/maintenance person, and other specialists (outlined below).
- Interdisciplinary work among architects, engineers, costing specialists, operations people, and other relevant persons right from the beginning of the design process.
- Discussion and documentation by the owners and the design team of the relative importance of various performance and cost issues, and the establishment of a consensus on these matters between client and designers, and among the designers themselves.
- Provision of a design facilitator (or EDC) to suggest strategies for the team to consider, as well as a CxA to raise performance issues throughout the process and to bring specialized knowledge to the table.
- Addition of an energy specialist to test various design assumptions through the use of energy and daylight simulations throughout the process and to provide relatively objective information on a key aspect of performance.
- Addition of subject specialists (e.g., for daylighting or thermal storage) for short consultations with the design team.
- Clear articulation of performance targets and strategies to be updated throughout the process by the owner and the design team.

Iterative Design Refinement

The design process requires the development of design alternatives. To come up with the most effective combination, these alternatives must be evaluated, refined, evolved, and finally optimized. This is the concept of iterative design, wherein the design is progressively refined over time, as shown in Figure 4-2.

Often fee and schedule pressures lead the designer to want to lock in a single design concept at the beginning of the project and stick with it throughout. But this precludes the opportunity to come up with a better system that reflects the unique combination of loads and design integration opportunities for this specific building. This better design usually evolves during schematics and early design development in the iterative process.

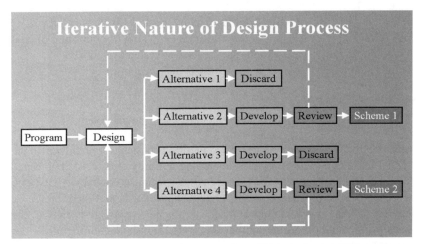

Image courtesy of Malcolm Lewis, CTG Energetics, Inc.

Figure 4-2 The iterative design process.

CONCEPT DEVELOPMENT

The Big Picture

Designers should always keep in mind the three major steps for achieving a sustainable/green design:

- Reduce the loads.
- Apply the most efficient systems.
- Look for synergies.

Reduce the Loads. If you have a building with a normal 500 ton cooling load, is it possible to provide a more comfortable environment with, say, only 300 tons? The team would have to really work to achieve this. Solar loads on the building would have to be reduced; lighting loads to the space would also have to be lowered; maybe the building could use daylight rather than electric light during the day, so the building shape would be influenced. The site for the building, its shape, its thermal mass, and its orientation could all work together to reduce the cooling load. Early and quick modeling can provide interesting information to assist decisions.

Similar things could be done with the heating load. Does the winter sun provide much of the building's heating needs during the day? With design changes, could the sun do more?

These considerations in a hierarchal design process are not typically brought to the attention of the HVAC&R engineer, who could significantly help improve the energy efficiency instead of just calculating the loads, and could apply energy-efficient systems. Significant reduction of utility consumption and environmental impact cannot occur by simply doing the same old job just a little bit better.

The HVAC&R or energy engineer can make a positive contribution to the success of a sustainable/green design. The value of the engineer to the project is significantly increased, and the results are reduced heating and cooling loads, as well as overall utility consumption.

Someone once suggested an attitudinal approach to building design that says the designer should strive toward making the building inherently work by itself. Building systems are there to fine tune the operation and pick up the extreme design conditions. In contrast, buildings are often traditionally designed like advanced fighter aircraft: if the flight computers are lost, the pilot cannot fly the plane.

Apply the Most Efficient Systems. This is the world of the energy-efficient engineer. This is the area where ASHRAE generally operates. While it is very important, it is not enough by itself.

Look for Synergies. The preceding two major steps have the potential of increasing capital costs. Therefore, you might have a wonderful, energy-efficient building that will not get built due to high first cost, or the value-engineering knives come out and cut the project back to a traditional, affordable project—proof perhaps that green cannot work. Part of the solution to get around this syndrome is to look for synergies of how building elements can work together. This also relates to the cost transfer mentioned earlier.

If a building has a large amount of southern exposure, exterior-shading devices might significantly reduce the summer solar load, while still admitting lower angle winter sun. Daylight (but not direct sun) would allow for shutting off the electric lights on sunny days. The HVAC system for the south perimeter zones could be significantly reduced in size and cost as the simultaneous solar and electric lighting loads are reduced. Indeed, the very nature of the HVAC system might well be simplified due to the significant load reduction. Resulting cost savings can be used to pay for some or all of the additional treatments.

A major benefit of an integrated design that is on budget is that you avoid wasting a lot of time on elemental payback exercises and value engineering (and cost cutting), because you are on budget. Many of the integrated solutions work so that if you save by cutting out an element, such as the exterior shades, there is an additional cost in another area such as the size of the HVAC system.

The Nitty-Gritty

The success of green design starts with establishing the project's goals and objectives, defining roles and responsibilities of each team member, fostering communication among design team members, developing a decision-making process, and clarifying the level of effort that will be required by each member of the team. It is recommended that a workshop be conducted to introduce the team to the process of integrating sustainable development principles and determining how decisions establish objectives and criteria that are documented in the OPR and provide guidance to the team in the delivery of the project. Objectives and criteria are tracked and used to form concise benchmarks to gage and document the team's success in meeting the established goals. Commercially available software can assist with cost-benefit analysis, design coordination, energy and daylight analysis, and organizing process design.

The creation of documentation supporting both the decision-making process and the results of decisions is important in guiding and determining the success of green design efforts, as well as in establishing what was or was not successful and the reasons why. Like a business plan or construction plan, it is important to measure milestones so that adjustments can be made to correct course deviations in reaching the goals. Sustainable/green design objectives and criteria defined in the OPR should also identify the criteria on which life-cycle cost analyses are based. Also, any assumptions made must be recorded in the basis of design document so comparison against actual performance can be measured. Learning from the deviations that occur will allow teams, as well as individuals, to grow from the experience.

The owner's sustainable/green design objectives and criteria documented in the OPR provide the organizational structure required for successful projects. Software tools available today also increase communication within a team, help stimulate innovative thinking, and help teams optimize design trade-offs by grouping related issues.

The team must develop consensus criteria that might include the following:

- Selecting a site that minimizes environmental impacts.
- Using existing infrastructure to the maximum extent possible to avoid building additional infrastructure to support the project.
- Minimizing the impact of automobiles and the infrastructure required to support them, such as parking, roads, and highways.
- Developing high-performance buildings that enhance occupant productivity and comfort, minimize energy and water consumption, and are durable and recyclable at the end of their useful service life.

Based on the consensus criteria selected, identify potential goals. Once goals are identified, develop tasks necessary to obtain these goals, including studying the impacts these goals will have upon:

- project cost, schedule, and energy and water usage;
- IEQ, operational and maintenance costs, life of the building, and occupant productivity; and
- environmental impacts at the end of the building's or whole facility's useful service life.

Next, assign roles and responsibilities by identifying who is responsible for each task, when the task must be completed, and in what chronological order tasks must be completed, so as to facilitate the tracking and management of the sustainable/ green design process. The design and construction commissioning plans and checklists can significantly assist a team in accomplishing their goals and minimizing wasted effort.

A good OPR provides the team the information needed to guide the team's decisions, measure the team's success, and document changes and the reasons for change in the project.

EXPRESSING AND TESTING CONCEPTS

Expressing concepts is very important in green design, because that is the way ideas and intentions are communicated to the owner and others on the design team. This is especially true since green design requires the close and active participation of many different parties.

There are three ways of expressing concepts in the design of buildings: the traditional verbal means and the diagrammatic or pictorial means, and the third (which has come of age more recently along with computers) is the modeling means.

Verbal

Both the written and the spoken word play an especially important part in green design. Because there are many meetings or charettes where ideas are explored and intentions voiced, getting across what is expressed accurately assumes significance. Then, succinctly and clearly putting down on paper what has been expressed (memorializing it) is also critical to the various team members, as they each go about filling their respective roles. To illustrate, one need only read Chapter 6, "Commissioning," for it to become apparent how important a written record of what happened during design (i.e., design intent, assumptions, etc.) is to the successful follow-through of a well-executed green design.

Diagrammatic/Pictorial

The use of diagrams, sketches, photos, renderings, etc., a tried and true method of communicating a lot of information, continues to be an essential part of green design (Figure 4-3). The old adage "one picture is worth a thousand words" most certainly applies here. But there is now a relatively new way of creating a picture (Figure 4-4) of a building, an energy system, or a year of operations—modeling.

Modeling

This computer-age technique plays such an important part in green design because of its speed, accuracy, and comprehensiveness.

Everyone is familiar with how speedy computers are, once the input data are entered. The slow part in this process is the human analyst, the one who converts intentions and ideas into computer-modeling program input, which is why it is so important for that analyst to be very conversant with the modeling process. This is especially true for load and energy calculations that impact HVAC&R systems. The team has an idea, and they want an answer fast as to how well that idea would work.

Most would also acknowledge that computers are accurate: they do not make careless mistakes. Again, if there are inaccuracies, they usually come from the human side, which is why the analyst must be an expert at avoiding garbage in.

Modeling programs have another advantage, especially the more sophisticated ones: they are comprehensive in what they can analyze simultaneously. The human mind can only accommodate so many ideas or concepts at once without getting confused and bogged down; a properly conceived model will not get confused and

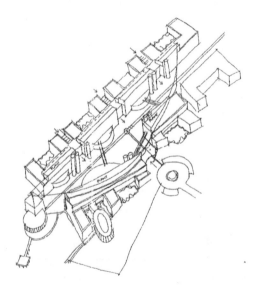

Image courtesy of Integrated Environmental Solutions (IES)

Figure 4-3 Example of diagrammatic building sketch.

can provide answers that may be counterintuitive. As an example, a good modeling program can track heat gain from lights, plug loads, and solar energy, along with heat loss from the building envelope and infiltration, do it for every hour or every day of the year in whatever weather conditions are assumed, take into account mass effects of the structure, and still yield an accurate answer. It would be impossible for the human mind to do this in a reasonable time, unless it was very good at guessing.

See Figure 4-5 for an example of daylighting analyses output.

BUILDING INFORMATION MODELING (BIM)

The approach to building design is moving away from conventional computer-aided design software to follow the way design software has evolved in the manufacturing sector. Your building can now be a working digital prototype. Sustainable design is driving this solution to ensure that the buildings we are erecting are designed, constructed, and operated in a manner that minimizes their environmental impact and are as close to self-sufficient as possible. This technology is known as *building information modeling* (BIM).

BIM is a software tool that uses a relational database together with a behavioral model that captures and presents building information dynamically. In the same way that a spreadsheet is automatically updated, a change in the parametric building modeler is immediately reflected everywhere. This means, for example, revising windows

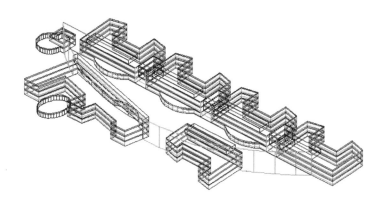

Image courtesy of Integrated Environmental Solutions (IES)

Figure 4-4 Example of computer simulation model derived from Figure 4-3.

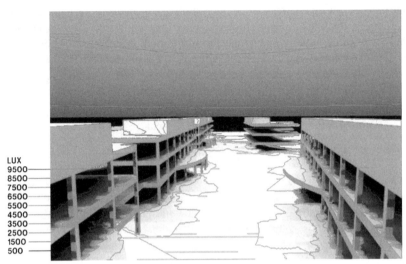

Figure 4-5 Example of daylight analysis software output—conceptual design.

from one type to another not only produces a visually different graphic representation, in all views of your building, but the insulation value of the glazing (R-values) is also revised. Due to the integration of BIM with existing tools of analysis, running energy calculations is greatly simplified. Visualization tools are sophisticated and allow three-dimensional views and walk-throughs of the building.

Multiple design options can therefore be developed and studied within a single model early in the design process to not only see the building and provide conventional documentation for construction, but also to interact with other software to perform energy analysis and lighting studies. (See Figure 4-6 for an example.)

Using BIM helps with the demanding aspects of sustainable design, such as solar applications and daylight harvesting, and also automates routine tasks such as documentation. Schedules are generated directly from the model. If the model changes, so do the schedules. Architects are able to filter and sort material quantities automatically, bypassing the manual extraction/calculation process required. Determining the percentages of material reuse, recycling, or salvage can be tracked and studied for various sustainability design options.

You can perform year-round sun studies to understand when your building is provided natural shading and, thus, optimize the orientation of the building to maximize afternoon shading from the hot summer sun and properly size roof overhangs to min-

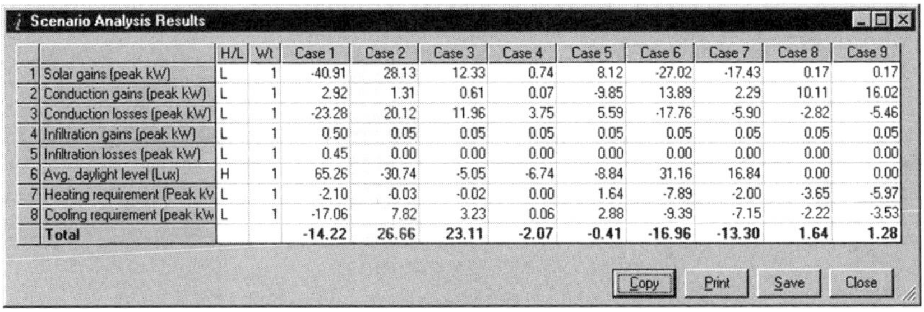

		H/L	Wt	Case 1	Case 2	Case 3	Case 4	Case 5	Case 6	Case 7	Case 8	Case 9
1	Solar gains (peak kW)	L	1	-40.91	28.13	12.33	0.74	8.12	-27.02	-17.43	0.17	0.17
2	Conduction gains (peak kW)	L	1	2.92	1.31	0.61	0.07	-9.85	13.89	2.29	10.11	16.02
3	Conduction losses (peak kW)	L	1	-23.28	20.12	11.96	3.75	5.59	-17.76	-5.90	-2.82	-5.46
4	Infiltration gains (peak kW)	L	1	0.50	0.05	0.05	0.05	0.05	0.05	0.05	0.05	0.05
5	Infiltration losses (peak kW)	L	1	0.45	0.00	0.00	0.00	0.00	0.00	0.00	0.00	0.00
6	Avg. daylight level (Lux)	H	1	65.26	-30.74	-5.05	-6.74	-8.84	31.16	16.84	0.00	0.00
7	Heating requirement (Peak kW)	L	1	-2.10	-0.03	-0.02	0.00	1.64	-7.89	-2.00	-3.65	-5.97
8	Cooling requirement (peak kW)	L	1	-17.06	7.82	3.23	0.06	2.88	-9.39	-7.15	-2.22	-3.53
	Total			-14.22	26.66	23.11	-2.07	-0.41	-16.96	-13.30	1.64	1.28

Image courtesy of Integrated Environmental Solutions

Figure 4-6 Example of multiple design options analysis.

imize solar heat gain. Engineers can then reduce the capacity of cooling systems, demonstrating the building is exceeding the baseline building energy requirements.

An energy analysis using a two-dimensional computer-aided design file requires manually removing the building values/areas from the floor plans and entering said data into an energy simulation application. The data for supporting green design are captured during the design process in BIM and are extracted as necessary.

The energy performance for the baseline model averages the results of four simulations during one year of operation. One simulation is based on the actual orientation of the building on the site; the others rotate the entire building by 90°, 180°, and 270°, which enables the proposed design to receive credit for a well-sited building. This is easily accomplished when using BIM.

The software carries all the data required for building a structure; it understands the data. It quantifies building materials so designers can move walls or insert windows and almost instantly have the building's data on energy performance, daylight harvesting, and, perhaps most importantly, costs shift accordingly in real time. Designers can test the life-cycle performance of brick walls versus concrete walls. The digital representations behave like buildings and not just drawings.

BIM is transforming the way we work and will enable further endeavors in the practice of creating sustainable, cost-effective buildings. A more detailed overview of how to utilize these tools during the conceptual design process is provided in Chapter 8.

Evaluating Alternative Designs

Modeling of alternative designs is made easier by the plethora of modeling tools available today. The chosen model should meet specific requirements depending on the level of accuracy needed. Error can be introduced into modeling if users forget the garbage in/garbage out rule. To reduce the chance of inappropriate or misunderstood input, modeling programs can use input and output formats that allow the user quick reality checks. Various stages of design, requirements, and associated tools are shown in Table 4-1.

Table 4-1: Summary of Available Analysis/Modeling Tools

Stage	Requirements	Tools	Reality Checks
Scoping	• Quick analysis • Comparative results • Reduce alternatives to consider • Control strategy modeling	• System Analyzer™ • Modified bin analysis (where load is not entirely dependent on ambient conditions) • eQUEST • IES VE	• Operation cost/ft² (m²) • Payback or other financial measure
System design	• Acccurate output • Industry-accepted methods	• HAP • TRACE 700 • Elite Design • IES VE	• cfm/ft² (L/s/m²) • cfm/ton (L/s/kWR)
Energy/ cost analysis	• Accurate • Complies with energy cost budget method requirements of Standard 90.1-2007 • Industry-accepted methods • Flexible • Allows modeling of complex control strategies	• EnergyPlus • DOE • HAP • TRACE 700 • SUNREL • IES VE • eQuest	• Btu/h·ft² (kWh/m²)·yr • Operation cost/ft² (m²) • Payback or other financial measure
Monitoring	• Simplicity • Intuitive interface • Systemwide • Interoperable	• BacNET® compatible automation systems	• Trended operating characteristics • Benchmark comparisons (such as system kW/ton [kW/kWR])

NATIONAL RENEWABLE ENERGY LABORATORY'S NINE-STEP PROCESS FOR LOW-ENERGY BUILDING DESIGN

1. Create a base-case building model to quantify base-case energy use and costs. The base-case building is solar neutral (equal glazing areas on all wall orientations) and meets the requirements of applicable energy efficiency codes such as Standard 90.1 (ASHRAE 2010) and *ANSI/ASHRAE Standard 90.2-2007, Energy Efficient Design of Low-Rise Residential Buildings* (ASHRAE 2007).

2. Complete a parametric analysis to determine sensitivities to specific load components. Sequentially eliminate loads from the base-case building, such as conductive losses, lighting loads, solar gains, and plug loads.

3. Develop preliminary design solutions. The design team brainstorms possible solutions that may include strategies to reduce lighting and cooling loads by incorporating daylighting or to meet heating loads with passive solar heating.

4. Incorporate preliminary design solutions into a computer model of the proposed building design. Energy impact and cost effectiveness of each variant are determined by comparing the energy with the original base-case building and with the other variants. Those variants having the most favorable results should be incorporated into the building design.

5. Prepare preliminary set of construction drawings. These drawings are based on the decisions made in Step 3.

6. Identify an HVAC system that will meet the predicted loads. The HVAC system should work with the building envelope and exploit the specific climatic characteristics of the site for maximum efficiency. Often, the HVAC system is much smaller than in a typical building.

7. Finalize plans and specifications. Ensure that building plans are properly detailed and that specifications are accurate. The final design simulation should incorporate all cost-effective features. Savings exceeding 50% from a base-case building are often possible with this approach.

8. Rerun simulations before design changes are made during construction. Verify that changes will not adversely affect the building's energy performance.

9. Commission all equipment and controls. Educate building operators. A building that is not properly commissioned will not meet the energy-efficiency design goals. Building operators must understand how to properly operate the building to maximize its performance.

Digging Deeper

Digging Deeper

ONE FIRM'S GREEN BUILDING DESIGN PROCESS CHECKLIST

- Create an integrated, cross-disciplinary design team that is committed to sustainability and is aware of environmental issues, especially those that the building impacts.
- Precharette and charette meetings should include the project owner, CxA, architects and landscape architects, engineers, an energy engineer with experience in computer simulation of building energy consumption, environmental consultant, facility occupants and users (including purchasing, human resources, and managers), facility manager, contractors (when hired), interior designer, local utility representatives, cost consultant, and other specialty consultants.
- Review how occupants will use the project and any of the client's unique operational characteristics. Based on the this information, assess and decide which sustainable/green design principles are aligned with the owner's overall objectives, criteria, and activities that will provide the most positive impact, in order to provide focus and priority.
- Define environmental standards, goals, and strategies early in predesign, and clearly state these in the OPR.
- Translate the owner's objectives and criteria into the construction documents.
- Channel development to urban areas with existing infrastructures, protecting greenfields and preserving habitat and natural resources.
- Increase localized density to conform to existing or desired density goals by utilizing sites that are located within an existing minimum development density of 60,000 square feet/acre (13,779 square meter/hectacre), or a 0.5 mile (0.8 kilometer) area, with at least ten services, such as banks, restaurants, retail businesses, etc.
- Channel development to areas with existing transportation infrastructure that provides nonautomobile-dependent choices.
- Select a location for the project within 0.5 miles (0.80 kilometers) of a rail station (e.g., commuter rail, light rail, or subway), within 0.25 miles (0.40 kilometers) of two or more bus lines, or in a live, work, walk, mixed-use environment.
- Reduce the overall building footprint and development area.
- Make important decisions on the mechanical load, daylighting, solar absorption, response to local climate and environment, and key building elements at the beginning to define subsequent decisions.
- Establish benchmarks/performance targets as a reference point.
- Integrate recycling systems into every aspect, from reusing existing building materials to purchasing new materials.

- Design for disassembly at the end of the building's useful life.
- Educate contractor and subcontractor in sustainable practices.
- Evaluate and benchmark OPR, including sustainable goals at the same intervals as budgets and schedules.
- Have a CxA as a team member to help ensure that owners' objectives and criteria, including sustainability goals, are met at each stage; benchmark and document success for future reference; and advocate for environmental choices during the course of the project.
- Tie compensation for the architect and design team to achieved building performance.

CANADA'S C-2000 PROGRAM

The C-2000 Program was designed in 1993 by Natural Resources Canada, a government agency, to demonstrate the feasibility of achieving very high levels of building performance. The program's technical requirements cover energy performance,[a] environmental impacts, indoor environment, functionality, and a range of other related parameters (Larson 1996). It was, therefore, expected that incremental costs for design and construction would be substantial. After a preliminary analysis of then-prevalent project costs and an informal survey of designers, provisions were made for support of incremental costs in both the design and construction phases. Contributions were provided according to a sliding scale, ranging from 7% in large projects to 12% in small projects.

Even though the program targeted a select group of clients known to have an interest in high performance, it was assumed that some level of financial incentive would be required to make the program a success. However, the extent of incentives required and the best point of intervention within the project development process were very much open to question.

The first two C-2000 projects received support according to this formula in the range of $400,000 to $750,000 CAN, and funding of this order of magnitude was also planned for subsequent projects.

a. At the time, the energy requirement was 50% better than the ASHRAE Standard 90.1 (ASHRAE 1999) (the benchmark is now the Model National Energy Code for Buildings [MNECB]). Both are North American standards for good practice.

Digging Deeper

However, after the first six projects were designed and two of them had been completed, it was found that incremental capital costs were less than expected, partly due to the fact that designers used technologies that were less sophisticated and expensive than anticipated.[b]

A careful investigation of the first two C-2000 projects constructed, Crestwood 8 (CETC 1996a) and Green on the Grand (CETC 1996b), indicated that the marginal costs for both projects, including design and construction phases, was 7% to 8% more than a conventional building, a rather modest increase. Even more interesting, the designers all agreed that application of the integrated design process (IDP) required by the C-2000 program was the main reason why high levels of performance could still be reached. It also appeared that most of the benefit of intervention was achieved during the design process.

C-2000, now called the IDP, emphasizes the following sequence:

- First minimize heating and cooling loads through orientation, building configuration, an efficient building envelope, and careful consideration of amount, type, and location of fenestration.
- Meet these loads through the maximum use of renewables and the use of efficient HVAC systems.
- Iterate the process to produce at least two, and preferably three, design concept alternatives.

The IDP contains no elements that are radically new but, rather, integrates well-proven approaches into a systematic total process. From an engineering perspective, the IDP allows the skills and experience of mechanical, electrical, and other engineers to be integrated at the design concept level from the very beginning of the design process. For example, reduced cooling loads will result in smaller and more economical systems, which, in turn, can reduce capital and replacement costs.

---

b. The conservative approach of designers is based primarily on their perception that they might face legal liability problems if they use exotic and unproven technologies.

When carried out in a spirit of cooperation among key persons, this results in a design that is highly efficient with minimal, and sometimes zero, incremental capital costs, along with reduced long-term operating and maintenance costs. Most project interventions are now focused on providing advice on the design process at the very early stage.

Six projects were constructed on this basis, and all have either achieved the C-2000 performance requirements or have come very close. Capital costs have been either slightly above or slightly below base budgets. The most hopeful sign that the IDP approach is taking root is that several owners have subsequently used the same process for buildings that have not benefited from any subsidy.

Simple software design support tools were produced to help design teams enrolled in the C-2000 program. One outlines generic design steps and provides a simple way for designers to record their performance targets and strategies; another facilitates the task of having the client and design team reach a consensus on the relative importance of various issues. The C-2000 IDP process is now being used as a model for development of a generic international model by Solar Heating and Cooling Task 23 of the International Energy Agency (IEA), and discussions are underway with the Royal Architectural Institute of Canada to see if the process can be accepted as an alternative form of delivery of professional services.

REFERENCES AND RESOURCES

Published

ASHRAE. 1999. *ANSI/ASHRAE/IESNA Standard 90.1-1999, Energy Standard for Buildings Except Low-Rise Residential Buildings.* Atlanta: American Society of Heating, Refrigerating and Air-Conditioning Engineers, Inc.

ASHRAE. 2005. *ASHRAE Guideline 0-2005, The Commissioning Process.* Atlanta: American Society of Heating, Refrigerating and Air-Conditioning Engineers, Inc.

ASHRAE. 2007. *ANSI/ASHRAE/IESNA Standard 90.1-2007, Energy Standard for Buildings Except Low-Rise Residential Buildings.* Atlanta: American Society of Heating, Refrigerating and Air-Conditioning Engineers, Inc.

ASHRAE. 2007. *ANSI/ASHRAE Standard 90.2-2007, Energy Efficient Design of Low-Rise Residential Buildings.* Atlanta: American Society of Heating, Refrigerating and Air-Conditioning Engineers, Inc.

ASHRAE. 2010. *ANSI/ASHRAE/IES Standard 90.1-2010, Energy Standard for Buildings Except Low-Rise Residential Buildings.* Atlanta: American Society of Heating, Refrigerating and Air-Conditioning Engineers, Inc.

CETC. 1996a. Technical report on Bentall Corporation Crestwood 8 C-2000 Building. CANMET Energy Technology Centre, Natural Resources Canada, Ottawa, Canada.

CETC. 1996b. Technical report on Green on the Grand C-2000 Building. CANMET Energy Technology Centre, Natural Resources Canada, Ottawa, Canada.

Larsson, N., ed. 1996. *C-2000 Program Requirements*. Natural Resources Canada, Ottawa, Canada.

Online

California Debt & Investment Advisory Commission document
www.treasurer.ca.gov/cdiac/publications/p3.pdf

Mondaq
www.mondaq.com/canada/article.asp?articleid=23737

CHAPTER FIVE

ARCHITECTURAL DESIGN AND PLANNING IMPACTS

One of an architect's primary functions as part of the design team is to create an environment. This environment has both a psychological and a physiological effect on the occupants, which, in turn, impacts human productivity, building operational efficiency, and effectiveness of natural resource use.

Before focusing on the building design, it is important that the overall planning impacts of campus and/or real estate development be assessed from a sustainability perspective. With a master plan in place, specific building projects will not only implement green concepts, as they relate directly to the design goals of a building project, but will also incorporate design elements that will contribute to localized sustainable development goals.

Site location, building orientation and geometry, building envelope, arrangement of spaces, and local climatic characteristics are all elements the design team must address, and the result will have a distinct impact on both the occupants' environment and the efficiency of the building. Buildings that effectively combine their surroundings with the application of green design principles generally provide a project with greater psychological and physiological benefits for the occupants. Buildings that also implement sustainability reduce carbon emissions, use fewer resources for construction and operation, are constructed for longer useful service life, and require less to maintain.

As described in Chapter 3, developing the Owner's Project Requirements (OPR) is an essential precursor to identifying a project's objectives and criteria, including sustainable/green design goals. The OPR creates the benchmarks used in assessing the various options a design team develops to meet the project's objectives and criteria during design. This chapter is intended to help designers understand the impacts some architectural decisions have and how these decisions affect sustainable/green project goals.

SUSTAINABILITY AND ENERGY MASTER PLANNING

Even when thinking about efficiencies at a building scale, it is critical to understand the local, regional, and national impacts. Very rarely are the buildings that we are designing for not tied to a larger infrastructural grid or utility network.

Master planning is looking at the issues beyond the one-plot building, and expanding to a larger, more interconnected network of buildings and facilities. Master planning can happen on a variety of scales, each with their own challenges and opportunities. It can occur when dealing with two buildings being tied to central power or mechanical systems, or in the redevelopment of 30 acres of a downtown urban center.

Sustainable master planning is a broad term that defines a variety of issues. It addresses resource use (i.e., energy and water consumption, waste, materials, and ecology), landscape concerns (i.e., transport, storm and sanitary, people flows, and cultural issues), and the Triple Bottom Line concept of environmental, economic, and social concerns (Savitz and Weber 2006). As a sustainable master planning professional, it is necessary to understand the impacts that one decision has on the plan as a whole. For instance, a renewable energy plan that does not have economic viability, or perhaps does not promote green jobs or local involvement across a variety of social levels, may not be the wisest recommendation.

As architects drive solutions toward building efficiency, working closely with building systems engineers, urban planners, landscape architects, and civil engineers must work closely with mechanical and power systems engineers. Decision making is not isolated to aesthetic concerns, and must be informed by a multidisciplinary team. We as designers need to embrace external microclimate issues, thermal comfort, outdoor air quality and day lighting.

Energy Concerns

Knowing that energy is just part of a sustainable master plan is important. As a smart building services engineer, one must be familiar with the flows of energy from generation, through transmission, to consumption. Understanding these flows is critical to being able to provide solutions that increase overall system efficiencies and facilitate energy reductions at all levels.

Energy systems should be the following:

- *Reliable.* The availability of a central power grid does not inherently mean that the grid power is reliable. What are the blackout issues? What are the load-shedding schemes? How is this 'grid' connected and backed up through adjacent systems? What percentage is fuels that are imported?
- *Cheap.* Understanding the economic trends of power supplies will help to further inform your decisions for fuel mixes to be used.
- *Clean.* As global climate change comes to the forefront of geopolitical agendas, understand carbon emission factors associated with electrical consumption of a grid, or by way of the combustion of on-site fuels, will continue to become a design driver.

- *Flexible.* In an increasingly volatile market, having a flexible energy plan will help to assure economic and energy security.

As we approach a tipping point in fossil fuel dependence, we are finding that it is increasingly difficult to achieve all of these four factors simultaneously. Moreover, energy systems are linked to nearly every other system of a master plan, from the architecture to the landscape. Understanding the interconnectedness of the power and mechanical systems will allow for more informed decisions.

Every master planning project is different and requires specialized solutions to solve the specific problems that the project presents. When master planning anything from a small district to a large-scale region, there are five guiding principles that should be considered. The following five questions can be used to guide your energy master plan:

1. Can the infrastructure perform more than one function, or multitask?
2. Will it draw on or complement natural systems?
3. Does it have some sociocultural value?
4. Can it contribute to reducing dependency on fossil fuels?
5. Is it able to respond/adapt to climate change scenarios?

Framework for Thinking

The following framework for thinking can help form a thought and decision process for the plan. This is not meant to be a linear decision making process, but instead is an iterative one of trial, testing, and weighing options. Here are the steps:

- *Establishing a Baseline.* Where are you now?
- *Sustainability Goals.* What do you want to accomplish?
- *Action Plans.* How do you get there and when?
- *Implementation.* How do you build and operate?
- *Verification.* How are you doing?

Frequently, there are very few options for design engineers to affect the supply chain of energy to their site. Although more often than not it cannot be controlled, that does not mean that it is not important to understand the origin of the power source and its composition. A snapshot of energy makeup is helpful in understanding the reliability, cost, cleanliness, and flexibility of an energy grid. However, a trend graph can help to further inform your decisions. There may be policy drivers such as carbon cap-and-trade issues that might further affect the grid.

In reviewing the power generation issues for a site, the following issues should be considered:

Decentralization. Thermodynamic losses and transmission losses associated with a traditional power generation and transmission system can near 65%. That is, if 100 units of energy are put into the system, only 35 units of useful energy will be available at the end-consumer.

Decentralization is the idea of replacing or supplementing these large-scale, centralized power generation systems that are located away from the end-users, with decentralized power generation at the end-user.

Relocating this generation will allow for the following benefits:

- Increased efficiencies, as it is now possible to implement cogeneration systems.
- Increased reliability, as power systems are not always reliable.
- Reduced transmission losses, which can near 7% in a traditional distribution system.
- Can often remove the need for standby power generation.

Renewable Energy Solutions. When studying various energy planning, implementation of renewable energy strategies can complement a plan in that they:

- are clean, negligible greenhouse gas emissions;
- flexible and provide diversity of fuel sources, and supplement traditional energy supply strategies; and
- reliable—the technology is proven.

The master planning team should identify potential larger scale opportunities, assess the economies of scale, explore district scale solution, and identify potential site-integrated opportunities.

Transmission Efficiency Assessment. The increase in efficiencies due to big conservation moves that deal with transmission losses include potentially exploring options for distributed generation, fuel switching, SMART Grid, and demand-side management. These assessments may or may not be a viable consideration depending on the scope of an energy master planning process.

SITE LOCATION

Consideration of the implications of site selection is essential to minimizing the negative environmental impacts that may accompany a project, from construction activities to those that will occupy the facility. Prudent site selection can lower first cost, operating and maintenance costs, environmental cost, and people cost. Sustainable/green design should consider the larger cost of projects that encroach on animal habitats, prime farmland, or public parks. Other considerations are transportation of materials and labor to construct the project; loss of land that supports biodiversity; the highways, roads, and bridges required to provide access to the facility; the infrastructure needed to support operation of the facility; and the proximity of the facility to residential and other services for building occupants to reduce natural resources needed for transportation.

While design engineers may have little say in the above considerations, it is wise for the architect to involve the engineers early in the site selection process, when possible. Matters such as building form and orientation, nearby pollution sources, ambient air quality, groundwater levels, site drainage, availability of or access to various energy sources (including renewables), and other not-so-obvious characteristics can have implications for a successful design in the later stages.

Further guidance is offered by various rating systems, one of which is the U.S. Green Building Council's (USGBC) Leadership in Energy and Environmental Design (LEED) rating systems for new construction, commercial interiors, core and shell, and existing buildings, which have specific information on site selection and other site-related concerns.

SITE ORIENTATION

Building orientation affects many aspects of green design, ranging from energy performance to visual stimulation of the building occupant. Considerations of solar orientation; prevailing winds; availability of natural light; shading created by natural vegetation, topography, or adjacent structures; and views all impact the designer's choice of how to orient the building on a site. Site orientation can also affect landscaping choices and irrigation water consumption. The benefits, drawbacks, and trade-offs should be weighed when choosing the orientation, and the engineer members of the design team can be particularly helpful here.

Buildings that minimize east and west exposures, especially where a lot of glass is used, are generally more energy efficient because of the huge solar heat gains associated with east- and west-facing elevations during cooling months. If a goal of the owner is to use natural breezes to help meet cooling requirements, then the building needs to be oriented with operable windows and the dominant elevations perpendicular to the prevailing breezes to capture windward/leeward effects and better draw outdoor air through the building. (In some instances this may conflict with minimizing east and west elevations to limit solar heat gain.)

Here is where computer simulations, performed by an experienced energy analyst and yielding fast and factual results, can assist the design team by evaluating nuances in building orientation and the effect various stacking and massing options have on building performance.

BUILDING FORM/GEOMETRY

A building's form (i.e., stacking, massing, and overall geometry) has a significant impact on a building's functionality, energy efficiency, and occupant performance. One of the most important considerations in green design is the effect form has on natural lighting.

Glazing size, orientation, and an occupant's distance from glazing, in addition to glazing characteristics, determine the quality and quantity of natural light reaching a building's interior, as well as occupant views of the surrounding environment. The most desirable natural light comes from the north; it has the least solar heat gain associated with it and is composed of diffused light, which does not cause glare.

The distance natural light will travel into the interior of a building is dependent on window and ceiling height. The quantity of light is dependent on the glazing area. The quality of light is determined by orientation and glazing characteristics. The usefulness of natural light to meet task lighting requirements is a function of light quality on task surfaces. All of these factors affect the form a building takes to meet the requirement for natural daylight harvesting.

Several sources of information are available to assist designers with daylight harvesting strategies. First, Chapter 13, offers some basic considerations on daylight harvesting, concentrating on applicability, pros and cons, and cost. Additional resources are listed in the "References and Resources" section at the end of this chapter.

Daylight harvesting is only one of many green factors that may influence building geometry. Buildings designed for natural ventilation could be configured in a form to best capture prevailing breezes and direct them for the most beneficial use. Stepping a building back as it rises in height could allow solar access to an adjacent property. The roof of a stepped building could also be vegetated, reducing the quantity and rate of stormwater to be treated.

BUILDING ENVELOPE

The building envelop performs the primary function of keeping the weather out (and, when feasible, letting its good aspects in), and its design is a key factor that defines how well a building and its occupants perform. (Examples of how the factors discussed in this chapter affect occupant performance are contained in productivity studies performed at a manufacturing facility designed to maximize the use of natural light [Heerwagen 2001].) Construction materials and techniques of the building envelope dictate the useful service life of the building, indoor air quality (IAQ), HVAC sizing, structural design, and maintenance costs, all of which have significant impact on the environment and the total cost of ownership.

Daylight Harvesting and Energy

Access to outdoor views and natural light have positive psychological and physiological effects on building occupants, but too much light and glare can have negative psychological and physiological impacts (Heerwagen 2001). Analysis of the building envelope utilizing daylight harvesting simulation programs can help a design team optimize building geometry, define glazing characteristics based on glazing orientation, and provide essential information needed in performing an energy analysis of the facility. (See Figures 5-1 and 5-2 for daylight harvesting examples.)

Daylight harvesting programs only provide one side of what a design team must consider when creating a building envelope. Honing it to minimize heating and cooling energy consumption requires energy modeling of the building, which is where the engineering side of the design team comes in. The books in the ASHRAE *Advanced Energy Design Guide* series also have tips and offer guidance on building envelope design without conducting energy modeling.

Several software programs exist that allow the results of the daylight harvesting model to be entered into the energy model. This combination of programs allows

Green roof
modular blocks

Green roof over
parking garage

Image courtesy of Tom Lawrence, University of Georgia

Figure 5-1 The Hauptmann Woodward Research Laboratory Building in Buffalo, New York, optimizes daylight harvesting with distinctive architectural geometry and building form.

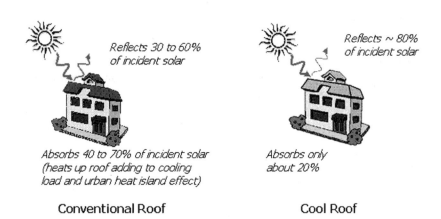

Reflects 30 to 60% of incident solar

Reflects ~ 80% of incident solar

Absorbs 40 to 70% of incident solar (heats up roof adding to cooling load and urban heat island effect)

Absorbs only about 20%

Conventional Roof

Cool Roof

Image courtesy of Tom Lawrence, University of Georgia

Figure 5-2 Example of north-facing assembly space that optimizes daylight harvesting while minimizing solar gain.

evaluation of different glazing characteristics, HVAC system types, and life-cycle costs of various combinations to determine which best meets project goals.

Moisture Intrusion

Although a primary function of the building envelope is protecting the building interior and its occupants from inclement weather, an astonishing fact is that 80% of insurance claims against architects are related to moisture intrusion through the building envelope. Further, moisture intrusion is a leading cause of sick-building syndrome. Water can enter through the building envelope by three methods: direct rainwater intrusion, water vapor transmission, and negative pressurization (unwanted infiltration).

Design teams often use belt-and-suspenders approaches to try to avoid direct rainwater intrusion but then fail to test the design and installation to ensure that the design intent is met. Chapter 3 discusses in detail how commissioning helps ensure that the building performs as intended and verifies that this aspect of green design intent is met.

Often overlooked in design is water vapor transmission into and across the building envelope. Appropriate members of the design team should examine each proposed building envelope assembly type and conduct a vapor transmission analysis for each. Calculation methods for evaluating vapor transmission and determining the likelihood of moisture collecting within the building envelope can be found in the 2009 *ASHRAE Handbook—Fundamentals* (ASHRAE 2009). IAQ problems and building failure resulting from moisture collecting within the building envelope has occurred in most areas of the United States and Canada.

While negative pressurization of a building in an arid climate generally has little air quality impact, IAQ problems can result when it occurs in a hot and humid—and sometimes even a moderate—climate. The resulting infiltration of humid air, in addition to being an added air-conditioning cost, can result in condensation in unexpected—and sometimes unseen—places. The ensuing problems (e.g., mold, mildew, spore production, etc.) can be so severe as to result in building evacuation and extensive remedial costs, sometimes even exceeding the original cost of the building. Design teams need to be very conscious of building pressurization and ensure that the building envelope is appropriately pressurized for the climate and intended building use. Here, in particular, coordination of HVAC design with building envelope design is critical to achieving good indoor environmental quality (IEQ) and in controlling energy consumption.

GREEN-ROOF AND COOL-ROOF TECHNOLOGIES

While similar in some respects, green-roof and cool-roof technologies can serve very different purposes.

Green Roofs

The practice of placing a living vegetative surface onto a building rooftop (hence, a green roof) is not new. The famous Hanging Gardens of ancient Babylon were built around 500 BC and were built of arched stone beams waterproofed with reeds and a thick tar coating. Modern materials allow for a wide range of vegetative system concepts for a green roof. Green-roof systems can be generally classified as intensive or extensive. An intensive green-roof system is, in essence, a miniature ecosystem built of several layers with drainage systems and, quite often, irrigation. Intensive green roofs would generally have a minimum of 12 in. (30 cm) of soil depth but can include even deeper soil substrates. These types of roofs can indeed be miniature parks with large trees, shrubs, and manicured landscapes. The resulting additional structural load can be large, in the range of 80 to 150 lb/ft^2 (390 to 732 kg/m^2).

In contrast, an extensive green roof involves a much smaller soil depth, from 1 to 6 in. (2.5 to 15 cm). Extensive green roofs are primarily installed for the environmental benefits and are commonly installed using modular plots. The additional load on the building structure is not nearly as much as with an intensive green roof, with typical values being on the order of 10 to 15 lb/ft^2 (49 to 73 kg/m^2).

One of the earlier benefits touted for green roofs was the potential for reduction in building HVAC energy consumption. Green roofs can reduce the heat flow into the building in summer and out of the building roof in winter due to the insulation properties of the added soil. The potential also exists for green roofs to act as an active cooling system to remove heat from the roof surface in the summer through evapotranspiration, but this generally would require the roof surface to be irrigated (and, hence, increase water consumption).

From an HVAC&R engineer's perspective for a green roof, the question is how exactly to analyze the green roof thermal transport properties. The green roof soil and other layers do add additional thermal insulation to the roof, and plant materials may shade the soil surface. In addition, the evapotranspiration effect of water leaving the green roof soil surface increases heat loss from the green roof, potentially keeping it cooler. Building energy simulation models are not well suited for analyzing the heat loss due to the effect of moisture evaporation from the soil. For example, in the eQUEST (DOE-2-based) simulation model, the only additional parameter available for manipulation beyond the soil thermal conductivity and capacitance is the soil absorptivity. In one study, it was proposed to adjust the absorptivity downward to account for rainwater evaporation effects (Hilten 2005). The recommended soil surface absorptivity values to use for various cities in the United States when analyzing the impact of a green roof on building energy loads are listed in Table 5-1. These values are compared to a normal soil surface absorptivitiy of approximately 0.7.

The primary benefit of green roofs that is driving the market acceptance, particularly in Europe, is that of reduced stormwater runoff. Several major cities in the United States have recently adapted roof vegetation requirements for new construction to reduce stormwater runoff. Table 5-2 summarizes potential benefits and drawbacks for green-roof systems. Green roofs are also considered to potentially reduce the urban heat island effect, but the exact influence and interaction of green roofs with the local thermal environment is not scientifically proven.

Cool Roofs

The primary intent of cool-roof technology is to reduce the amount of energy absorbed by a roof surface. New, advanced coating materials allow for the selective absorption and reflection of various spectral wavelengths. This allows for the design of roofing systems with visual coloring that can enhance a building's character, while still reflecting a good deal of the total incident solar energy (of which a significant portion extends beyond the visual wavebands to include infrared and ultraviolet light). The net result is that a lower fraction of the incident solar energy (only about 20% or less) is absorbed by the structure. This reduces the cooling load on the building's HVAC and significantly increases the expected life of the building's roof. The environmental benefits of cool roofs are that they can decrease the urban heat island effect by reflecting some of the incident solar energy back into space, as opposed to absorbing the heat and releasing it to the surroundings.

In summary, both technologies can have a positive environmental benefit but in somewhat different ways. A comparison of the various properties of each is given

Table 5-1:   Recommended Soil Surface Absorptivity Values to Use in Building Energy Analysis of Green Roofs

City	Absorptivity
Atlanta	0.46
Denver	0.58
Honolulu	0.56
Los Angeles	0.62
New York	0.39
Phoenix	0.67
Seattle	0.36

Table 5-2: Potential Benefits and Drawbacks of Green Roofs

Advantages	Disadvantages
Stormwater runoff reduction	Additional structural load
Reduced heat gains (in summer) and heat loss (in winter) to building structure	Cost
Longer life for the base roofing system (may not apply to an intensive green roof)	Additional maintenance, ranging from limited for an extensive green roof with low-maintenance plants to high for a manicured landscape intensive roof
Reduced noise transmission from outside	Optimal roof type, plant materials, and soil depths will vary depending on climate
Aesthetic benefits to people in or around the building with the additional green space	Documentation of benefits such as reduction in heat island effect has not been proven
Other general environmental benefits, such as reduced nitrogen runoff (source: bird droppings), air pollutant absorption, potential carbon sink, bird habitat	

in Table 5-3. Note that the net environmental impact of a technology should be taken into account for an individual project. For example, if adding a green roof requires additional building materials to strengthen the load-bearing capacity of the roof, then this would be a negative impact that must be considered. (For more information about green and cool roofs, see the references and resources listed at the end of the chapter.)

BUILDING MATERIALS

The types of materials specified for the integrated systems in a building have a significant impact on the other sustainability categories in the green design process. Green building materials are composed of renewable resources, and their environmental impacts are considered over the life of the product (Spiegel and Meadows, 1999). Depending upon project-specific goals, an assessment of green materials may involve an evaluation of one or more criteria. (These criteria and more information can be found at www.ciwmb.ca.gov/GreenBuilding/Materials/.)

While many of the green rating systems have excluded the consideration of the infrastructure materials in a building as part of the assessment in the green rating system process, the mechanical engineer can take a proactive role in specifying durable, non-toxic, high-performance, and low-waste materials for the minimum energy performance (MEP) systems in a building. The following link provides a detailed explanation of how one might start to assess this aspect of green design on a project: www.buildinggreen.com/auth/article.cfm?fileName=090101a.xml.

Table 5-3: Comparison of Green-Roof and Cool-Roof Technologies

Property	Green Roof	Cool Roof
Decrease roof surface temperature	Yes	Yes
Impact on cooling load	↓	↓
Impact on heating load	↓	↑
Building structural concern	Yes	No
Improved stormwater management	Yes	No
Reduce urban heat island impact	Yes	Yes
Cost impact	++	Minor

ARRANGEMENT/GROUPING OF SPACES

Although the owner's program, functional needs, daylight harvesting constraints, aesthetics, and many nonengineering green factors go into an architect's determination of how spaces are grouped and arranged in a building, what results can also impact how efficiently the HVAC system performs.

Good design practice for a typical floor layout optimizes scheduling capabilities and daylight harvesting while promoting interaction.

Avoiding unnecessary energy use by providing the capability to shut down or scale back the operation of systems serving building areas not being used is a basic green design principle (use only what is needed), and doing this depends, in part, on how spaces are arranged or grouped. If a department or group of occupants is known to work on a different schedule than others, having that area served by a separate air-handling system, for instance, would help designers avoid the need to run one or more large air-handling system to accommodate the needs of that one group.

While this is only one factor of many that an architect must consider, there is no reason why the HVAC engineer should not ensure that the architect is aware of this factor where it may be applicable. It is also important that the designers help educate the building operators on how the building is intended to be operated from the design perspective and provide strategies that can be used to reduce utility consumption.

CLIMATIC IMPACTS

Climatic factors are those conditions, features, or influences external to the building that can have an impact on the building. Some are natural and some are human-made. The key characteristics are ambient temperature and humidity patterns, ambient air quality, potential pollution sources, solar availability and intensity, wind patterns, soil conditions, freshwater availability and quality, and site drainage.

It is important to understand microclimate issues within a region. For example, there are different parts of San Francisco that have significantly different climates with respect to temperature, humidity, and sunshine.

The climatic characteristics of a site obviously have an impact on how the building performs, especially its energy performance and impact on its surroundings. The design team should be aware of such key characteristics, with each member examining them from the standpoint of his or her own expertise. The following questions should be asked:

- How will each affect my portion of the design?
- How will the climate affect the overall design?
- Can the local climate be used or accommodated in a way to further the goal of sustainable/green design for this building, including minimizing carbon emissions?

Additional sources for climatic data are located in the "References and Resources" section at the end of the chapter.

EXISTING BUILDINGS

The growth rate of commercial floor area in the United States is approximately 1% per year. This fact suggests that the greatest opportunity to reduce the overall environmental impacts of buildings is to renovate existing buildings. Extending the life of an existing building through a renovation project often means that the development of a new site can be avoided. A renovation project also requires fewer materials than a new construction project and provides the opportunity to make the building significantly more energy and water efficient.

Obviously, a renovation project does not permit the design team to change site location, building orientation, or (typically) building form. However, the remaining considerations outlined above (i.e., building envelope, daylight harvesting and HVAC systems, moisture intrusion, and grouping of spaces) can and generally should be addressed by a renovation project. Additionally, a renovation project can allow for the provision of greener finishes including low volatile organic compound (VOC)-emitting paints and sustainably harvested materials, water efficiency improvements by plumbing fixture upgrades, rainwater harvesting and the use of graywater, and the installation of renewable energy systems (e.g., building integrated photovoltaics and wind turbines).

The USGBC's LEED rating systems for new construction and existing buildings (LEED for new construction and LEED for existing buildings) both offer good guidance for renovating buildings. The former is focused on projects during which more than 50% of occupants remain in the building; the latter focuses on projects during which less than 50% of occupants remain in the building.

INTERDEPENDENCY

The site, resource availability, each element of the design, IEQ, and operability are all interdependently related. Focusing on any one element more than the others can compromise the effectiveness, performance, and cost. Defining the OPR in the predesign phase of a project that documents the owner's objectives and criteria, including sustainable/green goals, sets a solid foundation for integrated design and improves delivery efficiency, and balances sustainable principles with building function and the owner's needs.

BUILDING-TYPE GREENTIPS

The GreenTips in this chapter are called *Building-Type GreenTips*. The intent is to give the design engineer a very general idea of concepts to start with that are specific to certain building types. References are included for more detailed study and analysis of design options.

ASHRAE
Building-Type GreenTip # 1

Performing Arts Spaces

GENERAL DESCRIPTION

Performing arts spaces include dance studios, black box theaters, recital halls, rehearsal halls, practice rooms, performance halls with stage and fixed seating, control rooms, back-house spaces, and support areas.

HIGH-PERFORMANCE STRATEGIES

Acoustics

1. Understand different criteria for noise criteria levels to be achieved in different types of spaces.
2. Consider 2 and 4 in. (5 and 10 cm) liners for large ducts serving spaces with noise criteria levels of 25 and lower.
3. Locate equipment as far away from low noise criteria spaces as practical.
4. Work closely with the acoustic consultant, structural engineer, architect, and construction manager to integrate strategies that eliminate the distribution of vibration and equipment noise from the HVAC systems to the performance spaces.
5. Design duct distribution to eliminate noise transfer between acoustically sensitive spaces. This can be done by using duct liners, additional elbows to isolate sound travel, sound attenuators, etc.
6. Do not route piping systems through or above spaces that are acoustically sensitive.

Energy Considerations

1. Consider using demand-control ventilation for high-occupancy spaces.
2. Consider using heat recovery for spaces served by air-handling units (AHUs) with 100% outdoor air capability or over 50% outdoor air component.
3. Consider strategies that allow the significant heat gain from the theatrical lighting equipment to stratify, rather than handle all of the equipment heat gain within the conditioned space zones in the building.

4. Because of the significant variation in the cooling load through-out the day, incorporating a thermal energy storage system into the central plant design will reduce the size of the chiller plant equipment, saving capital costs and energy and operational costs.

Occupant Comfort

1. Consider underfloor supply air/displacement air strategies for large halls with fixed seating.
2. Consider stage air distribution separately from seating air distribution.
3. Consider humidification control for all spaces where musical instruments and vocalists will practice, store equipment, and perform.

KEY ELEMENTS OF COST

1. If properly integrated, an underfloor distribution system should not add significant capital costs to the project.
2. Heat recovery strategies should be assessed using life-cycle analyses. All components of the strategy must be taken into account, including the negative aspects such as adding fan static pressure and, therefore, using more fan energy when heat wheel or heat pipe strategies are considered.

SOURCES OF FURTHER INFORMATION

Bauman, F.S., and A. Daly. 2003. *Underfloor Air Distribution Design Guide*. Atlanta: American Society of Heating, Refrigerating and Air-Conditioning Engineers, Inc.

ASHRAE
Building-Type GreenTip #2

Health Care Facilities

GENERAL DESCRIPTION

Health care facilities are infrastructure-intensive and include many different types of spaces. The HVAC systems for these different types of spaces must be designed to address the specific needs of the spaces being served. The first considerations should always be safety and infection control. In addition, optimizing energy efficiency and positively affecting the patient experience should also be important design team goals.

HIGH-PERFORMANCE STRATEGIES

Safety and Infection Control

1. Consider high-efficiency particulate air (HEPA) filtration for all air-handling equipment serving the facility.
2. Consider air distribution strategies in operating rooms and trauma rooms that zone the spaces from most clean to least clean. Start with the most clean zone being the operation/thermal plume location at the patient, then the zone around the doctors, then the zone around the room, and then the zone outside the room.
3. Pressurize rooms consistent with American Institute of Architects (AIA) and/or ASHRAE guidelines.
4. Provide air exchange rates in excess of AIA guidelines in operating rooms, intensive care units, isolation rooms, trauma rooms, and patient rooms.
5. Provide redundancy of equipment for fail-safe operation and optimal full- and part-load energy-efficient operation.
6. Model intake/exhaust location strategies to ensure no reintroduction of exhaust into the building.

Energy Considerations

1. Consider utilizing heat recovery for spaces served by AHUs with 100% outdoor air capability.
2. Use variable-air-volume (VAV) systems in noncritical spaces working in conjunction with lighting occupancy sensors.

Occupant Comfort

1. Acoustics of systems and spaces must be designed with patient comfort in mind.
2. Daylight and views should be provided, while minimizing the HVAC load impact of these benefits.
3. Provide individual temperature control of patient rooms with the capability of adjustment by patient.
4. Building pressurization relationships/odor issues should be carefully mapped and addressed in the design and operation of the building.

KEY ELEMENTS OF COST

1. HEPA filtration costs are significant in both first cost and operating costs. The engineer should work closely with the infection control specialists at the health care facility to determine cost/benefit assessment of the filtration strategies.
2. Heat recovery strategies should be assessed using life-cycle analyses. All components of the strategy must be taken into account, including the negative aspects, such as adding fan static pressure and, therefore, using more fan energy when heat wheel or heat pipe strategies are considered.

SOURCES OF FURTHER INFORMATION

AIA. 2006. *Guidelines for Design and Construction of Health Care Facilities.* Washington, DC: American Institute of Architects.

American Society of Healthcare Engineering, *Green Guide for Health Care*
www.gghc.org

ASHRAE. 2003. *HVAC Design Manual for Hospitals and Clinics.* Atlanta: American Society of Heating, Refrigerating and Air-Conditioning Engineers, Inc.

The Center for Health Design
www.healthdesign.org

NFPA. 2005. *NFPA 99, Standard for Health Care Facilities.* Quincy, MA: National Fire Protection Agency.

ASHRAE
Building-Type GreenTip #3

Laboratory Facilities

GENERAL DESCRIPTION

Laboratory facilities are infrastructure-intensive and include many different types of spaces. The HVAC systems for these different types of spaces must be designed to address the specific needs of the spaces being served. The first considerations should always be safety and system redundancy to ensure the sustainability of laboratory studies. Life-cycle cost analyses for different system options is critical in developing the right balance between first cost and operating costs.

HIGH-PERFORMANCE STRATEGIES

Safety

1. Design fume hoods and associated air distribution and controls to protect the users and the validity of the laboratory work.
2. Pressurize rooms to be consistent with the *ASHRAE Laboratory Design Guide* (McIntosh et al. 2002) and any other code-required standards. Use building pressurization mapping to develop air distribution, exchange rate, and control strategies.
3. Optimize air exchange rates to ensure occupant safety, while minimizing energy usage.
4. Design chemical, biological, and nuclear storage, and handling exhaust and ventilation systems to protect against indoor pollution, outdoor pollution, and fire hazards.
5. Model intake/exhaust location strategies to ensure that lab exhaust air is not reintroduced back into the building's air-handling system.

Redundancy

1. Consider a centralized lab exhaust system with a redundant ($n + 1$) exhaust fan setup.
2. Redundant central chilled-water, steam, or hydronic heating, air-handling, and humidification systems should be designed for fail-safe operation and to optimize full-load and part-load efficiency of all equipment.

Energy Considerations

1. Heat recovery for spaces served by AHUs with 100% outdoor air capability or more than 50% outdoor air component.
2. Utilize VAV systems to minimize air exchange rates during unoccupied hours.
3. Consider low-flow fume hoods with constant volume controls where this concept can be properly applied.

Occupant Comfort

1. Air systems should be designed to allow for a collaborative working environment. Acoustic criteria should be adhered to in order to maintain acceptable levels of noise control.
2. Daylight and views should be considered where lab work will not be adversely affected.

KEY ELEMENTS OF COST

1. Heat recovery strategies should be assessed using life-cycle analyses. All components of the strategy must be taken into account, including the negative aspects, such as adding fan static pressure and, therefore, using more fan energy when heat wheel or heat pipe strategies are considered.
2. Low-flow fume hoods should be evaluated considering the impact of reducing the sizes of air-handling, heating, cooling, and humidification systems.

SOURCES OF FURTHER INFORMATION

Labs 21, Environmental Performance Criteria
    www.labs21century.gov
McIntosh, I.B.D., C.B. Dorgan, and C.E. Dorgan. 2002. *ASHRAE Laboratory Design Guide*. Atlanta: American Society of Heating, Refrigerating and Air-Conditioning Engineers, Inc.
NFPA. 2004. *NFPA 45, Standard on Fire Protection for Laboratories using Chemicals*. Quincy, MA: National Fire Protection Association.

ASHRAE
Building-Type GreenTip #4

Student Residence Halls

GENERAL DESCRIPTION

Student residence halls are made up primarily of living spaces (i.e., bedrooms, living rooms, kitchen areas, common spaces, study spaces, etc.). Most of these buildings also have central laundry facilities, assembly/main lobby areas, and central meeting/study rooms. Some of these spaces also include classrooms, central kitchen and dining facilities, etc. The strategies outlined below can also be applied to hotels and multiunit residential complexes, including downtown luxury condominium developments.

HIGH-PERFORMANCE STRATEGIES

Energy Considerations

1. Use heat recovery for spaces served by AHUs with 100% outdoor air capability serving living units (exhaust from toilet rooms/supply air to occupied spaces).
2. Use VAV systems or induction systems for public/common spaces.
3. Use natural ventilation and hybrid natural ventilation strategies.
4. Use electronically commutated motors (ECMs) for fan-coil units.
5. Use ground-source heat pumps (GSHPs) where feasible.

Occupant Comfort

1. Systems should be designed to appropriately control noise in occupied spaces.
2. Daylight and views should be optimized, while minimizing load impact on the building.
3. Consider providing occupant control in all bedrooms

KEY ELEMENTS OF COST

1. While there is a premium to be paid in first cost for ECMs, many utility companies have energy rebate programs that make this concept acceptable, even on projects with tight budgets.

2. Heat recovery strategies should be assessed using life-cycle analyses. All components of the strategy must be taken into account, including the negative aspects, such as adding fan-static pressure and, therefore, using more fan energy when heat wheel or heat pipe strategies are considered.

3. Hybrid natural ventilation strategies could be utilized such as using operable windows, properly designed vents, using the venturi effect to optimize natural airflow through the building, and the shutdown of mechanical ventilation and cooling systems during ambient temperature ranges between 60°F and 80°F (16°C and 27°C). This will significantly reduce operating costs. The costs of the operable windows and vents will need to be weighed against the energy savings.

SOURCES OF FURTHER INFORMATION

ASHRAE. 2005. *ASHRAE Handbook—Fundamentals*. Chapter 27, pp. 25.10–25.12. Atlanta: American Society of Heating, Refrigerating and Air-Conditioning Engineers, Inc.

BRESCU, BRE. 1999. *Natural Ventilation for Offices Guide and CD-ROM*. ÓBRE on behalf of the NatVent Consortium, Garston, Watford, UK, March.

Svensson C., and S.A. Aggerholm. 1998. Design tool for natural ventilation. ASHRAE IAQ 1998 Conference, October 24–27, New Orleans, LA.

ASHRAE
Building-Type GreenTip #5

Athletic and Recreation Facilities

GENERAL DESCRIPTION

Athletic and recreational spaces include pools, gymnasiums, cardio rooms, weight-training rooms, multipurpose rooms, courts, offices, and other support spaces, etc.

HIGH-PERFORMANCE STRATEGIES

Energy Considerations

1. Consider using demand-control ventilation for high-occupancy spaces.
2. Consider using heat recovery for spaces served by AHUs with 100% outdoor air capability or more than 50% outdoor air component.
3. Consider strategies that allow the significant heat gain in high-volume spaces to stratify, rather than handling all of the heat gain within the conditioned space zones in the building.
4. Consider heat recovery/no mechanical cooling strategy for the pool area in moderate climates.
5. Consider occupied/unoccupied mode for large locker room and toilet room areas to set back the air exchange rate in these spaces during unoccupied hours and save fan energy.
6. Consider heating pool water with waste heat from pool dehumidification system.

Occupant Comfort

1. Consider CO_2 sensors in all spaces that have infrequent, dense occupancy.
2. Consider high-occupancy and low-occupancy modes for air-handling equipment in gymnasiums utilizing a manual switch and variable-frequency drives.
3. Consider hybrid natural ventilation strategies in areas that do not have humidity control issues (i.e., pools, training rooms, etc.)

KEY ELEMENTS OF COST

1. The pool strategy described above should reduce first cost and operating costs.
2. Heat recovery strategies should be assessed using life-cycle analyses. All components of the strategy must be taken into account, including the negative aspects, such as adding fan static pressure and, therefore, using more fan energy when heat wheel or heat pipe strategies are considered.
3. Demand-control ventilation adds minimal first cost and often provides paybacks in one to two years.

ASHRAE
Building-Type GreenTip #6

Commercial Office Buildings

GENERAL DESCRIPTION

Commercial office buildings are made up primarily of office spaces, meeting rooms, and central core facilities such as toilet rooms, storage space, and utility rooms (including TelData). Some of these spaces also include central kitchen and dining facilities. The strategies outlined below can also be applied to most large-scale commercial office buildings.

HIGH-PERFORMANCE STRATEGIES

Energy Considerations

1. Use energy recovery for spaces served by AHUs with dedicated outside air (DOAS) 100% outdoor air capability serving occupied spaces.
2. Use high-efficiency fan coil units or chilled beam/induction systems in conjunction with the DOAS concept.
3. Use natural ventilation and hybrid natural ventilation strategies.
4. Use ECMs for fan-coil units.
5. Use GSHPs where feasible.
6. Incorporate energy-efficient lighting strategies that share integrated occupancy controls with the HVAC system.

Occupant Comfort

1. Systems should be designed to appropriately control noise in occupied spaces.
2. Daylight and views should be optimized, while minimizing load impact on the building.

KEY ELEMENTS OF COST

1. While there is a premium to be paid in first cost for ECMs, many utility companies have energy rebate programs that make this concept acceptable, even on projects with tight budgets.

2. Energy recovery/DOAS strategies should be assessed using life-cycle analyses. All components of the strategy must be taken into account, including the negative aspects, such as adding fan-static pressure and, therefore, using more fan energy when heat wheel or heat pipe strategies are considered.

3. Hybrid natural ventilation strategies could be utilized such as using operable windows, properly designed vents, using the venturi effect to optimize natural airflow through the building, and the shutdown of mechanical ventilation and cooling systems during ambient temperature ranges between 60°F and 80°F (16°C and 27°C). This will significantly reduce operating costs. The costs of the operable windows and vents will need to be weighed against the energy savings.

SOURCES OF FURTHER INFORMATION

ASHRAE. 2004. *Advanced Energy Design Guide for Small Office Buildings*. Atlanta: American Society of Heating, Refrigerating and Air-Conditioning Engineers, Inc.

ASHRAE. 2009. *ASHRAE Handbook—Fundamentals*. Chapter 27, pp. 25.10–25.12. Atlanta: American Society of Heating, Refrigerating and Air-Conditioning Engineers, Inc.

BRESCU, BRE. 1999. *Natural Ventilation for Offices Guide and CD-ROM*. ÓBRE on behalf of the NatVent Consortium, Garston, Watford, UK, March.

Svensson C., and S.A. Aggerholm. 1998. Design tool for natural ventilation. ASHRAE IAQ 1998 Conference, October 24–27, New Orleans, LA.

K-12 School Buildings

GENERAL DESCRIPTION

K-12 school buildings are made up primarily of classrooms, gymnasiums, libraries, an auditorium, a central kitchen and dining facilities, etc.

HIGH-PERFORMANCE STRATEGIES

Energy Considerations

1. Use heat recovery for spaces served by AHUs with 100% outdoor air capability serving occupied spaces.
2. Use DOAS with fan coils or chilled beam/induction systems for spaces.
3. Use natural ventilation and hybrid natural ventilation strategies.
4. Use ECMs for fan-coil units.
5. Use GSHPs where feasible.

Occupant Comfort

1. Systems should be designed to appropriately control noise in occupied spaces.
2. Daylight and views should be optimized while minimizing load impact on the building.

KEY ELEMENTS OF COST

1. While there is a premium to be paid in first cost for ECMs, many utility companies have energy rebate programs that make this concept acceptable, even on projects with tight budgets.
2. Energy recovery strategies should be assessed using life-cycle analyses. All components of the strategy must be taken into account, including the negative aspects, such as adding fan-static pressure and, therefore, using more fan energy when heat wheel or heat pipe strategies are considered.

3. Hybrid natural ventilation strategies could be used, such as using operable windows, properly designed vents, using the venturi effect to optimize natural airflow through the building, and the shutdown of mechanical ventilation and cooling systems during ambient temperature ranges between 60°F and 80°F (16°C and 27°C). This will significantly reduce operating costs. The costs of the operable windows and vents will need to be weighed against the energy savings.

SOURCES OF FURTHER INFORMATION

ASHRAE. 2009. *ASHRAE Handbook—Fundamentals*. Chapter 27, pp. 25.10–25.12. Atlanta: American Society of Heating, Refrigerating and Air-Conditioning Engineers, Inc.

BRESCU, BRE. 1999. *Natural Ventilation for Offices Guide and CD-ROM*. ÓBRE on behalf of the NatVent Consortium, Garston, Watford, UK, March.

Svensson C., and S.A. Aggerholm. 1998. Design tool for natural ventilation. ASHRAE IAQ 1998 Conference, October 24–27, New Orleans, LA.

ASHRAE
Building-Type GreenTip #8

Existing Buildings

GENERAL DESCRIPTION

Renovating an existing building can provide an excellent opportunity to reduce the environmental impact of that building. Significant improvements can be made in building energy and water efficiency. And, of course, extending the life of an existing building via a renovation project obviates the need to develop a new site, and uses fewer materials than would be required by a new building.

HIGH-PERFORMANCE STRATEGIES

Energy Considerations

1. Perform an audit of the building to determine the potential to reduce energy use and to identify specific opportunities to improve energy efficiency.
2. Retrocommission control and HVAC systems that will remain in place after completion of the renovation project.
3. Consider installing energy recovery systems for existing or new HVAC systems, particularly for AHUs providing 100% outdoor air.
4. Use air- and/or water-side free cooling (AHU economizer controls and plate and frame heat exchangers for existing or new cooling towers) where feasible.
5. Consider installing variable-speed drives on new or existing fan and pump motors to improve the match between air and water flows on the one hand and heating and cooling loads on the other.
6. Replace existing HVAC equipment and systems with more efficient equipment and systems where necessary to meet new owner requirements or where cost-justifiable.
7. Retrofit or replace existing lighting fixtures using current energy-efficient lamp and ballast technologies.
8. Consider the use of occupancy sensors to switch lamps off when not needed and dimming controls to take advantage of daylighting where feasible.

9. Consider incorporating renewable energy technologies into the renovation project, such as solar thermal, photovoltaics, and small-scale wind turbines.

Water Considerations

1. Address water use and efficiency concerns in the building audit.
2. Consider replacing existing plumbing fixtures (i.e., water closets, urinals, lavatory faucets, and shower heads) with new, more efficient plumbing fixtures to reduce both water and energy use.
3. Consider modifying landscapes to reduce outdoor water use (e.g., replace grass with native plants, pavers, or gravel).
4. Retrocommission or install new landscape irrigation controls where feasible.

Occupant Comfort

1. Be sure that existing or new control and HVAC systems are capable of meeting the requirements of *ANSI/ASHRAE Standard 55-2010, Thermal Environmental Conditions for Human Occupancy* (ASHRAE 2010) and *ANSI/ASHRAE Standard 62.1-2010, Ventilation for Acceptable Indoor Air Quality* (ASHRAE 2010).
2. Improve occupant comfort and performance with new lighting technologies and daylighting.
3. Provide occupant control over HVAC and lighting systems (i.e., operable windows, thermostats, and light fixture switches) where feasible.

KEY ELEMENTS OF COST

1. Energy and water cost savings are typically used to justify the installation costs of energy and water efficiency upgrades. Establishing cost savings requires a good understanding of baseline operating conditions, proposed operating conditions, utility rates, and interactions among conservation opportunities. It may be necessary to develop whole-building simulation models in order to estimate potential savings accurately.

2. Often, there are ancillary benefits to installing energy and water efficiency upgrades, such as improved comfort, improved maintainability, and extended system life. It is important to discuss these benefits thoroughly with the building owner or owner representative to prioritize energy and water conservation opportunities properly.

3. Alternative sources of funding may be available for energy and water efficiency upgrades. These include utility company rebates, state and federal grants and tax credits, and renewable energy credits. Obtaining access to such alternative funding sources may allow for an increase in renovation project scope.

SOURCES OF FURTHER INFORMATION

ASHRAE. 2010. *ANSI/ASHRAE Standard 55-2010, Thermal Environmental Conditions for Human Occupancy*. Atlanta: American Society of Heating, Refrigerating and Air-Conditioning Engineers, Inc.

ASHRAE. 2006. *ANSI/ASHRAE/IESNA Standard 100-2006, Energy Conservation in Existing Buildings*. Atlanta: American Society of Heating, Refrigerating and Air-Conditioning Engineers, Inc.

ASHRAE. 2007. *ASHRAE Handbook—HVAC Applications*. Chapter 35. Atlanta: American Society of Heating, Refrigerating and Air-Conditioning Engineers, Inc.

ASHRAE. 2010. *ANSI/ASHRAE Standard 62.1-2010, Ventilation for Acceptable Indoor Air Quality*. Atlanta: American Society of Heating, Refrigerating and Air-Conditioning Engineers, Inc.

REFERENCES AND RESOURCES

Published and Software

ASHRAE. 2009. *ASHRAE Handbook—Fundamentals*. Atlanta: American Society of Heating, Refrigerating and Air-Conditioning Engineers, Inc.

Evans, B. 1997. Daylighting design. In *Time-Saver Standards for Architectural Design Data*. New York: McGraw-Hill.

Heerwagen, J. 2001. Do green buildings enhance the well being of workers? www.edcmag.com.

Hilten, R.N. 2005. An analysis of the energetics and stormwater mediation potential of greenroofs. Master's thesis, University of Georgia, Athens, GA.

Savitz, A.W., and K. Weber. 2006. *The Triple Bottom Line*. San Francisco: John Wiley & Sons, Inc.

Spiegel and Meadows, 1999

Online

www.ciwmb.ca.gov/GreenBuilding/Materials/

www.buildinggreen.com/auth/article .cfm?fileName=090101a.xml

"Tips for Daylighting with Windows"
http://windows.lbl.gov/pub/designguide/designguide.html

Cool Roof Rating Council
www.coolroofs.org

Green Roof Industry Information Clearinghouse and Database
www.greenroofs.com

Regional Climate Data
www.wrcc.dri.edu/rcc.html

National Oceanic and Atmosphere Administration
www.noaa.gov

U.S. Environmental Protection Agency, Building Energy Analysis Tool, eQuest
www.energydesignresources.com/resource/130/

CHAPTER SIX

COMMISSIONING

The commissioning process and commissioning authority (CxA) provide a continuous thread from the predesign phase of the project throughout occupancy. *ASHRAE Guideline 0-2005, The Commissioning Process* (ASHRAE 2005) describes the process and provides guidance on implementation from predesign throughout the facility's lifetime. The commissioning process also provides the essential foundation for integrated design and delivery, modifications over the facility's lifetime, and benchmarks for evaluating achievement of the owner's defined goals and objectives as they change over time. Commissioning is applied to new projects and existing facilities to achieve and maintain a facility that meets the needs of the occupants to effectively and efficiently delivery the owner's daily mission, and the owner's financial goals. The true test of a high-performance facility is how it performs over its lifetime.

Achieving desired facility performance starts with clearly defining the Owner's Project Requirements (OPR) in predesign (before development of the architectural program). Many confuse the OPR with an architectural program. The OPR is different from the typical architectural program, which focuses on project floor area needs, adjacencies, circulation, cost, and structural predesign test results. The OPR documents what the owner needs from the facility to efficiently and effectively deliver the owner's daily mission. Specifically, it records the functional requirements associated with activities of this mission. For instance, an architectural program does not contain requirements for how the facility will be operated. It also does not contain operation and maintenance (O&M) training requirements, or documentation requirements for the facility, whereas the OPR does. A related example would be the requirement a scientist who works with a powerful microscope would find essential to efficient delivery of his or her mission—no vibration at the microscope. It is hard to analyze intricate information when the view looks like an earthquake in progress.

The OPR also includes sustainable development goals that are in harmony with the occupant's mission. Many teams focus on green rating system credits without knowing how these credit selections will affect the owner's daily mission. On a recent project, the design team selected use of native and adaptive plants to achieve a green rating system credit but neglected to understand that this conflicted with the military facility's mission and requirements for no vegetation that was 4 in. (10 cm) in height above the ground. There are hundreds of similar examples that could be provided that would not fit in this book. Developing the OPR ahead of the architectural program reduces programming effort and provides valuable information to the designers that they typically do not have. In combination with the architectural program, the OPR provides a strong foundation for a successful integrated design and delivery process and the facility's operational criteria.

The commissioning process focuses upon verifying and documenting that the facility and all of the systems and assemblies are planned, designed, installed, tested, operated, and maintained to meet the OPR. Commissioning is not only an important part of successful project delivery, but it's an essential and, in some cases, required part of green building design and construction. Chapter 4 of this Guide specifically addresses commissioning activities in design. Commissioning is not an exercise in blame. It is, rather, a collaborative effort to identify and reduce potential design, construction, and operational problems by resolving them early in the process, at the least cost to everyone. This chapter will include the selection and role of the commissioning provider, a discussion of various commissioning models, the choice of building systems for commissioning, and the long-term benefits afforded by implementing the commissioning process.

An important part of green design is verification that the goals defined by the owner are integrated by the design and construction team to achieve the owner's objectives for the lifetime of the facility, as defined in the OPR. The OPR is a living document that changes over time as the owner requires change. Once the facility is occupied, changes in owner/occupant mission occur that impact and modify the original project requirements. The original OPR is maintained for its historical value in marking the original project requirements. Using the original OPR as a starting point, the OPR is converted to the current facility requirements (CFR), which documents the changes the owner needs to match the changes in his or her daily mission. The OPR is the foundation for both the commissioning process and for defining the objectives and criteria that will guide a project team in delivering a new project. The CFR provides the foundation to guide the future project teams in modifications needed to meet the changing needs of the owner/occupant. Verification involves all stakeholders, from designers to construction contractors to operating staff to occupants.

Commissioning provides many benefits to the owner, the design and construction teams, building occupants, and building operators. What owner, particularly a long-term owner, does not want reduced risk, fewer change orders (and the resulting cost avoidance), improved energy efficiency, lower operating costs, satisfied tenants/occupants, and a building that operates as intended over the lifetime of the facility?

What contractor or designer does not dream of a project with few or no problems or callbacks and the additional costs that come with such problems? Although numerous commissioning service models exist, commissioning should be performed by a third-party provider or the owner's own commissioning team whenever possible. The process should also begin early in the predesign phase to ensure maximum benefits from commissioning. Starting early improves designer and contractor quality control processes, identifies and helps resolve problems during design (when corrective action is the least expensive), and during construction when the contractor has the materials and resources on site for efficient corrective action (minimizing postoccupancy repairs).

Commissioning for new construction projects can be broken down into five phases: predesign, design, construction, acceptance, and warranty/ongoing commissioning. Commissioning of existing buildings (retrocommissioning) also has four phases: investigation, analysis, recommendations, and implementation. Distinct commissioning activities occur during each of these phases. The process for new construction or renovation begins in the predesign phase with development of the OPR or acceptance of the CFR. During design, the CxA provides checklists to designers to assist them in their design quality control process and remind the designers about the specifics the CxA will be focusing on during commissioning design reviews. During construction, the CxA provides construction checklists to the contractors to assist them in their quality control process and, as in the design reviews, verifies that the contractor's quality control process is working. These efforts significantly improve the chances that the systems being commissioned will need minor modifications during performance testing and will reduce the delivery team's efforts. The acceptance phase verifies through testing that the systems perform as intended and helps resolve issues prior to occupancy. During the warranty phase, the CxA monitors system performance and verifies that training provided was understood by operators. The CxA assists operators in better understanding their systems and adjusting the systems for maximum performance, which helps prevent inappropriate modifications by the operators (due to lack of understanding). During the new construction process, the CxA specifies the deliverable from the project team needed for the systems manual. The systems manual is the repository for the OPR, basis of design, commissioning reports, location of O&M manuals, and as-built documentation and modifications made to the facilities systems and assemblies, along with the reasoning behind the modifications. Detailed information to be included in the systems manual is defined in ASHRAE Guideline 0 (ASHRAE 2005).

Ongoing commissioning in both new and existing projects provides the owner the tools necessary to efficiently manage financial and human resources to achieve desired returns on their investment, facility performance, and reduction of environmental impact. You cannot manage what is not measured. During occupancy, the CxA monitors the facility's performance and identifies deterioration of performance.

This deterioration typically falls into one of two categories: operator error or system malfunction. Monitoring-based, ongoing commissioning identifies the cause of the deterioration and recommendations can be made for correction. Operator errors resulting in deterioration of facility performance provide training opportunities to improve O&M staff understanding of correct facility operation, which helps prevent future operational mistakes. Monitoring-based, ongoing commissioning identification of degradation of facility performance due to system malfunction provides in-depth failure information, which lessens the O&M staffs' troubleshooting efforts and can verify that the repairs performed resolve the problem. Monitoring-based commissioning is easily implemented by the CxA when integrated into the OPR. Implementation in existing buildings does require more effort and some additional cost, but it provides significant financial benefits immediately and over the lifetime of the facility. Commissioning authorities can also help integrate measurement and verification (M&V) plans and procedures that can be used to identify when a building begins operating outside of allowable tolerances, signaling the owner that corrective action is needed to maintain performance.

How, and to what extent, an owner incorporates commissioning into their project generally depends on the owner's understanding of commissioning. Commonly, an owner might start with construction phase commissioning but may soon see how much more they would have benefited by starting in the predesign phase. Other key factors that determine the depth and breadth of commissioning incorporated in any given project are how long the owner holds the property, the owner's staff capabilities and funding methodology for design, construction, and operation, the project schedule, and ownership experience.

One of the most beneficial attributes of sustainable development principles contained in the U.S. Green Building Council's (USGBC) Leadership in Energy and Environmental Design (LEED®) rating system is the inclusion of commissioning. If a building's green design features do not function as intended, there is little benefit in having incorporated them into the design. Commissioning provides verification that the building systems will and do operate as intended.

CxA'S ROLE AND THE OPR DOCUMENT

It is the CxA's role to lead the collaborative team effort required to balance competing interests in the owner's favor. To accomplish this task, a benchmark is needed. This benchmark is the OPR.

The OPR is a written document that details the functional requirements of a project and expectations of how it will be used and operated. This should include project and design goals, measurable performance criteria, budgets, schedules, success criteria, and supporting information (i.e., specific information that should be included and can be found in ASHRAE Guideline 0 [ASHRAE 2005]). It also includes information necessary for all disciplines to properly plan, design, construct, operate, and maintain systems and assemblies.

In the predesign phase of a project, prior to engaging the design team, the owner needs to select a CxA to develop a draft commissioning plan. The draft commissioning plan defines the team's roles and responsibilities, suggested communication protocols, commissioning activities, and the schedule of the activities. Project success is dependent on each team member's understanding of what is expected of them and obtaining their buy-in. The commissioning plan provides the owner with clearly defined roles and responsibilities for each team member for inclusion in contractual agreements and for improved team efficiency. It is more economical to define these requirements early, before selecting and contracting the various project team members. After the project team selection, an owner may express orally (or in a formal written document) the basic requirements of the project that form the OPR and architectural program. This information may typically include justification for the project, program analysis/requirements, intended building use, basic construction materials and methods, proposed systems, project schedule, and general information (such as attaining LEED certification).

The OPR should not duplicate information contained in the architectural program. The OPR forms the basis from which the commissioning provider verifies that the developed project meets the needs and requirements of the owner. An effective commissioning process depends on a clear, concise, and comprehensive OPR with benchmarks for each of the objectives and criteria. This written document details the functional requirements of the facility and the expectations of how it will be used and operated.

If no formal program exists, the OPR document can be used to assist with identifying the criteria the design team is tasked with meeting. However, the main purpose of the OPR is to document the owner's objectives and criteria. The designer's basis-of-design documents, the assumptions the designers made to meet the OPR, and a summary of this information is provided to the operators of the project after the design and construction team have long left the project. As such, the OPR document provides the benchmark against which the design, construction, and project operating performance can be measured.

COMMISSIONING PHASES

The role of the CxA varies according to the phase of the project. Because of the nature of the delivery process, the further along the team is in the delivery process, the more difficult and expensive changes become (see Figure 6-1). Waiting until after predesign to define project end goals, occupant requirements, and team roles and responsibilities all can lead to increased project cost. The easiest time to reevaluate goals, objectives, and criteria is during the schematic design phase—and this is the best time to do these things to control cost. A steep decline in the sustainability potential line occurs after the schematic design phase. The ability to make significant cost-efficient changes ends when the project moves into design development.

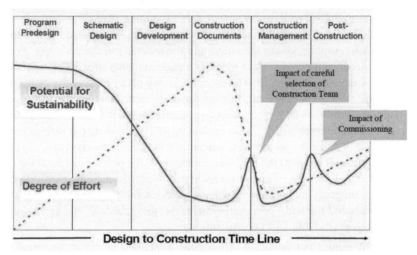

Image courtesy of Malcolm Lewis, CTG Energetics, Inc.

Figure 6-1 Design to construction time line.

Proper preparation prevents poor team and project performance, which summarizes the end goal of integrated design and high-performing facilities. Historically, owners and contractors set up a contingency fund intended to cover the unpredictable cost of changes in a project. If the design does not meet the owner's needs, the owner may be forced to accept the project as is, because changes needed to meet his or her requirements would be too costly at that point. If the CxA is engaged as late as the construction phase, there is some, but very limited, opportunity to address potential design problems. The longer an owner waits to engage in the commissioning process, the less influence the CxA has on resolving problems cost effectively.

Predesign

Commissioning is a team effort performed in a collaborative framework. The entire project team is part of the commissioning process. The commissioning plan defines the project team's roles and responsibilities, and execution of the commissioning process. It is essential that the owner clearly defines (contractually) the project team's commissioning roles and responsibilities and the OPR. The contrast between the quality and quantity of information provided by owners is often related to their development experience. Institutional owners who have developed many buildings and who have held properties for extended periods of time have over time developed the information that design teams need in order to understand an owner's basic needs. As previously stated, one of the greatest values of involving a CxA in the predesign phase is to develop a comprehensive OPR document that serves as the project benchmark, guiding all project team members. This improves project efficiency, because the requirements are clearly defined before the design process begins, reducing/eliminating the need for redesign.

Design Phase

During the design phase of a project, the CxA and project team execute the design phase commissioning plan. The CxA develops design checklists and specifications that incorporate commissioning into the project. The design checklists reflect objectives and criteria the designers should check during their quality control process, the amount and type of information to be provided at each stage of the commissioning design review, and the designer's assertion that items in the commissioning checklists are complete. Typically, three reviews occur in most design phases. The specifications identify the roles and responsibilities of the construction phase project team, the systems that will be commissioned, and the criteria for acceptance of the commissioned systems.

Commissioning design reviews focus on assessment of the design meeting the OPR. Typically, the OPR provides the project vision; expected service life; energy and water efficiency goals; maintainability; training of operational and maintenance personnel; infrastructure for monitoring-based, ongoing commissioning; expectations of the building envelope's ability to resist weather, air, and water infiltration; and other functional requirements needed for occupants to effectively and efficiently deliver their daily mission. Commissioning design reviews also randomly check the designer's quality control process by identifying systemic design issues that lead to potential change orders including missing or misleading information and insufficient detail needed for accurate pricing and completive bids. Commissioning design reviews reduce owner and project team risk, allow corrections to be made at the lowest possible cost, and reduce requests for information, supplemental instructions, and schedule impacts. Third-party commissioning provides great benefits to the project team and owner. (See further discussion in the "Commissioning Models" section later in this chapter.)

Design phase commissioning promotes communication, identifies disconnects, questions design elements that appear incorrect, and shares experience to produce a better set of contract documents and a better building.

Several engineering trade magazines and long-term owners, along with insurance companies who provide errors and omissions (E&O) coverage to the design community, have all voiced their concerns about the quality of construction documents and have charted how E&O premiums are affected as a result of judgments or settlements. Design phase commissioning reduces the risks of change orders, accompanying construction delays, and E&O claims, and helps clarify construction documents. Design phase commissioning, if correctly implemented, is a seamless process that provides benefits to the entire project team.

One of the roles of the CxA is to assemble a review team experienced in the type of facility being designed. Generally, the CxA has a team of reviewers with specific background and experience to review the disciplines selected for design phase commissioning. This process often requires the most senior individuals as part of the design phase commissioning provider team. (See "Selection of a CxA" later in this chapter.) A typical design review process is as follows:

- Written comments from the reviewers are provided to the design team and owner.
- Comments are reviewed, and the design team returns written responses.
- Meetings are scheduled with the review team and the designers to adjudicate comments as necessary, allowing the owner to understand the issues and have an opportunity to provide direction as needed.
- Design concerns, comments, and actions taken are recorded in the design review document. Changes are made as agreed and the commissioning review team verifies the change and closes the issue as appropriate.

Using a best practices approach, the design phase commissioning process could occur four different times during the project: at 100% of schematic design, 100% of design development, 95% complete construction documents, and 100% of construction documents. (Combining the review of the first two phases can be done on smaller projects.) An advantage of four reviews, however, is that the design is evaluated based on the OPR document goals before the design development phase starts.

Changes to optimize building performance, daylighting considerations, system selection, and stacking/massing synergies can best be addressed during schematic design review. Review during design development allows the team to identify potential problems and constructability perspectives early enough to resolve many issues before the construction documents phase starts.

The quantity of design concerns typically increases most in the 95% construction document phase because more detail is provided about each building system and component. The concerns identified at that point typically revolve around details—finishes, coordination conflicts, etc. Resolving these concerns provides clearer direction to the contractors, resulting in better cost and schedule predictions.

Depending on the schedule of the project, it is not uncommon that concerns identified at the 95% construction documents phase often go unaddressed by a design team. This is especially true in fast-track projects when designers, responding to owner and contractor demands for documents, struggle to finish and deliver their work product. This is why the 100% review is so important.

The financial benefits of design phase commissioning are immense. For example, on one project for the State of Louisiana, design phase commissioning was responsible for $3.4 million in first cost savings and $5 million in contingency savings on a $100 million project.

Construction Phase

The CxA's role during the construction phase is to review the 100% complete construction documents and submittals; develop and/or accept/integrate contractor construction checklists; identify and track issues to resolution; develop, direct, and verify functional performance tests; observe construction of commissioned systems; review the O&M manuals provided under the contract; and provide a systems manual. The purpose of these activities is to verify that the requirements of the OPR document have been met, commissioned systems are serviceable, commissioned systems perform as intended from the beginning, and operational personnel receive the training and documentation necessary for maintaining building performance.

The CxA's review of 100% construction documents is used to verify that the concerns and issues raised during the design reviews have been resolved, reducing the risk of contractors building flaws into the project. Sometimes, agreement between the designers and the commissioning design review team is not reached during the design phase. An example of this would be a disagreement over building pressurization control: the designer may feel that the design provides adequate control, and the CxA may disagree. The CxA must verify whether or not the building is correctly pressurized through performance tests. If the designer is correct, the CxA closes the issue after verification. If pressurization is an issue, then the team has the opportunity to correct the concern before more serious and costly ramifications can occur. Systems failing to perform are identified and the project team works to resolve the issue while the entire team is still engaged in the project.

The CxA reviews submittals to look for potential performance problems. An example of this would be contractor's ductwork shop drawings showing high-pressure loss fittings that would increase energy consumption. The CxA review activity does not, nor is it meant to, take the place of the designer's review, which should reveal whether the contractors are following the designer's intent. Several purposes can be combined by the CxA in his or her review of the submittals, depending on the role the owner defines for the CxA. For instance, if the CxA is also assisting the team with LEED certification, the CxA can verify that the sustainable development goals identified in the OPR document are being met.

At the start of construction, a CxA may choose to be part of prebid conference with the general contractor or construction manager to provide an oral description of commissioning activities, to describe the general roles and responsibilities the contractor will be asked to fulfill in the commissioning process, and to answer questions. Clear communication with the contractors during prebid has proven important in preventing high bids that reflect a fear factor from contractors who are unfamiliar with the commissioning process.

In the early stages of construction, the CxA develops a commissioning plan that defines the commissioning process, the roles and responsibilities of the project team, lines of communication, systems being commissioned, and a schedule of commissioning activities. The CxA conducts an initial commissioning scoping meeting where the commissioning plan is reviewed by the project team and, based on this information, a final commissioning plan is developed and implemented.

Throughout construction, the CxA observes the work to identify conditions that would impair preventive maintenance or repair, hinder operation of the system as intended and/or compromise useful service life, and to verify other sustainability goals (such as indoor air quality [IAQ] management) during construction. The CxA develops activities to help perfect installation procedures at the start of the specific construction activity. Then, the CxA coordinates activities to help ensure that the contractor's quality control process is working through verification of construction checklists, start-up procedures, and testing and balancing. When contractors have completed their construction checklist for a specific system being commissioned, they are stating that their systems will perform as intended. The CxA verifies this by directing and witnessing functional performance testing.

Acceptance Phase

The functional testing phase of the commissioning process is often referred to as the *acceptance phase*. With designer and contractor input, the CxA develops system tests (functional tests) to ensure that the systems perform as intended under a variety of conditions. Contractors under the CxA's direction execute the test procedures, while the CxA records results to verify performance. The tests should verify performance at the component level through inter- and intrasystem levels. Another practice is to have the contractors simulate failure conditions to verify alerts and alarms, as well as system reaction and interaction with associated systems. Problems identified are resolved while contractors and materials are still on site and the designers are engaged.

Warranty Phase

The first year of a project is critical to finding and resolving issues that arise, and the CxA plays an important role in helping ensure that a facility performs at its optimum. The warranty period is also the period when the contractors and manufacturers are responsible for the materials and systems installed, and is the only time the owner has to identify warranty repairs without additional construction costs. As such, the CxA has specific responsibilities to assist the owner and operational staff in identifying problems and assisting with resolution at the least interruption to the occupants during this critical period. This phase may also be coordinated with a postoccupancy evaluation, particularly if one is being done as part of the LEED green building program.

During the first several months, the CxA verifies that systems are performing as intended through monitoring of system operation. Many systems cannot be fully tested until the building is occupied or the systems are called to be operated during near-peak cooling or heating situations. There might be a small percentage of system components that pass functional testing but, under actual load, fail to perform as intended. These components must be identified in the warranty period and replaced or repaired as necessary. The CxA's role in conjunction with the operational staff is to search out problems that only become evident under actual load. To accomplish this, the commissioning provider performs several specific tasks.

The commissioning provider identifies system points to trend, verifying efficient system operation; installs independent data loggers to measure parameters beyond the capabilities of the building automation system (BAS); and monitors utility consumption. Using the trend system data from the selected BAS input points, the CxA analyzes the information, looking for operational sequences that consume resources unnecessarily and conditions that could compromise occupant satisfaction within the working environment. In addition, the CxA also looks for conditions that could result in building failure, such as high humidity in interstitial spaces in the building's interior, hot spots in the electrical distribution system, or analysis of electrical system harmonics where power quality is essential to the owner. These functions can only be tested after occupancy.

Some systems, such as the heating and cooling equipment, can only be fully tested when the season allows testing under design load conditions. The CxA works closely with the operational staff to identify and help resolve issues that become apparent in the warranty period and verifies that the operational staff fully understands and meets their warranty responsibilities. In addition, the CxA should provide operational staff with the specific functional test procedures developed for their use in maintaining building performance for the life of the facility. By having the CxA work with the operational staff during the warranty period, the operators gain valuable insight into how the building should operate and what to look for to ensure continued performance. This helps to overcome a typical industry problem: the bypassing of system components and controls because of a lack of understanding of how the systems are intended to operate.

Ongoing Commissioning Phase

The operational staff's knowledge and understanding of how the building should be operated, and their methods of operation in practice, typically determine the actual building system's performance. The most typical reason facilities fail to meet performance expectations or experience deterioration of performance is tied directly to how the building is operated. Changes in operational personnel often result in loss of the institutional knowledge needed to maintain the facility's performance and meet occupants' needs. The system manual is the repository for essential information needed by the operator to maximize occupant satisfaction and facility performance. Without this information, the operator is running blind, using only his or her instincts. The result is that it may be difficult to meet the owner's goals and objectives and operation costs may increase. Monitoring-based, ongoing commissioning provides regular monitoring and analysis of utility usage, system interaction, and operator performance. Performed on a regular basis, monitoring-based commissioning improves financial and operator performance by changing the culture from constantly responding to problems and replacing it with routine maintenance. It also helps to ensure that institutional knowledge is not lost through changes in personnel, occupant mission, and facility building modifications. For owners to get maximum performance from their facilities, they must know when systems fall outside of allowable performance tolerances or be aware of when operational personnel make changes that could negatively impact the facilities' performance. This is best done through monitoring-based, ongoing commissioning.

ASHRAE Guideline 14, Measurement of Energy and Demand Savings (ASHRAE 2002) provides several methods to establish operational benchmarks for energy consumption. Sustainable, healthy, high-performing facilities often measure other parameters including water consumption, waste generation, recycling, pesticide use, etc. The operational tracking of these parameters reduces total cost of ownership, impact on the environment, and building occupants' quality of life. An owner can obtain guidance on integrating sustainable operation practices by adopting the USGBC's LEED for Existing Buildings Operation and Maintenance program at this stage of the building's life.

SELECTION OF A CxA

There are several organizations that provide certification for CxAs. Two of these organizations, the Building Commissioning Association and The University of Wisconsin College of Engineering—Department of Engineering Professional Development, provide a comprehensive CxA certification program that requires several days of classroom instruction. To earn the certification, participants must pass an exam and provide proof of commissioning experience. Experience is determined through review of completed projects that demonstrate the participants' ability to commission and letters of recommendation from their peers and project owners that confirm their ability to implement the commissioning process on a small and large project. Other organizations generally conduct a one-day training class followed by an exam to receive a CxA certification. As with finding a doctor, lawyer, contractor, or other professional, the key element is that the commissioning provider should have experience in the types of systems an owner wants commissioned. In other words, an owner must match the experience with the job. A good CxA generally has a broad range of knowledge: hands-on experience in O&M,

design, construction, and investigation of building/system failures. CxAs must also be detail-oriented, good communicators, and able to provide a collaborative approach that engages the project team.

ASHRAE provides Commissioning Process Management Professional certification for owners implementing commissioning and engaging commissioning authorities. People who pass this certification understand how to apply the commissioning process and select commissioning providers, which helps ensure the owner gets what they paid for.

SELECTION OF SYSTEMS TO COMMISSION

Commissioning of all systems using the whole building approach has proven to be beneficial. However, due to budget constraints, owners may want to look at commissioning systems that will yield the greatest benefit to them. Long-term owners have an advantage and can apply their experience of where they have historically encountered problems and elect to commission only those systems. Others who do not have that depth of experience may wish to talk with long-term owners or insurance providers to gain perspective.

Commissioning was originally developed in areas where energy efficiency was a prime driver. The commissioning process has expanded beyond the original commissioning of HVAC systems to include building envelope, electrical, plumbing, security, etc. This expansion from HVAC is often referred to as *whole building commissioning*.

There are many factors that define which building systems should be commissioned, but there are no published standards yet to help guide owners through such selection. It often depends on the associated risk of not commissioning. E&O insurance providers publish graphs of claims against design professionals by discipline. Interestingly enough, 80% of the claims against architects are for moisture intrusion. Some organizations have suggested that up to 30% of new and remodeled buildings worldwide may be the subject of excessive complaints related to IAQ. The reasons for sick buildings include inadequate ventilation, chemical pollutants from both indoor and outdoor sources, and biological contaminates.

Commissioning provides several benefits, two of which are risk reduction and lower total cost of ownership. Based on a specific climate such as Phoenix, Arizona, the risk of not commissioning the building envelope is much less than in Atlanta, Georgia (due to humidity concerns). Based on functional requirements, not commissioning the security systems in a conventional office building may have minimum risk compared to a federal courthouse. So, what should be commissioned?

The best time for determining what systems should be commissioned is during the development of the OPR document. Generally, there are three main system categories that should be commissioned: building envelope, mechanical and plumbing systems, and electrical systems. Subsystems that could also be included are irrigation and/or process water systems. Depending on the functional requirements of a facility and the complexity of systems, additional systems that may be commissioned include security, voice/data, selected elements of fire and life safety, and daylighting controls.

The USGBC's LEED rating system recognizes the benefits of commissioning and its importance to green building design, construction, and operation. While the LEED reference guide does not specifically identify which building systems must be commissioned, it does point out that energy-efficient use of natural resources, indoor environmental quality, and productivity are important goals of sustainable/green projects. As such, the LEED reference guide implies that building systems that affect energy consumption, water usage, and indoor environmental quality should be commissioned.

Each element of green design needs verification to ensure that the design, construction, and operation of the high-performance facility meet the expectations of the team and realize the financial return envisioned by the owner.

COMMISSIONING MODELS

Independent third-party commissioning is the preferred commissioning approach, because it significantly reduces the potential for conflict of interest. It also allows for integration of commissioning professionals specialized to meet a project's specific needs concerning the building envelope, security systems, labs, etc.

Commissioning, as part of the project design professional's responsibility, does not typically result in an unbiased presentation of issues. Design teams do not intentionally provide bad designs; they are working with schedules, budgets, and multiple players in the process. Even if the CxA is a separate individual from the design team members, but is still within an organization or sister company with the same upper leadership, it may be common practice not to bring attention to negative issues. Commissioning conducted under this model has a high probability of minimizing design issues during design and passing responsibility on to the construction team during construction, resulting in after-the-fact solutions and corresponding cost increases and delays. This, in essence, differs little from the traditional model without any CxA input. The earlier an issue is identified and resolved, the more minimized the cost to the project is.

Commissioning as part of the general contractor's responsibility has many of the same problems as the model using the design professional. Contractors, by the very nature of the construction business, are focused on schedule and budget. This focus is not always in the owner's best long-term interest. Most contractors are quality-minded and do their best to identify problems and assist with resolutions (though often to their detriment because they inadvertently take responsibility for the design in doing so). If a constructability issue arises that will adversely affect the schedule or budget, the contractor may choose to fix the issue and hope that it does not create a warranty callback. The main problem is that many of the issues are discovered too late in the process, again resulting in change orders, construction delays, and additional costs.

Mechanical contractors have the same problems as general contractors when it comes to providing commissioning services. They work with a schedule and budget and review their own work or that of a supervisor or coworker. The mechanical contractor's knowledge and experience are usually limited to the mechanical field; thus, they lack the background to commission other systems.

To truly be an owner's advocate, the CxA must owe allegiance to no one but the owner. A third-party CxA will verify that the goals defined by the owner and integrated by the design and construction team are achieved as intended, from the first day of occupancy. If the CxA is separate from the design professional or contractor, he/she will provide unbiased reporting of issues to the team and will guide them toward timely solutions without finger-pointing, delays, and liability.

ONE FIRM'S COMMISSIONING CHECKLIST

- Begin the commissioning process during the design phase; carry out a full commissioning process from lighting to energy systems to occupancy sensors.
- Verify and ensure that fundamental building elements and systems are designed, installed, and calibrated to operate as intended.
- Engage a CxA that is independent of both the design and construction team.
- Develop an OPR document and review designer's basis of design to verify requirements have been met.
- Incorporate commissioning requirements into project contract documents.
- Develop and utilize a commissioning plan.
- Verify installation, functional performance, training, and O&M documentation.
- Complete a commissioning report.
- Perform additional commissioning:
  - Conduct a focused review of the design prior to the construction documents phase.
  - Conduct a detailed review of the construction documents when these are considered nearly complete and prior to their issuance for construction.
  - Conduct reviews of contractor submittals that are relevant to systems being commissioned.

Digging Deeper

Digging Deeper

- Provide information required for recommissioning systems in a single document to the owner.
- Have a contract in place to review with operations staff the actual building operation and any outstanding issues identified during commissioning, and to provide assistance resolving these issues within the warranty period.
- Encourage long-term energy management strategies.
  - Provide for the ongoing accountability and optimization of building energy and water consumption performance.
  - Design and specify equipment to be installed in base building systems to allow for comparison, management, and optimization of actual vs. estimated energy and water performance.
  - Use M&V functions where applicable.
  - Tie contractor final payments to documented M&V system performance and include in the commissioning report.
  - Provide for an ongoing M&V system maintenance and operating plan in building O&M maintenance manuals.
- Operate the building ventilation system at maximum fresh air for at least several days (and ideally several weeks) after final finish materials have been installed before occupancy.
- Provide for the ongoing accountability of waste streams, including hazardous pollutants.
- Use environmentally safe cleaning materials.
- Train O&M workers.

REFERENCES AND RESOURCES

Published

ASHRAE. 2002. *ASHRAE Guideline 14-2002, Measurement of Energy and Demand Savings*. Atlanta: American Society of Heating, Refrigerating and Air-Conditioning Engineers, Inc.

ASHRAE. 2005. *ASHRAE Guideline 0-2005, The Commissioning Process*. Atlanta: American Society of Heating, Refrigerating and Air-Conditioning Engineers, Inc.

CHAPTER SEVEN

GREEN RATING SYSTEMS, STANDARDS, AND OTHER GUIDANCE

There has been rapid growth in interest in green buildings over the past decade or so, and corresponding with that, a growth in the number, depth, and breadth of green building rating systems, standards, and other guiding documents that the HVAC&R engineer can use.

In the United States, the Leadership in Energy and Environmental Design (LEED®) Green Building Rating System, published by the U.S. Green Building Council (USGBC), has become a major force for encouraging the integration of green building principles and techniques into building projects. This chapter briefly discusses LEED along with the other related green building standards and design guidance available.

THE LEED PROGRAMS

Since its development and introduction in the late 1990s, the LEED program has become a major factor in the advancement of green buildings, as well as an influence on how all buildings are thought of in the design and construction process.

LEED is a voluntary program that uses a point-based rating system for a given building project. In 2009, USGBC released a significant revision to the program that, among other things, reworked the point ratings in order to provide a more effective focus to drive positive environmental and health benefits. Part of this revision was based on using the Tool for the Reduction and Assessment of Chemical and Other Environmental Impacts (TRACI) developed by the U.S. Environmental Protection Agency (EPA). An illustration of the impact of the various credit point option weightings is given in Figure 7-1.

Another 2009 change to the LEED program (for Version 3) was the introduction of regional credits, which are used to help put additional emphasis on design features that are particularly important in terms of the climate and area where the project is to be located. For example, in areas with known stormwater problems, the Sustainable Sites Credit 6.1 for Stormwater Design—Quantity Control may be included in this priority list. A full list of the Regional Priority credits can be

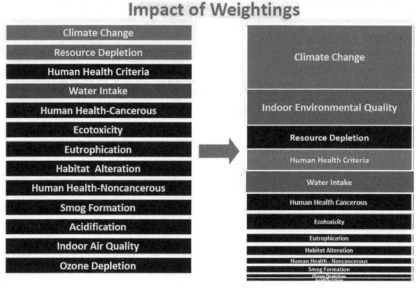

Image courtesy of Brendan Owens, U.S. Green Building Council.

Figure 7-1 The impact of weightings on revising the LEED credit point system.

found on the USGBC Web site (see the "References and Resources" section at the end of the chapter).

The breakdown of credits and points available under the LEED for new construction rating system is as follows:

- Sustainable Sites   8 credits/26 points
- Water Efficiency   3 credits/10 points
- Energy and Atmosphere   6 credits/35 points
- Materials and Resources   7 credits/14 points
- Indoor Environmental Quality (IEQ)   8 credits/15 points

Total core points   100
Innovation/design   6
Regional priority   4
TOTAL POSSIBLE   **110**

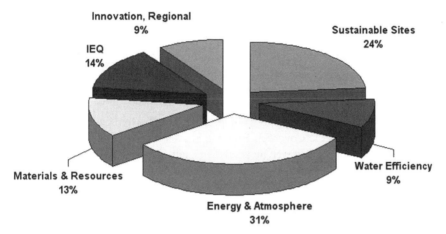

Image courtesy of Brendan Owens, U.S. Green Building Council.

Figure 7-2 The percentage distribution of LEED-NC Version 3.

The percentage distribution of these credits is illustrated in Figure 7-2. It can be seen that "Energy and Atmosphere" is the category with the highest number of points available, and this is in the direct purview of the HVAC&R engineer. The following discussion focuses on specific LEED credits that would be of most interest to HVAC&R engineers.

Sustainable Sites (SS) Credits
Affecting Minimum Energy Performance (MEP) Design

SS Credit 6—Stormwater Management. The focus in Credit 6 is minimizing the amount of stormwater runoff from the building site and maximizing the time lag between the stormwater impinging on the site and leaving the site. Often the techniques used are architectural (such as vegetative roofs), landscaping (pervious pavements or bioswales), and civil (detention basins or filtration). These systems may have added impacts on MEP in terms of design of roof drain systems and irrigation systems for roof vegetation.

However, there are also some MEP-focused techniques that have attained wide use, which focus on collecting the stormwater (and sometimes other recovered water) and storing it for future use on site. This technique is becoming more widely used in building designs. Examples include the Santa Monica Main Library project (Figure 7-3) and the Coverdell Building at the University of Georgia (Figure 7-4).

The Santa Monica system collects stormwater through the roof drain and area drain system and stores it in a cistern system of large-diameter, high-density poly-ethylene culvert pipes under the building. The water stored in the cistern is then used for landscape irrigation. Sizing of the storage cistern involves predictions of both water collection and water usage throughout the year. With the Coverdell Building, water is collected from stormwater from the roof drains and building perimeter sumps, and from condensate from building air-handling units. Since this building is located in a warm/humid climate, the potential for condensate collection is high. The water in the Coverdell Building is used for both internal flushing pur-poses as well as cooling tower makeup (with city water providing supplemental water when needed). Thus, this particular technique provides benefits in several LEED credit areas.

SS Credit 7—Heat Island Reduction. As every mechanical engineer knows, the color and reflectance of the building roof and of the surrounding paving can have a significant impact on cooling loads inside the building and on the local microclimate through the heat island effect. To the extent that the design team wants input on the options and impacts of improving reflectance and emissivity values of these materials, the mechanical engineer can provide assistance. These

Image courtesy of Moore Ruble Yudell Architects & Planners.

Figure 7-3 Santa Monica Main Library project.

values should also be integrated into the load calculations for the building, so as to take advantage of the improved exterior environment to reduce cooling loads and installed tonnage. However, the potential impact on increased heating loads should be considered as well.

SS Credit 8—Light Pollution Reduction. The impact of this credit is borne by the lighting designer and/or electrical engineer, and it involves both exterior lighting (on the building and site—see Figure 7-5) and interior lighting (which may project to the exterior).

Water Efficiency (WE) Credits Affecting MEP Design

WE Credit 2—Innovative Wastewater Technologies

WE Credit 3—Water Use Reduction

Image courtesy of Tom Lawrence, University of Georgia

Figure 7-4 Coverdell Building storage cistern (access hatch and piping).

With these credits, opportunities for the MEP designer primarily have to do with reducing the total potable water used by the building and minimizing the impact of that water use on the sanitary and stormwater systems.

The reduction of potable water usage through more water-efficient plumbing fixtures is relatively straightforward, as there are many fixtures and technologies available. The following is a list of water-efficient plumbing fixtures:

- Low-flow lavatory and shower aerators
- Auto-controls
- Dual-flush water closets
- Ultra-low-flow urinals
- Waterless urinals

Water closets and urinals are the biggest users of water in a typical office building, so focusing on these fixtures is the most effective use of design effort. LEED establishes a methodology for calculating the reduction of water usage for these fixtures that is a function of the number of building occupants and characteristics of the plumbing fixtures.

One of the technologies with the most impact is that of waterless urinals. This is an innovative concept that uses no water for flushing but instead uses a nontoxic

Image courtesy of Malcolm Lewis, CTG Energetics, Inc.

Figure 7-5 Light pollution reduction.

chemical to form the trap. The urine flows through the chemical to enter the drain. These fixtures are gradually attaining code approval and user acceptance in areas across the country.

Once the water usage is reduced to a minimum through earning water efficiency Credit 3, the opportunity exists to earn Credit 2 by treating the wastewater on site. This can have the effect of reducing the load on the municipal sanitary sewer system and offers the potential for using the treated wastewater within the project site. There are two basic approaches to this: a graywater treatment system, which clarifies that portion of the sewage that does not contain human fecal matter, and a tertiary treatment system that treats sewage regardless of its content. Both systems produce effluent, which can be used as reclaimed water for performing certain functions, such as toilet flushing or landscape irrigation. (Note that both of these uses are subject to rulings of the local building and health departments that have jurisdiction over the project, and these vary based on location.)

The graywater system collects the drainage from plumbing fixtures, such as lavatories and drinking fountains, as well as condensate from HVAC systems. The graywater is filtered and disinfected and then stored in a cistern or tank until needed. It is then piped in a special separate piping system for reclaimed water to the points of use, which can be toilets, urinals, or irrigation systems.

The on-site sewage treatment system approach can include traditional septic systems or more modern biological treatment systems that create a local natural wetland ecosystem that purifies wastewater after a biological digestion process is applied to the sewage.

Energy and Atmosphere (EA) Credits Affecting MEP Design

The single biggest area of potential LEED points is in the EA section of LEED. The MEP engineer may have influence on all credits in this category except for Green Power.

EA Credit 1—Optimize Energy Performance
EA Credit 2—On-Site Renewable Energy
EA Credit 3—Enhanced Commissioning
EA Credit 4—Enhanced Refrigerant Management
EA Credit 5—Measurement and Verification

One of the most profound effects of LEED in the areas of interest to the HVAC&R engineer is the requirement for building systems commissioning as a prerequisite for LEED certification. This is crucial because it ensures a focus on the actual performance of the building systems, as installed, and goes a long way toward ensuring that the MEP systems will provide the intended performance once the building is constructed.

EA Credits and Sustainable Design Measures. Energy efficiency is inextricably tied up in the sustainability of a building design, and this is illustrated by Figure 7-7, which shows how various energy measures impact the ability to earn points under the various LEED EA credits. Numerous building energy efficiency measures (i.e., envelope, HVAC, lighting, daylighting, etc.) impact the ability to earn points under EA Credit 1, but so does the use of renewable sources of energy including photovoltaic solar power and solar thermal heating. Because of the structure of LEED, which tends to encourage renewable energy, such renewable sources contribute to more than one credit, so they can be used to earn more points in multiple credits. The specifics of earning points under each credit are described in the sections that follow.

EA Credit 1—Optimize Energy Performance. This credit provides the single largest opportunity for earning points in the entire LEED rating system: up to 19 points are available for this single credit. Many projects earn substantial points under this credit.

To earn points under EA Credit 1, the project's energy performance must be simulated using an hourly energy simulation program. There is a sliding scale for points, based upon the extent to which the simulated design projects annual energy usage lower than the minimum required by the applicable local energy code. Note that as a minimum prerequisite, the building project must be shown to be at least 10% lower in energy cost than a baseline building, if built according to the minimum requirements in *ANSI/ASHRAE/IESNA Standard 90.1-2007, Energy Standard for Buildings Except Low-Rise Residential Buildings* (ASHRAE 2007). Credit points are earned for projects that exceed this 10% prerequisite, with 1 point for each additional 2% of energy cost reduction.

The energy simulation model provides a mechanism for assessing all of the energy features of the proposed design (i.e., building envelope, HVAC system, lighting, materials colors, etc.), in terms of their integrated impact on total energy usage and on the sizing of each of the systems. It is very important that this simulation process be used as an iterative design tool to optimize the overall building design and not just as an accounting tool for computing the LEED points earned by this credit. With this in mind, the simulation model should be developed in the early design phases and used to refine the design, rather than just at the end of the design to compute the percentage better than the baseline reference building.

There are numerous specific techniques that can contribute to earning points under EA Credit 1, including daylighting, high-efficiency lighting, high-efficiency HVAC, optimized building envelopes and orientations, and renewable energy. Each of these concepts is dealt with elsewhere in this book, so the primary point to be made here is that each of these has an impact on the other systems' energy usage. This provides an important opportunity for the HVAC&R engineer to contribute to the early evolution and optimization of the design but requires more involvement in the early design than is often done. As a result, it requires a more proactive approach on the part of the HVAC&R engineer to offer ideas and to perform energy analyses that can answer formative questions about the design. This is

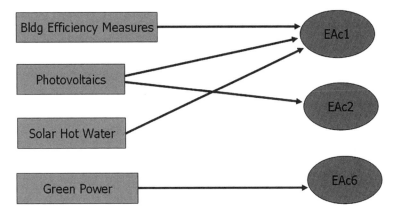

Image courtesy of Malcolm Lewis, CTG Energetics, Inc.

Figure 7-6 Energy efficiency is inextricably tied up in the sustainability of a building's design.

one of the aspects of green building design that is most challenging, as it requires redefinition of roles and scopes of work among the design team participants. Yet, it offers an exciting opportunity to the HVAC&R engineer to make a difference in the sustainability of the final design, so it is a highly desirable change in the process.

LEED requires a somewhat unique approach to energy simulation modeling in terms of the method of computing the actual energy savings on which the EA Credit 1 calculation is based. Conventionally, energy modeling computes the percent better than energy code, as measured in $Btu/ft^2 \cdot yr$ ($W/m^2 \cdot yr$ or similar annual energy metrics). By contrast, LEED requires the calculation of the percent annual energy cost reduction from Standard 90.1 (ASHRAE 2007), using the energy cost budget method, which is defined in Standard 90.1.

EA Credit 5—Measurement and Verification. In an effort to encourage efficient operation of LEED-certified buildings, LEED provides a credit for providing the building with the ability to measure its usage of energy and water over time. The requirements of this credit are for the permanent installation of sensors and a monitoring system to measure and track key HVAC system performance metrics, including airflow and indoor air quality (IAQ), energy consumption of major HVAC system components (i.e., fans, pumps, or chillers), and troubleshooting diagnostics. The LEED credit uses the International Performance Measurement and Verification Protocol (IPMVP) as a guide (www.evo-world.org).

INDOOR ENVIRONMENTAL QUALITY (IEQ) CREDITS AFFECTING MEP DESIGN

Minimum IAQ Performance (from *ANSI/ASHRAE Standard 62.1-2007, Ventilation for Acceptable Indoor Air Quality* [ASHRAE 2007])
EQ Credit 1—Outdoor Air Delivery Monitoring
EQ Credit 2—Increased Ventilation
EQ Credits 3.1 and 3.2—Construction IAQ Management Plan
EQ Credit 5—Indoor Chemical and Pollutant Source Control
EQ Credit 6.2—Controllability of Systems, Thermal Comfort
EQ Credits 7.1 and 7.2—Thermal Comfort
After the EA credits, the IEQ requirements of LEED provide HVAC&R engineers with the greatest opportunities to contribute to the green rating of a building. Many aspects of the indoor environment are governed by ASHRAE standards, which are cited by LEED in this group of credits. The emphasis of the IEQ credits is on the health and comfort of the building occupants.

The first IEQ prerequisite requires that the building mechanical systems comply with ASHRAE Standard 62.1 (ASHRAE 2007). This governs several HVAC system attributes, including:

- Placement of intakes vs. exhausts
- Reduced face velocities at coils
  - To eliminate condensate entrainment
  - To increase heat transfer efficiency
- Access to condensate pans
- Ductwork quality and workmanship
  - Cleanliness
  - Liner integrity
- IAQ Monitoring and Controls
  - CO_2, volatile organic compounds, particulates
  - Maintainability of IAQ over time

The first IEQ prerequisite also deals with the quality of the HVAC system installation and is meant to ensure that it is well built and functions as intended. These issues include the following quality construction practices:

- Duct sealing
- Condensate drains
- Functionality of dampers
- Accurate testing
- Collaboration and integration with commissioning activities

EQ Credit 1—Outside Air Delivery Monitoring. The focus of the first credit is on ensuring that adequate fresh (outdoor) air is delivered to maintain the CO_2 levels of the indoor air below accepted thresholds. The intent and requirements for this credit cover both mechanically and naturally ventilated buildings, and are as follows:

- INTENT: Provide capacity for ventilation system monitoring to help sustain occupant comfort and well-being.
- REQUIREMENTS: Install permanent monitoring systems that provide feedback on ventilation system performance to ensure that ventilation systems maintain design minimum ventilation requirements. Configure all monitoring equipment to generate an alarm if underventilation is detected, via either a building automation system alarm to the building operator or via an alarm that alerts building occupants.

EQ Credit 2—Increased Ventilation. LEED provides a credit for providing ventilation strategies that enhance occupant access to fresh air. This includes either mechanically ventilated or naturally ventilated spaces.

The MEP designer should take careful note to avoid causing unintended consequences, such as additional cooling or heating loads, or bringing in more outdoor air that might be polluted (such as in a large city during a smog alert).

EQ Credit 3—Construction IAQ Management Plan. In keeping with LEED's focus on actual construction and delivery processes, there are credits that focus on controlling construction impact on IAQ. This is done through a combination of a construction IAQ management plan for the periods during construction and the flushing or testing of the indoor air to minimize the level of pollutants prior to occupancy. This has obvious advantages for the occupants, in terms of improved IAQ, and is also a benefit to the HVAC&R engineer in terms of reduced liability and improved occupant satisfaction relative to IAQ.

For both of the credits (EQ Credit 3.1 and EQ Credit 3.2) related to construction IAQ, the intent of LEED is the same:

- INTENT: Reduce IAQ problems resulting from the construction/renovation process so as to help sustain the comfort and well-being of construction workers and building occupants.

EQ Credit 3.1 focuses on the construction phase, and EQ Credit 3.2 deals with the period prior to the end of construction activities but prior to occupancy of the building. Both require the development and implementation of a construction IAQ management plan, which coordinates the efforts to optimize IAQ.

(See Figures 7-7 and 7-8 for illustrations of bad construction IAQ management and good construction IAQ management, respectively.)

For the construction phase credit, EQ Credit 3.1 Construction IAQ Management Plan—During Construction, elements of the construction IAQ management plan will include a variety of good housekeeping procedures and protection of materials during construction, such as the following:

- Provide protection for all HVAC ducts and materials from deposition of dust and debris.
- Use chemicals responsibly and limit the offgassing of volatile organic compounds in the space.

Image courtesy of Malcolm Lewis, CTG Energetics, Inc.

Figure 7-7 Bad construction IAQ management.

Image courtesy of Malcolm Lewis, CTG Energetics, Inc.

Figure 7-8 Good construction IAQ management.

- Use filters with a minimum MERV-8 efficiency on all return air grilles if air handlers are operated during construction.

For the preoccupancy credit, EQ Credit 3.2 Construction IAQ Management Plan—Before Occupancy, the important elements are that the indoor air in the building be purged of contaminants, which can be demonstrated by one of two methods:

1. Thorough flushing of the air in the building interior with outdoor air (at a specified cumulative rate that will typically take eight to ten days to accomplish).
2. Through air quality testing to ensure that contaminant levels are below acceptable threshold levels (as specified by LEED).

EQ Credit 5—Indoor Chemical and Pollution Source Control. This is the final IAQ-related LEED credit, and it has the following intent:

- INTENT: Minimize exposure of building occupants to potentially hazardous particulates and chemical pollutants.

For the MEP engineer, this is typically accomplished with the following techniques:

- Deck-to-deck partition with separate exhaust system in areas of chemical use.
- Provision of exhaust systems and enclosures that keep copy machine rooms (and similar dirty environments) at negative pressures to reduce migration of contaminants into office areas.
- Use of minimum efficiency reporting value (MERV)-13 or better filters on all outdoor air and return air intakes of HVAC systems. (Note that this requires attention at the time of HVAC equipment selection to ensure that the filters will fit, as they are typically thicker than lower-efficiency filters.)

EQ Credit 6.2—Controllability of Systems—Thermal Comfort. Research by ASHRAE and others has documented the desirability of providing building occupants with the ability to control the HVAC system variables (i.e., temperature, airflow, and humidity) that affect their thermal comfort. LEED has honored this finding by providing a credit for systems that can provide this capability, with the specific credit intent as follows:

- INTENT: Provide a high level of thermal comfort system control by individual occupants or by specific groups in multioccupant spaces (i.e., classrooms or conference areas) to promote the productivity, comfort, and well-being of building occupants.

This intent is typically met by providing zoning of HVAC systems that, at a minimum, permits the separate control of interior and perimeter zones. It can be even better met through the use of underfloor air distribution (which allows a user-controlled diffuser for each workstation) or other work-station-level zoning techniques.

EQ Credit 7—Thermal Comfort. The next LEED IEQ credits require the design and validation of the HVAC system to meet the requirements of *ANSI/ ASHRAE Standard 55-2004, Thermal Environmental Conditions for Human Occupancy* (ASHRAE 2004), with specific intent and requirements as follows:

• INTENT: Provide a comfortable thermal environment that supports the productivity and well-being of building occupants.

EQ Credit 7.1—Thermal Comfort—Compliance. Credit EQ Credit 7.1 covers the design of the HVAC system and its ability to meet ASHRAE Standard 55 (ASHRAE 2004).

EQ Credit 7.2—Thermal Comfort—Monitoring. Credit EQ Credit 7.2 covers the actual performance of the HVAC system to validate that it meets comfort criteria established by ASHRAE Standard 55 (ASHRAE 2004).

Combined, these credits make it more likely that the HVAC system will satisfy the comfort needs of the occupants, which is a positive benefit to the HVAC&R engineer. The validation also provides a source of potentially valuable feedback to the designer regarding the actual performance of the HVAC systems designed.

ASHRAE/USGBC/IES STANDARD 189.1

The LEED program has been a tremendous tool that has advanced the cause of green building design and acceptance in the United States and beyond. Compliance with LEED is (in general) voluntary. In 2006, ASHRAE (in conjunction with the USGBC and the Illumination Engineering Society of North America) began a process to create a standard that would address a growing need within the industry. The need was for a code-language document for green buildings. *ANSI/ASHRAE/ USGBC/IES Standard 189.1-2009, Standard for the Design of High-Performance Green Buildings* (ASHRAE 2009) was developed during a more than three-year process with extensive public review, and was initially published in early 2010.

The standard differs from LEED or other products in that it is not a rating system, nor is it a design guideline per se. The purpose of Standard 189.1 is to provide minimum requirements for the siting, design, construction and plans for operation of high-performance green buildings, while attempting to balance environmental responsibility, resource efficiency, occupant comfort and well-being, and community sensitivity. One key point of this is that Standard 189.1 is not targeted for any building project, but rather for high-performance building projects. This document is intended to help fill a perceived gap in the evolving building codes in this area, as localities begin to adopt green building designs as a requirement. Standard 189.1 is also a jurisdictional compliance option of the International Green Construction Code™ (IGCC) (ICC 2010).

While many of the topics and criteria may overlap or seem similar to LEED for new construction, Standard 189.1 differs in that it establishes mandatory, minimal requirements across all topical areas. Since it is still new and many potential addenda are being considered, it will take time to see how this evolves and the impact that this standard will have on the industry. Besides the obvious intent of providing a vehicle for adoption into building codes, this standard may also be used by developers, corporations, universities, or governmental agencies to set requirements for their own building projects.

Standard 189.1 is not intended to do away with other ASHRAE standards. Rather, it builds upon key ASHRAE standards and adopts these with modifications when considered necessary to develop a document that deals with high-performance green buildings, as illustrated in Figure 7-10.

This standard includes mandatory criteria in all topical areas (such as water or energy) and provides for two compliance paths. The Prescriptive Path includes simple compliance criteria; simple in the sense that they are more like a checklist of technologies or system requirements. The Performance Path is more complicated in that it requires more analysis to verify that compliance is indeed achieved.

A brief overview of key differences in criteria in Standard 189.1 vs. the LEED program that the typical ASHRAE member or MEP professional should be aware of is given below. Since the standard is new and is sure to evolve as it continues to be scrutinized by the industry, this overview is just a cursory glance.

Water Use Efficiency

Standard 189.1 (ASHRAE 2009) puts limits on the number of cycles of water through a cooling tower. It also requires condensate collection on air-handling units above 5.5 tons of cooling capacity (19 kW).

Standard 189.1 is also unique in that it requires the installation of meters with data storage and retrieval capability on systems and areas above a given threshold in water usage. Similar provisions are included in the energy section for energy use and IEQ section for monitoring of outdoor airflow.

Energy Efficiency

There are significant changes and an increased stringency in requirements in the energy section of Standard 189.1 (ASHRAE 2009) when compared to Standard 90.1 (ASHRAE 2007). While the LEED program, through EA Credit 1, provides for a sliding scale of points awarded for energy efficiency improvements above Standard 90.1-2007, Standard 189.1 began with the intended goal of providing mandatory measures that would result in buildings using 30% less energy than what is designed according to Standard 90.1, including process loads.

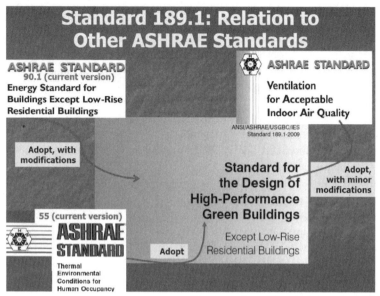

Image courtesy of Tom Lawrence and ASHRAE.

Figure 7-9 Relation of Standard 189.1 (ASHRAE 2009) to other key ASHRAE standards.

During the development of Standard 189.1, many concepts and requirements were considered for improvements. At the same time, addenda to Standard 90.1-2007 were proposed and approved that increased the overall efficiency levels of Standard 90.1. The net result is that the overall average energy utilization for buildings designed according to Standard 189.1 and Standard 90.1-2010 are not that great. It is ASHRAE's intent to have the energy efficiency levels for Standard 189.1 improve at a much faster rate than those for Standard 90.1, with an ultimate goal of both standards reaching net zero status by the year 2030.

One of the key considerations when developing the energy requirements for Standard 189.1 was whether to include on-site renewable energy, and if so, to what extent. Many renewable energy systems are not yet fully cost-competitive with conventional energy sources, particularly when excluding incentive programs that may go away at any time. Therefore, the standard only includes the provisions for being renewable ready as mandatory requirements. Exceptions are included for areas with low solar incidence or local shading. In the Prescriptive Path, on-site renewable energy is included, but a project can still comply with this standard using other methods that would have equivalent benefits.

Energy metering is required for systems (e.g., HVAC) above certain design load levels. This may influence the local wiring of systems like the HVAC to comply with this requirement.

Standard 189.1 makes numerous modifications to the requirements in Standard 90.1-2007 regarding HVAC systems. Here is a summary of key points:

- The threshold for occupancy levels requiring demand-controlled ventilation is lowered.
- Duct sealing requirements are increased to Level A.
- The climate zones requiring economizers is expanded upon.
- The volume of air allowed for reheating or recooling is restricted.
- Fan power limits (per volume of air moved) are lowered.
- The requirements for energy recovery from exhaust air are expanded.
- Unoccupied hotel/motel guest room controls are included.

Depending on the project approach, additional requirements for equipment efficiency beyond Standard 90.1-2007 may also be incorporated. In addition, requirements are set for reducing peak demand of the building.

The Performance Path for showing compliance with the energy section of ASHRAE Standard 189.1 includes demonstrating equivalent performance in terms of both energy cost and CO_2 equivalent emissions, compared to if the building project had been designed strictly to the criteria in the Prescriptive Path.

IEQ

There are four key criteria for outdoor airflow that are relevant to ASHRAE members: tobacco smoke control, outdoor air monitoring, filtration /air cleaning, and determination of outdoor airflow rate.

The minimum ventilation design for outdoor airflow is to be according to ASHRAE Standard 62.1 (ASHRAE 2010) using the Ventilation Rate Procedure. Outdoor air monitoring is to be done using permanently mounted, direct outdoor airflow measurement devices. In contrast to LEED, CO_2 monitoring in densely occupied zones is not included as part of Standard 189.1.

Tobacco smoke control is achieved by simply banning smoking within the building and near entrances, outdoor air intakes, or operable windows.

Construction and Plans for Operation

Standard 189.1 (ASHRAE 2009) includes provisions for not only how a building should be constructed, but also for planning for how it should be operated once occupied. Since it is written and intended for adoption into building codes, only items that would be expected to be developed and in place at the time a certificate of occupancy is issued could reasonably be considered for inclusion in this standard. The approach taken within Standard 189.1 is to set requirements for the development of plans for operation in critical areas.

This standard includes requirements for building acceptance testing and/or commissioning, erosion control, IAQ, moisture control and idling of construction vehicles to be implemented during construction. Commissioning is to be done according to requirements that in essence parallel those in ASHRAE guidelines. IAQ requirements during construction and before occupancy are similar to those in the LEED program but not identical and when different are generally more stringent.

Plans for operation are required in key areas that would be needed to help ensure the building performs as would be expected for a high-performance, green building. These include criteria in setting up long-term monitoring and verification of water and energy use, as well as IAQ through provisions such as outdoor air monitoring.

Maintenance and service life plans are required as well, and these involve equipment and systems relevant to the HVAC&R or MEP engineer.

GUIDELINES

ASHRAE has produced a number of publications that can help the inexperienced and experienced industry professional alike. These include:

- *ASHRAE Guideline 0-2005, The Commissioning Process* (ASHRAE 2005) and *ASHRAE Guideline 1.1-2007, HVAC&R Technical Requirements for the Commissioning Process* (ASHRAE 2007)
- The Advanced Energy Design Guide series
- *Indoor Air Quality Guide: Best Practices for Design, Construction and Commissioning* (ASHRAE 2009)
- *The ASHRAE Guide for Buildings in Hot and Humid Climates* (ASHRAE 2009)

Many of these are also discussed elsewhere in this Guide but are mentioned here as a reminder.

The *Advanced Energy Design Guide* series is a series of books that provide a set of prescriptive technical approaches to achieve significant energy savings. The documents are focused on specific building types, typically smaller building projects that may not have resources available for much engineering study and analysis of energy saving technologies (e.g., small retail stores). Recommendations are provided based on the climate zone the project is located in. The initial series of guides was targeted toward achieving 30% energy savings compared to Standard 90.1-1999, and the intent is to repeat the series with increasing efficiency levels leading to net zero designs. The target is to complete the net zero design series well before the year 2020.

These energy guides were produced in collaboration with the American Institute of Architects (AIA), the Illuminating Engineering Society of North America (IES), and the USGBC, with assistance provided by the U.S. Department of Energy (DOE). These guides are available for free from the ASHRAE Web site and have been widely distributed since their release.

The *Indoor Air Quality Guide* was released in January of 2010, and was developed in conjunction with AIA, the Building Owners and Managers Association (BOMA), the Sheet Metal and Air Conditioning Contractors National Association (SMACNA), the U.S. EPA and the USGBC. A summary of the guidance offered is available for free download from the ASHRAE Web site, while the detailed guidance document is available for purchase.

ASHRAE BUILDING ENERGY QUOTIENT (BUILDING eQ) PROGRAM

In 2009, ASHRAE unveiled a building energy labeling program known as the Building Energy Quotient (Building eQ) program. The program provides a method to rate a building's energy performance both "As Designed" (Asset Rating) and "As Operated" (Operational Rating). A pilot program was launched in 2010 that involves selected buildings from leading building owners and designers, real estate developers, and government agencies throughout the United States.

ASHRAE's Building eQ program will provide the general public, building owners and tenants, potential owners and tenants, and building operations and maintenance staff with information on the potential and actual energy use of buildings. This information is useful for the following reasons:

- Building owners and operators can see how their building compares to peer buildings to establish a measure of their potential for energy performance improvement.
- Building owners can use the information provided to differentiate their building from others to secure potential buyers or tenants.
- Potential buyers or tenants can gain insight into the value and potential long-term cost of a building.
- Operations and maintenance staff can use the results to inform their decisions regarding maintenance activities, influence building owners and managers to pursue equipment upgrades, and demonstrate the return on investment for energy efficiency projects.

Beyond the benefit received by individual building owners and managers, the increased availability of building data (specifically the relationship between the design and operation of buildings) will be a valuable research tool for the building community.

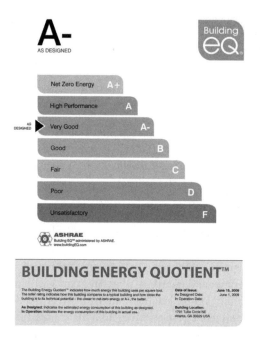

Figure 7-10 ASHRAE's Building eQ label.

REFERENCES AND RESOURCES

Published

ASHRAE. 2000. *ANSI/ASHRAE Standard 52.2-1999, Method of Testing General Ventilation Air-Cleaning Devices for Removal Efficiency by Particle Size.* Atlanta: American Society of Heating, Refrigerating and Air-Conditioning Engineers, Inc.

ASHRAE. 2004. *ANSI/ASHRAE Standard 55-2004, Thermal Environmental Conditions for Human Occupancy.* Atlanta: American Society of Heating, Refrigerating and Air-Conditioning Engineers, Inc.

ASHRAE. 2005. *ASHRAE Guideline 0-2005, The Commissioning Process.* Atlanta: American Society of Heating, Refrigerating and Air-Conditioning Engineers, Inc.

ASHRAE. 2007. *ASHRAE Guideline 1.1-2007, HVAC&R Technical Requirements for the Commissioning Process.* Atlanta: American Society of Heating, Refrigerating and Air-Conditioning Engineers, Inc.

ASHRAE. 2007. *ANSI/ASHRAE Standard 62.1-2007, Ventilation for Acceptable Indoor Air Quality*. Atlanta: American Society of Heating, Refrigerating and Air-Conditioning Engineers, Inc.

ASHRAE. 2007. *ANSI/ASHRAE/IESNA Standard 90.1-2007, Energy Standard for Buildings Except Low-Rise Residential Buildings*. Atlanta: American Society of Heating, Refrigerating and Air-Conditioning Engineers, Inc.

ASHRAE. 2009. *The ASHRAE Guide for Buildings in Hot and Humid Climates*. Atlanta: American Society of Heating, Refrigerating and Air-Conditioning Engineers, Inc.

ASHRAE. 2009. *Indoor Air Quality Guide: Best Practices for Design, Construction and Commissioning*. Atlanta: American Society of Heating, Refrigerating and Air-Conditioning Engineers, Inc.

ASHRAE. 2009. *ANSI/ASHRAE/USGBC/IES Standard 189.1-2009, Standard for the Design of High-Performance Green Buildings*. Atlanta: American Society of Heating, Refrigerating and Air-Conditioning Engineers, Inc.

ASHRAE. 2010. *ANSI/ASHRAE Standard 62.1-2010, Ventilation for Acceptable Indoor Air Quality*. Atlanta: American Society of Heating, Refrigerating and Air-Conditioning Engineers, Inc.

ASHRAE. 2010. *ANSI/ASHRAE/IES Standard 90.1-2010, Energy Standard for Buildings Except Low-Rise Residential Buildings*. Atlanta: American Society of Heating, Refrigerating and Air-Conditioning Engineers, Inc.

ICC. 2010. International green construction code, Public version 1.0. International Code Council, Washington, DC.

Jarnagin, R.E., R.M. Colker, D. Nail and H. Davies. 2009. ASHRAE Building EQ. *ASHRAE Journal* 51(12):18–21.

Taylor, S.T. 2005. LEED and Standard 62.1. *ASHRAE Journal Sustainability Supplement*, September.

USGBC. 2009. *LEED 2009 Green Building Design and Construction Reference Guide*. Washington, D.C.: U.S. Green Building Council.

Online

ASHRAE Building eQ
    www.buildingeq.com
International Performance Measurement and Verification Protocol
    www.evo-world.org
Tool for the Reduction and Assessment of Chemical and Other Environmental Impacts (TRACI)
    www.epa.gov/nrmrl/std/sab/traci/
U.S. Green Building Council, Regional Priority Credit Listing
    www.usgbc.org/DisplayPage.aspx?CMSPageID=1984

CHAPTER EIGHT

CONCEPTUAL ENGINEERING DESIGN— LOAD DETERMINATION

Economic benefits can be realized by focusing your efforts on reducing building loads. Reducing loads allow the designers to select smaller, less expensive HVAC equipment, which saves money. Plus, the reduced HVAC system's energy consumption leads to lower operational costs throughout the lifetime of the building.

The traditional load determination methods, such as the cooling load temperature difference method or rules of thumb, are rough, first approximations that are based on old correlations or simplified heat transfer calculations. Designing low-energy buildings requires the engineer to have a thorough understanding of the dynamic nature of the interactions of the building with the environment and the occupants. ASHRAE has published the *Load Calculation Applications Manual* (Spitler 2009), which focuses on the most current load calculation methods: the Heat Balance Method, and the Radiant Time Series Method. To optimize the design, detailed computer simulations that use these methods allow the engineer to accurately model the major loads and interactions.

Loads can be divided into those stemming from the envelope and those from internal sources. Envelope loads include the impact of the architectural features; heat and moisture transfer through the walls, roof, floor, and windows; and infiltration. Internal loads include lights, equipment, people, and process equipment. Examine all of the loads in two ways: separately, to determine their relative impact, and together, to determine their interactions.

The engineer must also understand the energy sources and flows in the building and their location, magnitude, and timing. Once the engineer understands these sources and flows, he or she can be creative in coming up with solutions. The charts in Figure 8-1 show how average energy use breaks down in commercial and residential buildings. As designs are developed, breakdowns such as these should be kept in mind so that the energy-using areas that matter most are given priority in the design process.

When trying to minimize energy use in buildings, the first step is to identify which aspects of building operation offer the greatest energy-saving opportunities.

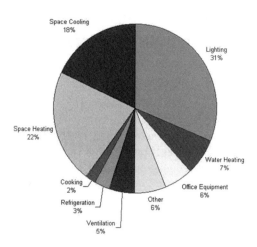

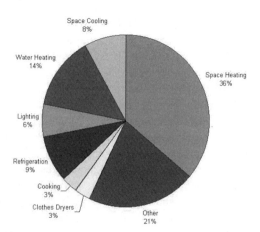

Image courtesy of CTG Energetics, Inc.

Figure 8-1 Average commercial and residential building energy use in the United States.

For example, as shown in Figure 8-1, space heating and cooling, lighting, and water heating make up a combined 78% of energy use in the average commercial building in the United States.

Another important aspect of this exercise in the design process is that it allows the design team, along with the owner, to set the appropriate goal for energy usage. Many organizations and institutions have adopted the Architecture 2030 Challenge. Conceptual load calculations help to determine if a specific building design concept meets these requirements.

To find energy end-use statistics for many types of buildings (e.g., office, education, health care, lodging, retail, etc.), based on building location, age, size, and principal energy sources, consult the Commercial Building Energy Consumption Survey data published by the U.S. Energy Information Administration at www.eia.doe.gov/emeu/cbecs/.

THE ROLE OF ENERGY MODELING DURING CONCEPTUAL DESIGN

To achieve the greatest possible energy reductions, energy modeling should begin during the early conceptual stage of the design process. Decisions about the building's form, orientation, percentage of glazing on each façade, and construction materials are generally made during this stage and can have a profound impact on how the building will perform.

Often, the architectural designers will develop several design options to present to the client. Perhaps one option has an elongated shape, another may be L-shaped, and a third may be rectangular with an interior courtyard. The options give the client the opportunity to provide feedback on the proposed design and interior space planning. Of course, if an energy use assessment of each option can be provided at this stage, then that will be another very important factor for the team to consider.

Commercially available energy simulation software can now give design teams the capability to directly read geometry from 3-D design models. This is a great time saver, and allows the design team to get feedback quickly on the performance of proposed designs rather than having to re-create geometry each time the design changes. For designs that have very complex geometry, this feature becomes especially important.

Once the geometry is created, the energy model can be populated with information on the loads. At the conceptual design phase, exact information is not yet likely to be determined, so engineering judgment is important to provide a realistic assessment

Suppose that the design team is working on a new office building. A massing model may be developed, however it is unlikely that specific office locations have been determined, so at this stage it would be reasonable for the energy model to be divided into simple block zones (for each exterior exposure) and interior zones. *ANSI/ASHRAE Standard 62.1-2010, Ventilation for Acceptable Indoor Air Quality.*

(ASHRAE 2010) provides data on typical occupancy densities and ventilation requirements, and *ANSI/ASHRAE/IESNA Standard 90.1-2010, Energy Standard for Buildings Except Low-Rise Residential Buildings* (ASHRAE 2010) provides data on typical lighting and equipment power densities for a wide range of different building types. Many energy simulation software tools have this information stored in a library (or allow creation of custom libraries) to allow users to quickly apply it to the energy model. Once this information is applied to the model, the design team can perform iterative simulations to determine the best performing massing scheme, the optimal orientation, the impact of different construction materials, and the impact of different window-to-wall ratios.

Since some assumptions must be made at this stage, the energy simulations may not predict energy consumption to the exact Btu (joule). However, if our assumptions are sound, we can get a good sense of the impacts of design decisions at an appropriate order of magnitude. Moving forward, we can be confident that the right concepts are in place and can then assess them in greater detail as the design progresses.

DETERMINING THE LOAD DRIVERS WITH PARAMETRIC SIMULATIONS

To gain an understanding of how the proposed design of the building affects energy use, the engineer should perform a series of parametric simulations. This process involves sequentially removing each load from the energy balance individually to determine the effect on overall energy use. The simulations that show the greatest energy reductions identify which loads are driving the building's energy consumption.

For instance, to effectively remove wall conductive heat transfer from the energy balance, set the wall thermal resistance to a very high value (such as R-100 [R-17.6]). Run the simulation model, and note the building energy requirements. Then, reset the wall insulation back to the actual R-value and proceed to the next parameter. Continue to do this individually with the floors, roofs, and windows. Then remove the window solar gain, daylighting, and other site-specific shading that may be involved. Assess the impact of infiltration and the effect of ventilation air by setting them sequentially to zero.

Parametric simulations should be completed for the internal loads in a process similar to that described in Chapter 5. Set the lighting load to zero, set the equipment load to zero, and then take all the people out of the building. In this manner, the engineer can understand what is driving the energy use in the building.

Plot the results for each case by annual energy use or by peak load to compare the impacts, as illustrated in Figure 8-1. A code building would be the building that meets the minimum requirements of the current Standard 90.1 (ASHRAE 2010), and the design building is a proposed building design.

Look for creative solutions to minimize the impact of each load, starting with those with the largest impact, or those that are the easiest to implement. From the parametric analysis example in Figure 8-2, adding underfloor air distribution results in the largest impact on annual energy use, so it should be one of the first solutions considered. Alternatively, a solution such as high-efficiency lighting may not result in as large of an impact, but may be easier to implement.

ENERGY IMPACTS OF ARCHITECTURAL FEATURES

It is important to collaborate with the architects to help guide decisions that will improve the thermal envelope's performance. Determine the greatest sources of heat gains and losses through the building's skin, and look for opportunities to minimize the effect.

Solar radiation through the windows can be one of the largest gains during the summer cooling season. Providing external shading can effectively minimize these gains. Horizontal shading, or overhangs, on the south face of the building will block the high sun during the day for much of the year, and vertical shading on the east and west can reduce gains early and late in the day as the sun rises and sets.

Another means to control solar gains is to specify high-performance glazing with a low solar heat gain coefficient. These glazing options can be either tinted glass, or spectrally selective glass. The benefit of the spectrally selective option is that they

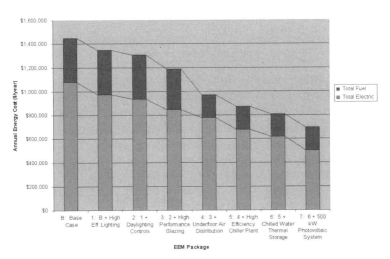

Image courtesy of CTG Energetics, Inc.

Figure 8-2 Sample parametric analysis to determine relative impacts of building envelope.

have a clear appearance and a high visible light transmittance, allowing for greater daylighting potential and views to the exterior. However, they are generally the more costly option.

In climates where heating the building is of primary concern, it can often be beneficial to allow solar heat gain into the building as it acts as a free heating source. In climates where heating and cooling are both significant concerns, use a building simulation software program to understand the trade-offs associated with various solar heat gain coefficient values.

Conduction gains through the building skin are also significant in the overall heat balance equation. Where possible, try to reduce the window-to-wall ratio. Even the best-performing glass selections cannot compare to the thermal characteristics of an insulated wall.

Glass selections with low U-factors will reduce the heat gains and losses. Also, try to minimize the U-factors of the walls and roof by using insulation with high R-values. Where thermal bridging may occur due to structural elements of the building, provide a continuous interior layer of insulation to minimize this effect.

Lastly, try to minimize infiltration gains from leakage of untreated air into the building. Positively pressurizing the building with the HVAC systems will minimize this impact; however, stack-driven and wind-driven pressure differentials will still cause exterior air to infiltrate the building. Opening and closing of doors to the exterior will also contribute to infiltration gains. Specify a continuous air barrier to minimize air infiltration through the building skin, and install entry vestibules or revolving doors to minimize airflow into the building through open doors.

THERMAL/MASS TRANSFER OF ENVELOPE

Basic, steady-state energy transfer through building envelopes is well known, well understood, and easy to calculate. Increased R-values are certainly beneficial in heating climates and can also help in cooling-load-dominated climates. Use as a minimum the recommended amounts spelled out in ASHRAE's energy standard (Standard 90.1 [ASHRAE 2010], latest approved edition). While values above those recommended can be beneficial in simple structures, high values can be counterproductive over a heating/cooling season in more complex structures. It is always wise to evaluate R-value benefits through the application of load and energy simulation programs.

The effects of thermal mass are sometimes not as easy to gauge intuitively. (See Figure 8-3.) Therefore, the above-mentioned simulation programs, when properly applied, are very useful in this regard. If thermal mass is significant in the building being planned (or if increased mass would be easy to vary as optional design choices), then such programs are essential for evaluating the flywheel effects of thermal mass on both loads and longer-term energy use.

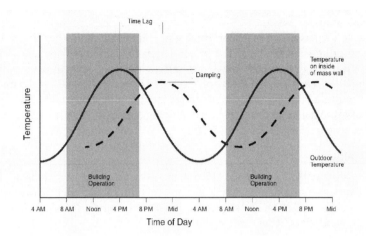

Image courtesy of U.S. Department of Energy Efficiency and Renewable Energy

Figure 8-3 The effects of thermal mass.

GreenTip #9 describes a technique for combining nighttime ventilation with a building's thermal mass to achieve load and/or energy savings.

ENGINEERING LOAD-DETERMINING FACTORS

Internal loads are significant contributors to the energy balance, but can be effectively reduced during the design phase. For office buildings, lights are usually the major culprits. Therefore, optimize the daylighting and electric lighting design.

Likewise, evaluate office equipment loads. Make recommendations about the effects of the choices of computers, monitors, printers, and other types of equipment. In many offices, this equipment is left on all night. An office building should have very few loads when the building is unoccupied. Leaving an office full of equipment powered up all night and on weekends can easily add up to large energy consumption.

For example, assume one 34,000 ft^2 (3159 m^2) office building has nighttime plug loads of 10 kW, and assume the building is unoccupied for 14 h/day during the week and 24 h/day on the weekend. This adds up to around 6000 h/yr and 60,000 kWh—or $4200 (at $0.07/kWh)—of electricity that could have easily been reduced. It is important for the engineer to bring up these issues during the design stage (and later, during the operation) of the building, because no one else may be paying attention to such details. Designing and building a great building is only half the job; operating it in the correct manner is the other—and often more important—half. The engineer can make better operation possible by designing piping, wiring, and controls capable of easily turning things off when not being used.

Educate owners about efficient office equipment and appliances to reduce plug loads, covering such things as flat screen computer monitors, laptops vs. desktop central processing units, copy machines, refrigerators, and process equipment (e.g., lab equipment, health care machinery, etc.). Consider measuring usage in one of the clients' existing buildings to get an accurate picture of load distribution and population profiles. Attempt to develop a total building electric load profile for every minute of one week.

LIGHTING

Good sustainable designs should not increase first cost over typical designs. More expensive equipment, glazing, and lighting should yield lower capacity requirements to offset those extra costs. Smaller equipment translates into smaller wiring, transformers, fuses, switchgear, etc.

The paragraphs below briefly outline some key considerations in lighting design, especially those involved in daylighting. Chapter 13 contains additional information for HVAC&R designers on lighting systems.

Electric Lighting

Work with electric lighting designers to lower connected and actual lighting loads while improving visual acuity. Collectively set the budget at less than the levels set in the current version of Standard 90.1 (ASHRAE 2010) (or local energy codes, whichever is more stringent). Typically, this will mean values less than 1 W/gross square foot connected load. Consider the following items: indirect, low ambient lighting levels; using task lights at workstations to allow lower area lighting levels; and using accent lighting in lieu of high area lighting levels to highlight relief, color, and areas of interest.

Daylight Harvesting

Studies on Daylight Harvesting. One of the principal rationales for the use of daylighting is the beneficial impact it has on the occupants of the building in terms of improved productivity and well-being. An example of the benefits is shown in one study of daylight harvesting impacts on retail sales, which showed a 40% improvement in sales. Another study of daylighting impacts on school performance showed a 20% improvement in math scores and a 26% improvement in reading scores. (These studies can be found at www.h-m-g.com/projects/daylighting/projects-PIER.htm.)

Daylight Harvesting Design Process: Some Key Points

Design Process/Design Options

• Study options in the schematic design phase.

- Integrate the design of all systems including:
  - Envelope
  - HVAC
  - Lighting
  - Interiors
- Take credit for HVAC downsizing to pay for daylight harvesting.
- Physical modeling can be useful.
- Address *all* the problems of daylit buildings including:
  - Direct insolation and glare control
  - Daylighting central cores
  - Heat gain—glazing selection, low-E glass
  - Heat loss—glazing selection, double-pane, interior shading
  - Owner awareness of design assumptions

Energy Conservation Regulation Compliance

- Prescriptive path vs. performance path (energy budget).
- A well-designed, daylit building will comply with Title 24 energy budgets.

Daylighting Considerations

- Envelope
- HVAC
- Lighting/controls
- Interiors/operations
- Implementation

Envelope Considerations

- Siting and orientation
- Fenestration/effective aperture area
  - Glass type
  - Area
- Shading and window management
  - External shading wherever possible
- Fenestration location

HVAC Loads

- Ensure realistic load assumptions among the design team.
- Design for actual load, not imaginary worst case.
- Take advantage of reduced internal loads to downsize.

- Select appropriate HVAC system.
- Capture skin loads before they enter the space.
  - Return air grilles over windows.
  - Returns or exhaust fans over skylights.

HVAC Zonation

- Upsize cooling capacity in zones near daylighting fenestration, if warranted.
- May need to upsize heating in such zones as well.
- Perimeter HVAC zones should be sized to be similar to daylighting zones (15–18 ft [4.6–5.5 m] deep).

Implementation

- Entire design has to be implemented.
- Cannot take out daylighting and not upsize HVAC to compensate.
- Cannot delete shading devices.
- Cannot delete controls.
- Cannot paint interiors black.
- Methods of operation need to be explained to occupants of the building.
- DON'Ts in the daylighting process:
  - (Avoid) partial design and specification.
  - (Avoid) partial implementation.
  - (Avoid) counterproductive building operation.
- Cost-benefit considerations:
  - Lighting energy savings
  - Energy savings due to reduced HVAC loads
  - Capital savings due to reduced equipment size
  - Capital savings from Southern California Edison Savings by Design
  - Improved comfort
  - Improved productivity and sales
  - Delight factor sells the space

SYSTEM/EQUIPMENT EFFICIENCIES

It is important to use cooling and heating equipment of the correct size. The old rule of thumb of 250 to 350 gross ft^2/ton (20 to 35 gross m^2/ton) cooling load does not apply to sustainable buildings. Recent high-performance building projects operate between 600 and 1000 gross ft^2/ton (55 to 90 gross m^2/ton). Set cooling equipment and system performance targets in terms of kW/ton (kW/kWR), such as the following:

Chiller	0.51 kW/ton (0.145 kW/kWR)
Cooling tower	0.011 kW/ton (0.003 kW/kWR)
Chilled-water pump	0.026 kW/ton (0.007 kW/kWR)
Condenser water pump	0.021 kW/ton (0.006 kW/kWR)
Air-handling unit	0.05 kW/ton (0.014 kW/kWR)

Industry standards such as Standard 90.1 (ASHRAE 2010) give minimum requirements for equipment efficiencies and system design and installation. Understand that these standards represent the least-efficient end of the spectrum of energy-conserving buildings that should be built. To be considered green, a building must exceed them.

In addition to ASHRAE, there are other sources of information on energy efficiency as related to green building design (see the "References and Resources" section at the end of this chapter). This Guide does not endorse any of them; the information is presented for informational purpose only. Readers should be aware that the sources use various methods to arrive at their final recommendations and that some of the guidance offered may have a hidden (or not so hidden) agenda. Some may use economics as a basis; however, the underlying economic assumptions should be understood prior to using the information. Others attempt to push energy efficiency to its technical limits. Therefore, before using any of these sources for guidance, investigate the premises used, the methods of analysis, and the background of the author.

LIFE-CYCLE COST ANALYSIS (LCCA)

As we can see, there are a wide range of strategies to achieve efficiency improvements, but which are the most cost effective? Life-cycle cost analysis (LCCA) can be used to compare various options to determine which will achieve the greatest net monetary savings over the building's life.

All of the costs associated with each option are considered including first cost, fuel costs associated with the building's operation, maintenance costs, and any other recurring costs. Escalation rates and increases in fuel prices are accounted for over the length of the study, and the totals are adjusted to calculate the total cost of each option in terms of today's dollars. This total is generally referred to as the *net present value*.

Interest rates and discount factors for performing these calculations are widely available. Additionally, there are numerous software programs available to perform LCCA studies. For additional resources, refer to the following Web sites:

* www1.eere.energy.gov/library/default.aspx?Page=3#lifecycle
* www.wbdg.org/resources/lcca.php

KEY CONSIDERATIONS IN THE HVAC DESIGN PROCESS

Design Intent

- Set goals for performance:
  - Energy performance
  - Environmental performance
  - Comfort
  - Operating cost
  - Determine how to achieve the goals
- System by system:
  - Integrated design

Verify that Design Intent is Met

- In design:
  - Verification of commissioning goals in design
  - Coordination between design disciplines
  - Include commissioning in design documents
- In construction:
  - Procurement of equipment and materials
  - Installation
- At start-up and testing
- In operations

Design Integration

- Integration with other disciplines
  - Architecture, lighting, interiors, and structural
  - Daylighting
  - Underfloor air distribution
  - Form-follows-function design
- Increased emphasis on HVAC performance
  - Thermal comfort
  - Indoor air quality (IAQ)
  - Energy efficiency

HVAC Systems

- High-efficiency equipment
- Systems responsive to partial loads
  - 80% of year, system operates at <50% of peak capacity.
- Emphasis on free cooling and heating
  - Economizers (i.e., air or water)

- Evaporative cooling (cooling towers or precooling)
- Heat recovery
- Emphasis on IAQ
- Underfloor air distribution is new wave

Load Reduction

- Reduce envelope loads
  - Solar loads
- Reduce lighting loads
  - Standard 90.1 (ASHRAE 2010) or local energy codes as a design maximum
- Reduce power loads
  - Site- and building-type specific, perhaps 1.0 to 1.5 W/ft^2 (16 W/m^2) as a maximum
- Reduced air-conditioning tonnage
  - Can provide higher air-conditioning efficiency for same cost

Cooling and Heating Load Reduction

- Envelope loads
  - Shading
  - Glass selection
  - Glass percentage
- Internal loads
  - Lighting power density
  - Equipment loads (advocate for ENERGY STAR®)
  - Controls/occupancy sensors

Digging Deeper

Another type of life-cycle assessment focuses on the environmental impact of products and processes. This is termed life-cycle environmental assessment (LCEA) or simply life-cycle assessment (LCA). This is a cradle-to-grave approach that evaluates all stages of a product's life to determine its cumulative environmental impact. This is very difficult to quantify, however many studies are underway to develop a standard approach to measuring LCA. A detailed description of the LCA approach has been developed by the U.S. Environmental Protection Agency (EPA), and can be found at www.epa.gov/nrmrl/lcaccess/lca101.html

ASHRAE
GreenTip #9

Night Precooling

GENERAL DESCRIPTION

Night precooling involves the circulation of cool air within a building during nighttime hours with the intent of cooling the structure. The cooled structure is then able to serve as a heat sink during the daytime hours, reducing the mechanical cooling required. The naturally occurring thermal storage capacity of the building is thereby utilized to smooth the load curve and for potential energy savings. More details on the concept of thermal mass on building loads are included in Chapter 5, "Architectural Design Impacts."

There are two variations on night precooling. One, termed *night ventilation precooling*, involves the circulation of outdoor air into the space during the naturally cooler nighttime hours. This can be considered a passive technique, except for any fan power requirement needed to circulate the outdoor air through the space. The night ventilation precooling system benefits the building IAQ through the cleansing effect of introducing more ventilation air. With the other variation, *mechanical precooling*, the building mechanical cooling system is operated during the nighttime hours to precool the building space to a setpoint that is usually lower than that of normal daytime hours.

Consider these key parameters when evaluating either concept:

- Local diurnal temperature variation
- Ambient humidity levels
- Thermal coupling of the circulated air to the building mass

The electric utility rate structure for peak and off-peak loads also is important when determining cost-effectiveness, in particular for a mechanical precooling scheme.

A number of published studies show significant reductions in overall operating costs by the proper precooling and discharge of building thermal storage. The lower overall costs result from load shifting from the day to the nighttime with its associated off-peak utility rates. For example, Braun (1990) showed significant energy cost savings of 10% to 50% and peak power requirements of 10% to 35% over a traditional nighttime setup control strategy. The percent savings were found to be most significant when lower ambient temperatures allowed night ventilation cooling to be performed.

For a system incorporating precooling to be considered a truly green design concept, the total energy used through the entire 24-hour day should be lower than without precooling. A system that uses outdoor air to do the precooling only requires the relatively lower power needed to drive the circulation fans, compared to a system that incorporates mechanical precooling. Electrical energy provided by the utility during peak demand periods also may be dirtier than that provided during normal periods, depending on the utility and circumstances.

The system designer needs to be aware of the introduction of additional humidity into the space with the use of night ventilation. Thus, the concept of night ventilation precooling is better suited for drier climates. A mechanical nighttime precooling system will prevent the introduction of additional humidity into the space by the natural dehumidification it provides, but at the expense of greater energy usage compared to night ventilation alone.

Both variations (i.e., night ventilation and night mechanical precooling) are not 100% efficient in the thermal energy storage in the building mass, particularly if the building is highly coupled (thermally) with the outside environment. Certain building concepts used in Europe are designed to increase the exposure of the air supply or return with the interior building mass (see, for example, Andersson et al. [1979]). This concept will increase the overall efficiency of the thermal storage mass.

For either type of system, the designer must carefully analyze the structure and interaction with the HVAC system air supply using transient simulations. A number of techniques and commercially available computer codes exist for this analysis (Balaras 1995).

WHEN/WHERE IT'S APPLICABLE

Night precooling would be applicable in the following circumstances:

- When the ambient nighttime temperatures are low enough to provide sufficient opportunity to cool the building structure through ventilation air. Ideally, a low ambient humidity level would also occur. A hot, dry environment, such as the southwestern U.S., is an ideal potential area for this concept.
- When the building occupants would be more tolerant of the potential for slightly cooler temperatures during the morning hours.

- When the owner and design team are willing to include such a precooling system concept and to commit to (1) a proper analysis of the dynamics of the building's thermal performance and (2) the refinement of the control strategy (upon implementation) to fine-tune the system performance.
- More massive buildings, or those built with heavier construction materials such as concrete or stone, have a greater potential for benefits. Just as important, is the interaction of the building mass with the building internal and HVAC system circulating air. This interaction may allow for more efficient transfer of thermal energy between the structure and the air space.

PROS

- Night ventilation precooling has good potential for net energy savings because the power required to circulate the cooler night-time air through the building is relatively low compared to the power required to mechanically cool the space during the day-time hours.
- Mechanical precooling could lead to net energy savings, although there will likely be a net increase in total energy use due to the less-than-100% thermal energy storage efficiency in the building mass.
- Both variations require only minor, if any, change to the overall building and system design. Any changes required are primarily in the control scheme.
- Night ventilation can provide a better IAQ environment, due to increased circulation of air during the night. A greater potential exists with the ventilation precooling concept. Both will be better than if the system was completely shut off during unoccupied hours.

CONS

- Temperature control should be monitored carefully. The potential exists for the building environment to be too cool for the occupants' comfort during the early hours of the occupied period. This will result in increased service calls or complaints and may end with the night precooling being bypassed or turned "off."

- The increased run time on the equipment could lead to lower equipment life expectancy or increased frequency in maintenance. Careful attention should be given to the resulting temperature profile through the day during the commissioning process. Adjustments to the control schedule may be necessary to keep the building within the thermal comfort zone.
- Proper orientation must be given to the building operator so he or she can understand how the control concept affects the overall system operation throughout the day.
- Future turnovers in building ownership or operating personnel could negatively affect how successfully the system performs.
- Occupants would probably need at least some orientation so that they would understand and be tolerant of the differences in conditions that may prevail with such a system. Future occupants may not have the benefit of such orientation.

KEY ELEMENTS OF COST

The following provides a possible breakdown of the various cost elements that might differentiate a nighttime precooling scheme from a conventional one and gives an indication of whether the net cost for the precooling option is likely to be lower (L), higher (H), or the same (S). This assessment is only a perception of what might be likely, but it may not be correct in all situations. There is no substitute for a detailed cost analysis as part of the design process. The listings below may also provide some assistance in identifying the cost elements involved.

First Cost

- Mechanical ventilation system elements   S
- Architectural design features   S
- System controls   H
- Analysis and design fees   H

Recurring Costs

- Energy for mechanical portion of system
  - Ventilation precooling   L
  - Mechanical precooling   S/H
- Total cost to operate cooling system   L

- Maintenance of mechanical ventilation and cooling system   S/H
- Training of building operators   H
- Orientation of building occupants   H
- Commissioning cost   H
- Occupant productivity   S

SOURCES OF FURTHER INFORMATION

Andersson, L.O., K.G. Bernander, E. Isfält, and A.H. Rosenfeld. 1979. Storage of heat and cool in hollow-core concrete slabs. Swedish experience and application to large, American style buildings. Second International Conference on Energy Use and Management, Lawrence Berkeley National Laboratory, LBL-8913.

Balaras, C.A. 1995. The role of thermal mass on the cooling load of buildings. An overview of computational methods. *Energy and Buildings* 24(1):1–10.

Braun, J.E. 1990. Reducing energy costs and peak electrical demand through optimal control of building thermal storage. *ASHRAE Transactions* 96(2):876–88.

Keeney, K.R., and J.E. Braun. 1997. Application of building pre-cooling to reduce peak cooling requirements. *ASHRAE Transactions* 103(1):463–69.

Kintner-Meyer, M., and A.F. Emery. 1995. Optimal control of an HVAC system using cold storage and building thermal capacitance. *Energy and Buildings* 23:19–31.

Ruud, M.D., J.W. Mitchell, and S.A. Klein. 1990. Use of building thermal mass to offset cooling loads. *ASHRAE Transactions* 96(2):820–29.

ASHRAE
GreenTip #10

Plug Loads

GENERAL DESCRIPTION

As the efficiency of various energy-using systems (i.e., HVAC, lighting, or building envelopes) improves, the impact of plug loads on the total annual building energy usage increases. This is accelerated by the rapidly growing use of computers and other electronic equipment in most building types. The purpose of this GreenTip is to identify some key issues to watch for that are relative to plug loads.

TYPICAL PLUG LOAD ENERGY BUDGETS

Historically, plug loads in office buildings have been designed to support connected loads in the 2 to 5 W/ft^2 (20 to 50 W/m^2) range. For laboratories or computing-intensive buildings, this can go up to 10 to 15 W/ft^2 (100 to 150 W/m^2). The electrical distribution system must be designed to support this level of load, in compliance with the National Electrical Code. Yet the actual diversified load exerted on the building electrical demand and upon the HVAC system will more likely be in the range of 1 to 1.5 W/ft^2 (10 to 15 W/m^2) or even less for highly efficient installations, as described below.

DIFFERENCE BETWEEN CONNECTED LOAD AND EFFECTIVE LOAD

The reason for this disparity is the fundamental difference between connected load for electrical equipment and the effective load imposed on the HVAC systems and electrical systems by the actual equipment when diversity of use is taken into account. The nameplate ratings of equipment are not representative of the actual energy usage of that equipment, which is typically a fraction of nameplate on average. Thus, if energy usage and cooling loads from office equipment and other plug loads are based upon nameplate, they can be overestimated by 200% to 500%.

There is debate about how much further plug loads are likely to drop in the future, as ever-improving efficiencies of equipment are being offset by increasing amounts of equipment being used. Programs like the U.S. EPA's Energy Star program will continue to improve the energy efficiency of individual pieces of equipment.

CONTROLS OF PLUG LOADS

One of the key factors in reducing effective plug loads is the impact of controls on the equipment loads. The primary issue is the power management controls now built into all computers and most other office equipment—putting the equipment in standby mode or completely shutting it off after preset intervals of nonactivity. Another way to accomplish this is through the use of occupancy sensors connected to plug strips that control equipment at a workstation, so it can be shut off when not occupied. This also works well for task lighting, which is not otherwise equipped with power management.

SOURCES OF FURTHER INFORMATION

M. Piette et al. June 1995 and subsequent updates. Office technology energy use and savings potential in New York. Lawrence Berkeley National Laboratory, Berkeley, CA.

REFERENCES AND RESOURCES

Published

ASHRAE. 1998. *Fundamentals of Water System Design*. Atlanta: American Society of Heating, Refrigerating and Air-Conditioning Engineers, Inc.

ASHRAE. 2007. *ASHRAE Handbook—HVAC Applications*. Atlanta: American Society of Heating, Refrigerating and Air-Conditioning Engineers, Inc.

ASHRAE. 2010. *ANSI/ASHRAE Standard 62.1-2010, Ventilation for Acceptable Indoor Air Quality*. Atlanta: American Society of Heating, Refrigerating and Air-Conditioning Engineers, Inc.

ASHRAE. 2010. *ANSI/ASHRAE/IESNA Standard 90.1-2010, Energy Standard for Buildings Except Low-Rise Residential Buildings*. Atlanta: American Society of Heating, Refrigerating and Air-Conditioning Engineers, Inc.

Spitler, J. 2009. *Load Calculation Applications Manual*. Atlanta: American Society of Heating, Refrigerating and Air-Conditioning Engineers, Inc.

Trane. 2000. *Multiple-Chiller-System Design and Control Manual*. Lacrosse, WI: Trane Company.

Online

Air-Conditioning, Heating and Refrigeration Institute
www.ahrinet.org/

Alliance to Save Energy
http://ase.org

American Council for an Energy-Efficient Economy
www.aceee.org

Architecture 2030 Challenge
www.architecture2030.org/

California Energy Commission
www.energy.ca.gov

CoolTools Chilled Water Plant Design Guide
www.hvacexchange.com/cooltools/

ENERGY STAR®
www.energystar.gov

Geoexchange
www.geoexchange.org

Heschong Mahone Group
www.h-m-g.com/projects/daylighting/projects-PIER.htm

Savings by Design
www.savingsbydesign.com

U.S. Department of Energy, Federal Energy Management Program
www.eere.energy.gov/femp

U.S. Energy Information Administration,
   Commercial Building Energy Consumption Survey
   www.eia.doe.gov/emeu/cbecs/
U.S. Environmental Protection Agency
   www.epa.gov

CHAPTER NINE

INDOOR ENVIRONMENTAL QUALITY

WHY A CHAPTER ON THIS?

This Guide is not intended to be a complete compilation of all interactions that buildings, and HVAC systems in particular, have with the environment. Many of the issues are known to be important to green building design among engineers and lay people alike. Areas such as energy consumption, location of buildings, and the construction process are prime examples. This Guide is primarily intended to convey ideas on how to improve buildings and their systems. There are, however, some areas that are either not intuitively obvious as being potential impacts of HVAC systems or are items that some may not consider to be true sustainability issues. Regardless of your definition of *sustainability* or the various labels and compartmentalization, it is assumed that the reader of this Guide is interested in designing buildings and their systems in a way that provides for the needs of the occupants, while minimizing the adverse impacts. Therefore, this chapter provides examples of several areas that the HVAC engineer may not initially think are important when minimizing environmental impacts—but they are.

In this chapter, we describe how building HVAC systems interact with the local environment and methods for mitigating or reducing their impact. We particularly focus on issues generally not considered by HVAC engineers but that are still HVAC-related. The issues discussed include the interaction with the local outdoor and indoor environments.

INDOOR ENVIRONMENTAL QUALITY (IEQ)

The terms *IEQ* and *indoor air quality* (IAQ) are sometimes confused as being one and the same. In reality, IEQ is a broader, more encompassing concept that includes IAQ as one of the key factors. The quality of indoor air for well-being is sometimes wrongly understood as the absence of pollution and pollutant emissions. One of the key factors for IEQ is the perception of indoor air as being naturally fresh and not artificial, in order to enhance well-being. Thermal and olfactory comfort go hand-and-hand, and therefore should be looked at in a combined manner (see section on olfactory comfort below). The following five areas are considered key to providing good IEQ:

- Indoor air quality and ventilation
- Thermal comfort
- Acoustics and noise
- Lighting levels
- Visual perception

IAQ and Ventilation

This is one area where the outdoor environment can have a negative impact on the building HVAC and the indoor environment, or vice versa, depending on the specific situation. Location of outdoor air intakes near a known contamination source (such as a loading dock with potential idling engines) can seriously degrade the IAQ by introducing, rather than removing, contaminants. Similarly, building exhausts can contaminate the local area near the exhaust discharge, making this air unsuitable for human exposure or intake into the building. Chapter 44, "Building Air Intake and Exhaust Design," of the 2007 *ASHRAE Handbook—Applications* (ASHRAE 2007) contains more information on this topic.

Assuming there is no contamination of the local air surrounding the building, good IAQ is possible by providing adequate ventilation and distribution within the space. In addition, a green building design will reduce the amount of indoor and outdoor air contaminants that have adverse impacts on the environment and human health. The following steps provide suggested items for consideration:

- Evaluate and preferentially specify materials that are low-emitting, nontoxic, and chemically inert.
- Do not install combustion appliances unless they are sealed-combustion or power-vented types; avoid gas ranges.
- Prevent exposure of building occupants and systems to environmental tobacco smoke.
- Use effective moisture control to curb humidity and prevent mold problems.
- Avoid using hard-to-seal building cavities, such as dropped ceiling plenums, for air movement unless these areas can be properly constructed and sealed. Given the fact that ceiling plenums will be used on many projects, attention should be paid to ensure that exterior elements (e.g., fluted roof deck to exterior wall) are properly sealed.
- Establish minimum IAQ performance to prevent the development of IAQ problems in the building, maintaining the health and well-being of the occupants.

- Meet the minimum requirements of voluntary consensus standard *ANSI/ASHRAE Standard 62.1-2010, Ventilation for Acceptable Indoor Air Quality* (ASHRAE 2010) and approved addenda.
- Provide IAQ monitoring to sustain long-term occupant health and comfort.
- Power-vent equipment that emits volatile organic compounds (VOCs) and ozone.
- Consider natural or liquefied petroleum (LP) gas with vented hoods, as gas ranges are less greenhouse-gas-emitting than grid-supply electric ranges.

Other Air Quality Considerations during Design and Operation

- Determine the condition of the ductwork system, and develop methodologies to meet current standards for occupant comfort and well-being.
- Inspect, evaluate, and document hygiene factors, microbial contamination, leakage, and thermal qualities according to the American Conference of Governmental Industrial Hygienists' *Bioaerosols: Assessment and Control* (Macher 1999). If the standard is not met, proceed with required remediation.
- Clean ductwork in accordance with the National Air Duct Cleaning Association's *General Specification for the Cleaning of Commercial Heating, Ventilating and Air Conditioning Systems* (NADCA).
- Achieve ductwork leakage class as described in Table 6 of the 2009 *ASHRAE Handbook—Fundamentals* (ASHRAE 2009), Chapter 21. This can also be referenced with the Sheet Metal and Air Conditioning Contractors' National Association *HVAC Duct Construction Standards, Third Edition 2005* (SMACNA 2005), Table 1-3, Chapter 1.

Thermal Comfort

Thermal comfort affects the occupants perception of overall building IEQ. A thermally comfortable environment that supports the productive performance of the building occupants is paramount to green building design. Maintaining this environment can be one of the biggest challenges for HVAC&R systems designers and operators. Generally, systems do not offer adequate control of the following thermal environmental factors:

- Drafts
- Thermal radiation
- Vertical air temperature
- Warm or cold floors
- Air speed

These factors affect the occupants' perception of comfort within the space. *ANSI/ASHRAE Standard 55-2010, Thermal Environmental Conditions for Human Occupancy* (ASHRAE 2010), the primary reference standard for designing a space that meets these criteria, defines thermal comfort as "that condition of mind which expresses satisfaction with the thermal environment." The standard acknowledges that thermal comfort is based on a specific individual's perception, and it is difficult to satisfy all occupants. Therefore, the standard addresses conditions that will satisfy a majority of the occupants within the space. It also allows for adaptation of individuals (e.g., they can wear warmer or cooler clothing depending on the season).

An HVAC system designed in accordance with the latest approved edition of ASHRAE Standard 55 will maintain a uniform thermal environment, or at least sufficiently uniform as not to adversely affect the occupants' perception of comfort. This supports the productive performance of the building occupants, which is one of the major objectives of green buildings. To achieve these criteria, the HVAC system will comply with the following thermal environmental factors:

- Temperature
- Thermal radiation
- Humidity
- Air Speed

While thermal comfort is also affected by other factors (e.g., activity level, clothing, and personal expectation), general acceptable ranges have been established to account for varying levels of clothing, activity level within a building, and different levels of thermal comfort based on the type of HVAC system and the expectation of the building occupants.

In addition to designing the HVAC system to meet the requirements of ASHRAE Standard 55, installing permanent temperature and humidity monitoring systems will assist in maintaining an acceptable thermal environment. The systems will also be configured to provide control over thermal comfort performance as well as the effectiveness of the humidification and/or dehumidification systems in the building. Ideally, a system designed to provide optimum environmental controls, as expected of green buildings, will have individual controls that allow variation to suit individual preferences and will shut down when individual spaces are unoccupied.

Occupied Space Energy and Air Delivery Means

The HVAC system is designed to provide both thermal control for comfort and outdoor air for ventilation. Thus, differing criteria are in play, and these occasionally may come in conflict.

Designing the HVAC system should be done in a way that allows for the rate of outside air intake to be measured. In some cases, it may be advisable to have permanent minimum IAQ performance monitoring for CO_2, CO, O_3, NO_x, and VOCs. As a minimum, the design should include a permanently installed device for monitoring the total amount of outdoor air at the intake. The air intake points should be located away from sources of contamination, as described in ASHRAE Standard 62.1 (ASHRAE 2010). The use of CO_2 as a surrogate method for outdoor airflow monitoring is widely discussed but not universally accepted as a proper method. Lawrence (2008) provides guidance on maximum CO_2 concentrations to expect during normal building and system operation.

In buildings with variable-air-volume (VAV) ventilation systems, special controls may be required to maintain minimum outside air intake at all times. VAV control units must have a minimum open position to ensure required distribution of outside air to all portions of the building. Industry practice is moving toward using dedicated outdoor air systems instead, which provide for better control of outdoor airflow to each occupied zone. A typical dedicated outdoor air system design would deliver the required outdoor airflow directly to each occupied space, which can be controlled to adjust as occupancy levels change (i.e., demand-controlled ventilation). Additional sensible cooling or heating in the space is provided by other means (e.g., a chilled beam, fan coil units, or radiant floor heating).

A green design should employ architectural and HVAC strategies to increase ventilation effectiveness and prevent short-circuiting of airflow delivery. For mechanically or naturally ventilated spaces, design ventilation systems that result in a zone air change effectiveness E of at least 0.9 under both heating and cooling modes using accepted reference standards of testing, design, or analysis (see Table 6-2 of ASHRAE Standard 62.1 [ASHRAE 2010]). This requires special attention when heating from overhead.

Acoustics and Noise

Sound and vibration are the often unheralded contributors to occupant comfort and health that should be an integral part of green building design and should not be forgotten. While noise is not always an obvious problem, current research into the effect of noise on human productivity and performance has shown noise to be an important parameter affecting a worker's performance (Waye et al. 2002). In addition to worker productivity, relatively low levels of indoor noise can also adversely affect workers' well-being. Outdoors, increasing environmental noise levels lower the general quality of life and degrade the environment. Unforeseen effects due to sound reflections can have serious adverse affects after a project is completed.

Noise Criteria. There are three basic criteria (that are in wide use today) for indoor noise: noise criteria (NC), room criteria (RC), and A-weighting (dB[A]). A full description of these criteria and how they are used can be found in the 2007 *ASHRAE Handbook—HVAC Applications* (ASHRAE 2007), Chapter 47. The graphs Figure 9-1 show the sound pressure levels associated with various sound frequency levels for both the noise and room criteria.

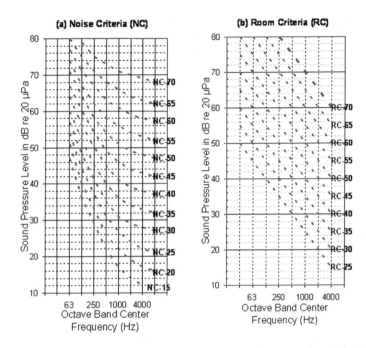

Image courtesy of Neil Moiseev

Figure 9-1 Noise criteria (NC) and room criteria (RC) levels.

There is one basic criterion used for rating outdoor noise: dB(A). The criterion can be stated in terms of a maximum sound level (L_{max}) or as an energy average sound level—the equivalent sound level (L_{eq}).

Indoor Sound Sources

1. *Fan and Mechanical Equipment Noise and Vibration*
   - Paths—There are two paths by which sound travels to people: airborne and structureborne. Airborne sound travels through the air and through windows, and is how we hear other people's voices. Structureborne sound is how we hear ourselves (through the bones in our skulls) and is what happens when you hear someone walking on the floor above, or an elevator passing by, or the hum of a pump on the floor above. In Figure 9-2, a typical floor fan room is shown, along with the many paths by which sound reaches the occupants of the space it serves. Paths A, B, and C are airborne transmission paths, while Path D is a structureborne path. All are important

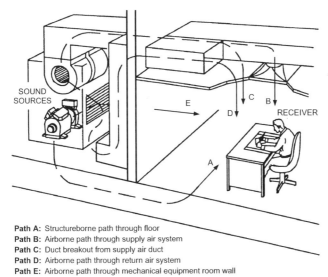

Path A: Structureborne path through floor
Path B: Airborne path through supply air system
Path C: Duct breakout from supply air duct
Path D: Airborne path through return air system
Path E: Airborne path through mechanical equipment room wall

Source: 2007 ASHRAE Handbook—HVAC Applications, Chapter 47

Figure 9-2 Typical floor fan room sound transmission paths.

in securing the comfort of the occupants. See 2007 *ASHRAE Handbook—HVAC Applications* (ASHRAE 2007), Chapter 47, for more information.

2. *Sources.* There are many sources of mechanical noise in a building:

   • Equipment—fans, pumps, chillers, compressors, and vacuum pumps.
   • Duct system airflow—regenerated noise due to high-flow velocities, close spacing of successive duct elements, too rapid transitions. Anytime static pressure is lost, there is noise generated. The greater the loss, the higher the noise.
   • Pipe system flow noise and vibration—excessive flow velocities; air in the fluid, closely spaced successive valves, turns, and junctions can all contribute to noise in occupied spaces.

3. *Noise and Vibration Control.* There is extensive information on controlling noise and vibration generated by building mechanical equipment in the "References and Resources" section at the end of this chapter.

Outdoor Sound Sources

1. *Cooling Towers.* This equipment comes in a variety of sizes from small units to great behemoths that service industrial plants. There are three sources of noise

from this equipment: fans, motors, and water. The two primary types are cross-flow, induced-draft tower, and forced-draft centrifugal fan towers.

- Fan noise can be controlled in the induced-draft fans through the use of larger units with slower fan speeds. Recent innovations include the wide-blade, hatchet-shaped fans that move more air at slower speeds, due to their larger, shaped-blade surfaces and the newer multiple-blade fans that achieve much the same effect by using more blades at slower speeds to move the same air as a conventional fan. In forced-draft towers, fan noise is controlled through the use of sound attenuators, since these towers can handle the additional pressure loss without losing cooling capacity.
- Newer, more efficient, and quieter motors with variable-speed controls have served to eliminate the start-up whine associated with older equipment.
- While fan noise can be controlled through speed and innovative fan designs, water noise can still be a problem in very quiet environments. To control water noise requires interrupting the path of the noise from the tower to the listener using barriers or silencers. The alternative is to reduce the water noise generated by reducing the height from which the water drops fall or by having them fall onto a quieter surface than the water in the sump basin.
- Using of a thermal energy storage (TES) system can result in the cooling towers and associated condenser pumps shutting down during daytime operation, thereby eliminating the outdoor noise levels associated with this equipment.

2. *Direct Expansion Condensing Units.* This equipment is air-cooled, primarily with propeller fans that are the main noise source. Depending on the type of compressor, the compressor noise adds annoying tonal components.
   - Centrifugal compressors are the traditional type and generate noise in the lower-frequency bands (31.5, 63, and 125 Hz).
   - Scroll compressors have higher-frequency noise.
   - Screw compressors have come into wide use in recent years and have serious pure-tone issues on which manufacturers have made significant strides, but great care still needs to be taken with these types of units. Enclosing the compressor in a sound-sealed compartment or wrapping the compressor in a sound barrier of composite material can contain the compressor noise.

3. *Dry Coolers.* This equipment is largely associated with computer room air conditioners (CRACs), coils, and fans. In addition to the fan noise, fan vibration often excites the casing of the units, which radiates more noise. Larger, slower-moving fans can reduce much of this noise. Applying damping compounds and stiffening the casing sheet metal can reduce the casing-radiated noise. Larger versions of the closed-circuit drycoooler are being provided with sumpless evaporative cooling to provide an alternative for cooling towers. The latest versions of the closed-circuit coolers either spray or evaporate water directly onto the dry cooler coil or dispense the water onto a pad where it is evaporated before the dry cooler. Generally, these

units are provided with larger inverter-driven motors, complete with soft-start capabilities. The housing is structurally solid to reduce casing-radiated noise.

4. *Exhaust Fans.* These fans and their ventilation supply counterparts can be inside the building (with only the discharge infusing noise into the environment) or located outside (where the radiated noise also contributes to the noise in the environment). Low-noise fan selection and the use of duct silencers can significantly reduce this noise.

5. *Sound Reflections.* An expected sound reflection can double or quadruple (four times) the sound energy. Each surface within about 10 ft (3 m) (in addition to the ground or the roof) will increase the resulting noise from a source by 3 dB (see Figure 9-3). One also needs to be aware of potential sound-reflecting structures that are more distant. These can reflect sound around a barrier directly to a noise-sensitive receiver.

Suggestions for Green Design for Acoustical Concerns

1. Lower fan tip speeds result in lower noise levels; this applies generally to all fans but is most pertinent to propeller ventilation fans, small centrifugal exhaust fans, and cooling tower fans. For example, consider two fans at 10,000 cfm (4720 L/s) and 2 in. (498 Pa) static pressure: one is a 24 in. (610 mm) backward-inclined centrifugal fan at 1610 rpm (26.8 rps), and the other is a 22 in. (559 mm) fan at 1953 rpm (32.6 rps). The difference in sound power is approximately 5 dB and lower for the larger, slower moving fan.

2. Use variable-speed drives instead of inlet guide vanes or volume dampers. This reduces energy use as well as generated noise levels. A fan without inlet guide vane can be up to 10 dB quieter.

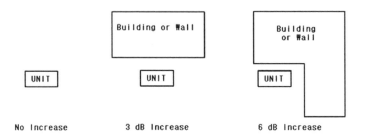

Image courtesy of Neil Moiseev

Figure 9-3 Effect of reflecting surfaces.

3. The use of a variable-frequency drive (VFD) on cooling tower fans can reduce noise levels by 6 dB during the more sensitive nighttime periods as well as eliminate the whine associated with a motor ramping up to speed.

4. Locating sound sources near reflective surfaces can result in adverse increases in the effective sound level of equipment. Try to keep sound sources a minimum of 10 ft (3 m) from a wall if at all possible. Be aware of the relative location of a sound source and a wall and to where sound may be reflected.

5. Using of a thermal storage system (TES) can cause the cooling towers and associated condenser pumps to shut down during daytime operation, thereby eliminating the outdoor noise levels associated with this equipment.

Lighting Levels

Adequate lighting levels are required for the building occupants. The lighting levels required vary according to the design purpose of the room or building zone. The local environment, in the form of trees, landscaping, or other buildings, can influence the lighting that may enter the space and, hence, affect the lighting levels inside. Lighting and its impact on HVAC load determination, along with daylighting, are discussed in more detail in Chapter 13 of this Guide.

Lighting is more than just providing the amount of light. It is also the overall perception and quality of that light. That includes, in some situations, the avoidance of glare. New lighting technologies, such as the large scale use of light-emitting diode (LED) lighting, are on the horizon, which could change lighting system design. These technologies also may change the definition of lighting fixtures and how these are integrated within the occupied space.

Visual

This is another area that influences how a person perceives the IEQ. The HVAC system will rarely interact with visual perception of the indoor space, except possibly when there is exposed ductwork. However, the engineering team can be a key part of the evaluation of trade-offs between window size and location with energy considerations (i.e., HVAC and lighting) in the integrated design process. The issues with visual perception should be jointly worked out with the project architect.

DESIGNING HEALTHY BUILDINGS

The science of green building design implicitly includes the design of healthy building environments, and this concept can and should be extended to address the aerobiology of the indoor environment. The field of aerobiological engineering includes technologies that incorporate active, passive, or natural means of disinfecting air and surfaces indoors (Kowalski 2006). The field of green building design bears a lot in common with aerobiological engineering, since they both aim at providing healthy habitats in the most practical or feasible manner (ASHE 2002). The U.S. Green Building Council (USGBC) has created the Leadership in Energy and

Environmental Design (LEED®) Green Building Rating System (USGBC 2002). This voluntary rating system provides guidance to building owners, occupants, interior designers, architects, and others who design and install building interiors. It addresses topics related to sustainable design including space usage, water and energy efficiency, and IEQ. See Chapter 7 for more information on LEED and other rating systems.

For aerobiological engineering, several technologies fall into the category of green building design, including passive solar disinfection, vegetation air cleaning, biofiltration of air, material selectivity, and architectural design for hygienic living. These are all primarily developmental technologies that may have limitations in terms of application and effectiveness. But when combined with other green building systems, they may contribute to an integrated solution to IAQ problems and healthy living.

Ventilation Air Cleaning

Currently, the LEED rating system doesn't focus much on air treatment systems (other than for air filters used during and after construction), but it is likely the matter will receive increasing attention in the future. The incorporation of air-cleaning systems in any building requires some investment in design, labor, equipment, and maintenance, and, like all building systems, the matter needs to be evaluated in economic terms. At present, however, there is insufficient information to fully establish the cost/benefits of indoor air cleaning or the actual requisite level of indoor aerobiological quality necessary for healthy living. It could be assumed, however, that the presence of any air-cleaning system is likely to provide a higher quality of health than the absence of air cleaning. Since even some minimal amount of air cleaning (e.g., a minimum efficiency reporting value (MERV) 8 filter) will provide noticeable improvement in air quality, especially for atopic or allergic individuals, it is recommended that some modest level of air filtration be provided in all buildings. It is also recommended that individuals who require higher levels of air cleanliness should consider designing and installing combined air filtration and ultraviolet germicidal irradiation systems (insofar as budgets permit).

Incorporating sustainable air-cleaning technologies into the design of a green building is a field that requires research. There are currently no formal requirements for air-cleaning systems in commercial or residential buildings, but there are some proposed guidelines for such applications (IUVA 2005). Natural ventilation could be considered a green building technology due to the low energy consumption, but natural ventilation systems must be designed to facilitate airflow through a building. When climate permits, natural ventilation may provide an adequate number of air exchanges but cannot easily provide for filtration of outdoor spores. The use of 100% outdoor air with enthalpy recovery wheels is one green building option, but it is necessary to filter outdoor air to remove environmental spores. The minimization of biological contamination through envelope design is another green approach, provided it can be accomplished economically (Rosenbaum 2002).

Various technologies exist in the marketplace for cleaning of air being circulated in buildings. This can involve both particulate and gas phase cleaning. Types of technologies and products can range from the well-established passive particle filtration to newer concepts such as air ionization, ultraviolet treatment, and ozone removal systems.

Material Selectivity for Health

The appropriate selection of building materials to avoid those that may contribute to microbial growth is a developing science that begs attention. The use of sustainable materials and renewable energy resources does not necessarily conflict with the objective of providing aerobiologically clean indoor environments, but there are areas of overlapping concerns and some considerations that need to be addressed.

Carpets often contain various chemical by-products that may act as indoor pollutants. Carpets and rugs also provide a substrate that may both collect and grow mold and mildew under moist conditions. Since mold spores tend to settle over time, they inevitably collect in carpets, and the problem is exacerbated by traffic. A wet spill is sufficient to initiate mold spore germination.

Passive Solar Disinfection

The subject of daylighting does receive some LEED credit, however, and maximizing daylighting can provide natural disinfection to building air and surfaces. Passive exposure to solar irradiation as a means of destroying airborne pathogens is based on the fact that sunlight contains some ultraviolet radiation and is lethal to airborne human pathogens (El-Adhami et al. 1994; Fernandez 1996; Beebe 1959). Sunlight in which all Ultraviolet B (UVB) and Ultraviolet A (UVA) was removed showed no significant disinfection within the first 120 minutes. Partially filtered sunlight that passes at least some of the UVA or UVB wavelengths can have a potentially significant disinfection effect over periods of days or weeks. Maximum fenestration will enhance this effect.

Generous quantities of sunlight and skylight are available even in the most northern latitudes, and careful attention to the design of indoor illumination via maximized fenestration may enhance the self-disinfection of buildings. When window space cannot be maximized, it may be possible to use UV-transmittant glass. In a hypothetical design for a building using passive solar exposure to control airborne microbes, the windows form a plenum for return air, with the outside panes being UV-transmitting glass (Ehrt et al. 1994).

Vegetation Air Cleaning

Large amounts of living vegetation can act as a natural biofilter, reducing levels of airborne microorganisms (Darlington et al. 1998; Rautiala et al. 1999). Winter gardens may act as buffer zones in moderating the indoor climate (Watson and Buchanan 1993). The surface area of large amounts of vegetation may absorb or adsorb microbes or dust. The oxygen generation of the plants may have an oxidative effect on microbes. The increased humidity may have an effect on reducing some microbial species, although it may favor others. The presence of symbiotic microbes such as streptomyces, may aid disinfection of the air. Natural plant defenses against bacteria may operate against mammalian pathogens. Finally, gardens and vegetation may have an effect on the psyche of occupants that may stimulate a sense of well-being. A number of houseplants have been identified that may contribute to passive cleaning of indoor air pollutants, but their effects on airborne microbes are not known (Wolverton 1996).

Although houseplants are often considered a source of potential fungal spores, a study by Rautiala et al. (1999) indicated that no significant increase in concentrations of fungi in air or surface samples occurred when houseplants were added to indoor environments. In a vegetation air-cleaning system, air flows through areas filled with vegetation or through entire greenhouses before entering the ventilation system. Often, such vegetation areas include waterfalls, which may also have an effect on local ionization levels. One downside to keeping large amounts of vegetation indoors is that the potting soil may include potentially allergenic fungi.

Vegetation has also been shown to have the capability of removing indoor pollutants and chemicals (Darlington et al. 2001). Atriums can provide solutions to IAQ problems in commercial and institutional buildings (when large spaces are provided in multistory buildings) but also present complex interfacing with ventilation and environmental control systems (Kainlauri and Vilmain 1993).

Biofiltration

Biofiltration has been in successful use in the water industry for some time and offers a potential alternative method for controlling indoor aerobiology through the use of filtration material containing bacteria that are antagonistic to pathogens. In this sense, it is similar to aspects of vegetation air cleaning. In one suggested approach, the building structure is used as the biofilter (Darlington et al. 2000). Before biofiltration was accepted as a means for dealing with VOCs and CO_2, efforts were made to determine if this amount of biomass in the indoor space could impact IAQ. A relatively large, ecologically complex biofilter composed of a bio-scrubber of about 110 ft^2 (10 m^2), 325 ft^2 (30 m^2) of vegetation, and a 925 gal (3500 L) aquarium was incorporated in an airtight 1720 ft^2 (160 m^2) room in a newly constructed office building in downtown Toronto. This space maintained about 0.2 ach compared to the 15 to 20 ach (with 30% outdoor air) of other spaces in the same building. Total VOCs and formaldehyde levels in the biofilter room were the same as, or significantly lower than, other spaces in the building. Aerial spore levels were slightly higher than other indoor spaces but were well within reported values for healthy indoor spaces. Levels appeared to be dependent on horticultural management practices within the space. Most of the fungal genera identified were either common indoor spores or other genera associated with living or dead plant material, or soil.

Olfactory Comfort: The Hedonic Impact on the Environment

The hedonic impact of the environment, and therefore the occupants' well-being is determined by the harmonization of all senses: smell, taste, vision, hearing, and touch. Smell has an immediate impact on well-being and is described in Chapter 12 of the 2009 *ASHRAE Handbook—Fundamentals* (ASHRAE 2009), which explains the importance and impact of olfaction. The nose (as the biggest air intake for humans) decides if the air is perceived as positive or negative and determines the hedonic value of the IAQ. It is known that the orthonasal or retronasal intake of air is liable for various health issues. Therefore, olfactory and thermal comfort have to be treated as an entity, since temperature and humidity can act together to affect the perception of odors. For well-being, receptors of the nose demand a positive stimulation due to the amygdale within the brain structures, which is involved in the sense of smell. Some of the IAQ complaints can involve emotional responses completely out of proportion to the concentration of odorant or intensity of the odor it produces. The sense of smell is directly connected to the emotional center in the brain.

One of the major goals in the design of a green building should be to achieve a positive feeling when breathing. The perception of natural, fresh, stimulating air, and not conditioned artificial air, should be a requirement for a healthy green building. The cost benefits of well-being, achieved by a positive hedonic environment, are enormous and result in increased productivity, reduced absenteeism, and diminished health factors. Energy costs are far less than human capital costs.

HVAC, BUILDING ENVELOPE AND MATERIALS, AND IAQ INTERACTION

Recent years have seen a marked increase in recognition of the impact that building materials (i.e., envelope, furniture, paints, flooring, etc.) have on IAQ. This was the primary reason for changes in the outdoor air ventilation requirements in 2004 in ASHRAE Standard 62.1 (ASHRAE 2010).

The IAQ can be negatively affected by offgassing of chemicals in building materials or chemicals used during the construction or fabrication of the components. The LEED program contains a number of credit point items that relate to reducing the introduction of potentially harmful materials into a building environment. It also describes methods to help ensure that key HVAC components, such as ductwork, do not become contaminated during construction and act as a source of indoor pollution after occupancy.

REFERENCES AND RESOURCES

Published

ARI. 1997. *ARI STANDARD 275-97, Standard for Application of Sound Rating Levels of Outdoor Unitary Equipment*. Arlington, VA: Air-Conditioning and Refrigeration Institute.

ASHE. 2002. Green healthcare design guidance statement. American Society of Healthcare Engineering, Chicago.

ASHRAE. 2010. *ANSI/ASHRAE Standard 55-2010, Thermal Environmental Conditions for Human Occupancy*. Atlanta: American Society of Heating, Refrigerating and Air-Conditioning Engineers, Inc.

ASHRAE. 2007. *ASHRAE Handbook—HVAC Applications*. Atlanta: American Society of Heating, Refrigerating and Air-Conditioning Engineers, Inc.

ASHRAE. 2009. *ASHRAE Handbook—Fundamentals*. Atlanta: American Society of Heating, Refrigerating and Air-Conditioning Engineers, Inc.

ASHRAE. 2010. *ANSI/ASHRAE Standard 62.1-2010, Ventilation for Acceptable Indoor Air Quality*. Atlanta: American Society of Heating, Refrigerating and Air-Conditioning Engineers, Inc.

ASHRAE. 2010. *ANSI/ASHRAE Standard 62.2-2010, Ventilation and Acceptable Indoor Air Quality in Low-Rise Residential Buildings*. Atlanta: American Society of Heating, Refrigerating and Air-Conditioning Engineers, Inc.

Beebe, J.M. 1959. Stability of disseminated aerosols of *Pastuerella tularensis* subjected to simulated solar radiations at various humidities. *Journal of Bacteriology* 78:18–24.

Darlington, A., M. Chan, D. Malloch, C. Pilger, and M.A. Dixon. 2000. The biofiltration of indoor air: Implications for air quality. *Indoor Air 2000* 10(1):39–46.

Darlington, A.B., J.F. Dat, and M.A. Dixon. 2001. The biofiltration of indoor air: Air flux and temperature influences the removal of toluene, ethylbenzene, and xylene. *Environ Sci Technol* 35(1):240–46.

Darlington, A., M.A. Dixon, and C. Pilger. 1998. The use of biofilters to improve indoor air quality: The removal of toluene, TCE, and formaldehyde. *Life Support Biosph Sci* 5(1):63–69.

Ehrt, D., M. Carl, T. Kittel, M. Muller, and W. Seeber. 1994. High performance glass for the deep ultraviolet range. *Journal of Non-Crystalline Solids* 177:405–19.

El-Adhami, W., S. Daly, and P.R. Stewart. 1994. Biochemical studies on the lethal effects of solar and artificial ultraviolet radiation on *Staphylococcus aureus*. *Arch Microbiol* 161:82–87.

Fernandez, R.O. 1996. Lethal effect induced in *Pseudomonas aeruginosa* exposed to ultraviolet-A radiation. *Photochem & Photobiol* 64(2):334–39.

IUVA. 2005. General guideline for UVGI air and surface disinfection systems. IUVA-G01A-2005, International Ultraviolet Association. Ayr, Ontario, Canada.

Kainlauri, E.O., and M.P. Vilmain. 1993. Atrium design criteria resulting from comparative studies of atriums with different orientation and complex interfacing of environmental systems. *ASHRAE Transactions* 99(1):1061–69.

Kowalski, W.J. 2006. *Aerobiological Engineering Handbook: Airborne Disease and Control Technologies.* New York: McGraw-Hill.

Lawrence, T. 2008. Selecting CO_2 criteria for space monitoring. *ASHRAE Journal* 50(12):18–27.

Macher, J., ed. 1999. *Bioaerosols: Assessment and Control.* Cincinatti, Ohio: American Conference of Governmental Industrial Hygenists.

Rautiala, S., S. Haatainen, H. Kallunki, L. Kujanpaa, S. Laitinen, A. Miihkinen, M. Reiman, and M. Seuri. 1999. Do plants in office have any effect on indoor air microorganisms? *Indoor Air 99: Proceedings of the 8th International Conference on Indoor Air Quality and Climate, Edinburgh, Scotland*, pp. 704–709.

Rosenbaum, M. 2002. A green building on campus. *ASHRAE Journal* 44(1):41–44.

Schaffer, M. 2004. *Practical Guide to Noise and Vibration Control for HVAC Systems, Second Edition.* Atlanta: American Society of Heating, Refrigerating and Air-Conditioning Engineers, Inc.

SMACNA. 2005. *HVAC Duct Construction Standards,* 3d ed., Chapter 1. Chantilly, VA: Sheet Metal and Air Conditioning Contractors National Association, Inc.

von Kempski, D. 2003. Air and well being—A way to more profitability. *Proceedings of Healthy Buildings 2003, Singapore*, pp. 248–354.

von Kempski, D. 2009. Going beyond green—green perception A paradigm change in IAQ for the well-being and health of the occupants. *Proceedings of Healthy Buildings 2009, Syracuse, New York,* paper 138.

Watson, D., and G. Buchanan. 1993. *Designing Healthy Buildings.* Washington DC: American Institute of Architects.

Waye, K.P., J. Bengtsson, R. Rylander, F. Hucklebridge, P. Evans, and A. Clow. 2002. Low frequency noise enhances cortisol among noise sensitive subjects during work performance. *Life Science* 70(7):745–58.

Wolverton, B.C. 1996. *How to Grow Fresh Air: 50 Plants That Purify Your Home of Office.* Baltimore, MD: Penguin Books.

Online

NADCA. *General Specifications for the Cleaning of Commercial Heating, Ventilating and Air Conditioning Systems.* National Air Duct Cleaners Association, Washington, D.C.

U.S. Green Building Council, Leadership in Energy and Environmental Design, Green Building Rating System[TM]
www.usgbc.org/DisplayPage.aspx?CategoryID=19

CHAPTER TEN

ENERGY DISTRIBUTION SYSTEMS

For there to be heating, cooling, lighting, and electric power throughout a building, the energy required by these functions is usually distributed from one or more central points. The most common media used to distribute energy are steam, hydronics, air, and electricity. Refrigerants are also used as a means of energy transfer between components of refrigeration equipment. Usually, except for with industrial and certain specialized applications, the length of refrigerant piping runs is not great.

ENERGY EXCHANGE

Distributing energy throughout a building is usually accomplished through the flow of steam or a hydronic fluid, air, electrons (electricity), and sometimes a refrigerant. Air and hydronic flows in particular also serve the function of disposition of used air (exhaust) or liquid waste. Since the air and hydronic media being moved are often at different thermal levels (i.e., warm or cold), opportunities are offered to incorporate green design techniques. There are several practical techniques whereby energy from one flow stream can be transferred usefully to another. Several GreenTips on energy recovery systems are included in this chapter.

Cooling and Dehumidifying

Chilled Water (CHW). Circulating CHW is generally the least energy-efficient process for refrigerated air conditioning. But, in many cases it is the most cost-effective, particularly for large buildings. The relatively low thermal efficiency results from it being a two-step process. The most common process uses a refrigerant circulated at a low temperature through an electrical recycling vapor-compression system. The CHW then chills a secondary refrigerant (water) to the temperature needed for cooling or both cooling and dehumidifying the air supplied to the occupied zones.

CHW can also be produced by a heat-driven absorption process that uses a mixture of water with lithium bromide or ammonia.

197

Some installations can benefit from energy reduction by using thermal storage using either CHW or ice, if further reduced in temperature and melted for later use.The CHW is pumped through air-conditioning coils that may be in a central plant room, in several building zones, or in individual rooms. Further energy losses result from heat gained through insulation on the CHW piping.

Liquid Desiccant (LD). Circulating LD is a single-step process that uses heat (i.e., that from natural gas or from liquid petroleum gas [LP], solar, or waste heat sources) when available. LD generally does not need piping to be insulated.

Synthetic Refrigerant (SR). Circulating SR from an electrical recycling vapor-compression system can be directly used in A/C coils that are in the same housing or plant room. Alternatively, the SR can be distributed to A/C coils in several building zones or in individual rooms (rooms with variable refrigerant flow [VRF] or volume systems).

Natural refrigerant (NR). Ammonia, hydrocarbons, and CO_2 should also be considered.

Leakage

There are differing hazards and costs associated with refrigerant leaks, and all should be considered serious faults.

- *CHW.* Leaks mainly cause building damage. Pressure testing procedures must be specified.
- *LD.* Some can have minor toxicity and can also cause building damage. Piping, being uninsulated, allows ready inspection.
- *SR.* Different types of SR damage the ozone layer and increase global warming potential. These leaks can be hard to detect, especially in systems with extended piping, and may develop long after installation. As Pearson (2003) noted, high losses have been reported, leading to concern that SR should perhaps be confined to plant room or factory-certified, leak-free systems.
- *NR.* Hydrocarbons are highly flammable, and ammonia is toxic and has limited flammability. These refrigerants are required by relevant codes to be confined to plant rooms having appropriate ventilation and spark protection.

ENERGY DELIVERY METHODS

Media Movers (Fans/Pumps)

Basics: Power, Flow, and Pressure. If air conditioning (heating/cooling) could be produced exactly where it is needed throughout a building, overall system efficiency would increase, because there would be no additional energy used to move (distribute) conditioned water or air. For acoustic, aesthetic, logistic, and a variety of other reasons, this ideal seldom is realized. Therefore, fans and pumps are used to move energy in the form of water and air. Throughout this process, the goal is to minimize system energy consumption.

Minimization of a media mover's power at full-load and part-load conditions is the goal. Understanding how fan and pump power change with flow and pressure is imperative. (Refer also to Chapter 2, "Background and Fundamentals.")

$$Power \sim Flow \times \Delta Pressure$$

As flow drops, so does the pressure differential through pipes, chillers, and coils. Pressure drop through these devices varies approximately with $flow^{1.85}$. This, in turn, means that the power required to cause flow through these devices varies approximately as $flow^{2.85}$. In an ideal world, power changes with the cube of the flow. While the 2.0 and 3.0 exponent is not fully achieved in practical application, it is nevertheless clear that reducing flow can drastically reduce energy use.

However, there are some pressure drops in typical systems that do not change as flow decreases. These include:

• the pressure differential setpoint that many system controls use,

• cooling tower static lift, and

• pressure drop across balancing devices.

Therefore, for flow through these system components, power will vary directly with flow.

To reduce pressure drop, the pipe or duct size should be maximized and valve and coil resistance minimized. (Duct and pipe sizes are discussed later in this chapter.) Coil sizes should be maximized within the space allowed to reduce pressure drop on both the water side and the air side. The ideal selection will require striking an economic balance between first cost and projected energy savings (i.e., operating cost).

Chilled-Water Pumps. Historically, a design chilled-water temperature differential (ΔT) across air-handling unit cooling coils of 10°F (5.5°C) was used, which resulted in a flow rate of 2.4 gpm/ton (2.6 L/min per kW). In recent years, the 60% increase in required minimum chiller efficiency from a 3.8 coefficient of performance (*ASHRAE Standard 90-75, Energy Conservation in New Building Design* [ASHRAE 1975]) to a 6.1 coefficient of performance (*ANSI/ASHRAE/IESNA Standard 90.1-2004, Energy Standard for Buildings Except Low-Rise Residential Buildings* [ASHRAE 2004]) has led to a reexamination of the assumptions used in designing hydronic media flow paths and in selecting movers (pumps) with an eye to reducing energy consumption.

The CoolTools team came to the following conclusion:

> ...the trend for most applications is that higher chilled water delta-Ts result in lower energy costs, and they will always result in the same or lower first costs. (Taylor et al. 1999).

Simply stated, increase the temperature difference in the chilled-water system to reduce the chilled-water pump flow rate and increase chiller efficiency with warmer return water. This reduces installed cost and operating costs. *The CoolTools Chilled Water Plant Design and Performance Specification Guide* (Taylor et al. 1999) recommends starting with a chilled-water temperature difference of 12°F to 20°F (7°C to 11°C). It is important to understand that in order for the chiller plant to utilize a higher chilled-water ΔT, you must start at the load coils (i.e., the air-handling units).

Condenser Water Pumps. In the same manner, design for condenser water flow has traditionally been based on a 10°F (5.6°C) ΔT, which equates to 3 gpm/ton (3.2 L/min/kW). Today's chillers will give approximately a 9.4°F (5.2°C) ΔT with that flow rate. The CoolTools guide states, "Higher delta-Ts will reduce first cost (because pipes, pumps, and cooling towers are smaller), but the net energy-cost impact may be higher or lower depending on the specific design of the chillers and tower."

The CoolTools team, in their summary, state:

> In conclusion, there are times you can "have your cake and eat it too." In most cases larger DT's and the associated lower flow rates will not only save installation cost but will usually save energy over the course of the year. This is especially true if a portion of the first cost savings is reinvested in more efficient chillers. With the same cost chillers, at worst, the annual operating cost with the lower flows will be about equal to "standard" flows but still at a lower first cost (Taylor et al. 1999).

The CoolTools Chilled Water Plant Design and Performance Specification Guide recommends a design method that starts with a condenser water temperature difference of 12°F to 18°F (7°C to 10°C).

Thus, reducing chilled- and condenser-water flow rates (conversely, increasing the ΔTs) can not only reduce operating cost but, more importantly, can free funds from being applied to the less-efficient infrastructure and allow them to be applied toward increasing overall efficiency elsewhere.

Variable Flow Systems. The above discussion suggests that variable-flow air and water systems are an excellent way to reduce system energy consumption. Variable flow (either air or water) is required by Standard 90.1 (ASHRAE 2004) for many applications, but it may be beneficial in even more applications than the standard requires. Today's most used technology for reducing flow is the variable-frequency drive.

Distribution Paths (Ducts/Pipes/Wires)

Ducts, pipes, and wires are used to move media. Proper sizing is a balancing act between energy use and cost and between material use and first cost. In terms of space consumed in running these carriers, in terms of the energy carried for the cross section of the carrier involved, wires (through electricity) have the capacity for carrying the most energy, followed by pipes (hydronics), and followed, in turn, by ducts (air). Another consideration is that the different energy-carrying media have different characteristics and capabilities in terms of meeting the requirements of the spaces served. The above factors will have some influence on determining the type of HVAC system to be used.

Sizing Considerations. The previous section, "Media Movers," stated that reducing flow rates may reduce both installed cost (by reducing duct, pipe, fan, and pump sizes) and operating cost (by reducing pump and fan energy use). Decreased duct and pipe sizes also lead to less insulation. However, if the incremental installed cost savings would be relatively small, the design professional may want to leave pipe and duct sizes larger to minimize energy cost. The best designs begin with generalized ranges (as were stated above for chilled and condenser water) that are fine-tuned for the specific application. This fine-tuning may be done with commonly available analysis and design software.

To reduce pressure drop, pipes and ductwork should be laid out prior to locating pumps, chillers, and air handlers.

Hydronic Fluid Selection. Fluid properties can greatly affect system performance. Antifreeze generally increases pressure drop and decreases heat transfer effectiveness. This leads to reduced system efficiency and perhaps increased cost due to the need for larger components. So, the design professional should first examine the system to determine if antifreeze is an absolute necessity or whether water, with proper antifreeze safeguards, could not be used.

If antifreeze is truly necessary, remember the following:

- Determine whether it is freeze or burst protection that is being sought. If an affected component (such as a chiller) does not need to be operated during freezing conditions, perhaps only burst protection is necessary. The amount of antifreeze needed can be greatly reduced, although slush may form in the pipes.
- Use only the minimum antifreeze necessary to provide protection; higher concentrations will simply reduce performance.
- Balance all environmental aspects of the antifreeze. Understand that while some antifreeze solutions are viewed as less toxic, they can significantly increase system installation and operating costs. Often the greatest environmental cost of a particular antifreeze is the increased energy consumption.
- Consult the manufacturer for more information on burst and freeze protection.

STEAM

Advantages

- Steam flows to the terminal usage point without aid of external pumping.
- Steam systems are not greatly affected by the height of the distribution system, which has a significant impact on a water system.
- Steam distribution can readily accommodate changes in the system terminal equipment.
- Major steam distribution repair does not require piping draindown.
- The thermodynamics of steam utilization are effective and efficient.

Disadvantages

- Steam traps, condensate pumps, etc., require frequent maintenance and replacement.
- Steam piping systems often have dynamic pressure differentials that are not easily controlled by typical steam control appurtenances.
- Returning condensate by gravity is not always possible. Lifting the steam back to the source can be a challenge due to pressure differential dynamics, space constraints, wear and tear on equipment, etc.
- Venting of steam systems (through pressure relief valves, flash tanks, boiler feed tanks, condensate receivers, safety relief valves, etc.) must be done properly and must be brought to the outside of the building.
- High-pressure steam systems require a full-time boiler plant operator, which adds to operating costs.

With the advantages listed, steam is often a logical choice for commercial and industrial processes, and for large-scale distribution systems, such as on campuses and in large or tall buildings. However, steam traps require periodic maintenance and can become a source of significant energy waste. Condensate return venting issues can add to operation and design challenges. Venting of flash steam can also cause significant energy to be wasted. (See subsequent section on steam traps, condensate return, and pressure differential.)

Classification

Steam distribution is either one-pipe or two-pipe. One-pipe distribution is defined to be where both the steam supply and the condensate travel through a single pipe connecting the steam source and the terminal heating units. Two-pipe distribution is defined to be where the steam supply and the steam condensate travel through separate pipes. Two-pipe steam systems are further classified as gravity return or vacuum return.

Steam systems are also classified according to system operating pressure:

- Low pressure is defined to be 15 psig (103 kPa) or less.
- Medium-pressure steam is defined to be between 15 and 50 psig (103 and 345 kPa).
- High pressure is defined to be over 50 psig (345 kPa).

Selection of steam pressure is based on the constraints of the process served. The level of system energy rises with the system pressure. Higher steam pressure may allow smaller supply distribution pipe sizes, but it also increases the temperature difference across the pipe insulation and may result in more heat loss. Higher steam pressure also dictates the use of pipes, valves, and equipment that can withstand the higher pressure. This translates to higher installation costs.

Piping

Supply and return piping must be installed to recognize the thermodynamics of steam and to allow unencumbered steam and condensate flow. Piping that does not slope correctly—that is, it is installed with unintended water traps or has leaks—will not function properly and will increase system energy use. Careful installation will result in efficient and effective operation. If steam or condensate leaks from the piping system, additional water must be added to make up for the losses. Makeup water is chemically treated and is an operating cost.

Control

Control of steam flow at the terminal equipment is very important. Steam control valves are selected to match the controlled process. If steam flow varies over a wide range, it may be necessary to have multiple control valves. On large-terminal heat exchange units, a single control valve usually cannot provide effective control. In such cases, multiple control valves of various sizes operated in a sequential manner are used. Consult sizing data available from manufacturers.

Condensate Return and Flash Steam

The energy conservation and operational problems that come up when utilizing steam often occur because the system design and/or installation does not properly address the issue of returning condensate to the boiler or cogeneration plant. The simplest and most efficient way to return condensate is via gravity. When this is not possible, the designer needs to clearly understand issues of lift, condensate rate, and pressure differential to ensure that operational problems (e.g., water hammer and reduction in capacity) do not occur.

In addition, the proper sizing and routing of vents for both the condensate receiver and the flash tank need to be clearly understood by the designer and the operator.

When considering recovery of flash steam, it is important to accurately calculate the expected operating pressure of the flash steam to ensure that the system or equipment served by the flash steam will be able to operate under all system conditions. Alternatively, if the flash tank is to be vented to atmosphere, the designer must fully understand the amount of energy that will be relieved and wasted by venting the flash tank to the atmosphere.

Steam Traps

Selection of steam traps is related to the function of the terminal device or pipe distribution served. Steam traps have the function of draining condensate from the supply side of the system to the condensate return side of the system without allowing steam to flow into the return piping. The flow of steam into return piping unnecessarily wastes energy, and significant energy waste can occur if periodic maintenance is not performed. Properly sized and installed steam traps allow terminal heat exchange equipment to function effectively. If condensate is not fully drained from the terminal heat exchange equipment, the heat transfer area is reduced, resulting in a loss of capacity.

Efficient Steam System Design and Operation Tips

* Preheat boiler plant makeup water with waste heat.
* Use ecofriendly chemical treatment.
* Recover flash steam, making sure to understand pressure differential of flash steam compared to system pressure serving equipment where flash steam recovery is used.
* Minimize use of pumped condensate return.
* Do not use steam pressure for lifting condensate return.
* Consider clean steam generators where steam serves humidification or sterilization equipment.

Sources of Further Information

Manufacturers of equipment—control valves, steam traps, and other devices—are valuable resources. There are multiple Web sites that contain system design information. Perform a search on the Internet for *steam piping design*. "Steam Systems" is Chapter 10 of the 2008 *ASHRAE Handbook—HVAC Systems and Equipment* (ASHRAE 2008). See the "References and Resources" section at the end of this chapter for additional resources.

HYDRONICS

Pumping heated water and chilled water is common system design practice in many buildings. Water is often diluted with an antifreeze fluid to avoid freezing in extremely cold conditions (thus, referring to these systems as *hydronic*.) There are many approaches in utilizing these systems.

Classification

Hot-water heating systems are classified as low-temperature water, medium-temperature water, or high-temperature water.

- Low-temperature water systems operate at temperatures of 250°F (121°C) and below.
- Medium-temperature water systems operate at temperatures between 250°F and 350°F (121°C and 177°C).
- High-temperature water systems operate at temperatures above 350°F (177°C).

Chilled-water systems distribute cold water to terminal cooling coils to provide dehumidification and cooling of conditioned air or cooling of a process. They can also serve cooling panels in occupied spaces. Chilled-water panels, which serve as a heat sink for heat radiated from occupants and other warm surfaces to the radiant panel, can be used to reduce the sensible load normally handled solely by mechanical air cooling. The percentage by which the load can be reduced depends upon the panel surface area and dew-point limitations, which are necessary to avoid any possibility of condensation.

Condenser water systems connect mechanical refrigeration equipment to outdoor heat dissipation devices (e.g., cooling towers or water- or air-cooled condensers). These, in turn, reduce the temperature of the condenser water by rejecting heat to the outdoor environment.

Piping, Flow Rates, and Pumping

Each of these systems uses two pipes—a supply and a return—to make up the piping circuit, and each uses one or more pumps to move the water through the circuit. Information on the design and characteristics of these various systems can be found in Chapters 12, 13, and 14 of the 2008 *ASHRAE Handbook—HVAC Systems and Equipment* (ASHRAE 2008).

Cost-effective design depends on consideration of the system constraints. Piping must be sized to provide the required load capacities and arranged to provide necessary flow at full- and part-load conditions. Design will be determined by several system characteristics and selections including:

- supply and return water temperatures,
- flow rates at individual heat transfer units,
- system flow rate at design condition,
- piping distribution arrangement,
- system water volume,
- equipment selections for pumps, boilers, chillers, and coils, and
- temperature control strategy.

Pumping energy can be a significant portion of the energy used in a building. In fact, pumping energy is roughly equal to the inverse fifth power of pipe diameter, so a small increase in pipe size has a dramatic effect on lower pumping energy (horsepower or kW). Traditionally, it was common to select heating water flow for coils based on a temperature difference of 20°F (11.1 K) between the supply and return. Flow rate in gal/min (gpm) was calculated by dividing the heating load in Btu/h by 10,000 (1 Btu/lb·°F·8.33 lb/gal·60 min/h·20°F temperature difference) (L/s was calculated by dividing the kW heating load by 4.187 [specific heat capacity of water, kJ/kg·K] · 11.1 K). As long as the cost of energy was cheap, this method was widely used.

Flow rate can easily be reduced by one-half of the 20°F (11.1 K) value by using a 40°F (22.2 K) temperature difference. The impact on pump flow rate is significant. The temperature difference selected depends upon the ability of the system to function with lower return water temperatures. Certain types of boilers can function with the low return water temperatures, while others cannot. Care must be taken in selecting the boiler type, coupled with supply and return water design temperatures. In specific instances, a low return water temperature could damage the boiler due to the condensation of combustion gases.

Lower flow rates could allow smaller pipe sizes, and pipe size, along with flow, affects pumping energy. A goal should be established for the pump horsepower to be selected. A small increase in some or all of the pipe distribution sizes could reduce the pump energy (hp or kW) horsepower needed for the system. When this goal is established and attained in the finished design, the concept and energy usage will be achieved. A reasonable goal can be expressed using the water transport factor equation adjusted to reflect kW (multiply hp by 0.746). Measurements of efficient designs indicate a performance of 0.026 kW/ton (0.007 kw/kWR [with kWR being refrigeration cooling capacity]) being served as a reasonable goal for 10°F (5.6 K) ΔT systems. Adjusting the flow rate and ΔP variables in this formula will quickly show the benefits of larger pipes or lower flow rates (greater ΔT).

For instance, let us calculate the energy (kW) required with the modified water transport factor equation:

$$\text{pump kW} = \frac{(Q)(\Delta P)(0.746)}{(3960)(nP)(nM)} \quad \text{or} \quad \text{mkW} = \frac{(L/s)(\Delta P \text{ kPa})(sg)}{(1000)E_{pump}E_{motordrive}}$$

where nP (E_{pump}) is pump efficiency and nM ($E_{motordrive}$) is electric motor efficiency.

We can create a performance index by solving the equation for 1 ton of cooling. That would produce an answer in kW/ton (kW/kWR). A typical condenser system might use 3 gpm/ton (0.054 L/s/kWR) of cooling and a ΔP of 100 ft (300 kPa) with an 82% efficient pump and a 92% efficient motor. If we insert these variables into the above equation, the derived kW answer for 1 ton (3.5 kWR) of cooling would be 0.075 kW or 0.075 kW/ton (0.021 kW/kWR).

Now, let's compare this index to the performance of an efficient design that increases piping and fitting size, and therefore reduces ΔP to, say, 30 ft (90 kPa) total dynamic head (TDH), keeps the gpm the same, and uses an 85% efficient pump with a 92% efficient motor. (Since the most efficient motors cost the same as less efficient motors, almost everyone is now using premium efficiency motors.) If we solve again for kW, we get 0.022 kW/ton (0.006 kW/kWR).

This shows us we can reduce pumping energy by 71% by lowering the TDH from 100 to 30 ft (300 to 90 kPa) and selecting a more efficient pump. One author of this Guide has personally measured systems with the characteristics indicated above. If the average cost per kWh of electricity is $0.08, and we are pumping for a 1000 ton (3517 kWR) chiller, the annual operating cost difference would be more than $37,000/yr.

If the system lasts 20 years, the improved system would save $740,000 in electricity costs. Of course, the obvious question is: "How much does it cost to increase pipe and fitting size and pump efficiency?" The answer will vary by project, but keep in mind that efficient pumps cost no more than inefficient ones. Larger pipes and fittings cost more than smaller pipes and fittings and, in one author's experience, the cost of increasing the pipe size one size (going from a 10 in. [250 mm] pipe to a 12 in. [300 mm] pipe) is recovered in electrical cost in less than 18 months.

Using the formula above and carefully measuring existing projects, we can establish performance goals for our designs such as the ones in Table 10-1.

At times, reductions in pipe sizes to reduce first cost are suggested as value engineering. However, energy usage of the building may be greatly impacted: pump size and horsepower could well be increased. In order to be truly valid, value engineering should also include refiguring the life-cycle cost of owning and operating the building. These factors can also be applied to chilled-water systems, except that chilled-water systems have a smaller range of temperatures within which to work.

System Volume

In small buildings, water system volume may relate closely to boiler or water-chiller operation. When pipe distribution systems are short and of small water volume, both boilers and water chillers may experience detrimental operating effects. Manufacturers of water chillers state that system water volume should be a minimum of 3 to 10 gal/installed ton of cooling (0.054 to 0.179 L/s/kWR). In a system less than this and under light cooling load conditions, thermal inertia coupled with the reaction time of chiller controls may cause the units to short-cycle or shut down on low-temperature safety control.

Table 10-1: Example Performance Goals

Component	Typical kW/ton (kW/kWR)	Efficient kW/ton (kW/kWR)	Delta	% Savings
Chiller	0.62 (0.1763)	0.485 (0.1379)	0.135 (0.0384)	22%
Cooling tower	0.045 (0.0128)	0.012 (0.0034)	0.033 (0.0094)	73%
Condenser-water pump	0.0589 (0.0167)	0.022 (0.0063)	0.0369 (0.0104)	63%
Chilled-water pump	0.0765 (0.0218)	0.026 (0.0074)	0.0505 (0.0144)	66%
Total water side system	0.8004 (0.2276)	0.545 (0.155)	0.2554 (0.0726)	32%

Similar detrimental effects may occur with small modular boilers in small systems. Under light load conditions, boilers may experience frequent short cycles of operation. An increase in system volume may eliminate this condition.

Energy Usage

There are many opportunities to reduce energy usage in the design of hydronic systems. Here is a list of some of the ways:

- Reduce flow rates by using larger supply-to-return temperature differences. For example, consider 30°F (16.7 K) ΔT on hot-water systems and 14°F (7.8 K) or greater ΔT on chilled-water systems. Reduction of pipe sizes could be considered to reduce first cost. However, to minimize energy usage, consider sizing systems at 3 ft/s (0.915 m/s).
- Reduce pumping horsepower based on flow reduction and responsible sizing of piping. In today's electrical rate environment, cost of increases in pipe size can be offset with lower energy costs, providing investment rate of returns of more than 25%.
- Utilize the reverse return concept to minimize pumping energy.
- Minimize water pressure drop across coils.
- Utilize two-way valves, variable-speed pumping, and variable/low-flow heat generating and/or heat rejection equipment.

- Minimize the use of glycol and three-way valve applications, except where necessary for freeze protection or other design and operating considerations.

Sources of Further Information

Manufacturers of equipment—pumps, boilers, water chillers, control valves, and other devices—are valuable sources. There are also multiple Web sites that contain system design information. (Perform a search on the Internet for *hydronic piping design.*)

AIR

Using air as a means of energy distribution is almost universal in buildings, especially as a means of providing distributed cooling to spaces that need it. A key characteristic that makes air so widely used, however, is its importance in maintaining good indoor air quality. Thus, air distribution systems are not only a means for energy distribution, they serve the essential role of providing fresh or uncontaminated air to occupied spaces.

That being said, it is important to understand that properly distributing air to heat and cool spaces in a building is less efficient, from an energy usage perspective, than using hydronic or steam distribution. Air-distribution systems are often challenging to design because, for the energy carried per cross-sectional area, they take up the most space in a ceiling cavity and are frequent causes of space conflicts among disciplines (i.e., structural members, plumbing lines, heating/cooling pipes, light fixtures, etc.). Many approaches have been tried to better coordinate duct runs with other services—or even to integrate them in some cases.

Another tricky aspect of air system design is that there are temperature limitations on supply air (due to the fact that air is the energy medium that directly impacts space occupants). While care must always be taken in how air is introduced into an occupied space, it is especially critical the colder the supply temperature gets. Low-temperature air supply systems offer many advantages in terms of green design, but an especially critical design aspect is avoiding occupant discomfort at the supply air/occupant interface.

Most of the same principles that were discussed under hydronic energy distribution systems apply to air systems, with respect to temperature differences, carrier size, and driver power and energy. Thus, there are plenty of opportunities for applying green design techniques to such systems and for seeking innovative solutions.

Energy Usage

Here are some of the ways to reduce energy usage when designing air-distribution systems:

- Size duct to minimize pressure drop.
- Require SMACNA's Seal Class "A" for all duct systems.
- Use variable-air-volume concepts for constant-volume-type systems.
- Utilize static pressure reset logic for all variable-air-volume applications.
- Minimize pressure drops of air-handling unit components and duct-mounted accessories (e.g., sound attenuators, dampers, diffusers, filter, energy wheels, etc.).

Sources of Further Information

Manufacturers of equipment—fans, ductwork, air-handling units, dampers, and other air devices—are valuable sources. There are also multiple Web sites that contain system design information. Air systems are also discussed in Chapters 20 and 21 of the 2009 *ASHRAE Handbook—Fundamentals* (ASHRAE 2009), and in Chapters 18 through 27 of the 2008 *ASHRAE Handbook—HVAC Systems and Equipment* (ASHRAE 2008). Another source for information includes SMACNA, www.smacna.org.

ELECTRIC

From the standpoint of space consumed, distribution of energy by electric means (e.g., wire, cables, etc.) is the most efficient. This advantage has often overcome the usual higher cost of electricity (per energy unit) as an energy form and has been one of the major reasons for electing to design all-electric buildings. The relative inefficiencies of electric resistance heating no longer make it a viable choice from an environmental or life-cycle cost perspective. However, when used in conjunction with a heat pump system, electrical energy as a source is efficient and less costly from an operating perspective.

ASHRAE
GreenTip #11

Variable-Flow/Variable-Speed Pumping Systems

GENERAL DESCRIPTION

In most hydronic systems, variable flow with variable-speed pumping can be a significant source of energy savings. Variable flow is produced in chilled- and hot-water systems by using two-way control valves and in condenser-water cooling systems by using automatic two-position isolation valves interlocked with the chiller machinery's compressors. In most cases, variable flow alone can provide energy savings at a reduced first cost, since two-way control valves cost significantly less to purchase and install than three-way valves. In condenser-water systems, even though two-way control valves may be an added first cost, they are still typically cost-effective, even for small (1 to 2 ton [3.5 to 7 kWR]) heat pump and air-conditioning units. (Standard 90.1 [ASHRAE 1999] requires isolation valves on water-loop heat pumps and some amount of variable flow on all hot-water and chilled-water systems.)

Variable-speed pumping can dramatically increase energy savings, particularly when it is combined with demand-based pressure reset controls. Variable-speed pumps are typically controlled to maintain the system pressure required to keep the most hydraulically remote valve completely open at design conditions. The key to getting the most savings is placement of the differential pressure transducer as close to that remote load as possible. If the system serves multiple hydraulic loops, multiple transducers can be placed at the end of each loop, with a high-signal selector used to transmit the signal to the pumps. With direct digital control (DDC) systems, the pressure signal can be reset by demand and controlled to keep at least one valve at or near 100% open. If valve position is not available from the control system, a trim-and-respond algorithm can be employed.

Even with constant-speed pumping, variable-flow designs save some energy, as the fixed-speed pumps ride up on their impeller curves, using less energy at reduced flows. For hot-water systems, this is often the best life-cycle cost alternative, as the added pump heat will provide some beneficial value. For chilled-water systems, it is typically cost-effective to control pumps with variable-speed drives. It is very important to right size the pump and motor before applying a variable-speed drive, as a means of keeping drive cost down and performance up.

WHEN/WHERE IT'S APPLICABLE

Variable-flow design is applicable to chilled-water, hot-water, and condenser-water loops that serve water-cooled, air-conditioning, and heat-pump units. The limitations on each of these loop types are as follows:

- Chillers require a minimum flow through the evaporators. (Chiller manufacturers can specify flow ranges if requested.) Flow minimums on the evaporator side can be achieved via hydronic distribution system design using either a primary/secondary arrangement or primary-only variable flow with a bypass line and valve for minimum flow.
- Some boilers require minimum flows to protect the tubes. These vary greatly by boiler type. Flexible bent-water-tube and straight-water-tube boilers can take huge ranges of turn-down (close to zero flow). Fire-tube and copper-tube boilers, on the other hand, require a constant-flow primary pump.

Variable-speed drives on pumps can be used on any variable-flow system. As described above, they should be controlled to maintain a minimum system pressure. That system pressure can be reset by valve demand on hot-water and chilled-water systems that have DDC control of the hydronic valves.

PROS

- Both variable-flow and variable-speed control save significant energy.
- Variable-speed drives on pumps provide a "soft" start, extending equipment life.
- Variable-speed drives and two-way valves are self-balancing.

- Application of demand-based pressure reset significantly reduces pump energy and decreases the occurrence of system overpressurization, causing valves near the pumps to lift.
- Variable-speed systems are quieter than constant-speed systems.

CONS

- Variable-speed drives add cost to the system. (They may not be cost-effective on hot-water systems.)
- Demand-based supply pressure reset can only be achieved with DDC of the heating/cooling valves.
- Variable flow on condenser-water systems with open towers requires that supplementary measures be taken to keep the fill wet on the cooling towers. Cooling towers with rotating spray heads or wands can accept a wide variation in flow rates without causing dry spots in fill. Fitting the cooling tower with variable-speed fans can take advantage of lower flow rates (there's more free area) to reduce fan energy while providing the same temperature of condenser water.

KEY ELEMENTS OF COST

The following provides a possible breakdown of the various cost elements that might differentiate a variable-flow/variable-speed system from a conventional one and an indication of whether the net cost for the hybrid option is likely to be lower (L), higher (H), or the same (S). This assessment is only a perception of what might be likely, but it obviously may not be correct in all situations. There is no substitute for a detailed cost analysis as part of the design process. The listings below may also provide some assistance in identifying the cost elements involved.

First Cost

- Hydronic system terminal valves: two-way vs. three-way (applicable to hot-water and chilled-water systems)   L
- Bypass line with two-way valve or alternative means (if minimum chiller flow is required)   H
- Hydronic system isolation valves: two-position vs. none (applicable to condenser-water systems)   H

- Cooling tower wet-fill modifications (condenser-water systems)   H
- Variable-speed drives and associated controls   H
- DDC system (may need to allow demand-based reset)
  or pressure transducers   H
- Design fees   H

Recurring Costs

- Pumping energy   L
- Testing and balancing of hydronic system   L
- Maintenance   H
- Commissioning   H

SOURCES OF FURTHER INFORMATION

ASHRAE. 1999. *ANSI/ASHRAE/IESNA Standard 90.1-1999, Energy Standard for Buildings Except Low-Rise Residential Buildings.* Atlanta: American Society of Heating, Refrigerating and Air-Conditioning Engineers, Inc.

CEC. 2002. *Part II: Measure Analysis and Life-Cycle Cost 2005, California Building Energy Standards*, P400-02-012. Sacramento, CA: California Energy Commission.

Taylor, S.T. 2002. Primary-only vs. primary-secondary variable flow chilled water systems. *ASHRAE Journal* 44(2):25–29.

Taylor, S.T., and J. Stein. 2002. Balancing variable flow hydronic systems. *ASHRAE Journal* 44(10):17–24.

ASHRAE
GreenTip #12

Variable Refrigerant Flow (VRF) Systems

GENERAL DESCRIPTION

VRF systems have been used in Asia and Europe for almost 25 years. The main advantage of a VRF system is its ability to respond to fluctuations in space load conditions. By comparison, conventional direct expansion (DX) systems offer limited or no modulation in response to changes in the space load conditions. The problem worsens when conventional DX units are oversized, or during part-load operation (because the compressors cycle frequently). A simple VRF system is composed of an outdoor condensing unit and several indoor evaporators. The systems are interconnected by refrigerant piping with integrated oil and refrigerant management controls, which allows each individual thermostat to modulate its corresponding electronic expansion valve to maintain its space temperature setpoint.

There are two basic types of VRF multisplit systems: heat pump and heat recovery (Figure 10-1). Both heat pump and heat recovery VRF systems are available in air-to-air and water-source (water-to-refrigerant) configurations. Heat pumps can operate in heating or cooling mode. A heat recovery system, by managing the refrigerant through a gas flow device, can simultaneously heat and cool—some indoor fan coil units in heating and some in cooling, depending on the requirements of each building zone. The majority of VRF systems are equipped with variable-speed compressors. Often called variable-frequency drives or inverter compressors, this component responds to indoor temperature changes, varying the speed to operate only at the levels necessary to maintain a constant and comfortable indoor environment. Heat recovery systems increase VRF efficiency because, when operating in simultaneous heating and cooling, energy from one zone can be transferred to meet the needs of another.

WHEN/WHERE IT'S APPLICABLE

VRF systems offer controls that match the space heating/cooling loads to that of the indoor coil over a range of operation. Variable speed compressors and fans in the outdoor units modulate their speed, saving energy at part-load conditions.

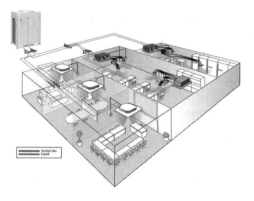

Image courtesy of Daikin AC (www.daikinac.com)

Figure 10-1 Heat-pump system in cooling mode.

VRF systems are best suited to buildings with diverse zoning especially buildings requiring individual control, such as office buildings, residential, schools, or hotels.

PROS

- A single condensing unit can serve multiple indoor units.
- VRF systems are generally modular and can easily be modified, which makes it easy to adapt the system to expansion and/or reconfiguration.
- VRF indoor unit capacities are generally smaller, allowing more individual zones and individual zone controls. Systems can be designed with individual space zoning and controls.
- Variable speed compressors enable capacity modulation, which translates to higher part load efficiencies in VRF systems.

CONS

- Indoor units on VRF systems generally do not have high latent capacities and are not suitable for applications requiring a high percentage of outdoor air.

- The external static pressure available for ducted indoor sections is limited. For ducted indoor sections, the permissible ductwork lengths and fittings must be kept to a minimum.
- There is the potential for refrigerant leaks in the building.

KEY ELEMENTS OF COST

The following provides a possible breakdown of the various cost elements that might differentiate a VRF system from a conventional one and an indication of whether the net cost for the hybrid option is likely to be lower (L), higher (H), or the same (S). This assessment is only a perception of what might be likely, but it obviously may not be correct in all situations. There is no substitute for a detailed cost analysis as part of the design process. The listings below may also provide some assistance in identifying the cost elements involved.

First Cost

- Conventional heat pumps/DX systems   H
- Ground-source heap pumps   L
- Refrigerant piping   L
- Installation costs   H
- Controls   S
- Design fees   H

Recurring Costs

- Overall energy cost   L
- Maintenance   L

SOURCES OF FURTHER INFORMATION

Afify, R. 2008. Designing VRF systems. *ASHRAE Journal* 52–55.

Aynur, T., Y. Hwang, and R. Radermacher. 2008. Experimental evaluation of the ventilation effect on the performance of a VRV system in cooling mode—Part I: Experimental evaluation. *HVAC&R Research* 14(4):615–30.

Aynur, T., Y. Hwang, and R. Radermacher. 2008. Simulation evaluation of the ventilation effect on the performance of a VRV system in cooling mode—Part II: Simulation evaluation. *HVAC&R Research* 14(5):783–95.

Cendón, S.F. 2009. *New and Cool: Variable Refrigerant Flow Systems*. AIArchitect.

Goetzler, W. 2007. Variable refrigerant flow systems. *ASHRAE Journal* 24–31.

REFERENCES AND RESOURCES

Published

ASHRAE. 1975. *ASHRAE Standard 90-75, Energy Conservation in New Building Design.* Atlanta: American Society of Heating, Refrigerating and Air-Conditioning Engineers, Inc.

ASHRAE. 1999. *ANSI/ASHRAE/IESNA Standard 90.1-1999, Energy Standard for Buildings Except Low-Rise Residential Buildings.* Atlanta: American Society of Heating, Refrigerating and Air-Conditioning Engineers, Inc.

ASHRAE. 2004. *ANSI/ASHRAE/IESNA Standard 90.1-2004, Energy Standard for Buildings Except Low-Rise Residential Buildings.* Atlanta: American Society of Heating, Refrigerating and Air-Conditioning Engineers, Inc.

ASHRAE. 2008. *ASHRAE Handbook—HVAC Systems and Equipment.* Atlanta: American Society of Heating, Refrigerating and Air-Conditioning Engineers, Inc.

ASHRAE. 2009. *ASHRAE Handbook—Fundamentals.* Atlanta: American Society of Heating, Refrigerating and Air-Conditioning Engineers, Inc.

ASHRAE. 2010. *ANSI/ASHRAE/IES Standard 90.1-2010, Energy Standard for Buildings Except Low-Rise Residential Buildings.* Atlanta: American Society of Heating, Refrigerating and Air-Conditioning Engineers, Inc.

NADCA. *General Specifications for the Cleaning of Commercial Heating, Ventilating and Air Conditioning Systems.* Washington, DC: National Air Duct Cleaners Association.

Pearson, F. 2003. ICR 06 Plenary Washington. *ASHRAE Journal* 45(10).

SMACNA. 2005. *HVAC Duct Construction Standards,* 3d ed., Chapter 1. Chantilly, VA: Sheet Metal and Air Conditioning Contractors National Association, Inc.

Taylor, S., P. Dupont, M. Hydeman, B. Jones, and T. Hartman. 1999. *The CoolTools Chilled Water Plant Design and Performance Specification Guide.* San Francisco, CA: PG&E Pacific Energy Center.

Online

Armstrong Intelligent Systems Solutions
www.armstrong-intl.com

Spirx Sarco Design of Fluid Systems, Steam Learning Module
www.spiraxsarco.com/learn/modules.asp

CHAPTER ELEVEN

ENERGY CONVERSION SYSTEMS

HEAT GENERATORS (HEATING PLANTS)

Considerable improvements in the seasonal efficiency of conventional heating plant equipment (e.g., boilers and furnaces) were made over the last several decades. Designers should verify claims of equipment manufacturers by reviewing documented data of this equipment to prove the efficiency ratings are accurate.

Some unconventional equipment and techniques to achieve greater efficiency or other possible green building design goals are described in the GreenTips at the end of this chapter.

COOLING GENERATORS (CHILLED-WATER PLANTS)

Chilled-water plants are most often used in large facilities. Their benefits include higher efficiency, reduced maintenance costs, and redundant capacity (in comparison to decentralized plants).

Generally, a chilled-water plant consists of

- Chillers
- Chilled-water pumps
- Condenser-water pumps (for water-cooled systems)
- Cooling towers (for water-cooled systems) or air-cooled condensers
- Associated piping, connections, and valves.

Because chilled-water temperature can be closely controlled, chilled-water plants have an advantage over direct-expansion systems, because they allow air temperatures to be closely controlled.

Often, chilled-water plant equipment will be in a single, central location, allowing system control, maintenance, and problem diagnostics to be performed efficiently. Chilled-water plants also allow redundancy to be easily designed into the system by designing for firm capacity. Firm capacity is calculated with the largest piece of equipment not operating. With firm capacity, one piece of equipment can be maintained or repaired and the system still has the ability to meet peak loads.

Chiller Types

Electric chillers used within chiller plants employ either a scroll-, reciprocating-, screw-, or centrifugal-type compressor (in order of increasing size). Models can be offered with both air-cooled or water-cooled condensers, with the exception that today's centrifugal compressors are water-cooled only.

Steam-driven turbines or absorption chillers, powered by steam, hot water, natural gas, or other hot gases, are used in many central plants to balance steam and electric demands in combined heat and power plants, and to offset high electric demand or consumption charges.

The various chiller types are used most often, though not exclusively, in the following situations.

Electric Motor-Driven Chillers:

• When low to moderate electric consumption and demand charges prevail.
• When air-cooled heat dissipation is preferred.
• When condenser heat recovery is desired.

Steam-Driven and Absorption Chillers:

• When part of a combined heat and power plant.
• When low fuel (e.g., natural gas) costs prevail.
• When high electric demand charges prevail.
• When there is a plentiful source of heat available (its main use usually being for other functions).

Heat Pumps. A heat pump is another means of generating cooling, as well as heating, using the same piece of equipment. There is usually an array of them used for a project, and they are generally distributed throughout the building (i.e., they're not part of a central plant). Buildings that have consistent demands for both chilled and hot water, such as hospitals, are good candidates to utilize a larger heat pump as a central plant. (See the GreenTips at the end of this chapter on various heat-pump system types.)

Thermal Energy Storage (TES). TES is a technique that has been encouraged by electricity pricing schedules where the off-peak rate is considerably lower than the on-peak rate. Cooling, in the form of chilled water or ice, is generated during off-peak hours and stored for use during on-peak hours. Although not refrigeration equipment per se, the technique can usually reduce the size of refrigeration equipment—or obviate the need for adding a chiller to an existing plant.

The characteristics, merits, and cost factors of TES for cooling, as well as numerous reference sources, are presented in GreenTip #20.

System Design Considerations

When a designer puts together a chilled-water plant, there are many design parameters to optimize. They include fluid flow rates and temperatures, pumping options, plant configuration, and control methods. For each specific application, the design professional should understand the client's needs and desires and implement the chiller plant options that best satisfy him or her.

Fluid Flow Rates. Flow rates were discussed in the "Media Movers" section of Chapter 10.

Fluid Temperatures. To allow the aforementioned lower flow rates, the chiller must be able to supply colder chilled-water temperatures and to tolerate higher condenser-leaving temperatures.

Pumping Options. Pumps may be selected to operate with a specific chiller or they may be manifolded.

Pump-per-chiller arrangement advantages include

* Hydronic simplicity
* Chiller and pump are controlled together
* Pumps and chillers may be sized for one another

Manifolded-pump arrangement advantages include
* Simpler redundancy
* Pumps may be centrally located

Plant Configuration (Multiple Chillers). The most prevalent chiller plant configuration is the primary-secondary (decoupled) system. This system allows the flow rate through each chiller to remain constant, yet accommodates a reduction in pumping energy, since the system water flow rate varies with the load.

Becoming more common are variable-primary-flow systems that also vary the flow through the chiller evaporators. New chiller controls allow this. Often these systems can be installed at a reduced cost when compared to primary-secondary systems since fewer pumps (and their attendant piping, connections, valves, fittings, and electrical draws) are required. These systems can also save energy in comparison to the primary-secondary configuration, due to more efficient chiller operation and reduced pumping energy.

(The subjects of plant configuration, pumping options, and control methods are discussed in detail in ASHRAE's *Fundamentals of Water System Design* [ASHRAE 1998], Trane's *Multiple-Chiller-System Design and Control Manual* [Trane 2000], and the *Chilled Water Plant Design Guide* from Energy Design Resources [EDR 2009].)

The designer should always review the overall use of energy within a facility and employ systems (including heat recovery systems) that interact with one another so as to minimize the overall energy consumption of the entire chilled-water plant.

COOLING SYSTEM HEAT SINKS

Building HVAC systems exchange a significant amount of thermal energy between the building and the surrounding environment; that is their function. This chapter describes technical details of heating and cooling systems and their interaction with the environment as a heat source or heat sink.

Green design features are available that provide high energy efficiency but have the potential for adversely impacting the environment. For example, systems have been installed that use deep water in a lake or nearby ocean as a heat sink, which results in significant energy savings. This technique has been used in Scandinavian systems for approximately 20 years and more recently in colder regions in North America. The possible net energy savings are impressive, but these must be balanced against potential adverse impacts on local aquatic environment.

COOLING TOWER SYSTEMS

Cooling towers are a very efficient method of cooling. Cooling towers remove heat by evaporation and can cool close to the ambient wet-bulb temperature (the difference between the leaving water and ambient wet-bulb being defined as the *approach temperature*). Unless the air is totally saturated (i.e, 100% relative humidity), the wet-bulb temperature is always lower than the dry-bulb. Thus, water cooling allows more efficient condenser operation than air cooling. In a typical cooling tower operation, about 1% of the recirculated water flow is evaporated. This evaporation will cool the remaining 99% of the water for reuse. In addition to evaporation, some recirculated water must be bled from the system to prevent soluble and semisoluble minerals from reaching too high of a concentration. This bleed or blowdown is usually sent to a publicly owned treatment works (POTW).

Water Treatment

The water in the evaporative cooling loop must be treated to minimize biological growth, scaling, and corrosion. Typically, a combination of biocides, corrosion inhibitors, and scale inhibitors are added to the system.

Corrosion inhibitors are usually phosphate or nitrogen based (e.g., fertilizers) or molybdenum- or zinc-based (e.g., heavy metals). These inhibitors are more effective when added in combinations. These materials have low vapor pressures, and thus, do not evaporate from the system. The inhibitors simply need to remain in the solution at the proper concentration to maintain a protective film on the metal components. Their only loss is through blowdown and drift.

Most scaling inhibition is accomplished using polymer-based chemicals, organic phosphorous compounds (phosphonates), or by acid addition. The acid reacts with the alkalinity in the water to release CO_2 and is used up. The polymer and phosphonate scale inhibitors remain in the solution to delay scaling; their major loss is through blowdown and drift. Some polymers are designed to be biodegradable, easily broken down by bacteria in the environment, while others are not.

There are very wide assortments of biocides. A typical system will maintain an oxidizing biocide (e.g., bromine or chlorine) at a constant level and should be given a dose of a nonoxidizing biocide once a week. Chlorine and bromine have a high vapor pressure, and thus, easily volatilize from the water. Much of the chlorine and bromine added to the tower is stripped from the water into the air; a small quantity actually reacts with organics in the tower. Drift and blowdown will contain all of the nonoxidizing biocides, a small quantity of oxidizing biocides, and the reaction products of the biocides.

Drift

To promote efficient evaporation, cooling towers force intimate contact of outdoor air with warm water. Besides removing heat by evaporation, dust, pollen, and gas components of the air will become entrained in the water, while some high vapor pressure components of the water (e.g., bromine or chlorine) as well as entrained water drops, will migrate to the air. Airborne dust and pollen that are captured by the water can promote biological growth in the tower.

Small water droplets entrained and carried out with the air passing through the tower are called *drift*. Drift is always present when operating a cooling tower. Since drift is actually just small droplets of the cooling tower water, it contains all of the dissolved minerals, microbes, and water treatment chemicals in the tower water. Drift is a source of PM_{10} emission (particulate matter less than 10 μ in diameter) and is as well a suspected vector in Legionella transmission.

Drift is usually reported as a percentage of the recirculating water, though it may also be described in terms of parts per million (ppm) of the air passing through the tower. Tower designs use drift eliminators to capture some of this entrained water. A typical value for drift from cooling towers is 0.005% of the recirculating water; many tower designs have drift values as low as 0.001%.

To put these values in perspective, consider an example of a 400 ton cooling system with a particular treatment program. A 400 ton system would circulate approximately 1200 gpm (4543 L/min) through the tower and chiller. At nominal rates, 12 gpm (45.4 L/min) would be lost to evaporation, 0.06 gpm (0.23 L/min) would be lost to drift (0.005%), and, at four cycles of concentration, 4 gpm (15.1 L/min) would be intentionally bled from the system. Chlorine addition would be 0.09 gal/h (0.34 L/h) of 12.5% liquid bleach, equivalent to 0.06 lb/h or 0.027 kg/h of Cl_2. This chlorine addition should maintain about 0.2 ppm free chlorine and 0.2 ppm combined chlorine. The combined chlorine is from the reaction of chlorine with organic molecules and may include some hazardous by-products, such as chloroform. For corrosion and scale protection, the water would be maintained with 2 ppm zinc, 3 ppm triazole, and 20 ppm polyphosphate. Once a week 4 lb. of a 1.5% solution of isothiazoline, a nonoxidizing biocide, will be fed to the system for biofilm control. The drift and bleed will contain the same quantity of minerals and chemicals as are maintained in the recirculated water.

Table 11-1 shows monthly results for operating this tower at an assumed 75 h/ week (300 h/month). From the Table 11-1, it can be seen that most of the chlorine used in this tower is unaccounted for. Some of this loss is due to oxidation of organic and inorganic material in the cooling system, resulting in nonhazardous chloride ions; much of the chlorine is released into the atmosphere as chlorine gas. While it is hard to be quantitative, over the course of one year, this tower could release more than 100 lb (45.4 kg) of chlorine gas into the immediate building environment. If less-effective drift eliminators were used, 12,000 gal (45.4 kL) of contaminated tower water would also be released every year and 800,000 gal (3028 kL) of water containing heavy metals, phosphates, and biocides would be sent to a POTW system. Most POTW systems are designed to handle only organic waste; much of these cooling tower chemicals would pass through the system untreated or would be released later as gaseous emissions at the POTW.

Over the lifetime of the building, these releases could be among the most significant impacts that the building would have on the local environment. This example highlights what could happen if the issue is not addressed.

Table 11-1: Material Release from Example Cooling Tower Operation

	Release Rate	Total per Month
Evaporation	12 gpm (45.4 L/min)	216,000 gal (817,560 L)
Bleed at four cycles	4 gpm (15.1 L/min)	72,000 gal (272,520 L)
Drift	0.060 gpm (0.23 L/min) (0.005%) 0.012 gpm (0.05 L/min) (0.001%)	1080 gal (4088 L) 216 gal (818 L)
Chlorine addition	0.06 lb/h (0.027 kg/h)	18.0 pounds Cl_2 (8.2 kg)
Chlorine in bleed	Free—about 0.2 ppm Combined—about 0.2 ppm	0.12 lb free (0.055 kg) 0.12 lb combined (0.055 kg)
Unaccounted chlorine		17.7 lb Cl_2 (8.0 kg)

Green Choices—Water Treatment

The water treatment plan illustrated above is not the only choice. There are many ways to treat the system that will have a less negative impact on the environment. Besides being rapidly stripped into the air, chlorine and bromine may react with organic molecules to produce very hazardous daughter products; however, other oxidizing biocides (e.g., hydrogen peroxide) do not have this issue. By continuous monitoring of the cooling system, chemical additions can be added only when needed. This technique can yield equivalent performance with less-added chemicals. Also, the U.S. Environmental Protection Agency (EPA) maintains a Web site on green chemistry, www.epa.gov//greenchemistry/, which contains criteria on how to evaluate the life-cycle environmental impact of a particular chemical.

Nonchemical water treatment has the potential to be a powerful method for water treatment; however, its success depends on the water chemistry, operating procedures, and degree of pollution of the specific system. There are several different nonchemical technologies available, including those based on pulsed electric fields, mechanical agitation, and ultrasound. Each of these technologies has developed a widespread following. ASHRAE has investigated the scale prevention effectiveness of some of these nonchemical technologies and has published the results from ASHRAE's Research Project RP-1155 (Cho et al. 2003). These technologies offer an alternative to the storage and handling of toxic chemicals at the site, eliminating the risk caused by any spills or leaks of cooling tower water, the issues of the bleed water at the POTW, and much of the concern with drift. Bleed water, instead of being sent to the POTW, could be used on site for irrigation or other nonpotable needs. The pulsed-field technology is the subject of GreenTip #13.

Green Choices—Tower Selection

All cooling tower designs are efficient at removing heat from water through evaporation; however, not all designs perform as well environmentally. Some tower designs are more prone to splashout, spills, drift, and algae growth than others. Splashout involves tower water splashing from the tower. This happens most often in no-fan conditions (i.e., when tower water is circulated with the fans off) when there are strong winds. Cross-flow towers are more prone to this issue since, in a no-fan condition, some water will fall outside of the fill.

Spills can happen from the cold-water basin from overflowing at shutdown when all of the water in the piping drains into the basin. Proper water levels will prevent this. Some tower designs use hot-water basins to distribute water at the top of the tower, while other designs use a spray header pipe. The hot-water basin design can overflow if the nozzles clog; a spray header pipe never overflows.

Algae are a nuisance in basins and can contribute to microbial growth. Algae control requires harsher chemical treatment than typical biological control. Since algae are plants, they need sunlight to grow. Some tower designs are light-tight, virtually eliminating algae as an issue, while other designs are more open and algae growth can be an issue.

The amount of drift varies extensively in tower design. Some tower designs have very little drift. The less the drift from a tower, the lower the amount of water containing minerals, water treatment chemicals, and microbes that will be released into the surrounding environment.

Fan-power draw also varies between designs. There are two general types of fans: axial and centrifugal. With axial fans, the fan blades are mounted perpendicular to the axis like propellers on a plane or boat. All induced-draft cooling towers and some forced-draft designs use axial fans. With centrifugal fans, the fan blades are mounted parallel to the axis, along the outside of the shaft hub. Centrifugal fans are only used in forced-draft towers and typically use twice the energy to achieve the same amount of airflow as an axial fan.

Maintenance

An often overlooked method for minimizing environmental impact is maintenance. Cooling towers operate outdoors under changing conditions. Wind damage to inlet air louvers, excessive airborne contamination, clogging of water distribution nozzles, and mechanical problems can best be prevented and quickly corrected with periodic inspections and maintenance.

DISTRICT ENERGY SYSTEMS

District energy (DE) systems involve the provision of thermal energy (heating and/or cooling) from one or more central energy plants to multiple buildings or facilities via a network of interconnecting thermal piping. Generally, district heating systems deliver heat as steam or hot water, while district cooling systems deliver cooling as chilled water or chilled secondary coolant (such as an aqueous glycol or an aqueous sodium nitrite solution) or even as a refrigerant.

DE systems often deliver multiple significant positive impacts to the local building environments that they serve. These typical impacts include the areas outlined in the following sections.

Energy Consumption

Heating and/or cooling buildings using DE systems can affect overall energy consumption in various ways, from modest increases or decreases to very dramatic decreases in fuel and energy consumption. The energy consumed within the boundaries of DE-served buildings will, of course, be dramatically reduced compared to a baseline building with its own dedicated boilers and chillers. This energy reduction within the buildings will be offset by the energy consumed in the central DE plants and in distributing the thermal energy from the central plants to the customer buildings. If the central DE plant utilizes similar technology (e.g., gas boilers and electric chillers) as otherwise used in the individual buildings, there may be little or no net reduction in energy use. However, the larger (and generally more efficient) DE plant equipment more than offsets extra energy consumed in the distribution of the thermal energy to the buildings for at least a slight net reduction in overall energy consumption. Reductions in overall fuel and energy consumption are achieved through the ability of DE plants to more readily and more economically utilize alternative technologies than is the case for individual buildings. These technologies include, but are not limited to, dual-fuel boilers; alternative fuel boilers (including renewable fuels such as low-Btu landfill gas, municipal solid waste, wood waste, etc.); high-efficiency boilers; high-efficiency chillers; alternative energy-efficient refrigerants (e.g., ammonia); nonelectric chiller plants (e.g., absorption chillers, engine-driven chillers, or turbine-driven chillers); hybrid chiller plants (with various combinations of electric and nonelectric chillers); energy-efficient series or series-parallel chiller configurations for high ΔT systems; thermal energy storage (TES); cogeneration of combined heating and power (CHP); trigeneration or combined cooling, heating, and power (CCHP); and the use of natural renewable thermal energy (such as geothermal heat for district heating systems and cold deep water sources [e.g., lakes or oceans] for district cooling systems). In addition, DE plants are better able to meet the changing loads of the system.

Emissions

As is the case with energy consumption, DE serves to eliminate many emissions from the local building environment, such as boiler exhausts and chiller plant heat rejection. Some emissions are of course relocated to the site of the central DE plant. However, just as DE plants tend to have higher levels of energy efficiency, they tend to have lower levels of emissions vs. those associated with individually heated and cooled buildings. And for DE systems utilizing one or more of the alternative technologies (as cited above), the overall emissions can be significantly reduced in terms of air pollutants (i.e., SO_X, NO_X, and precipitates) and greenhouse gases (i.e., CO_2, NO_X, and some refrigerants).

Noise and Vibration

Through the avoidance of needing boilers and/or chillers in the buildings, the occupants of DE-served buildings experience a local building environment that is free from the potential noise and vibrations associated with such equipment.

Chemical Supplies and Blowdown

Due to the avoidance of needing boilers and/or chiller plants in each building, DE systems can eliminate or greatly mitigate the presence of potentially harmful fuel and chemicals to be handled within the occupied buildings. With the use of DE, the storage, handling, and disposal of fuel, boiler water treatment chemicals, refrigerants, condenser water treatment chemicals, and chilled-water treatment chemicals can all be removed to the location of the central DE plants. Thus, the potential for related chemical spills, disruptions, and associated hazards are avoided within the occupied building environments.

Efficiency and Reliability

Central energy plants associated with DE systems, compared to the alternative of dispersed, multiple, smaller boilers and chiller plants within individual buildings, generally have higher levels of operational efficiency and reliability. This is because larger DE plants can more easily justify sophisticated design, automated optimized control systems, more attentive maintenance programs, and more highly trained and focused operations and maintenance personnel. Central energy plants are also better able to match the system load with central equipment vs. part load performance of multiple equipment throughout a campus.

Space Utilization and Aesthetics

By not needing heating and/or chilling plants in the buildings, DE systems provide improved space utilization for the occupants of the individual buildings. Also, there is no longer a need for local boiler exhaust stacks and/or for local chiller plant heat rejection via, for example, roof-mounted cooling towers. In addition to the improved aesthetics of having buildings without such stacks and towers, multiple and sometimes unsightly exhaust plumes from stacks and towers are also removed from the local building environment.

Other Factors for Consideration

District energy systems do require additional infrastructure (e.g., a piping distribution network from the central plant to the various buildings within the network). A full-fledged, life-cycle assessment of the net benefits from a DE system should take items including construction of the additional piping network and additional space requirements of distributed equipment into consideration.

Where DE Systems are Used

DE systems are routinely utilized on university campuses; DE systems are also often used for other institutional applications (including schools, hospital and medical facilities, airports, military installations, and other federal, state, and local government facilities), for privately owned multibuilding commercial/industrial facilities, and for thermal utilities serving urban business districts. DE systems serve as few as two buildings or as many as many hundreds of buildings. The ideal times to consider utilizing DE for serving the heating and/or cooling needs of a building are either during master planning and new construction or during expansion or renovation of buildings or their HVAC systems.

COOLING SYSTEM HEAT SINKS

Building HVAC systems exchange a significant amount of thermal energy between the building and the surrounding environment; that is their function. This chapter describes technical details of heating and cooling systems and their interaction with the environment as a heat source or heat sink.

Green design features are available that provide high energy efficiency but have the potential for adversely impacting the environment. For example, systems have been installed that use deep water in a lake or nearby ocean as a heat sink, which results in significant energy savings. This technique has been used in Scandinavian systems for approximately 20 years and more recently in colder regions in North America. The possible net energy savings are impressive, but these must be balanced against potential adverse impacts on local aquatic environments.

DISTRIBUTED ELECTRICITY GENERATION

One opportunity for energy conservation in buildings is the use of on-site generation systems to provide both distributed electric power and thermal energy (otherwise wasted heat from the generation process), which can be used to meet the thermal loads of the building.

Distributed generation (DG) provides electricity directly to the building's electrical systems to offset loads that would otherwise have to be met by the utility grid (see Figure 11-1). The waste heat from that generation process goes through a heat recovery mechanism where it may be provided as heat to meet loads for conventional heating (such as space heating, reheat, and domestic water heating) or for specialized processes. Alternatively, that heat energy, if at a sufficiently high temperature, can be used to power an absorption chiller to produce chilled water to meet either space-cooling or process-cooling loads. This is shown in Figure 11-2.

Any timing differences between the generation of the waste heat from the DG system and the thermal needs of the building can be handled utilizing a chilled-water TES system. This concept may also permit downsizing the absorption cooling system (so it does not need to be sized for the peak cooling load).

The overall usable energy value from the fuel input to the generation process is only about 30% (or less) if there is no waste heat recovery, but it can be more than 70% if most or all the waste heat is able to be utilized. This increased system efficiency can have a radical impact on the economics of the energy systems, because almost two-and-one-half times the useful value is obtained from the fossil fuel purchased. System sizing is generally done by evaluating the relative electrical and thermal loads over the course of the typical operating cycle and then selecting the system

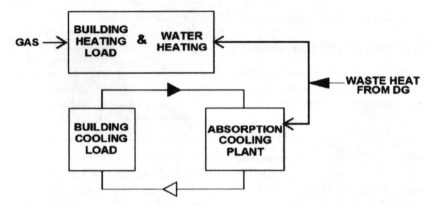

Figure 11-1 Thermal energy storage and waste heat usage.

capacity to meet the lesser of the thermal or electrical loads. See Figure 11-3 showing comparative thermal and electrical energy for typical office buildings.

If the DG system is sized for the greater of the two, then there will be a net waste of energy produced, since it is seldom economical to sell electricity back to the grid. A key design issue that arises here is whether or not the system is being designed to improve efficiency, as discussed above, or as a baseload on-site generation system for purposes of improving the reliability of the electric and/or thermal energy supply. Either of these is a legitimate design criterion, although the goal, from a green design standpoint, almost always focuses on the energy-efficient strategy.

DG Technologies

Technologies that can be used for this type of generation include engine-driven generators, microturbine-driven generators, or fuel cells. Typically, each uses natural gas as the input fuel. There are advantages and disadvantages associated with these technologies, which are summarized briefly in Table 11-2.

Engine-Driven Generator (EDG). This technology has been around the longest of the three and is in many ways the least-expensive option. It produces a relatively high temperature of waste heat that can be more effectively utilized by the heat recovery systems. Disadvantages, however, include air pollution, acoustical impacts, and noise/vibration from the engines. EDG sets are available in sizes ranging from approximately 40 kW to several thousand kW.

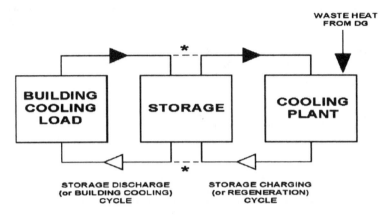

Image courtesy of Malcolm Lews, CTG Energetics, Inc.

Figure 11-2 Thermal uses of waste heat.

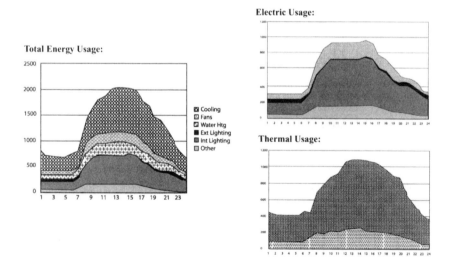

Image courtesy of Malcolm Lews, CTG Energetics, Inc.

Figure 11-3 Relationship between electric and thermal energy.

Table 11-2: Comparison of Power Generation Options

Generation Option	Efficiency (%)	Typical Size	Installed Costs ($/kW)	Operations and Maintenance Costs ($/kWh)	Life-Cycle Costs (assumes 20-year life cycle) ($/kWh)
Wind turbine	N/A	5–600 kW	$750–$1250	$0.001–$0.007	$0.036
Hybrid fuel cell—gas turbine with heat recovery	56%–80%	5–3 kW	$1300–$1500	$0.005–$0.010	$0.048
Natural gas cogen on site with heat recovery	40%–48%	30–300 kW	$600–$1000	$0.003–$0.010	$0.052
Natural gas power plant (combustion turbine)	28%–45%	500–150 kW	$600–$900	$0.003–$0.008	$0.052
Fuel cell without heat recovery	30%–60%	5–3 kW	$1900–$3500	$0.005–$0.010	$0.072
Natural gas cogen on site without heat recovery	20%–28%	30–300 kW	$600–$1000	$0.003–$0.010	$0.072
Photovoltaic	8%–13%	1–50 kW	$3500–$6000	$0.003–$0.005	$0.166

Note the following:
* Life-cycle costs assume the same cost for gas as for all technologies. Central technologies will likely have lower rates.
* As of summer 2010, hybrid fuel cell microturbine plants are just coming into production. Costs are estimated.

Microturbine Generator. At the moment, micro-turbine generators are somewhat more expensive in first cost than EDGs, but they have less air pollution and less severe acoustic and vibration impacts than EDGs. They also have longer operating lives and a projected lower cost. However, at the moment they are only available in sizes less than 100 kW per unit compared to EDGs, which can be up in the several-hundreds-per-unit range.

Fuel Cells. Fuel cells are the most advanced form of power generation in terms of being a clean and green technology. They generate virtually no air pollution, have minimal acoustic and vibration impacts, and are considered the wave of the future. At this point, however, the cost of fuel cell equipment is high, so it's the least attractive of these options, from an economic standpoint. It is anticipated that this will change as continued development of the technology evolves over the next several years.

CCHP Systems

Combined heating and power is also referred to as *cogeneration*, and when combined with cooling they are called *trigeneration*. The larger, industrial-scale versions of such integrated energy systems have been in use through most of the twentieth century. More recently, with the focus shifting to distributed power generation for the reasons cited above (and with the California energy crisis of 2000), a new scale of CCHP has emerged, involving more integrated design of the components. These CCHP systems typically consist of one of the DG technologies described above (e.g., reciprocating engines or microturbines [possibly fuel cells, in the future] fired by natural gas, a heat exchanger to recover heat from the exhaust stream and/or jacket water, and, if there is a cooling demand, an absorption chiller). An intermediate medium such as hot water can be used to transfer heat between the exhaust stream of the prime-mover and the chiller (Figure 11-4), but lately a lot of development has gone into a dedicated heat recovery unit that also forms the generator of the absorption chiller (Rosfjord et al. 2004). Such integrated energy systems are admittedly in their infancy in the United States, but there is a significant drive by organizations including the U.S. Department of Energy (DOE) toward commercializing these systems as packaged systems.

The traditional application of CHP has been to directly utilize the waste heat for space heating and/or domestic hot-water heating. Larger central CCHP facilities use the waste heat to produce space or process cooling. The former is put together of off-the-shelf equipment, while the latter follows an integrated design approach with a better opportunity at optimization.

To illustrate the benefits of the DG-based CCHP systems, the following elementary view of the energy efficiencies, both at the component and system level, is offered. A typical reciprocating gas-fired engine has a thermal efficiency of about 35%; 65% of the energy in the fuel is ordinarily not utilized and wasted through the stack. The exhaust temperatures leaving the engine (>500°F or 260°C) are typically high enough to drive, at the very least, a single-effect

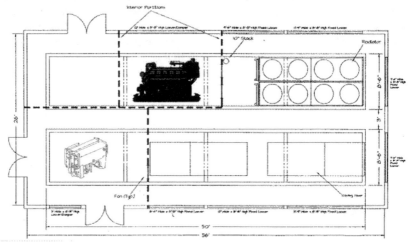

Image courtesy of Vikas Patnaik.

Figure 11-4 Schematic of actual CHP system consisting of a reciprocating engine and an indirect-fired absorption chiller, along with other ancillary equipment (Patnaik 2004).

absorption chiller with a coefficient of performance (COP) in the vicinity of 0.7. Factoring in the actual amount of available heat in the exhaust stream (temperature/enthalpy and flow rate), this translates to overall fuel utilization rates/efficiencies that are as high as 80%. The ratio of electrical to thermal load carrying capability shifts a bit when the prime mover is a microturbine or a fuel cell, with typical generation efficiencies being 25% (based on higher heating value) and 40%, respectively. However, the overall fuel utilization rate is relatively unchanged. The waste heat can also be directly utilized for desiccant dehumidification (regeneration).

So, the integrated energy systems have done the following:

- Brought the power generation closer to the point of application/load (through distributed generation), eliminating transmission and distribution losses, etc.

- Removed or reduced the normal electric and primary fuel consumption by independent pieces of equipment providing cooling, heating, and/or dehumidification (e.g., separate electric chiller and boiler), thereby substantially improving overall fuel utilization rates, inclusive of the power generation process.

- Removed or reduced emissions of CO_2 and other combustion by-products associated with the operation of the cooling, heating, and/or dehumidification equipment.

Challenges include the matching of electrical and thermal loads, given the diversity of energy usage patterns in buildings. The consultant/contractor can determine if the heating/cooling components of the CCHP system will play a primary or complementary role (the latter involving other, more conventional equipment to fill in the missing thermal load). Numerous studies were done in this regard, including one by William A. Ryan (Ryan 2003). Further resources are given in GreenTip #14.

WATER CONSUMPTION DUE TO COOLING SYSTEM OPERATION

Trade-offs between energy consumption and water consumption must be carefully considered. In many cases, site energy can be saved at the expense of using site water. Examples of this include using evaporative cooling compared with direct expansion cooling. Likewise, chillers with water-based cooling towers are more efficient than air-based systems—but this energy saving comes with using water. Further complicating the analysis, is that water does not arrive at the site without treating and pumping. Much of the electricity production is produced with thermal electric plants that use evaporative cooling for the condenser part of the Rankine cycle. As additional environmental pressures are applied, more power plants are using water evaporation through towers, rather than discharging the heat to rivers, lakes, and oceans. Even hydroelectric power plants evaporate water because of the large lake surface areas compared to free-running rivers.

We have just begun to understand these interactions and know that the numbers vary considerably by climate and location—many of the variations are because of variations in power plant designs. In the United States, a national average of 0.50 gal (1.9 L) of water is consumed for every kWh of electricity produced. An additional breakdown by region and for energy mixes is provided in Torcellini et al. (2004).

Because of the variations in climate and HVAC design, no rules of thumb exist to compare water and electrical consumption. Hourly computer simulations can be used to compare systems, with the water consumption calculated based on water and energy balances.

Other uses or sources of water should also be considered. For example, condensate from cooling coils can be collected and reused (see GreenTip #36 in Chapter 14). In some cases, blowdown from cooling towers can also be used, depending on the levels of dissolved solids and chemical treating.

ASHRAE
GreenTip #13

Pulse-Powered, Chemical-Free Water Treatment

TECHNOLOGY DESCRIPTION

Pulse-powered physical water treatment uses pulsed, electric fields (a technology developed by the food industry for pasteurization) to control scaling, biological growth, and corrosion. This chemical-free approach to water treatment eliminates environmental and health and safety issues associated with water treatment chemicals. Pulse-powered systems do not require pumps or chemical tanks. Pulse-powered systems tend to be forgiving of operational upsets and promote cooling tower operation at higher cycles of concentration (so there's less blowdown and less water usage) than standard chemical treatment. Independent studies have shown that not only is the method effective for cooling towers, the performance of pulse-powered systems is superior to standard chemical treatment in biological control and water usage. The performance results of pulse-powered technology for chemical-free water treatment, as documented by various independent evaluations, support the objectives of green buildings and have earned LEED points for certification in a number of projects.

WHEN/WHERE IT'S APPLICABLE

Pulse-powered technology is applicable on the recirculating lines of cooling towers, chillers, heat exchangers, boilers, evaporative condensers, fluid coolers, and fountains.

The technology produces a pulsed, time-varying, induced electric field inside a PVC pipe that is fit into the recirculating water system. The electric signal changes the way minerals in the water precipitate, totally avoiding hard-lime scale by instead producing a nonadherent mineral powder in the water that does not adhere. The powder is readily filterable and easily removed. Bacteria are encapsulated into this mineral powder and cannot reproduce, thereby resulting in low bacteria populations. The water chemistry maintained by pulse-powered technology is noncorrosive, since the water is operating at the saturation point of calcium carbonate (a cathodic corrosion-inhibiting environment). The low bacteria count and reduction or elimination of biofilm reduces concern about microbial influenced corrosion. The absence of aggressive oxidizing biocides eliminates the risk of other forms of corrosion.

PROS

1. The potential for lower bacterial contamination while providing scale and corrosion control.
2. Lower energy and water use than in traditional chemical treatment.
3. Blowdown water is environmentally benign and recyclable.
4. Potentially lower life-cycle cost savings compared to chemical treatment.
5. Reduction or elimination of biofilm.
6. Removes health and safety concerns about handling chemicals.
7. Eliminates the environmental impact of blowdown, air emissions, and drift from toxic chemicals.

CONS

1. It does not work effectively on very soft or distilled water, since the technology is based on changing the way minerals in the water precipitate.
2. Water with high chloride or silica content may limit the cycles of concentration obtainable to ensure optimum water savings, since the technology operates at the saturation point of calcium carbonate.
3. Energy usage is still required to operate.

KEY ELEMENTS OF COST

The following economic factors list the various cost elements associated with traditional chemical treatment that are avoided with chemical-free water treatment. This is a general assessment of what might be likely, but it may not be accurate in all situations. There is no substitute for a detailed cost analysis as part of the design process.

- *Direct Cost of Chemicals.* This item is the easiest to see and is sometimes considered the only cost. For cooling towers in the United States, this direct cost usually runs between $8.00 and $20.00 per ton ($2.27 and $5.69 per kWR) of cooling per year.

- *Water Softener.* Water softeners have direct additional costs for salt, media, equipment depreciation, maintenance, and direct labor.
- *Occupational Safety and Health Administration (OSHA) and General Environmental Requirements.* Many chemicals used to treat water systems are OSHA-listed hazardous materials. Employees in this field are required to have documented, annual training on what to do in the event of a chemical release or otherwise exposed contamination.
- *General Handling Issues.* Chemical tanks, barrels, salt bags, etc., take space. A typical chemical station requires 100 ft (9.3 m) of space.
- *Equipment Maintenance.* Lower overall maintenance for the systems as a whole may be possible.
- *Water Savings.* Cooling towers are often a facility's largest consumer of water. Most chemically controlled cooling towers operate at two to four cycles of concentration. Cycles of concentration can often be changed to six to eight cycles with chemical-free technology, with an annual reduction in water usage costs and the associated environmental impacts.
- *Energy Savings.* Energy is required to operate the pulse-powered system, but overall energy usage can be lower. The reduction or elimination of biofilm (a slime layer in a cooling tower) results in energy savings vs. chemical treatment due to improved heat transfer. Biofilm has a heat transfer resistance that is four times that of scale and is also the breeding ground for Legionella amplification. Thus, preventing this amplification saves money.

SOURCES OF FURTHER INFORMATION

Bisbee, D. 2003. Pulse-power water treatment systems for cooling towers. Energy Efficiency & Customer Research & Development, Sacramento Municipal Utility District.

PG&E. 2002. *Codes and Standards Enhancement Report, Code Change Proposal for Cooling Towers.* California: Pacific Gas & Electric.

HPAC. 2004. Innovative grocery store seeks LEED certification. *HPAC Engineering* 27:31.

Torcellini, P.A., N. Long, and R. Judkoff. 2004. Consumptive water use for U.S. power production. *ASHRAE Transactions* 110(1):96–100.

Trane. 2005. *Trane Installation, Operation, and Maintenance Manual: Series R® Air-Cooled Rotary Liquid Chillers*, RTAA-SVX01A-EN. Lacrosse, WI: Trane Company. www.trane.com/Commercial/Uploads/Pdf/1060/RTAA-SVX01A-EN_09012005.pdf.

ASHRAE
GreenTip #14

CHP Systems

GENERAL DESCRIPTION

Other abbreviations that have been used to describe such integrated energy systems are CCHP (includes *cooling*) and BCHP (building cooling, heating, and power). The goal, regardless of the abbreviation, is to improve system efficiencies or source fuel utilization by availing of the low-grade heat that is a by-product of the power generation process for heating and/or cooling duty. Fuel utilization efficiencies as high as 80% were reported (Adamson 2002). The resulting savings in operating costs, relative to a conventional system, are then viewed against the first cost, and simple payback periods of less than four years have been anticipated (LeMar 2002). This is particularly important, from a marketing perspective, for both the distributed-generation and the thermal equipment provider. This is because, by themselves, a microturbine manufacturer and an absorption chiller manufacturer, for example, would find it difficult to compete with a utility and an electric chiller manufacturer, respectively, as the provider of low-cost power and cooling. Last, but by no means least, the higher (fossil-)fuel utilization rates result in reduced emissions of CO_2, the greenhouse gas with a more than 55% contribution to global warming (Houghton et al. 1990).

Gas engines, microturbines, and fuel cells have been at the center of CHP activity as the need for reliable power and/or grid independence has recently become evident. These devices are also being promoted to reduce the need for additional central-station peaking power plants. As would be expected, however, they come at a first cost premium, which can range from $1000 to $4000/kW (Ellis and Gunes 2002). At the same time, operating (thermal) efficiencies have remained in the vicinity of those of the large, centralized power plants, even after the transmission and distribution losses are taken into account. This is particularly true of engines and microturbines (which have a 25% to 35% thermal efficiency), while fuel cells promise higher efficiencies (of ~50%), albeit at the higher cost premiums ($3000 to $4000/kW).

On the thermal side, standard gas-to-liquid or gas-to-gas heat exchanger equipment can be used for the heating component of the CHP system. This transfers the heat from the exhaust gases to the process/hydronic fluid or air, respectively. For the cooling component, the size ranges of distributed power generators offer a unique advantage, in terms of flexibility, in the selection of the chiller equipment. These can be smaller-end (relative to commercial), water-lithium bromide single- or double-effect absorption chillers or larger-end (relative to residential) single-effect or generator-absorber heat exchange ammonia-water absorption chillers (Erickson and Rane 1994). Such chillers have a typical coefficiency of performance of 0.7, and, as a rule of thumb, for thermal-to-electrical load matching, for every 4 kW of power generated, 1 ton of cooling may be achieved (Patnaik 2004). Figure 11-5 illustrates typical operating conditions that an absorption chiller would see with a reciprocating engine.

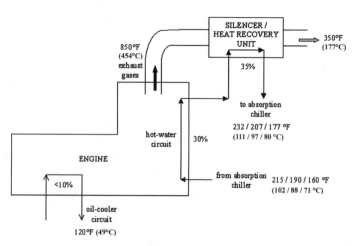

Image courtesy of Vikas Patnaik.

Figure 11-5 Schematic of CHP system consisting of a gas-fired reciprocating engine showing typical operating temperatures (Patnaik 2004).

WHEN/WHERE IT'S APPLICABLE

CHP is particularly suited for applications involving distributed power generation. Buildings requiring their own power generation, either due to a stringent power reliability and/or quality requirement or remoteness of location, must also satisfy various thermal loads (i.e., space heating or cooling, water heating, dehumidification). A conventional fossil-fuel-fired boiler and/or electric chiller can be displaced, to some extent if not entirely, by a heat recovery device (e.g., standard heat exchanger) and/or an absorption chiller driven by the waste heat from the power generator. Since the source of heating and/or cooling is waste heat that would ordinarily have been rejected to the surroundings, the operating cost of meeting the thermal demand of the building is significantly mitigated if not eliminated.

Economic analyses suggest that CHP systems are ideally suited for base-loaded distributed power generation and steady thermal (heating and/or cooling) loading. This is also the desirable mode of operation for the absorption chiller. Peak-loading is then met by utility power. Alternatively, if utility power is used for base-loading and the DG meets the peaking demand, the thermal availability may be intermittent and require frequent cycling of the primary thermal equipment (i.e., the boiler and/or chiller).

PROS

- One of the primary advantages of CHP systems is the reduction in centralized (utility) peak-load generating capacity. This is especially true, because one of the biggest contributors to summer peak loads is the demand for air conditioning. If some of this air-conditioning demand can be met by chillers fired by essentially free energy (waste heat), there is a double benefit.
- Additionally, DG-based CHP systems enable the following:
  - They bring the power generation closer to the point of application/load (i.e., distributed generation), eliminating transmission and distribution losses, etc.
  - They remove or reduce the normal electric and primary fuel consumption by independent pieces of equipment providing cooling, heating, and/or dehumidification (e.g., a separate electric chiller and boiler), thereby substantially improving overall fuel utilization rates, inclusive of the power generation process.

- They remove or reduce emissions of CO_2 and other combustion by-products associated with the operation of the cooling, heating, and/or dehumidification equipment.

CONS

- If the CHP system is to replace a conventional boiler/electric chiller system, the ratio of electrical to thermal load of the building must closely match the relative performance (i.e., efficiencies) of the respective equipment.
- Start-up times for absorption chillers are relatively longer than those for vapor-compression chillers, particularly when coupled to microturbines, which themselves have large time constants. Such systems would require robust and sophisticated controls that take these transients into account.

KEY ELEMENTS OF COST

The following provides a possible breakdown of the various cost elements that might differentiate a CHP system from a conventional one and an indication of whether the net cost for the alternative system is likely to be lower (L), higher (H), or the same (S). This assessment is only a perception of what might be likely, but it obviously may not be correct in all situations. There is no substitute for a detailed cost analysis as part of the design process. The listings below may also provide some assistance in identifying the cost elements involved.

First Cost

- Distributed power generator   H
- Heat recovery device/heat exchanger   L
- Absorption chiller   H
- Integrating control system   H

Recurring Costs

- Distributed power generator
  (engine/microturbine/fuel cell)   S/H/L
- Heat recovery device/heat exchanger   None
- Absorption chiller   None
- Integrating control system   H

SOURCES OF FURTHER INFORMATION

In keeping with the spirit of overlapping themes being promoted by ASHRAE, a number of technical sessions in recent meetings have been devoted to CHP, generally sponsored by technical committees on cogeneration systems (TC 1.10) and absorption/sorption heat pumps and refrigeration systems (TC 8.3). Presentations from these should be available on the ASHRAE Web site. The following is a link to recently sponsored programs by TC 8.3, including a couple of viewable presentations: http://tc83.ashraetcs.org/programs.html.

REFERENCES

Adamson, R. 2002. Mariah Heat Plus Power™ Packaged CHP, applications and economics. Second Annual DOE/CETC/CANDRA Workshop on Microturbine Applications, January 17–18, University of Maryland, College Park, MD.

Ellis, M.W., and M.B. Gunes. 2002. Status of fuel cell systems for combined heat and power applications in buildings. *ASHRAE Transactions* 108(1):1032–44.

Erickson, D.C., and M. Rane. 1994. Advanced absorption cycle: Vapor exchange GAX. ASME International Absorption Heat Pump Conference, January 19–21, New Orleans, LA.

Houghton, J.T., G.J. Jenkins, and J.J. Ephraums, eds. 1990. *Climate Change: The IPCC Scientific Assessment.* Intergovernmental Panel on Climate Change. New York: Cambridge UP.

LeMar, P. 2002. Integrated energy systems (IES) for buildings: A market assessment. Final report by Resource Dynamics Corporation for Oak Ridge National Laboratory, Contract No. DE-AC05-00OR22725.

Patnaik, V. 2004. Experimental verification of an absorption chiller for BCHP applications. *ASHRAE Transactions* 110(1):503–507.

ASHRAE
GreenTip # 15

Low-NO$_x$ Burners

GENERAL DESCRIPTION

Low-NO$_x$ burners are natural gas burners with improved energy efficiency and lower emissions of NO$_x$. When fossil fuels are burned, nitric oxide and nitrogen dioxide are produced. These pollutants initiate reactions that result in the production of ozone and acid rain. The NO$_x$ come from two sources: high-temperature combustion (thermal NO$_x$) and nitrogen bound to the fuel (fuel NO$_x$). For clean-burning fuels such as natural gas, fuel NO$_x$ generation is insignificant.

In most cases, NO$_x$ levels are reduced by lowering flame temperature. This can be accomplished by modifying the burner to create a larger (and therefore lower temperature) flame, injecting water or steam into the flame, recirculating flue gases, or limiting the excess air in the combustion process. In many cases a combination of these approaches is used. In general, reducing the flame temperature will reduce the overall efficiency of the boiler. However, recirculating flue gases and controlling the air-fuel mixture can improve boiler efficiency so that a combination of techniques may improve total boiler efficiency.

Natural-gas-fired burners with lowered NO$_x$ emissions are available for commercial and residential heating applications. One commercial/residential boiler has a burner with inserts above the individual burners; this design reduces NO$_x$ emissions by 30%. The boiler also has a wet base heat exchanger to capture more of the burner heat and reduce heat loss to flooring.

NO$_x$ production is of special concern in industrial high-temperature processes, because thermal NO$_x$ production increases with temperature. Processes include metal processing, glass manufacturing, pulp and paper mills, and cement kilns. Although natural gas is the cleanest-burning fossil fuel, it can produce emissions as high as 100 ppm or more.

A burner developed by the Massachusetts Institute of Technology and the Gas Research Institute combines staged-introduction combustion air, flue gas recirculation, and integral reburning to control NO$_x$ emissions. These improvements in burner design result in a low-temperature, fuel-rich primary zone, followed by a low-temperature, lean secondary zone; these low temperatures result in lower NO$_x$ formation.

In addition, any NO_x emission present in the recirculated flue gas is

reburned, further reducing emissions. A jet pump recirculates a large volume of flue gas to the burner; this reduces NO_x emissions and improves heat transfer.

The low-NO_x burner used for commercial and residential space heating is larger in size than conventional burners, although it is designed for ease of installation.

WHEN/WHERE IT'S APPLICABLE

Low NO_x burners are best applied in regions where air quality is affected by high ground-level ozone and where required by law.

PROS

- Lowers NO_x and CO emissions, where that is an issue.
- Increases energy efficiency.

CONS

- High cost.
- Higher maintenance.

KEY ELEMENTS OF COST

The following provides a possible breakdown of the various cost elements that might differentiate a low-NO_x system from a conventional one and an indication of whether the net cost for the alternative system is likely to be lower (L), higher (H), or the same (S). This is only a perception of what might be likely, but it may not be correct in all situations. There is no substitute for a detailed cost analysis as part of the design process. The listings below may provide some assistance in identifying the cost elements involved.

First Cost

- Conventional burner   L
- Low NO_x burner   H

Recurring Costs

- Maintenance   H
- Possible avoidance of pollution fines   L

SOURCE OF FURTHER INFORMATION

American Gas Association
    www.aga.org

ASHRAE
GreenTip # 16

Combustion Air Preheating

GENERAL DESCRIPTION

For fuel-fired heating equipment, one of the most potent ways to improve efficiency and productivity is to preheat the combustion air going to the burners. The source of this heat energy is the exhaust gas stream, which leaves the process at elevated temperatures. A heat exchanger, placed in the exhaust stack or ductwork, can extract a large portion of the thermal energy in the flue gases and transfer it to the incoming combustion air.

With natural gas, it is estimated that for each 50°F (10°C) the combustion air is preheated, overall boiler efficiency increases by approximately 1%. This provides a high leverage boiler plant efficiency measure, because increasing boiler efficiency also decreases boiler fuel usage. And, since combustion airflow decreases along with fuel flow, there is a reduction in fan-power usage as well.

There are two types of air preheaters: recuperators and regenerators. Recuperators are gas-to-gas heat exchangers placed on the furnace stack. Internal tubes or plates transfer heat from the outgoing exhaust gas to the incoming combustion air while keeping the two streams from mixing. Regenerators include two or more separate heat storage sections. Flue gases and combustion air take turns flowing through each regenerator, alternatively heating the storage medium and then withdrawing heat from it. For uninterrupted operation, at least two regenerators and their associated burners are required: one regenerator is needed to fire the furnace while the other is recharging.

WHEN/WHERE IT'S APPLICABLE

While theoretically any boiler can use combustion preheating, flue temperature is customarily used as a rough indication of when it will be cost-effective. However, boilers or processes with low flue temperatures but a high exhaust gas flow may still be good candidates and must be evaluated on a case-by-case basis. Financial justification is based on energy saved rather than on temperature differential. Some processes produce dirty or corrosive exhaust gases that can plug or attack an exchanger, so material selection is critical.

PROS

- Lowers energy costs.
- Increasing thermal efficiency lowers CO_2 emissions.

CONS

- There are additional material and equipment costs.
- Corrosion and condensation can add to maintenance costs.
- Low specific heat of air results in relatively low U-factors and less economical heat exchangers.
- Increasing combustion temperature also increases NO_x emissions.

KEY ELEMENTS OF COST

The following provides a possible breakdown of the various cost elements that might differentiate a building with a combustion pre-heat system from one without and an indication of whether the net cost is likely to be lower (L), higher (H), or the same (S). This assessment is only a perception of what might be likely, but it obviously may not be correct in all situations. There is no substitute for a detailed cost analysis as part of the design process. The listings below may also provide some assistance in identifying the cost elements involved.

First Cost

• Equipment costs	H
• Controls	S
• Design fees	H

Recurring Costs

• Overall energy cost	L
• Maintenance of system	H
• Training of building operators	H

SOURCES OF FURTHER INFORMATION

DOE. 2002. *Energy Tip Sheet #1*, May. U.S. Department of Energy, Office of Industrial Technologies, Energy Efficiency, and Renewable Energy, Washington, D.C.

Fiorino, D.P. 2000. Six conservation and efficiency measures reducing steam costs. *ASHRAE Journal* 42(2):31–39.

ASHRAE
GreenTip #17

Combination Space/Water Heaters

GENERAL DESCRIPTION

Combination space and water heating systems consist of a storage water heater, a heat delivery system (e.g., a fan coil or hydronic baseboards), and associated pumps and controls. Typically gas-fired, they provide both space and domestic water heating. The water heater is installed and operated as a conventional water heater. When there is a demand for domestic hot water, cold city water enters the bottom of the tank, and hot water from the top of the tank is delivered to the load. When there is a demand for space heating, a pump circulates water from the top of the tank through fan coils or hydronic baseboards.

The storage tank is maintained at the desired temperature for domestic hot water (e.g., 140°F [60°C]). Because this temperature is cooler than conventional hydronic systems, the space heating delivery system needs to be slightly larger than typical. Alternatively, the storage tank can be operated at a higher water temperature; this requires tempering valves to prevent scalding at the taps.

The water heater can be either a conventional storage-type water heater (either naturally venting or power vented) or a recuperative (condensing) gas boiler. Conventional water heaters have an efficiency of approximately 60%. By adding the space heating load, the energy factor increases because of longer runtimes and reduced standby losses on a percentage basis. Recuperative boilers can have efficiencies approaching 90%.

WHEN/WHERE IT'S APPLICABLE

These units are best suited to buildings that have similar space and water heating loads including dormitories, apartments, and condos. They are suited to all climate types.

PROS

- Reduces floor space requirements.
- Lowers capital cost.
- Improves energy efficiency.
- Increases tank life.

CONS

- They are only available in small sizes.
- All space heating piping has to be designed for potable water.
- No ferrous metals or lead-based solder can be used.
- All components must be able to withstand prevailing city water pressures.

KEY ELEMENTS OF COST

The following provides a possible breakdown of the various cost elements that might differentiate a combination space and water heating system from a conventional one and an indication of whether the net cost for the hybrid option is likely to be lower (L), higher (H), or the same (S). This assessment is only a perception of what might be likely, but it obviously may not be correct in all situations. There is no substitute for a detailed cost analysis as part of the design process. The listings below may also provide some assistance in identifying the cost elements involved.

First Cost

- Conventional heating equipment   L
- Combination space/domestic water heater   H
- Sanitizing/inspecting space heating system   H
- Piping and components able to withstand higher pressures   H
- Floor space used   L

Recurring Costs

- Heating energy   L
- Maintenance   L

SOURCES OF FURTHER INFORMATION

Sustainable Sources
    www.greenbuilder.com
UG. 2010. Wise Energy Guide. Chatham, ON: Union Gas. www.uniongas.com/residential/energyconservation/education/ wiseEnergyGuide/WEG_Booklet_Web_Final.pdf/.
U.S. Department of Energy, Energy Efficiency and Renewable Energy www.eere.energy.gov/

ASHRAE
GreenTip #18

Ground-Source Heat Pumps (GSHPs)

GENERAL DESCRIPTION

A GSHP extracts solar heat stored in the upper layers of the earth; the heat is then delivered to a building. Conversely, in the summer season, the heat pump rejects heat removed from the building into the ground rather than into the atmosphere or a body of water.

GSHPs can reduce the energy required for space heating, cooling, and service water heating in commercial/institutional buildings by as much as 50%. GSHPs replace the need for a boiler in winter by utilizing heat stored in the ground; this heat is upgraded by a vapor-compressor refrigeration cycle. In summer, heat from a building is rejected to the ground. This eliminates the need for a cooling tower or heat rejector and also lowers operating costs, because the ground is cooler than the outdoor air. (See Figure 11-6 for an example of a GSHP system.)

There are numerous types of GSHP loop systems. Each has its advantages and disadvantages. Visit the Geoexchange Geothermal Heat Pump Consortium Web site (www.geoexchange.org/about/how.htm) for a more detailed description of the loop options.

Water-to-air heat pumps are typically installed throughout a building with ductwork serving only the immediate zone; a two-pipe water distribution system conveys water to and from the ground-source heat exchanger. The heat exchanger field consists of a grid of vertical boreholes with plastic U-tube heat exchangers connected in parallel.

Simultaneous heating and cooling can occur throughout the building, as individual heat pumps, controlled by zone thermostats, can operate in heating or cooling mode as required.

Unlike conventional boiler/cooling, tower-type, water-loop heat pumps, the heat pumps used in GSHP applications are generally designed to operate at lower inlet water temperature. GSHPs are also more efficient than conventional heat pumps, with higher COPs and energy efficiency ratios. Because there are lower water temperatures in the two-pipe loop, piping needs to be insulated to prevent sweating. In addition, a larger circulation pump is needed because the units are slightly larger in the perimeter zones, requiring larger flows.

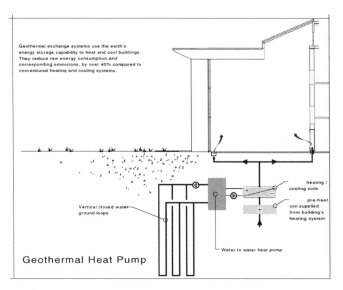

Image courtesy of Buro Happold.

Figure 11-6 Schematic example of GSHP closed-loop system.

GSHPs reduce energy use and, hence, atmospheric emissions. Conventional boilers and their associated emissions are eliminated, since no supplementary form of energy is usually required. Typically, single-packaged heat pump units have no field refrigerant connections and have significantly lower refrigerant leakage compared to central chiller systems.

GSHP units have life spans of 20 years or more. The two-pipe water-loop system typically used allows for unit placement changes to accommodate new tenants or changes in building use. The plastic piping used in the heat exchanger should last as long as the building itself.

When the system is disassembled, attention must be given to the removal and recycling of the hydrochlorofluorocarbons or hydrofluorocarbon (HFC) refrigerants used in the heat pumps and the antifreeze solution typically used in the ground heat exchanger.

WHEN/WHERE IT'S APPLICABLE

The most economical application of GSHPs is in buildings that require significant space/water heating and cooling over extended hours of operation. Examples are retirement communities, multifamily complexes, large office buildings, retail shopping malls, and schools. Building types not well-suited to the technology are buildings where space and water heating loads are relatively small or where hours of use are limited.

PROS

- Requires less mechanical room space.
- Requires less outdoor equipment.
- Does not require roof penetrations, maintenance decks, or architectural blends.
- Relatively little operational noise.
- Reduces operation and maintenance costs.
- Requires simple controls only.
- Requires less space in ceilings.
- Loop piping, carrying low-temperature water, does not have to be insulated.
- Installation costs are lower than for many central HVAC systems.

CONS

- Requires surface area for heat exchanger field.
- Higher initial cost.
- Requires additional site coordination and supervision.

KEY ELEMENTS OF COST

The following provides a possible breakdown of the various cost elements that might differentiate a GSHP system from a conventional one and an indication of whether the net cost for it is likely to be lower (L), higher (H), or the same (S). This assessment is only a perception of what might be likely, but it obviously may not be correct in all situations. There is no substitute for a detailed cost analysis as part of the design process. The listings may also provide some assistance in identifying the cost elements involved.

First Cost

- Conventional heating/cooling generators   L
- Heat pumps   H
- Outside piping system   H
- Heat exchanger field   H
- Operator training   H
- Design fees   H

Recurring Costs

- Energy cost (fossil fuel for conventional)   L
- Energy cost (electricity for heat pumps)   H
- Maintenance   L

SOURCES OF FURTHER INFORMATION

ASHRAE. 1995. *Commercial/Institutional Ground-Source Heat Pump Engineering Manual*. Atlanta: American Society of Heating, Refrigerating and Air-Conditioning Engineers, Inc.

Earth Energy Society of Canada
www.earthenergy.ca

Kavanaugh, S.P., and K. Rafferty. 1997. *Ground-Source Heat Pumps: Design of Geothermal Systems for Commercial and Institutional Buildings*. Atlanta: American Society of Heating, Refrigerating and Air-Conditioning Engineers, Inc.

Natural Resources Canada, RETScreen
(software for renewable energy analysis)
www.retscreen.net

ASHRAE
GreenTip #19

Water-Loop Heat Pump Systems

GENERAL DESCRIPTION

A water-loop heat pump system consists of multiple water-source heat pumps serving local areas within a building that are tied into a neutral-temperature (usually 60°F to 90°F [15.5°C to 32°C]) water loop that serves as both heat source and heat sink. The loop is connected to a central heat source (e.g., a small boiler) and a central heat dissipation device (e.g., a closed-circuit evaporative condenser or open-circuit cooling tower isolated from the building loop via the heat exchanger). These operate to keep the temperature of the loop water within range.

The water-source heat pump itself is an electric-driven, self-contained, water-cooled heating and cooling unit with a reversible refrigerant cycle (i.e., a water-cooled air-conditioning unit that can run in reverse). Its components include a heat exchanger, heating/cooling coil, compressor, fan, and reversing controls, all in a common casing. The heat exchanger and coil are designed to accept hot and cold refrigerant liquid or gas. The units can be located either within the space (e.g., low, along the outside wall) or remotely (e.g., in a ceiling plenum or in a separate nearby mechanical room).

Piping all of the water-to-refrigerant heat exchangers together in a common loop yields what is essentially an internal source heat recovery system. In effect, the system is capable of recovering heat energy (through the cooling process) and redistributing it where it is needed.

During the cooling mode, heat energy is extracted from room air circulated across the coil (just like a room air conditioner) and rejected to the water loop. In this mode, the unit's heat exchanger acts as a condenser and the coil as an evaporator. In the heating mode, the process is reversed: specifically, a reversing valve allows the heat exchanger to function as the evaporator and the coil as the condenser so that heat extracted from the water loop is rejected to the air being delivered to the occupied space, thus heating the space.

In addition to the components mentioned above, the system includes equipment and specialties normally associated with a closed hydronic system (e.g., pumps, filters, air separator, expansion tank, makeup system, etc.)

WHEN/WHERE IT'S APPLICABLE

A water-source heat pump system is well qualified for applications where simultaneous heating and cooling needs/opportunities exist. (An example might be a building where, in certain seasons, south-side or interior rooms need cooling at the same time north-side rooms require heating.) Appropriate applications may include office buildings, hotels, schools, apartments, extended care facilities, and retail stores.

The system's characteristics may make it particularly suitable when a building is to be air conditioned in stages, perhaps due to cost constraints. Once the basic system is in, additional heat pumps can be added as needed and tied into the loop. Further, since it uses low-temperature water, this system is an ideal candidate for mating with a hydronic solar collection system (since solar hydronic systems are more efficient when generating lower water temperatures).

PROS

- It can make use of energy that would otherwise be rejected to the atmosphere.
- Loop piping, carrying low-temperature water, does not have to be insulated.
- When applied correctly, the system can save energy. (Note: that some factors tend to decrease energy cost, and some tend to increase it, which prevails will determine whether savings result.)
- It is quieter than a system utilizing air-cooled condensers (e.g., through-the-wall room air conditioners).
- Failure of one heat pump unit does not affect others.
- It can condition (heat or cool) local areas of a building without having to run the entire system.

CONS

- Multiple compressors located throughout a building can be a maintenance concern because of their being noncentralized and sometimes difficult to access (e.g., above the ceiling).
- Effective water filtration is critical to proper operation of heat exchangers.

- There is an increased potential for noise within the conditioned space from heat pump units.
- Some of the energy used in the heating cycle is derived from electricity (used to drive the heat pump compressors), which may be more expensive than energy derived from fossil fuel.

KEY ELEMENTS OF COST

The following provides a possible breakdown of the various cost elements that might differentiate a water-loop heat pump system from a conventional one and an indication of whether the net incremental cost for the alternative option is likely to be lower (L), higher (H), or the same (S). This assessment is only a perception of what might be likely, but it obviously may not be correct in all situations. There is no substitute for a detailed cost analysis as part of the design process. The listings below may also provide some assistance in identifying the cost elements involved.

First Cost

- Equipment costs (will vary depending on what type of conventional system would otherwise be used)   S/L
- Controls   S
- Design fees   S

Recurring Costs

- Overall energy costs   L
- Maintenance of system   H
- Training of building operators   H

SOURCES OF FURTHER INFORMATION

Tri-State Generation and Transmission Association, Inc.
    http://www.tristategt.org/
Trane. 1994. *Trane Water-Source Heat Pump System Design Application Engineering Manual,* SYS-AM-7. Lacrosse, WI: Trane Company.

ASHRAE
GreenTip #20

TES for Cooling

GENERAL DESCRIPTION

There are several suitable media for storage of cooling energy, including:

* Chilled water
* Ice
* Calcium chloride solutions (brine)
* Glycol solutions
* Concentrated desiccant solutions

Active thermal storage systems utilize a building's cooling equipment to remove heat, usually at night, from an energy storage medium for later use as a source of cooling. The most common energy storage media are ice and chilled water. These systems decouple the production of cooling from the demand for cooling, (i.e., the plant output does not have to match the instantaneous building cooling load). This decoupling increases flexibility in design and operations, thereby providing an opportunity for a more efficient air-conditioning system than with a nonstorage alternative. Before applying active thermal storage, however, the design cooling load should be minimized.

Although many operating strategies are possible, the basic principle of a TES system is to reduce peak building cooling loads by shifting a portion of peak cooling production to times when the building cooling load is lower. Energy is typically charged, stored, and discharged on a daily or weekly cycle. The net result is an opportunity to run a chiller plant at peak efficiency during the majority of its operating period. A nonstorage system, on the other hand, has to follow the building cooling load, and the majority of its operation is at part-load conditions. Part-load operation of chiller plants comes at the expense of efficiency.

Several buildings have demonstrated site energy reductions with the application of TES, as discussed in both the "Pros" and "Sources of Further Information" sections that follow.

In addition to the potential for site energy reduction, operation of TES systems can reduce energy resource consumption. This reduction is due to a shift toward using energy during periods of low aggregate electric utility demand. As a result, transmission and distribution losses are lower and power plant generating efficiencies can be higher because the load is served by base-load plants. Thermal storage can also have beneficial effects on CHP systems by flattening thermal and electric load profiles.

The ASHRAE *Design Guide for Cool Thermal Storage* (Dorgan and Elleson 1993) covers cool storage application issues and design parameters in some detail.

WHEN/WHERE IT'S APPLICABLE

TES systems tend to perform well in situations where there is variability in loads. Successful applications of TES systems have included commercial office buildings, schools, worship facilities, convention centers, hotels, health care facilities, industrial processes, and turbine inlet air cooling.

PROS

- Because TES allows downsizing the refrigeration system, the resulting cost savings (which may include avoiding having to add such equipment on an existing project) may substantially or entirely cover the added incremental cost of the storage system proper (also see the first con in the next section). However, if the first cost is more than another design option, there are still life-cycle cost benefits due to a significant reduction in utility costs.
- The addition of a TES system allows the size of refrigerating equipment to be reduced, since it will have to meet an average cooling load rather than the peak cooling load. Reduced refrigeration equipment size means less on-site refrigerant usage and a lower probability of environmental impacts due to direct effects.
- Because TES allows operation of the refrigeration system at or near peak efficiency during all operating hours, the annual energy usage may be lower than nonstorage systems that must operate at lower part-load ratios to meet instantaneous loads. In addition, since off-peak hours are usually at night when lower ambient temperatures prevail, lower condensing temperatures

required for heat rejection would tend to increase refrigeration efficiency. A number of carefully documented examples of energy savings can be found in the literature, including Bahnfleth and Joyce (1994), Fiorino (1994), and Goss et al. (1996).

- Because TES systems shift the consumption of site energy from on-peak to off-peak periods, the total energy resources required to deliver cooling to the facility will be lower (Reindl et al. 1995; Gansler et al. 2001). In addition, in some electric grids, the last generation plants to be used to meet peak loads may be the most polluting per kW of energy produced (Gupta 2002). In such cases, emissions would be further reduced by the use of TES.
- TES enables the practical incorporation of other high-efficiency technologies such as cold-air distribution systems and nighttime heat recovery.
- TES can be effective at preventing or delaying the need to construct additional power generation and transmission equipment.
- Liquid desiccant can be circulated in plastic pipes and does not need insulation.

CONS

- Compared to a conventional system, the thermal storage element proper (i.e., the water tank or ice tank) and any associated pumping, piping accessories, and controls add to the incremental capital cost. If the system's refrigeration equipment can be reduced in size sufficiently (see the first pro listed in the previous section), this burden may be mitigated substantially or balanced out.
- The need to generate cooling at evaporator temperatures lower than conventional ones tends to decrease refrigeration efficiency. This reduction may be overcome, however, by factors that increase efficiency (see the third pro).
- Successful TES systems require additional efforts in the design phase of a project.
- TES systems will require increased site space usage. The impact of site space usage can be mitigated by considering ice storage technologies.
- Because a thermal storage system departs from the norm of system operation, continued training of facility operations staff is required, as are procedures for propagating system knowledge through a succession of facilities personnel.

- Ice requires special control of the melt rate to prevent uneven melting and to maximize performance.
- Calcium chloride brine needs management to prevent corrosion. Glycol needs management to prevent corrosion and toxicity.
- Liquid desiccant needs small resistant heating to be above 77°F (25°C) to prevent crystallization (similar to compressor sumps to prevent condensation).

KEY ELEMENTS OF COST

The following provides a possible breakdown of the various cost elements that might differentiate a TES system above from a conventional one and an indication of whether the net cost for the alternative option is likely to be lower (L), higher (H), or the same (S). This assessment is only a perception of what might be likely, but it obviously may not be correct in all situations. There is no substitute for a detailed cost analysis as part of the design process. The listings below may also provide some assistance in identifying the cost elements involved.

First Cost

- Storage element (e.g., chilled water, ice, glycol, and brine tanks) (Desiccant cost is higher than chilled water and brine but similar to glycol)   H
- Additional pumping/piping re-storage element   H
- Chiller/heat rejection system   L
- Controls   H
- Electrical (regarding chiller/heat rejection system)   S/L
- Design fees   H
- Operator training   H
- Commissioning   S/H
- Site space   H

Recurring Costs

- Electric energy   L
- Gas supply with low electrical demand   H
- Operator training (ongoing)   H
- Maintenance training   L

SOURCES OF FURTHER INFORMATION

Bahnfleth, W.P., and W.S. Joyce. 1994. Energy use in a district cooling system with stratified chilled water storage. *ASHRAE Transactions* 100(1):1767–78.

CEC. 1996. Source energy and environmental impacts of thermal energy storage. Completed by Tabors, Caramanis & Assoc. for the California Energy Commission.

Dorgan, C., and J.S. Elleson. 1993. *Cool Storage Design Guide.* Atlanta: American Society of Heating, Refrigerating and Air-Conditioning Engineers, Inc.

Duffy, G. 1992. Thermal storage shifts to saving energy. *Eng. Sys.* July/August: 32–38.

Elleson, J.S. 1996. *Successful Cool Storage Projects: From Planning to Operation.* Atlanta: American Society of Heating, Refrigerating and Air-Conditioning Engineers, Inc.

Fiorino, D.P. 1994. Energy conservation with stratified chilled water storage. *ASHRAE Transactions* 100(1):1754–66.

Galuska, E.J. 1994. Thermal storage system reduces costs of manufacturing facility (Technology Award case study). *ASHRAE Journal*, March.

Gansler, R.A., D.T. Reindl, T.B. Jekel. 2001. Simulation of source energy utilization and emissions for HVAC systems. *ASHRAE Transactions* 107(1):39–51.

Goss, J.O., L. Hyman, and J. Corbett. 1996. Integrated heating, cooling and thermal energy storage with heat pump provides economic and environmental solutions at California State University, Fullerton. *Proceedings of the EPRI International Conference on Sustainable Thermal Energy Storage, Minneapolis, MN,* pp. 163–67.

Lawson, S.H. 1988. Computer facility keeps cool with ice storage. *HPAC* 60(88):35–44.

Mathaudhu, S.S. 1999. Energy conservation showcase. *ASHRAE Journal* 41(4):44–46.

O'Neal, E.J. 1996. Thermal storage system achieves operating and first-cost savings (Technology Award case study). *ASHRAE Journal* 38(4).

Reindl, D.T., D.E. Knebel, and R.A. Gansler. 1995. Characterising the marginal basis source energy and emissions associated with comfort cooling systems. *ASHRAE Transactions* 101(1):1353–63.

ASHRAE
GreenTip #21

Double-Effect Absorption Chillers

GENERAL DESCRIPTION

Chilled-water systems that use fuel types other than electricity can help offset high electric prices, whether those high prices are caused by consumption or demand charges. Absorption chillers use thermal energy (rather than electricity) to produce chilled water. A double-effect absorption chiller using high-pressure steam (115 psig [793 kPa]) has a COP of approximately 1.20. Some double-effect absorption chillers use medium-pressure steam (60 psig [414 kPa]) or 350°F to 370°F (177°C to 188°C) hot water, but with lower efficiency or higher cost.

Double-effect absorption chillers are available from several manufacturers. Most are limited to chilled-water temperatures of 40°F (4.3°C) or above, since water is the refrigerant. The interior of the chiller experiences corrosive conditions; therefore, the manufacturer's material selection is directly related to the chiller life. The more robust the materials, the longer the life.

WHEN/WHERE IT'S APPLICABLE

Double-effect absorption chillers can be used in the following applications:

- When natural gas prices (used to produce steam) are significantly lower than electric prices.
- When the design team and building owner wish to have fuel flexibility to hedge against changes in future utility prices.
- When there is steam available from an on-site process; an example is steam from a turbine.
- When a steam plant is available but lightly loaded during the cooling season. Many hospitals have large steam plants that run at extremely low loads and low efficiency during the cooling season. By installing an absorption chiller, the steam plant efficiency can be increased significantly during the cooling season.
- At sites that have limited electric power available.
- In locations where district steam is available at a reasonable price (e.g., New York City).

PROS

- Reduces electric charges.
- Allows fuel flexibility, since natural gas, No. 2 fuel oil, propane, or waste steam may be used to supply thermal energy for the absorption chiller.
- Uses water as the refrigerant, making it environmentally friendly.
- Allows system expansion even at sites with limited electric power.
- When the system is designed and controlled properly, it allows versatile use of various power sources.

CONS

- Cost of an absorption chiller will be roughly double that of an electric chiller of the same capacity, as opposed to 25% more for a single-effect absorption machine.
- Size of an absorption chiller is larger than an electric chiller of the same capacity.
- Although absorption chiller efficiency has increased in the past decade, the amount of heat rejected is significantly higher than that of an electric chiller of similar capacity. This requires larger cooling towers, condenser pipes, and cooling tower pumps.
- Few plant operators are familiar with absorption technology.

KEY ELEMENTS OF COST

The following provides a possible breakdown of the various cost elements that might differentiate an absorption chiller system from a conventional one and an indication of whether the net cost for the hybrid option is likely to be lower (L), higher (H), or the same (S). This assessment is only a perception of what might be likely, but it obviously may not be correct in all situations. There is no substitute for a detailed cost analysis as part of the design process. The listings below may also provide some assistance in identifying the cost elements involved.

First Cost

- Absorption chiller   H
- Cooling tower and associated equipment   H
- Electricity feed   L

- Design fees   H
- System controls   H

Recurring Costs

- Electric costs   L
- Chiller maintenance   S
- Training of building operators   H

SOURCES OF FURTHER INFORMATION

ASHRAE. 2008. *ASHRAE Handbook—HVAC Systems and Equipment*, Chapter 50. Atlanta: American Society of Heating, Refrigerating and Air-Conditioning Engineers, Inc.

ASHRAE. 2010. *ASHRAE Handbook—Refrigeration*, Chapter 43. Atlanta: American Society of Heating, Refrigerating and Air-Conditioning Engineers, Inc.

Trane Co. 1999. *Trane Applications Engineering Manual, Absorption Chiller System Design*, SYS-AM-13. Lacrosse, WI: Trane Company.

ASHRAE
GreenTip #22

Gas Engine-Driven Chillers

GENERAL DESCRIPTION

Chilled-water systems that use fuel types other than electricity can help offset high electric prices, regardless of whether those high prices are caused by consumption or demand charges. Gas engines can be used in conjunction with electric chillers to produce chilled water. Depending on chiller efficiency, a gas engine-driven chiller may have a cooling COP of 1.6 to 2.3.

Some gas engines are directly coupled to a chiller's shaft. Another option is to use a gas engine and switchgear. In such cases, the chiller may be operated either by using electricity from the engine or from the electric utility.

WHEN/WHERE IT'S APPLICABLE

A gas engine is applicable in the following circumstances:

- When natural gas prices are significantly lower than electric prices.
- When the design team and building owner wish to have fuel flexibility to hedge against changes in future utility prices.
- At sites that have limited electric power available.

PROS

- Reduces electric charges.
- Allows fuel flexibility if installed as a hybrid system (i.e., part gas engine and part electric chiller, so the plant may use either gas engine or electricity from utility).
- Allows system expansion even at sites with limited electric power.
- When the system is designed and controlled properly, these chillers allow for use of various fuel sources.
- May be used in conjunction with an emergency generator if switchgear is provided.

CONS

- Added cost of gas engine.
- Additional space required for engine.

- Due to the amount of heat rejected being significantly higher than for similar capacity electric chiller, larger cooling towers, condenser pipes, and cooling tower pumps may be required.
- Site emissions are increased.
- Noise from engine may need to be attenuated, both inside and outside.
- Significant engine maintenance costs.

KEY ELEMENTS OF COST

The following provides a possible breakdown of the various cost elements that might differentiate a gas engine-driven chiller from a conventional one and an indication of whether the net cost is likely to be lower (L), higher (H), or the same (S). This assessment is only a perception of what might be likely, but it obviously may not be correct in all situations. There is no substitute for a detailed cost analysis as part of the design process. The listings below may also provide some assistance in identifying the cost elements involved.

First Cost

- Gas engine   H
- Cooling tower and associated equipment   H
- Electricity feed   L
- Site emissions   H
- Site acoustics   H
- Design fees   H
- System controls   H

Recurring Costs

- Electric costs   L
- Engine maintenance   H
- Training of building operators   H
- Emissions costs   H

SOURCE OF FURTHER INFORMATION

NBI. 1998. *Gas Engine Driven Chillers Guideline*. Fair Oaks, CA: New Buildings Institute and Southern California Gas Company. http://newbuildings.org/sites/default/files/AbsorptionChiller-Guideline.pdf.

ASHRAE
GreenTip #23

Gas-Fired Chillers/Heaters

GENERAL DESCRIPTION

Chilled-water systems that use fuel types other than electricity can help offset high electricity prices, whether those high prices are caused by consumption or demand charges. Absorption chillers use thermal energy (rather than electricity) to produce chilled water. Some gas-fired absorption chillers can provide not only chilled water but also hot water. They are referred to as *chiller heaters*.

A gas-fired absorption chiller has a cooling COP of approximately 1.0 and a heating efficiency of about 80%.

Gas-fired chiller heaters are available from several manufacturers. Most are limited to chilled-water supply temperatures of 40°F (4.3°C) or above, since water is the refrigerant. Some manufacturers offer dual-fuel capability (e.g., can handle natural gas or No. 2 fuel oil).

WHEN/WHERE IT'S APPLICABLE

Gas-fired chiller heaters are applicable in the following circumstances:

- When natural gas prices are significantly lower than electric prices.
- At sites where a boiler can be eliminated by using the chiller heater.
- When the design team and building owner wish to have fuel flexibility to hedge against changes in future utility prices.
- At sites that have limited electric power available.

PROS

- Reduces electric charges.
- Allows fuel flexibility, since either natural gas or No. 2 fuel oil may be used to supply thermal energy for the absorption chiller.
- May allow for a boiler to be eliminated.
- Uses water as the refrigerant, making it environmentally friendly.

- Allows system expansion even at sites with limited electric power.
- When the system is designed and controlled properly, allows versatile use of various fuel sources.

CONS

- Cost will be roughly double that of the same capacity electric chiller.
- Size of absorption chiller will be larger than the same capacity electric chiller, and added space is required.
- The amount of heat rejected is significantly higher than that from an electric chiller of similar capacity, approximately double that of a single-stage absorption machine, and 50% greater for a two-stage unit.
- Larger cooling towers, condenser pipes, and cooling tower pumps are required compared with electric-drive machines.
- Few plant operators are familiar with absorption technology.

KEY ELEMENTS OF COST

The following provides a possible breakdown of the various cost elements that might differentiate the gas-fired chiller/heater system from a conventional system and an indication of whether the net cost for the hybrid option is likely to be lower (L), higher (H), or the same (S). This assessment is only a perception of what might be likely, but it obviously may not be correct in all situations. There is no substitute for a detailed cost analysis as part of the design process. The listings below may also provide some assistance in identifying the cost elements involved.

First Cost

- Absorption chiller   H
- Possible boiler elimination   L
- Cooling tower and associated equipment   H
- Electricity feed   L
- Design fees   H
- System controls   H

Recurring Costs

- Electric costs   L
- Chiller maintenance   S
- Training of building operators   H

SOURCES OF FURTHER INFORMATION

AGCC. 1994. *Applications Engineering Manual for Direct-Fired Absorption*. Washington, D.C.: American Gas Cooling Center.

ASHRAE. 2008. *ASHRAE Handbook—HVAC Systems and Equipment*, Chapter 50. Atlanta: American Society of Heating, Refrigerating and Air-Conditioning Engineers, Inc.

ASHRAE. 2010. *ASHRAE Handbook—Refrigeration*, Chapter 43. Atlanta: American Society of Heating, Refrigerating and Air-Conditioning Engineers, Inc.

Trane. 1999. *Trane Applications Engineering Manual, Absorption Chiller System Design*, SYS-AM-13. Lacrosse, WI: Trane Company.

Desiccant Cooling
and Dehumidification

GENERAL DESCRIPTION

There are two basic types of open-cycle desiccant process: solid and liquid desiccant. Each of these processes has several forms, and these should be investigated to determine the most appropriate for the particular application. Both of these systems need to have the air being conditioned come in good contact with the desiccant, during which moisture is absorbed from the air and the temperatures of both the air and desiccant are coincidently raised.

The moisture absorption process is caused by desiccant having a lower surface vapor pressure than the air. As the temperature of the desiccant rises, its vapor pressure rises, and its useful absorption capability lessens. Some systems, particularly liquid types, have cooling of air and desiccant coincident with dehumidification. This can allow the need for less space and equipment.

The dehumidified air then has to be cooled by other means. Two supply air arrangements are available. One method uses a mixture of recycled return air and dehumidified outdoor ventilation air as supply air to the building. Moisture and contaminants such as volatile organic compounds can be absorbed by the desiccant and recycled; particles of solid or liquid desiccant may also be carried over into the ducts and to building occupants.

The other arrangement combines energy recovery from building exhaust air that is typically much cooler and less humid than outdoor ventilation air. By dehumidifying the exhaust air to a sufficiently low humidity ratio (i.e., moisture content), it can be used to indirectly cool outdoor air for supply to the building that has not contacted desiccant. Using the recovered energy, this arrangement can be used to process the total ventilation air requirement, even up to 100% from outside.

So that desiccant can be reused, it has to be re-dried by a heating process generally called *reactivation* or *regeneration* (for solid types) or *reconcentration* (for liquid types). The re-drying can be either direct (by contact with heated outdoor air with the desiccant) or indirect. Indirect may be preferable, particularly in high humid climates, because of the higher temperature needed to maximize the vapor difference and drying potential. The energy storage benefit for liquid desiccant was discussed in GreenTip #20.

Rotary desiccant dehumidifiers use solid desiccants such as silica gel to attract water vapor from the moist air. Humid air, generally referred to as *process air*, is dehumidified in one part of the desiccant bed while a different part of the bed is dried for reuse by a second airstream known as *reactivation air*. The desiccant rotates slowly between these two airstreams, so that dry, high-capacity desiccant leaving the reactivation air is available to remove moisture from the moist process air.

Process air that passes through the bed more slowly is dried more deeply, so for air requiring a lower dew point, a larger unit (and slower velocity) is required. The reactivation air inlet temperature changes the outlet moisture content of the process air. In turn, if the designer needs dry air, it is generally more economical to use high reactivation temperatures. On the other hand, if the leaving humidity need not be especially low, inexpensive, low-grade heat sources (e.g., waste heat or rejected cogeneration heat) can be used.

The process air outlet temperature is higher than the inlet temperature primarily because the heat of sorption of the moisture removed is converted to sensible heat. The outlet temperature rises roughly in proportion to the amount of moisture that is removed. In most comfort applications, provisions must be made to remove excess sensible heat from the process air following reactivation. Cooling is accomplished with cooling coils, and the source of this cooling affects the operating economics of the system.

WHEN/WHERE IT'S APPLICABLE

In general, applications that require a dew point at or below 40°F (4.3°C) may be candidates for active desiccant dehumidification. Examples of such candidates include facilities handling hygroscopic materials; film drying; the manufacturing of candy, chocolate, or chewing gum; the manufacturing of drugs and chemicals; the manufacturing of plastic materials; packaging of moisture-sensitive products; and the manufacturing of electronics. Supermarkets often use desiccant dehumidification to avoid condensation on refrigerated casework. And when there is a need for a lower dew point and a convenient source of low-grade heat for reactivation is available, rotary desiccant dehumidifiers can be especially economical.

PROS

- Desiccant equipment tends to be very durable.
- Often this is the most economical means to dehumidify below a 40°F (4.3°C) dew point.
- It eliminates condensate in the airstream, in turn, limiting the opportunity for mold growth.

CONS

- Desiccant usually must be replaced, replenished, or reconditioned every five to ten years.
- In comfort applications, simultaneous heating and cooling may be required.
- The process is not especially intuitive, and the controls are relatively complicated.

KEY ELEMENTS OF COST

The following provides a possible breakdown of the various cost elements that might differentiate a building with a rotary desiccant dehumidification system from one without and an indication of whether the net cost is likely to be lower (L), higher (H), or the same (S).

First Cost

- Equipment costs   H
- Regeneration (heat source and supply)   H
- Ductwork   S
- Controls   H
- Design fees   S

Recurring Costs

- Overall energy cost   S/H
- Maintenance of system   H
- Training of building operators   H
- Filters   H

SOURCE OF FURTHER INFORMATION

ASHRAE. 2008. *ASHRAE Handbook—HVAC Systems and Equipment*. Atlanta: American Society of Heating, Refrigerating and Air-Conditioning Engineers, Inc.

Indirect Evaporative Cooling

GENERAL DESCRIPTION

Evaporative cooling of supply air can be used to reduce the amount of energy consumed by mechanical cooling equipment. Two general types of evaporative cooling—direct and indirect—are available. The effectiveness of either of these methods is directly dependent on the extent that dry-bulb temperature exceeds wet-bulb temperature in the supply airstream.

Direct evaporative cooling introduces water directly into the supply airstream, usually with a spray or wetted media. As the water absorbs heat from the air, it evaporates. While this process lowers the dry-bulb temperature of the supply airstream, it also increases the air moisture content.

Two forms of indirect evaporative cooling (IEC) are described below.

1. **Coil/cooling Tower IEC.** This type uses an additional water-side coil to lower supply air temperature. The added coil is placed ahead of the conventional cooling coil in the supply airstream and is piped to a cooling tower where the evaporative process occurs. Because evaporation occurs elsewhere, this method of precooling does not add moisture to the supply air, but it is somewhat less effective than direct evaporative cooling. A conventional cooling coil provides any additional cooling required.

2. **Plate Heat Exchanger IEC.** This is composed of sets of parallel plates arranged into two sets of passages separated from each other. In a typical arrangement, exhaust air from a building is passed through one set of passages, during which it is wetted by water sprays. A stream of outdoor air is coincidently passed through the other set of passages and is cooled by heat transfer through the plates by the wetted exhaust air before being supplied to the building. Alternatively, the exhaust air may be replaced by a second stream of outdoor air. The wetted air is reduced in dry-bulb temperature to be close to its wet-bulb temperature. The stream of dry air is cooled to be close to the dry-bulb temperature

of the wetted exhaust air. In some applications, the cooled stream of outdoor air is passed through the coil of a direct expansion refrigeration unit, where it is further cooled before being supplied to the building. This system is an efficient way for an all outdoor air supply system. The plates in the heat exchanger can be formed from various metals and polymers. Consideration needs to be given to preventing the plate material from corroding.

WHEN/WHERE IT'S APPLICABLE

This may be used in climates with low wet-bulb temperatures where significant amounts of cooling are available. In such climates, the size of the conventional cooling system can also be reduced.

In more humid climates, indirect evaporative cooling can be applied during nonpeak seasons. It is especially applicable for loads that operate 24 h/day for many days of the year.

PROS

- Indirect evaporative cooling can reduce the size of the conventional cooling system.
- It reduces cooling costs during periods of low wet-bulb temperature.
- It does not add moisture to the supply airstream (in contrast, direct evaporative cooling does add moisture).
- It may be designed into equipment such as self-contained units.
- There is no cooling tower or condenser piping in the plate heat exchanger IEC that is described.

CONS

- Air-side pressure drop (typically 0.2 to 0.4 in. w.c. [50 to 100 Pa]) increases due to an additional coil in the airstream.
- To make water cooler in the coil/cooling tower IEC, the cooling tower fans operate for longer periods of time and consume more energy.
- For the coil/cooling tower IEC, condenser piping and controls must be accounted for during the design process.

KEY ELEMENTS OF COST

The following provides a possible breakdown of the various cost elements that might differentiate an IEC system from a conventional one and an indication of whether the net cost for the hybrid option is likely to be lower (L), higher (H), or the same (S). This assessment is only a perception of what might be likely, but it obviously may not be correct in all situations. There is no substitute for a detailed cost analysis as part of the design process. The listings below may also provide some assistance in identifying the cost elements involved.

First Cost

- Indirect cooling coil   H
- Decreased conventional cooling system capacity   L
- Condenser piping, valves, and control   H

Recurring Costs

- Cooling system operating cost   L
- Supply fan operating cost   H
- Tower fan operating cost   H
- Maintenance of indirect coil   S

SOURCES OF FURTHER INFORMATION

ASHRAE. 2007. *ASHRAE Handbook—HVAC Applications*, pp. 53.3–5. Atlanta: American Society of Heating, Refrigerating and Air-Conditioning Engineers, Inc.

ASHRAE. 2008. *ASHRAE Handbook—HVAC Systems and Equipment*, pp. 4.5; 40.2–4. Atlanta: American Society of Heating, Refrigerating and Air-Conditioning Engineers, Inc.

REFERENCES AND RESOURCES

Published

ASHRAE. 1998. *Fundamentals of Water System Design*. Atlanta: American Society of Heating, Refrigerating and Air-Conditioning Engineers, Inc.

ASHRAE. 2008. *ASHRAE Handbook—HVAC Systems and Equipment*, Chapter 11. Atlanta: American Society of Heating, Refrigerating and Air-Conditioning Engineers, Inc.

Cho, Y.I., S. Lee, and W. Kim. 2003. Physical water treatment for the mitigation of mineral fouling in cooling-tower water applications. *ASHRAE Transactions* 109(1):346–57.

EDR. 2009. *Chilled Water Plant Design Guide*. Energy Design Resources. www.energydesignresources.com/Resources/Publications/DesignGuidelines/tabid/73/articleType/ArticleView/articleId/422/Default.aspx.

Patnaik, V. 2004. Experimental verification of an absorption chiller for BCHP applications. *ASHRAE Transactions* 110(1):503–507.

Rosfjord, T., T. Wagner, and B. Knight. 2004. UTC microturbine CHP product development and launch. Presented at the 2004 DOE/CETC Annual Workshop on Microturbine Applications, January 20–22, Marina del Rey, CA.

Ryan, W.A. 2003. CHP: The concept. Midwest CHP Application Center, Energy Resources Center, University of Illinois, Chicago. www.chpcentermw.org/presentations/WI-Focus-on-Energy-Presentation-05212003.pdf

Torcellini, P.A., M. Longm, and R. Judkoff. 2004. Consumptive water use for U.S. power production. *ASHRAE Transactions* 110(1):96–100.

Trane. 2000. *Multiple-Chiller-System Design and Control Manual*. Lacrosse, WI: Trane Company.

Online

U.S. Environmental Protection Agency, Green Chemistry www.epa.gov/greenchemistry/

CHAPTER TWELVE

ENERGY/WATER SOURCES

RENEWABLE/NONRENEWABLE ENERGY SOURCES

There are often discussions about using renewable energy sources as a way to power the world but little is done to actually implement it. This chapter focuses on ways to use renewable energy to offset nonrenewable energy sources. By definition, a renewable energy source (RES) is a fuel source that can be replenished in a short amount of time. The common renewable sources are solar, wind, hydro, and biomass. This is in contrast to the common nonrenewable energy sources such as coal, oil, natural gas, and nuclear.

The use of renewable energy is separated between using the energy source on site versus paying for the renewable resource. Today, many utility companies offer the ability to purchase renewable energy mixes from their generation portfolio. These utilities generate their own renewable energy with either large-scale wind or solar facilities. Note that quite often, large-scale hydroelectric plants are not considered a renewable resource because of the size of the environmental impact of such facilities. *Green energy*, as it is sometimes called, can also be purchased by third-party resellers of energy. The concept is that renewable energy is put into the utility grid and you, as the end user, can purchase that power somewhere else on the grid. The bottom line is that you can, in most areas, purchase green power, and you are not limited by the default utility offering. According to the U.S. Department of Energy's (DOE) National Renewable Energy Lab (NREL), "in 2009 total utility green power sales exceeded 6 billion kWh, a 60% increase since 2006. More than 850 utilities are participating in programs nationwide" (NREL 2010). The U.S. Environmental Protection Agency (EPA) has a publication, *Guide to Purchasing Green Power*, which is a good overview of the green power market and steps to take for participating.

According to Europe's Energy Portal, in the European Union (EU), renewables contribute 9.2% of the final energy consumption in 2006 (www.energy.eu/ #renewable). More than 4 million European consumers have already switched to a green power.

To further strengthen the exploitation of RES, the EU officially adopted a 20-20-20 Renewable Energy Directive on December 17, 2008, setting the following ambitious targets for 2020: cutting greenhouse gas emissions by at least 20% of 1990 levels; cutting energy consumption by 20% through improved energy efficiency; and boosting the use of RES to 20% of total energy production (currently at about 8.5%). Under the terms of the directive, for the first time each member state has a legally binding renewables target for 2020 and by June 2010 each state will have drawn up a National Action Plan detailing plans to meet their 2020 targets (EU 2008).

The designer has little say over how energy at the source will be provided. Electricity may be generated from coal, imported oil, natural gas, or uranium, and each source may have broad implications for national or industry interests, the environment, and/or economics. However, there is little a designer can do about it—at least in choosing between conventional nonrenewable energy sources. This subject is addressed in more detail in the Chapter 34 of the 2009 *ASHRAE Handbook—Fundamentals* (ASHRAE 2009), and the designer is referred to that source for more specific data.

What designers do have influence over is creating a building that is designed to minimize energy consumption, which is the focus of most of this book. Passive solar techniques—that is, those with minimal moving parts—can be incorporated into the design of a building. Daylighting, trombe walls, passive cooling, and natural ventilation are all methods for using the natural environment to help heat, light, and cool the building.

Other techniques can be used, such as solar water heating, solar ventilation preheat, photovoltaic (PV) systems, and wind systems, although these active systems tend to be a little more complicated to integrate into a building's operation.

In many cases, renewable energy can be considered free. The issue is that this free energy source usually needs some capital equipment to concentrate the diffuse nature of renewable energy into a useful form for the building. One way to illustrate this characteristic is to think of a gallon jug of, say, fuel oil compared to an array of hydronic solar collectors. The fuel oil could provide hot water, on demand, for hours in a simple water heater in a corner of a boiler room, but the fuel oil will consume fossil fuels and produce emissions. The equivalent job done by solar collectors would require an array of collectors on a roof, plus a tank, piping, and some controls (a simple thermosiphon-type solar collector can operate without controls) but would produce no emissions and would operate with free solar energy.

While consideration of renewables is a highly touted element of green design, the design team should be well aware of the key characteristics of whichever renewable is being considered and develop creative strategies accordingly. In the next sections, we focus on two main renewable energy sources (other than hydro-power) in the world today.

SOLAR

Solar energy is the primary energy source that fuels the growth of the Earth's natural capital and drives wind and ocean currents that also can provide alternative energy sources. Since the beginning of time, solar energy has been successfully harnessed for human use. Early civilizations and some modern ones used solar energy for many purposes: food and clothes drying, heating water for baths, heating adobe and stone dwellings, etc. Solar energy is free and available to anyone who wishes to use it.

Solar thermal heating for domestic hot-water and space heating has grown considerably over the years and is well established in several countries. Global installed capacity is estimated at about 348×10^9 Btu/h (102 gigawatts of thermal energy [GW$_{th}$]) for glazed flat-plate (144×10^9 Btu/h [42.2 GW$_{th}$] or 649×10^6 ft^2 [60.3 $\times 10^6$ m^2]) and evacuated-tube collectors (204×10^9 Btu/h [59.9 GW$_{th}$] or 921.4×10^6 ft^2 [85.6 $\times 10^6$ m^2]), at 84×10^9 Btu/h (24.5 GW$_{th}$) for unglazed plastic collectors (376.7×10^6 ft^2 [35 $\times 10^6$ m^2]), and 4.1×10^9 Btu/h (1.2 GW$_{th}$) (17.2×10^6 ft^2 [1.6 $\times 10^6$ m^2]) for glazed and unglazed air collectors (Weiss et al. 2008). In North America (i.e., United States and Canada), swimming pool heating is dominant with an installed capacity of about 66.9×10^9 Btu/h (19.6 GW$_{th}$) of unglazed plastic collectors. In other countries, flat-plate and evacuated-tube collectors are used to generate hot water for sanitary use and space heating. These countries include China and Taiwan (225×10^9 Btu/h [66 GW$_{th}$]), Europe (51×10^9 [15 GW$_{th}$]), and Japan (17×10^9 Btu/h [5 GW$_{th}$]).

According to the European Solar Thermal Industry (ESTIF 2010), at the end of 2009, the total capacity of glazed collector area in operation in the European Union reached 73.7×10^9 Btu/h (21.6 GW$_{th}$) (about 334×10^6 ft^2 [31 $\times 10^6$ m^2]). Germany is the leader with 41% of the European market followed by Greece (13%), Austria (11.6%), and Spain (6.5%). In terms of capacity in operation per capita, Cyprus, where more than 90% of all buildings are equipped with solar collectors, leads Europe with 2.2×10^6 Btu/h (646 kW$_{th}$) per 1000 capita, followed by Austria at 1.0×10^6 Btu/h (301 kW$_{th}$) per 1000 capita, and Greece at 0.86×10^6 Btu/h (253 kW$_{th}$) per 1000 capita, with the European average at 0.15×10^6 Btu/h (44 kW$_{th}$) per 1000 capita.

According to the International Energy Agency (Weiss and Mauthner 2010), China dominates the world market (66%), with annual domestic sales of about 334×10^6 ft^2 (31 $\times 10^6$ m^2) in 2008 (74×10^9 Btu/h [21.7 GW$_{th}$]).

For many, a key impediment to increased solar use is economics. The cost of some solar technologies is perceived to be high compared to the fossil-based energy source it is offsetting. For example, while the simple payback of solar PV systems tends to be rather long (although much improvement has occurred over the past couple of decades), the recent increase in the cost of energy and advances in solar energy justify a fresh look at the applications and the engineering behind those applications. In addition, public policy in many areas encourages solar and other renewable energy applications through tax incentives and encouraging or requiring repurchase of excess electrical energy generated by the utility provider.

The applicability and, consequently, the economics and public policy incentives available with different solar energy system types and applications depend greatly on the location, which determines the technical factors (such as solar resources available), as well as the nontechnical (such as the country's political situation).

Solar Thermal Applications

Solar energy thermal applications range from low-temperature applications (e.g., swimming pool heating or domestic water) to medium- to high-temperature applications (e.g., space heating, absorption cooling or steam production for electrical generation). (See Figure 12-1 for examples of typical installations.)

The most common solar energy thermal application is for domestic hot water (DHW) production. However, the same solar collectors can be used to deliver thermal energy for space heating. A typical installation for the combined production of DHW and space heating (i.e., solar combi systems) includes the solar collectors, the heat storage tank, and a boiler used as an auxiliary heater. Combi systems require a larger collector area than a DHW system to meet the higher loads. It is possible to use a heat storage tank and a DHW storage vessel, but it may also be suitable to combine them in a single storage tank (with a high vertical stratification) to meet the different operating temperatures for space heating and DHW. To assess and compare performances of different designs for solar combi systems, the International Energy Agency (IEA) launched Task 26 to address issues in this area (www.iea-shc.org/task26). Standardized classification and evaluation processes and design tools were developed for these systems, along with proposals for the international standardization of combi system test procedures.

The main drawback of solar combi systems has been the fact that during summer, the available high solar radiation and the heat produced from the solar collectors cannot be fully used, thus making the system financially less attractive and limiting its use to the low DHW summer demand. In addition, there are some technical problems related to stagnation (i.e. the condition when the medium in the solar collector loop vaporizes as a result of high solar radiation availability and low thermal demand). Since high building cooling loads generally coincide with high solar radiation, the readily available solar heat from the existing solar collectors can be exploited by a heat-driven cooling machine, thus extending the use of the solar field throughout the year (solar hot water [SHW] and space heating in winter and SHW and cooling in summer). Combining solar heating and cooling is usually referred to as a solar combi-plus system that can increase the total solar fraction.

Europe has the most sophisticated market for different solar thermal applications, including systems for hot-water production, plants for space heating of

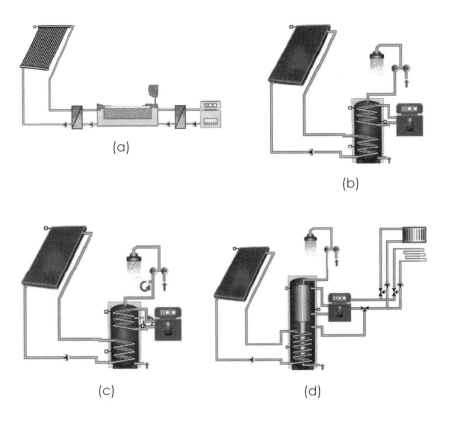

Figure 12-1 Examples of typical solar installations: (a) swimming pool, (b) domestic hot water, (c) domestic hot water for dwellings, and (d) solar combi systems for domestic hot water and space heating for houses. (Images generated using T-SOL 4.5 Expert; Valentin Energie software, www.valentin.de.)

single- and multifamily houses and hotels, large-scale plants for district heating, and a growing number of systems for air-conditioning, cooling, and industrial applications.

The capital cost of solar thermal systems generally increases with higher working fluid temperatures. The higher the delivery temperature, the lower the efficiency, and the more solar collector area is generally required to deliver the same net energy. This is due to parasitic thermal losses that are inherent in solar collector design. Different solar collector types provide advantages and disadvantages, depending on the application, and there are significant cost differences among each solar collector type. Some common collector types are discussed here. (See Figure 12-2 for examples of hardware.)

Flat-Plate Solar Collectors. These are best suited for processes requiring low-temperature working fluids (80°F to 160°F or 27°C to 71°C) and can deliver 80°F (27°C) fluid temperatures, even during overcast conditions. The term *flat-plate collector* generally refers to a hydronic coil-covered absorber housed in an insulated

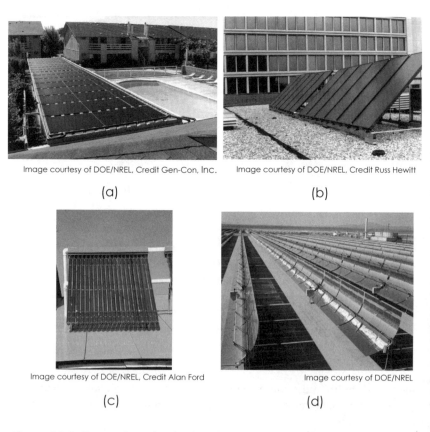

Image courtesy of DOE/NREL, Credit Gen-Con, Inc.

(a)

Image courtesy of DOE/NREL, Credit Russ Hewitt

(b)

Image courtesy of DOE/NREL, Credit Alan Ford

(c)

Image courtesy of DOE/NREL

(d)

Figure12-2 Examples of solar hardware: (a) unglazed plastic collector, (b) glazed flat-plate collector, (c) evacuated-tube collector, and (d) concentrating collectors.

box with a single- or double-glass cover that allows solar energy to heat the absorber. Heat is removed by a fluid running through the hydronic coils. Its design makes it more susceptible to parasitic losses than an evacuated tube collector, but more efficient in solar energy capture, because flat-plate collectors convert both direct and indirect solar radiation into thermal energy. This makes flat-plate collectors the preferred choice for domestic hot-water and other low-temperature heating applications. Coupling a water-source heat pump with low fluid temperatures with solar collectors provides heating efficiencies that are higher than ground-source heat pump (GSHP) applications and standard natural gas furnaces.

Evacuated-Tube Collectors. These are a series of small absorbers consisting of small-diameter (approximately 3/8 in. or 10 mm) copper tubing encased in a clear, cylindrical, evacuated thermos bottle that minimizes parasitic losses even at elevated temperatures. Because of the relatively small absorber area, significantly more collector area is required than with the flat-plate or concentrating collector.

Typical flat-plate solar collector performance curves are illustrated in Figure 12-3. The collector's efficiency (η) is expressed as a function of the solar collector's working fluid inlet temperature (T_{in}), the ambient temperature (T_o), and the total solar radiation incident on the collector's surface (G_T).

Concentrating Collectors. This refers to the use of a parabolic reflector that focuses the solar radiation falling within the reflector area onto a centrally located absorber. Concentrating collectors are best suited for processes requiring high-

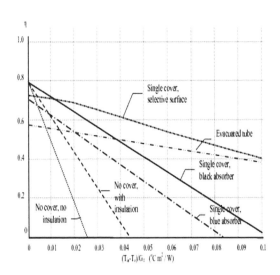

Image courtesy of C.A. Balaras

Figure 12-3 Typical flat-plate solar collector performance curves.

temperature working fluids (300°F to 750°F or 150°C to 400°C) and do not operate under overcast conditions. This type of collector converts only direct solar radiation, which varies dramatically with sky clearness and air quality (e.g., smog). Concentrating collectors rotate on one or two axes to track the sun and collect the available direct solar radiation.

Pros and cons of different solar collector types and other limitations of active solar systems can be found in a number of sources. Many of the key contributions came during the initial energy concerns of the 1970s, and a few are listed in the "References and Resources" section at the end of this chapter.

The percentage of energy a solar system can provide is known as the solar fraction. The F-Chart method (Klein and Beckman 2001) developed by Sanford Klein at the University of Wisconsin provides an accurate assessment of the amount of energy a solar thermal system will provide. This modeling provides the designer the ability to vary system parameters (e.g., collector area, storage volume, operating temperature, and load) to optimize system design. The method was originally developed to aid engineers who did not have computer resources available to do the complex analyses required for solar thermal calculations. This method has since been adapted for automated computer analysis using modern tools.

The cost-effectiveness of thermal solar systems is also dependent on having a constant load for the energy the solar system provides. Since space heating requirements are generally seasonal in most climates, it is advisable that energy from the solar system have more uses than space heating alone. Domestic water heating is usually a much steadier year-round load, though typically not very substantial. Solar cooling can extend utilization of solar collectors during the summer. The fact that peak cooling demand in summer is associated with high solar radiation availability offers an excellent opportunity to exploit solar energy with heat-driven cooling machines.

Solar hot water can be used as the sole source of domestic hot water or to preheat incoming supply water. This can be as simple as having an uninsulated tank in a hot attic in a southern climate to having a batch water heater on the roof of a building. Pool heating is the reason for the vast majority of current sales of hot-water-based systems in most markets in the United States. Water is taken from the pool and pumped through an unglazed collector and then returned back into the pool. In many climates, most of the energy for pool heating can be offset with this technique. Solar energy is a major source for domestic hot-water heating in several countries (i.e., China, Israel, Australia, and Greece) and is currently widely used in states such as Hawaii and Florida. Although it is an economically viable option for practically all areas of the United States, a barrier to increased market acceptance is the current lack of trained installation contractors and limited information available in most areas.

Besides preheating water, solar energy can be used to preheat incoming air—before it is introduced to a building—using systems integrated with the overall building design or collectors. This is a simple technological approach that can be economically viable and is well suited for northern climates or areas with high building heating load. The DOE has published a bulletin on these transpired solar collectors (DOE 2006).

The main heat-driven cooling technologies that can be used for solar cooling include:

- Closed-cycle systems (e.g., LiBr/H_2O and H_2O/NH_3 absorption systems [see Chapter 41 of 2006 *ASHRAE Handbook—Refrigeration* (ASHRAE 2006)] and adsorption [see Chapter 32 of 2009 *ASHRAE Handbook—Fundamentals* (ASHRAE 2009)] cycles). They produce chilled water that can be used in combination with any air-conditioning equipment, such as an air-handling unit, fan-coil systems, chilled ceilings, etc.
- Open cycles (e.g., desiccant systems [see Chapter 32 of 2009 *ASHRAE Handbook—Fundamentals* (ASHRAE 2009)]). The term *open cycle* is used to indicate that the refrigerant is discarded from the system after it provides the cooling effect. New refrigerant is supplied in its place in an open-ended loop.

Solar-assisted cooling systems employ solar thermal collectors connected to thermal-driven cooling devices. They consist of several main components (Figure 12-4), namely, the solar collectors, heat storage, heat distribution system, heat-driven cooling

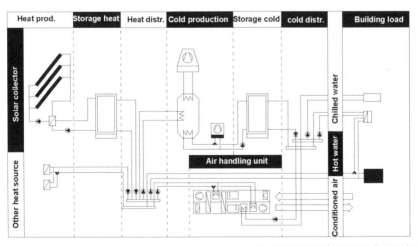

Image courtesy of Hans-Martin Henning

Figure 12-4 Schematic description of a solar air-conditioning system describing the integration of different component options.

unit, optional cold storage, an air-conditioning system with appropriate cold distribution, and an auxiliary subsystem (which is integrated at different places in the overall system and is used as an auxiliary heater parallel to the collector or the collector/storage, as an auxiliary cooling device, or both). International research and development efforts, along with monitoring data from several installations are available from Task 38 on solar air conditioning and refrigeration from the International Energy Agency (IEA) (www.iea-shc.org/task38).

Due to their low first cost, common flat-plate solar collectors are used for reaching a driving temperature of 140°F to 194°F (60°C to 90°C) (Balaras et al. 2006). With selective-surface, flat-plate solar collectors, the driving temperature can be up to 248°F (120°C); however, the collector efficiency will be quite low at this temperature level. Stationary flat-plate, evacuated tube solar collectors are typically used for 175°F to 250°F (79°C to 121°C) applications, and can reach higher temperatures but at a lower collector efficiency. Compound parabolic concentrators can reach 207°F to 329°F (97°C to 165°C).

The average specific solar collector area averages 136 ft^2/ton (3.6 m/kW refrigeration), ranging from 19 to 208 ft^2/ton (0.5 to 5.5 m^2/kW refrigeration), depending on the employed technology. Adsorption and absorption systems typically use more than 76 ft^2/ton (2 m^2/kW refrigeration) and usually less than 189 ft^2/ton (5 m^2/kW refrigeration). Overall, H_2O/NH_3 systems require larger specific collector areas than LiBr/H_2O systems, and, as a result, the installations are usually more expensive. The initial overall cost per installed cooling capacity in averages about 4000 Euro/kWR, excluding the cost for distribution networks among the system and the application and the delivery units.

Each technology has specific characteristics that match the building's HVAC design, loads, and local climatic conditions. A good design must first exploit all available solar radiation and then cover the remaining loads from conventional sources. Proper calculations for collector and storage size depend on the employed solar cooling technology. Hot-water storage may be integrated between the solar collectors and the heat-driven chiller to dampen the fluctuations in the return temperature of the hot water from the chiller. The storage size depends on the application: if cooling loads mainly occur during the day, then a smaller storage unit will be necessary than when the loads peak in the evening. Heating the hot-water storage by the backup heat source should be strictly avoided. The storage's only function is to store excess heat of the solar system and to make it available when sufficient solar heat is not available. An overview of European efforts on solar combi and combi-plus systems, summarizing their main design, and operational and performance characteristics, is available in Balaras et al. (2010).

Solar-Electric Systems

The direct conversion from sunlight to electricity is accomplished with PV systems. These systems continue to drop in price, and many states (as well as the federal government) offer tax incentives for the installation of these systems. The most common application is a grid-tied system where electricity is directly fed into the grid.

Other applications of PV may be attractive and provide additional value beyond the cost of offsetting utility power. Whenever power lines must be extended, PV should be investigated. It is cost-effective to use stand-alone PV applications for signs, remote lights, and blinking traffic lights. Many times, if an existing small grid line is available and additional power is needed, it is less expensive to add the PV system rather than increase the power line. This may be true of remote guard shakes, restroom facilities, or other outbuildings. PV should also be considered as part of the uninterruptible power system for a building. Every building has battery backup for certain equipment. Batteries can be centralized and the PV fed directly into this system. The cost can be less than other on-site generation and fuel storage.

Technical and legal factors have generally been worked out that have hindered the use of grid-tied solar PV systems in the past. In temperate climates, grid-tied PV systems provide a good method to reduce peak summer electrical demand, since peak solar gains generally correspond to peak air-conditioning demand. This was a major factor that led to the passing of the California Million Solar Roofs initiative in early 2006. The German 100.000 rooftops—HTDP program, which began in early 1999, had a goal of 300 MW. It was successfully completed in 2003 with the parallel introduction of the German Renewable Energy Resources Act (EEG) that came into effect in 2000. The EEG and HTDP program secured commercially oriented PV investors (because they received a full payback of their investment).

According to the European Photovoltaic Industry Association (EPIA 2010), by the end of 2009, the cumulative installed capacity of PV systems around the world had reached about 23 GWp (peak gigawatts), which produce about 25 TWh of electricity on an annual basis. Europe is leading the way with almost 16 GWp of installed capacity in 2009, representing about 70% of the global cumulative PV power installed at the end of 2009, while Japan (2.6 GWp) and the United States (1.6 GWp) are following behind. China (0.3 GWp) is expected to become a major player in the coming years. The German market almost doubled in one year from 1.8 GWp in 2008 to about 3.8 GWp installed in 2009 (representing more than 52% of the world PV market), followed by Italy (711 MWp), Japan (484 MWp), and 477 MWp (including 40 MW of off-grid applications) in the United States.

The economic viability of PV systems is dependent on many factors. Improvements in technology have lowered the cost per peak watt from $5.14 and $3.08 in 1989 (in nominal dollars) to $3.49 for modules and $1.94 for cells in 2008, according to the DOE (EIA [see the "References and Resources" section]).

The module cost represents about 50%–60% of the total installed cost of a solar energy system. Therefore, the solar module price is the key element in the total price of an installed solar system. All prices are exclusive of sales taxes, which, depending on the country or region, can add 8%–20% to the prices, with the highest sales tax rates being in Europe. The typical PV cell efficiencies (i.e., the ratio of electrical energy produced by a solar cell to the incident solar irradiance) currently range from less than 5% for the first generation of thin-film cells to more than 24% for the most advanced crystalline-silicon cells in laboratory conditions.

The integration of PV systems with building materials is a new development that may, in the long run, help make PV systems viable in most areas. One of the key ways to incorporate solar energy technologies is to incorporate them directly into the architecture of the building (see Figure 12-5). Trombe walls can replace spandrel panels and other glass facades; PV panels can become overhangs for the building or parking shading structures. Using these elements as part of the building doubles the value of the systems. An example of these technologies is the concept called *building-integrated PVs*. A picture of one concept is shown in Figures 12-5 and 12-6. These are being developed by the National Renewable Energy Laboratory (NREL), among others.

Finally, PV is very visible and can be used as a marketing tool for a building project. PV collectors are addressed in GreenTip #28.

WIND

Using prevailing breezes and wind energy is one of the most promising alternative technologies today. Wind turbine design and power generation have become more reliable over the last 30 years. Consistency and velocity of available breezes are essential to successful application of wind for electrical generation and natural ventilation in buildings. Information on velocities, durations, and direction of winds in a project area is generally available from the National Oceanic and Atmospheric Administration (NOAA).

Image courtesy of DOE/NREL, Credit Ben Kroposki

(a)

Image courtesy of DOE/NREL, Credit Lawrence Berkeley Lab

(b)

Figure 12-5 Building-integrated PVs.

Global wind energy installations reached about 158.5 GW at the end of 2009, with more than 38 GW of new wind power generation capacity coming online in 2009, according to the Global Wind Energy Council (GWEC 2010). The United States maintains its global leadership in total installed grid-connected capacity (35 GW), covering 2% of the country's total electricity demand. In the United States, 36 states have utility-scale wind installations, and 14 states have more than 1 GW installed. Texas remains the leading state, with more than 9 GW of total installed capacity. Iowa is second (3.67 GW), followed by California, Washington, and Minnesota. China was the world's largest market in 2009, more than doubling its capacity from 12.1 GW in 2008 to 25.8 GW. Europe, which has traditionally been the world's largest market for wind energy development, continued to see strong growth by 10.5 GW in 2009, reaching a total wind power capacity of 76.2 GW, of which 25.78 GW was in Germany (generating 38 TWh in 2009 or 7% of the country's total power consumption) and 19.15 GW in Spain (generating 36.2 TWh in 2009, covering 14.5% of the country's electricity demand). A total of nine European Union member states exceeded 1 GW installed.

From a natural-ventilation perspective for passive cooling of buildings, other factors (e.g., temperature and relative humidity) must also be taken into consideration. Many areas can use outdoor air/natural breezes to provide passive cooling only during a limited period of the year, requiring designers wanting to use natural ventilation to carefully analyze both climatic conditions and cost to implement. The benefits of using natural ventilation must be weighed against the consistency of breezes, potential for higher relative humidity levels (which may affect indoor air quality), and the impact on occupant comfort and HVAC operation.

There are many excellent examples where natural ventilation provides the cooling needed throughout the year, but most are located in cool, arid climates. Even in moderate climates, such as that in Atlanta, Georgia, natural ventilation can provide

Image courtesy of DOE/NREL, Credit United Solar Ovonic

Figure 12-6 Building-integrated PV roofing.

passive cooling during some periods of the year, but in doing so, the designer must consider the impact on HVAC operation and building control. These elements may be very difficult to get to work effectively with operable windows. Additional programming and control points are required for successful operation. The potential of natural ventilation, its appropriate use, the design and dimensioning methodologies, the need for an integrated design approach, and how to overcome barriers are available in a handbook by Alvarez et al. (1998).

Incorporating one or more wind turbine generators at a building site is a more active approach. Initially, it should be recognized that there is a disadvantage of scale: one or two wind turbines alone are destined to be less cost-effective than a wind farm with hundreds. Wind turbines should first be evaluated by looking at the wind resource at the site. For most small-scale wind turbines, steady winds over 20 mph (9 m/s) are preferred to maximize the cost effectiveness. Other issues include noise, vibration, building geometry (if on the building), wind pattern interrupters, wildlife effect, periodic maintenance, safety, visual impact, and community acceptance; these must also be taken into account.

HYDRO

According to the International Hydropower Association (www.hydropower.org/downloads/F1_the_contribution_of_hydropower.pdf), hydropower already produces one sixth of the world's power. In all of its forms, from conventional power generation to emerging technologies like ocean and wave energy, hydrokinetic, and tidal power, there is a role of all types and scales of hydropower. According to the National Hydropower Association, wave energy conversion devices capture mechanical power from the waves and use it to directly or indirectly power a turbine and a generator. The flow from the tides of an ocean or stream may also be harvested to produce power. Pumped storage may be combined with other RES systems to meet power demand variations. The water may be pumped from a lower reservoir to an upper reservoir when demand for electricity is low (the power for pumping may be supplied from RES systems or the grid). The water is then released from the upper reservoir back to the lower reservoir to generate power using the hydrokinetic energy of the water flow through a generator (this is done during peak power demand or low generating output from RES systems).

The ability to use hydro is limited on an individual building scale. On rare occasions, older building renovations can take advantage of existing river dams and generate hydroelectric on site. This is especially true in the northeastern United States, where the primary power supply in the 1800s was hydro. In some cases, small streams can be diverted and small turbines installed—this is called *low-impact hydro*, as a minimal dam is needed and water is returned to the same stream.

In some cases, pressure reduction values can be replaced with small turbines. Although this is not really free energy from the big picture, as the water was pressurized before being distributed to the site, it is better to recover some of the energy rather than essentially waste it during pressure reduction.

BIOMASS

Biomass is the conversion of plant and animal matter into useful energy. Several ideas should be investigated to be considered as an energy source in a building. According to the DOE Biomass program's Resources for Consumers Web page (www1.eere.energy.gov/biomass/for_consumers.html), biomass currently supplies about 3% of total U.S. energy consumption in the form of electricity, process heat, and transportation fuels. In the European Union, bioenergy contributes about 3.7% of the total primary energy supply, according to the European Biomass Industry Association (www.eubia.org/about_biomass.0.html). However, it plays a considerable role in several European countries, such as Finland and Sweden, where its contribution amounts to 20% and 16% of the gross inland consumption, respectively.

Wood chip conversion to heat (and possibly then electricity) can replace boiler systems in buildings. Automatic feed systems can now take wood chips and make hot water as conveniently as oil and natural gas systems can. In many locations, wood chips are free for the cost of the transportation, saving further cost. Pellet burners are a similar concept, except for the additional cost of the wood pellets. Burners are also available for corn cobs. In some cases, manufacturers will lease equipment for the energy savings, resulting in no additional cost to the end user.

The production and distribution of bio-oils and biodiesel fuels derived from bio-based materials is growing in momentum. Heating systems are available to burn used vegetable oils. These systems are useful near the point of production of used vegetable oil—usually the food service industry. Grocery stores and restaurants may benefit from such technologies. Most diesel-fueled machines can run on biodiesel without any (or minor) modifications. In addition, hauling and waste costs for the oil are eliminated, increasing the attractiveness of the technology.

WATER

This section deals with water as a resource for consumption or use, not as an energy source. Since 70% of our planet is covered with water, it may seem that water is an inexhaustible source. However, 97% of the water on Earth consists of seawater, and about 2% is ice. Much of the remaining part is either located at great depths underground or is heavily polluted. Less than 0.01% can be immediately used for the supply of drinking water (Shiklomanov 1993).

The importance of this natural base material is still increasing: the presence of fresh drinking water contributes to the social and cultural structure and the level of development of a country. Therefore, it seems logical that this natural resource would be valued, protected, and safeguarded for future generations. Still, this does not happen. Water continues to be wasted, polluted, and misused. As a consequence, global water shortage is already a reality in many countries around the world and is projected to increase with the demands of a growing population.

Water is also a resource to buildings. Energy is required to treat and pump water as it is brought to the site. As with renewable energy sources, conservation is the first step in minimizing environmental impact. Water is no different. We will focus here on how to supply water to a building system. Rainwater collection and storage can be used to meet irrigation needs. In some areas, this water can be filtered and used for other nonpotable uses (e.g., fountains and some limited washing). Other sources of water are the collection of cooling tower bleeds and collection of condenser water. These make good sources for irrigation systems and minimize the need for purchased water and wastewater treatment.

Passive Solar Thermal Energy Systems

GENERAL DESCRIPTION

Passive solar thermal energy systems utilize solar energy (mainly for space heating) via little or no use of conventional energy or mechanisms other than the building design and orientation. All above-grade buildings are passive solar. Making buildings collect, store, and use solar energy wisely then becomes the challenge for building designers. A building that intentionally optimizes passive solar heating can visually be a solar building, but many reasonably sized features that enhance energy collection and storage can be integrated into the design without dominating the overall architecture.

To be successful, a well-designed passive solar building needs (1) an appropriate thermal load (e.g., space heating); (2) aperture (e.g., clear, glazed windows); (3) thermal storage to minimize overheating and to use heat at night; (4) control, either manual or automatic, to address overheating; and (5) night insulation of the aperture so that there is not a net heat loss.

HIGH-PERFORMANCE STRATEGIES

The following strategies are general in nature and are presented as guidelines to help maximize the performance of a passive thermal solar design:

- Think about conservation first. Minimizing the heating load will reduce conventional and renewable heating systems' sizes and yields the best economics. Insulate, including the foundation, and seal the building well. Use quality exterior windows and doors.
- In the northern hemisphere, the aperture must face due south for optimal performance. If this is not possible, make it within ±10 degrees of due south. In the southern hemisphere, this solar aperture looks north.
- Minimize use of east- and west-facing glazing. They admit solar energy at nonoptimal times, at low angles that minimize storage, and are difficult to control by external shading. Also, reduce north glazing in the colder regions of the northern hemisphere, because this can lead to high heat loss rates.

- Use optimized and/or moveable external shading devices, such as overhangs, awnings, and side fins. Internal shading devices should not be relied upon for passive solar thermal control—they tend to cause overheating.

- Use high-mass direct gain designs. The solar collector (windows) and storage (floors and potentially walls) are part of the occupied space and typically have the highest solar savings fraction, which is the percent of heating load met by solar. Directly irradiated thermal masses are much more effective than indirect, thus floors or trombe walls are often best.

- Use vertical glazing. Horizontal or sloped windows and skylights are hard to control and insulate.

- Calculate the optimal thermal mass—it is often around 8 in. thick (about 20 cm)—high-density concrete for direct-gain floors over conditioned basements. The optimization should direct the designer to a concept that will capture and store the highest amount of solar energy without unnecessarily increasing cost or complexity. For all direct-gain surfaces, make sure they are of high-absorptivity (dark color) and are not covered by carpet, tile, much furniture, or other items that prevent or slow solar energy absorption. Be sure the thermal mass is highly insulated from the outdoor air or ground.

- Seeking a very high annual solar savings fraction (f_s) often leads to disappointment and poor economics, so keep expectations reasonable. Even a 15% annual fraction represents a substantial reduction in conventional heating energy use. A highly optimized passive solar thermal single-family house, in an appropriate climate, often only has about a 40% solar fraction. Combining passive with active solar, PVs, wind, and other renewable energy sources is often the most satisfactory way to achieve a very high annual solar savings fraction.

- An old solar saying, of unknown origin, is "the more passive a building, the more active the owner." Operating a passive solar building to optimize collection has thus been called *solar sailing* and requires time and experience. Be sure that passive solar and the building operator are good matches for each other.

KEY ELEMENTS OF COST

Passive solar energy systems must be engineered; otherwise, poor performance is likely.

Window sizes are typically larger than for conventional design. Some operable windows and/or vents, placed high and low, are needed for overheat periods. Proper solar control must also be foreseen.

Concrete floors and walls are commonly thicker in the storage portion of a passive solar building. A structural engineer's services are likely required.

Conventional backup systems are still needed. They will be used during cloudy and/or cold weather, so select high-efficiency equipment with low-cost fuel sources.

Night insulation must be used consistently or else there will be a net heat loss. Making the nightly installation and removal automatic is recommended, but costly.

SOURCES OF FURTHER INFORMATION

ASHRAE. 2007. *ASHRAE Handbook—HVAC Applications*, Chapter 33. Atlanta: American Society of Heating, Refrigerating and Air-Conditioning Engineers, Inc.

Balcomb, J.D. 1984. *Passive Solar Heating Analysis: A Design Manual*. Atlanta: American Society of Heating, Refrigerating and Air-Conditioning Engineers, Inc.

Crosbie, M.J., ed. 1998. *The Passive Solar Design and Construction Handbook*, Steven Winter Associates. New York: John Wiley & Sons, Inc.

ASHRAE
GreenTip #27

Active Solar Thermal Energy Systems

GENERAL DESCRIPTION

Both passive and active solar thermal energy systems rely on capture and use of solar heat. Active solar thermal energy systems differ from passive systems in the way that they use solar energy, as they use it primarily for space and water heating. This can allow for greatly enhanced collection, storage, and use of solar energy.

To be successful, a well-designed active solar system needs (1) an appropriate thermal load (e.g., potable water, space air, or pool heating); (2) collectors such as flat-plate solar panels; (3) thermal storage to use the heat at a later time; and (4) control, typically automatic, to optimize energy collection and storage and for freeze and overheat protection.

The working fluid or coolant that moves heat from the collectors to the storage device is typically water, a water/glycol solution, or air. The heat storage medium is often water but could be a rock-bed or a high-mass building for air-coolant systems.

The solar energy collectors are most often of fixed orientation and nonconcentrating, but they could be tracking and/or concentrating. Flat-plate collectors are most common and are typically installed as fixed and nonconcentrating. Large surface areas of collectors, or mirrors and/or lens for concentration, are needed to gather heat and to achieve higher temperatures.

There are many different types of active solar thermal energy systems. For example, one type often used for potable water heating is flat-plate, pressurized water/glycol coolant, and two-tank storage. An internal double-wall heat exchanger is typically employed in one tank, known as the preheat tank, and the other tank, plumbed in series, is a conventional water heater. These preheat tanks are now widely available due to nonsolar use as indirect water heaters. One-tank systems typically have an electric-resistance heating element installed in the top of the special tank.

HIGH-PERFORMANCE STRATEGIES

The following strategies are general in nature and are presented as a guideline to helping maximize the performance of an active thermal solar design:

- Think about conservation first. Minimizing the heating load will reduce conventional and renewable heating systems' sizes, and yield the best economics.
- In the northern hemisphere, the solar collectors must face due south for optimal performance. If not possible, make them within ±10 degrees of due south. In the southern hemisphere, the solar collectors look north.
- When using flat-plate collectors for space heating, mount them at an angle equal to the local latitude plus 15 to 20 degrees. For water heating, use the local latitude plus 10 degrees.
- Calculate the optimal thermal storage—about one day's heat storage (or less) often yields the best economics. Place the thermal storage device within the heated space, and be sure it is highly insulated, including under its base.
- Seeking a very high annual solar savings fraction (f_s) often leads to disappointment and poor economics, so keep expectations reasonable. Even a 25% annual fraction represents a substantial reduction in conventional energy use. A highly optimized, active solar thermal domestic water-heating system, in an appropriate climate, often has about a 60% solar fraction. Combining active solar with passive, PVs, wind, and other renewable energy sources is often the most satisfactory way to achieve a very high annual solar savings fraction.

KEY ELEMENTS OF COST

Active solar energy systems must be engineered; otherwise, poor performance is likely. Fortunately, good design tools, such as F-Chart software (Klein and Beckman 2001), are readily available.

Well-designed, factory-assembled collectors are recommended, but are fairly expensive. Site-built collectors tend to have lower thermal performance and reliability.

Storage tanks must be of high quality and be durable. Water will eventually leak, so proper tank placement and floor drains are important. For rock storage, moisture control and air-entrance filtration are important for mold growth prevention.

Quality and appropriate pumps, fans, and controls can be somewhat expensive. Using surge protection for all the electrical components is recommended. Effective grounding, for lightning and shockmitigation, is normally required by building code. For liquid coolants in sealed loops, expansion tanks and pressure relief valves are needed. For domestic water heating, a temperature-limiting mixing valve is required for the final potable water to prevent scalding; even nonconcentrating systems can produce 180°F (82°C) or so water at times. All thermal components require insulation for safety and reduced heat loss.

Installation requires many trades: a contractor to build or install the major components, a plumber to do the piping and pumps (i.e., water systems), an HVAC contractor to install ducts (i.e., air systems) and/or space-heating heat exchangers, an electrician to provide power, and a controls specialist.

Conventional backup systems are still needed. They will be used during cloudy and/or cold weather, so select high-efficiency equipment with low-cost fuel sources.

SOURCES OF FURTHER INFORMATION

ASHRAE. 1988. *Active Solar Heating Systems Design Manual.* Atlanta: American Society of Heating, Refrigerating and Air-Conditioning Engineers, Inc.

ASHRAE. 2007. *ASHRAE Handbook—HVAC Applications*, Chapter 33. Atlanta: American Society of Heating, Refrigerating and Air-Conditioning Engineers, Inc.

Howell, J., R. Bannerot, and G. Vliet. 1982. *Solar-Thermal Energy Systems: Analysis and Design.* New York: McGraw-Hill.

Klein, S., and W. Beckman. 2001. *F-Chart Software.* The F-Chart Software Company., Madison, WI. www.fchart.com.

ASHRAE
GreenTip #28

Solar Energy System—PV

GENERAL DESCRIPTION

Light shining on a PV cell, which is a solid-state semiconductor device, liberates electrons, which are collected by a wire grid, to produce direct-current electricity.

The use of solar energy to produce electricity means that PV systems reduce greenhouse gas emissions, electricity costs, and resource consumption. Electrical consumption can be reduced. Because the peak generation of PV electricity coincides with peak air-conditioning loads (if the sun shines), peak electricity demands (from the grid) may be reduced, though it is unlikely without substantial storage capacity.

PV can also reduce electrical power installation costs where the need for trenching and independent metering can be avoided. The public appeal of using solar energy to produce electricity results in a positive marketing image for PV-powered buildings and, thus, can enhance occupancy rates in commercial buildings.

While conventional PV design has focused on the use of independent applications in which excess electricity is stored in batteries, grid-connected systems are becoming more common. In these cases, electricity generated in excess of immediate demand is sent to the electrical grid, and the PV-powered building receives a utility credit. Grid-connected systems are often integrated into building elements. Increasingly, PV cells are being incorporated into sunshades on buildings for a doubly effective reduction in cooling and electricity loads.

PV power is being applied in innovative ways. Typical economically viable commercial installations include the lighting of parking lots, pathways, signs, emergency telephones, and small outbuildings.

A typical PV module consists of 33 to 40 cells, which is the basic block used in commercial applications. Typical components of a module are aluminum, glass, tedlar, and rubber. The cell is usually silicon, with trace amounts of boron and phosphorus.

Because PV systems are made from a few relatively simple components and materials, the maintenance costs of PV systems are low. Manufacturers now provide 20-year warranties for PV cells.

PV systems are adaptable and can easily be removed and re-installed in other applications. Systems can also be enlarged for greater capacity through the addition of more PV modules.

WHEN/WHERE IT'S APPLICABLE

PV is well suited for rural and urban off-grid applications and for grid-connected buildings with air-conditioning loads. The economic viability of PV depends on the distance from the grid, electrical load sizes, power line extension costs, and incentive programs offered by governmental entities or utilities.

PV applications include prime buildings, outbuildings, emergency telephones, irrigation pumps, fountains, lighting for parking lots, pathways, security, clearance, billboards, bus shelters or signs, and remote operation of gates, irrigation valves, traffic signals, radios, telemetry, or instrumentation.

Grid-connected PV systems are better-suited for buildings with peak loads during summer cooling operation but are not as well-suited for grid-connected buildings with peak wintertime loads.

Note that a portion of a PV electrical system is direct current, so appropriate fusing and breakers may not be readily available. A PV system is also not solely an electrical installation; other trades, such as roofing and light steel erectors, may be involved with a PV installation. When a PV system is installed on a roof or wall, it will likely result in envelope penetrations that will need to be sealed.

PROS

- Reduces greenhouse gas emissions.
- Reduces nonrenewable energy demand, with the ability to help offset demand on the electrical grid during critical peak cooling hours.
- Enhances green-image marketing.
- Lowers electricity consumption costs and may reduce peak electrical demand charges.
- Reduces utility infrastructure costs.
- Increases electrical reliability for the building owner. May be used as part of an emergency power backup system.

CONS

- Relatively high initial capital costs.
- Requires energy storage in batteries or a connection to electrical utility grid.
- May encounter regulatory barriers.
- High-capacity systems require large-building envelope areas that are clear of protuberances and have uninterrupted access to sunshine.
- Capacity to supply peak electrical demand can be limited, depending on sunshine during peak hours.

KEY ELEMENTS OF COST

The following provides a possible breakdown of the various cost elements that might differentiate a PV system from a conventional one and an indication of whether the net cost for this system is likely to be lower (L), higher (H), or the same (S). This assessment is only a perception of what might be likely, but it obviously may not be correct in all situations. There is no substitute for a detailed cost analysis as part of the design process. The listings below may also provide some assistance in identifying the cost elements involved.

First Cost

- PV modules   H
- Wiring and various electrical devices   H
- Battery bank   H
- Instrumentation   H
- Connection cost (if grid-connected)   H

Recurring Costs

- Electricity   L

SOURCES OF FURTHER INFORMATION

California Energy Commission, Renewable Energy Program
    www.energy.ca.gov/renewables/

The Canadian Renewable Energy Network
www.canren.gc.ca/
ecoENERGY for Renewable Power
www.ecoaction.gc.ca/ecoenergy-ecoenergie/power-electricite/
index-eng.cfm
National Renewable Energy Laboratory, Building-Integrated PV
www.nrel.gov/pv/building_integrated_pv.html
NRC. *Photovoltaic Systems Design Manual.* Ottawa, Ontario, Can-
ada: Natural Resources Canada, Office of Coordination and
Technical Information.
NRC. RETScreen (Renewable Energy Analysis Software). Natural
Resources Canada, Energy Diversification Research Laboratory,
Ottawa, Ontario, Canada. www.retscreen.net.
Photovoltaic Resource Site
www.pvpower.com
School of Photovoltaic and Renewable Energy Engineering,
University of New South Wales
www.pv.unsw.edu.au
Solar Energy Industries Association
www.seia.org
Sustainable Sources
www.greenbuilder.com
Watsun. 1999. *WATSUN-PV—A computer program for simulation
of solar photovoltaic systems, User's Manual and Program
Documentation,* Version 6.1. Watsun Simulation Laboratory,
University of Waterloo, Ontario, Canada.

ASHRAE
GreenTip #29

Solar Protection

GENERAL DESCRIPTION

Shading the building's transparent surfaces from solar radiation is mandatory during summer and sometimes even necessary during winter. This way, it is possible to prevent solar heat gains when they are not needed and to control daylighting to minimize glare problems. Depending on the origin of solar radiation (i.e., direct, diffuse, reflected), it may be possible to select different shading elements that provide more effective solar control.

Depending on the specific application and type of problem, there may be different options for selecting the optimum shading device. The decision can be based on several criteria, from aesthetics to performance and effectiveness or cost. Different types of shading elements are suitable for a given application, result in varying levels of solar control effectiveness, and have a different impact on indoor daylight levels, natural ventilation, and overall indoor visual and thermal comfort conditions.

There are basically three main groups of solar control devices. The first group is external shading devices, which can be fixed and/or movable elements. They have the most apparent impact on the aesthetics of the building. If properly designed and accounted for, they can become an integral part of the building's architecture, as they are integrated into the building envelope. Fixed types are typically variations of a horizontal overhang and a vertical side fin, with different relative dimensions and geometry. When properly designed and sized, fixed external shading devices can be effective during summer, while during winter they allow the desirable direct solar gains through the openings. This is a direct positive outcome given the relative position of the sun and its daily movement in winter (when there is low solar elevation) and summer (when there is high solar elevation). Movable types are more flexible, since they can be adjusted and operated either manually or automatically for optimum results and typically include various types and shapes of awnings and louvers.

The second group is interpane shading devices, which are usually adjustable and retractable louvers, roller blinds, screens, or films that are placed within the glazing. This type of a shading device is more suitable for solar control of scattered radiation or sky diffuse radiation. Given that the incident solar radiation is already absorbed by the glazing, thus increasing its temperature, one needs to take into account the heat transfer component to the indoor spaces.

The third group, which is internal shading devices, is very common because of indoor aesthetics. They offer privacy control and easy installation, accessibility, and maintenance. Although on the interior they are very practical and, most of the time, necessary, their overall thermal behavior needs to be carefully evaluated, since the incident solar radiation is trapped inside the space and will be absorbed and turn into heat if not properly controlled (i.e., reflecting solar radiation outward through the opening). Numerous types or combinations of the various shading devices are also possible, depending on the application.

HIGH-PERFORMANCE STRATEGIES

- Use natural shading. Deciduous plants, trees, and vines offer effective natural shading. It is critical for their year-round effectiveness not to obstruct solar radiation during winter (in order to increase passive solar gains). Plants also have a positive impact on the immediate environment surrounding the building (i.e., the microclimate) because of their evaporative cooling potential. However, the plants need some time to grow, may cause moisture problems if they are too close to opaque elements, and can suffer from various diseases. The view can be restricted and some plants, especially large leafless trees, can still obstruct solar radiation during winter and may reduce natural ventilation. In general, for deciduous plants, the shading effect is best for east and west orientations, along with southeast and southwest.
- Incorporate louvers into the design. These are also referred to as *venetian blinds* and can be placed externally (which is preferable) or internally (which allows for easier maintenance and installation in existing buildings). The external louvers can be fixed in place with rotating or fixed tilt of the slats. The louvers can also be retractable. The slats can be flat or curved. Slats from

semitransparent material allow for outdoor visibility. The louvers can be operated manually (i.e., slat tilt angle, up or down movement) or they can be electrically motor driven. Adjusting the tilt angle of the slats or raising/lowering the panel can change the conditions from maximum light and solar gains to complete shading. Louvers can also be used to properly control air movement during natural ventilation. Slat curvature can be utilized to redirect incident solar radiation before entering into the space. Slat material can have different reflective properties and can also be insulated. During winter, fully closed louvers with insulated slats can be used at night for providing additional thermal insulation at the openings.

• Incorporate awnings into the design. External or internal awnings can be fixed in place, operated manually, or driven electrically by a motor that can also be automated. Light-colored materials are preferable, as they allow for high solar surface reflectivity. Awnings are easily installed on any type and size of opening and may also be used for wind protection during winter to reduce infiltration and heat losses.

KEY ELEMENTS OF COST

Natural shading usually is a cost-effective strategy that reduces glare, and, depending on the external building façade, can improve aesthetics. Plants should be carefully selected to match local climatic conditions (in order to optimize watering needs).

External electrically driven and automated units have a higher cost and it takes money to maintain the motors, but they are more flexible and effective. Louvers are difficult to clean on a regular basis. Nonretractable louvers somewhat obstruct outward vision.

Awning fabric needs periodic replacement, depending on local wind conditions. Electrically driven and automated units have a higher cost and it takes money to maintain the motors.

SOURCES OF FURTHER INFORMATION

Argiriou, A., A. Dimoudi, C.A. Balaras, D. Mantas, E. Dascalaki, and I. Tselepidaki. 1996. *Passive Cooling of Buildings.* M. Santamouris and A. Asimakopoulos, eds. London: James & James Science Publishers Ltd.

Baker, N. 1995. *Light and Shade: Optimising Daylight Design.* European Directory of sustainable and energy efficient building. London: James & James Science Publishers Ltd.

Givoni, B. 1994. *Passive and Low Energy Cooling of Buildings.* New York: Van Nostrand Reinhold.

Stack, A., J. Goulding, and J.O. Lewis. Shading systems: Solar shading for the European climates. DG TREN, Brussels, Belgium. http://erg.ucd.ie/down_thermie.html.

REFERENCES AND RESOURCES

Published

Alvarez, S., E. Dascalaki, G. Guarracino, E. Maldonado, S. Sciuto, and L. Vandaele. 1998. *Natural Ventilation of Buildings—A Design Handbook.* F. Allard, ed. London: James & James Science Publishers Ltd.

ASHRAE. 2006. *ASHRAE Handbook—Refrigeration.* Atlanta: American Society of Heating, Refrigerating and Air-Conditioning Engineers, Inc.

ASHRAE. 2009. *ASHRAE Handbook—Fundamentals.* Atlanta: American Society of Heating, Refrigerating and Air-Conditioning Engineers, Inc.

Balaras, C.A., E. Dascalaki, P. Tsekouras, and A. Aidonis. 2010. High solar combi systems in Europe. *ASHRAE Transactions* 116(1).

Balaras, C.A., H.-M. Henning, E. Wiemken, G. Grossman, E. Podesser, and C.A. Infante Ferreira. 2006. Solar cooling—An overview of European applications and design guidelines. *ASHRAE Journal* 48(6):14–22.

Beckman, W., S.A. Klein, and J.A. Duffie. 1977. *Solar Heating Design.* New York: John Wiley & Sons, Inc.

DOE. 2006. Solar buildings. Transpired air collectors ventilation preheating. DOE/GO-102001-1288, U.S. Department of Energy, Washington, DC.

EIA. Table 10.8, Photovoltaic cell and module shipments by type, trade, and prices, 1982–2008. U.S. Energy Information Administration. www.eia.doe.gov/aer/txt/stb1008.xls.

EPA. 2010. *Guide to Purchasing Green Power.* Washington, DC: U.S. Environmental Protection Agency. www.epa.gov/grnpower/buygreenpower/guide.htm.

EPIA. 2010. 2014 global market outlook for photovoltaics until 2014. European Photovoltaic Industry Association. www.epia.org/fileadmin/EPIA_docs/public/Global_Market_Outlook_for_Photovoltaics_until_2014.pdf.

ESTIF. 2010 Solar thermal markets in Europe—Trends and market statistics 2009. www.estif.org/fileadmin/estif/content/market_data/downloads/2009%20solar_thermal_markets.pdf.

EU. 2008. Climate change: Commission welcomes final adoption of Europe's climate and energy package. Europa press release IP/08/1998, European Union, Brussels.

GWEC. 2010. Global wind 2009 report. Global Wind Energy Council, Brussels, Belgium. www.gwec.net/index.php?id=167.

Henning. H.-M., ed. 2004. *Solar Assisted Air-Conditioning in Buildings—A Handbook For Planners.* Wien: Springer-Verlag.

Klein, S., and W. Beckman. 2001. *F-Chart Software.* The F-Chart Software Company., Madison, WI. www.fchart.com.

Kreith, F., and J. Kreider. 1989. *Principles of Solar Engineering*, 2d ed. Wasington, DC: Hemisphere Pub.

NREL. 2010. NREL highlights utility green power leaders. NREL press release NR-1910. Golden, CO: National Renewable Energy Laboratory.

Shiklomanov, I.A. 1993 World fresh water resources. In *Water in Crisis*. Gleick, P.H., ed. New York: Oxford University Press.

Weiss, W., I. Bergmann, and G. Faninger. 2008. *Solar Heat Worldwide*. Solar Heat & Cooling Programme, International Energy Agency, Paris, France. www.iea-shc.org/publications/statistics/IEA-SHC_Solar_Heat_Worldwide-2008.pdf.

Weiss, W., and F. Mauthner. 2010. Solar heat worldwide—Markets and contribution to the energy supply 2008. www.iea-shc.org/publications/statistics/IEA-SHC_Solar_Heat_Worldwide-2010.pdf.

Online

AGORES—A Global Overview of Renewable Energy Sources (the official European Commission renewable energy information centre and knowledge gateway, with a global overview of RES)
www.agores.org

American Solar Energy Society
www.ases.org

American Wind Energy Association
www.awea.org

Building Energy Efficiency Research Project at the Department of Architecture, The University of Hong Kong
www.arch.hku.hk/research/beer/

Centre for Analysis and Dissemination of Demonstrated Energy Technologies
www.caddet-re.org

Global Wind Energy Council
www.gwec.net

Green Energy In Europe
www.ecofys.com/

Green Venture
www.greenventure.on.ca

Europe's Energy Portal
www.energy.eu/#renewable

European Biomass Association
www.aebiom.org

European Biomass Industry Association
www.eubia.org/about_biomass.0.html

European Photovoltaic Industry Association
www.epia.org

European Renewable Energy Centres Agency
www.eurec.be

European Solar Thermal Industry
www.estif.org

European Wind Energy Association
www.ewea.org

EUROSOLAR—The European Association for Renewable Energies e.V.
www.eurosolar.org

International Energy Agency, Bioenergy
www.ieabioenergy.com

International Energy Agency, Photovoltaic Power Systems Programme
www.iea-pvps.org

International Energy Agency, Solar Heating And Cooling Programme
www.iea-shc.org

International Energy Agency, Task 38
www.iea-shc.org/task38

International Hydropower Association
www.hydropower.org

International Hydropower Association Fact Sheet
www.hydropower.org/downloads/F1_the_contribution_of_hydropower.pdf

International Solar Energy Society
www.ises.org

National Hydropower Association
www.hydro.org

National Oceanic and Atmospheric Administration
www.noaa.gov

National Renewable Energy Laboratory, Solar Energy Research Facility
www.nrel.gov/pv/facilities_serf.html

North Carolina Solar Center, DSIRE
www.dsireusa.org/

North Carolina Cooperative Extension Service, Water Quality and Waste Management
www.bae.ncsu.edu/programs/extension/publicat/wqwm

Oak Ridge National Laboratory, Bioenergy Feedstock Information Network
http://bioenergy.ornl.gov/

Solar Energy Industries Association
www.seia.org

U.S. Department of Energy, Energy Efficiency and Renewable Energy,
Biomass program, Resources for Consumers Web page
www1.eere.energy.gov/biomass/for_consumers.html

World Meteorological Organization, World Radiation Data Centre
http://wrdc-mgo.nrel.gov/

The World's Water
www.worldwater.org

CHAPTER THIRTEEN

LIGHTING SYSTEMS

This chapter is not intended to make you a lighting expert but rather to familiarize you with the basic goals and process of lighting design. It's meant to enable HVAC&R design engineers to interact effectively with lighting designers and architects so that visually effective and energy-efficient systems are created.

Lighting has a significant impact on building loads and energy usage. Therefore, it is important that the HVAC&R designer understand the role and objectives of the lighting designer. The productive interaction between a professional lighting designer and the HVAC&R engineer can enhance the overall energy and the environmental performance of buildings.

ELECTRIC LIGHTING

Energy-Effective Lighting Design

The lighting design profession is increasingly focused on providing high-quality visual environments, with an emphasis on energy efficiency. As lighting technologies have become more efficient and interior illuminance (footcandles [Lux]) expectations have moderated, it is now possible to design high-quality lighting at connected power levels that are much lower than 25 years ago.

All buildings can be efficiently and comfortably illuminated using carefully selected, standard lighting equipment. Successful lighting systems with lighting power densities of 0.7 to 1.0 W/ft² (8 to 11 W/m²) can be applied to most building types by following basic application design criteria set forth by the Illuminating Engineering Society of North America (IES) and lighting equipment manufacturers. For offices and schools, lighting quality is generally defined as visually comfortable, low-glare, relatively uniform lighting with appropriate illuminance for the task performed. This includes balancing both the horizontal and vertical brightness.

Most energy codes have lighting power limits between 0.9 and 1.4 W/ft² (10 and 15 W/m²). Some exceptions are storage buildings (lesser limit), retail stores (higher limit), and hospitality facilities (higher limit). However, even in many stores and hospitality buildings, the same efficient lighting approaches suitable for schools,

313

offices, and most other common building types can also be applied. The fundamental guide for lighting professionals is the IES *Lighting Handbook* (IESNA 2000). (The tenth edition should be available in 2011.) It is a highly recommended resource for designers and engineers involved in the design and specification of lighting systems. It comprehensively describes recommended design approaches, illuminance and uniformity levels, power density targets, daylighting integration strategies, luminaire efficiency, and other lighting-related information necessary to provide appropriate lighting.

Efficient Lighting Systems

Tables 13-1, 13-2, and 13-3 contain a listing of one state's standard fluorescent lighting systems and related criteria that will generally satisfy current IES light level recommendations, as well as comply with energy codes and meet a modest project budget. Table 13-1 lists two common lighting systems that can be used for a wide variety of project types at very low costs. Table 13-2 lists lighting systems suitable for private and open office areas and similar spaces (e.g., exam rooms in

Table 13-1: General Use Systems

Primary Application	Luminaire Type	Lamps or Total Lamp Watts	Spacing between Luminaries (in Plan View)	Lamp Ballast System
General use spaces of all types	Nominal 4 ft (1.2 m) recessed or surface-mounted fluorescent troffer (e.g., basket, lensed, etc.) with high-efficiency electronic ballast	(two) F32T-8 lamps	No less than 8 ft (2.4 m) OC*	Maximum 56 W, 45–48 W, low-ballast-factor ballast preferred
General use spaces of all types	Nominal 2 ft (0.6 m) recessed or surface-mounted fluorescent troffer (e.g., basket, lensed, etc.) with electronic ballast	(three) F17T-8 lamps	No less than 8 ft (2.4 m) OC*	Maximum 52 W

*OC = on center

Table 13-2: Lighting for Offices
(including Commercial, Academic, and Institutional)

Primary Application	Luminaire Type	Lamps or Total Lamp Watts	Spacing between Luminaires (in Plan View)	Lamp Ballast System
Open offices	Suspended linear fluorescent fixtures, consisting of nominal 4 ft (1.2 m) sections in continuous rows with electronic ballast(s) (ceiling heights 9 ft [2.7 m] or above)	One F54T-5HO, two F32T-8, or two F28T-5	Continuous rows no closer than 15 ft (4.6 m) apart	Maximum 60 input W/4 ft (1.2 m) unit,
	Nominal 4 ft (1.2 m) recessed or surface-mounted fluorescent troffers (ceiling heights below 9 ft [2.7 m])	Two F32T-8 lamps	Regular grid 8 ft (2.4 m) OC*	Maximum 48 input W/ luminaire
Very small private offices < 105 ft^2 (10 m^2)	One recessed or suspended 4 ft (1.2 m) linear fluorescent fixture (minimum ceiling height 9 ft [2.7 m] for suspended fixtures)	Three F32T-8 lamps	One luminaire per office	Maximum 90 input W
mall private offices 105–125 ft^2 (10–12 m^2)	Two recessed or suspended 4 ft (1.2 m) linear fluorescent fixtures (minimum ceiling height 9 ft [2.7 m] for suspended fixtures)	Two F32T-8 lamps per fixture	No less than 6 ft (1.8 m) OC*	Maximum 48 input W to each luminaire
mall private offices 125–160 ft^2 (10–15 m^2)	Two recessed or suspended 4 ft (1.2 m) linear fluorescent fixtures (minimum ceiling height 9 ft [2.7 m] for suspended fixtures)	Two F32T-8 lamps per fixture	No less than 6 ft (1.8 m) OC*	Maximum 56 input W to each luminaire

*OC = on center

Table 13-2: Lighting for Offices
(including Commercial, Academic, and Institutional) (Continued)

Primary Application	Luminaire Type	Lamps or Total Lamp Watts	Spacing between Luminaires (in Plan View)	Lamp Ballast System
Medium private offices 160–200 ft^2 (15–19 m^2)	Two recessed or suspended 4 ft (1.2 m) linear fluorescent fixtures Three recessed or suspended 4 ft (1.2 m) linear fluorescent fixtures Four recessed 2 ft (0.6 m) linear fluorescent fixtures (minimum ceiling height 9 ft [2.7 m] for suspended fixtures)	Three F32T-8 lamps/fixture Two F32T-8 lamps/fixture Two F17T-8 lamps/fixture	No less than 6 ft (1.8 m) OC*	Maximum 7 input W to each luminaire Maximum 4 input W to each luminaire Maximum 3 input W per fixture
Executive offices and conference rooms 200-250 ft^2 (19–23 m^2)	Four recessed or suspended 4 ft (1.2 m) linear fluorescent fixtures Four recessed 2 ft (0.6 m) linear fluorescent fixtures (minimum ceiling height 9 ft [2.7m] for suspended fixtures)	Two F32T-8 lamps/fixture Two F32T-8U lamps/fixture	No less than 8 ft (2.4 m) OC*	Maximum 4 input W to each luminaire

*OC = on center

Table 13-3: Other Common Lighting Systems

Primary Application	Luminaire Type	Lamps or Total Lamp Watts	Spacing between Luminaires (in Plan View)	Lamp Ballast System
Lobbies, atriums, etc. Industrial spaces	Metal halide, induction, or multiple compact fluorescent lamps (of equivalent lamp watts with electronic ballasts), downlights, pendants, etc.	100 W or less 150 W or less 250 W or less 400 W or less	No less than 12 ft (3.7 m) OC* No less than 15 ft (4.6 m) OC* No less than 18 ft (5.5 m) OC* No less than 22 ft (6.7 m) OC*	Mounting height at least 12 ft (3.7 m) above-finished door; only recommended for high-bay spaces
Corridors, lobbies, meeting rooms, etc.	Compact fluorescent (including twin tube, quad tube, or triple tube) or metal halide downlights, wallwashers, monopoints, and similar directional luminaires Wall sconces using any of the above light sources	40 W or less 60 W or less 80 W or less 100 W or less	No less than 6 ft (1.8 m) OC* No less than 8 ft (2.4 m) OC* No less than 10 ft (3.0 m) OC* No less than 12 ft (3.7 m) OC*	Any space height
Undercabinet and undershelf task lighting	Hardwired undercabinet or undershelf fluorescent or LED luminaires, nominal 2, 3, or 4 ft (0.6, 0.9, or 1.2 m) in length and employing an electronic ballast (fluorescent sources)	No greater than 8.5 W/ft (27.09 W/m) of luminaire	No typical spacing requirements. Must be addressed specifically for each application.	Luminaires may be mounted end-to-end if needed to accommodate cabinet length

*OC = on center

Table 13-3: Other Common Lighting Systems *(Continued)*

Primary Application	Luminaire Type	Lamps or Total Lamp Watts	Spacing between Luminaires (in Plan View)	Lamp Ballast System
Lobby, executive office, and conference room accent lighting	Low-voltage down-lights, accent lights, or monopoint lights having an integral transformer	Rated at 50 W or less	No less than 8 ft (2.4 m) OC*	For accent lighting only; should not be used for general lighting
Copyroom, storeroom, etc.	Nominal 4 ft (1.2 m) recessed or surface-mounted fluorescent troffer, wraparound, strip lights, etc., with electronic ballast	One or two lamps totaling 64 W or less	No less than 8 ft (2.4 m) OC*	Maximum 60 input W to each luminaire
Small utility, storage, and closet spaces	Single-lamp fluorescent with electronic ballast (strip, wrap, industrial, or other fixture)	32 W	One luminaire in a closet, electric room, or other small space	Maximum 35 input W to each luminaire
Storage and utility spaces	Industrials, wraparounds, strip lights, etc., consisting of nominal 4 ft (1.2 m) sections	Two F32T-8	Individual 12-lamp luminaires 8 ft (2.4 m) OC* Continuous single-lamp rows no closer than 8 ft (2.4 m) apart	48 input W per two lamp

*OC = on center

Table 13-3: Other Common Lighting Systems (Continued)

Primary Application	Luminaire Type	Lamps or Total Lamp Watts	Spacing between Luminaires (in Plan View)	Lamp Ballast System
Bathroom vanities and stairwells	Two-lamp fluorescent with electronic ballast (wrap, cove, troffer, corridor, vanity, valence, or other fixture)	Two F32T-8	One luminaire per vanity in a toilet or locker room	Maximum 48 input W to each luminaire
Exit signs	LED	No greater than 3.5 W per sign	One luminaire per landing in a stairwell	Maximum 48 input W to each luminaire

*OC = on center

clinics and hospitals). Table 13-3 lists a variety of common lighting systems that can be used in industrial and commercial applications.

For most spaces, designers should use lighting layouts that conform to these criteria. Spacing measurements are taken from the plan-view center of the luminaire. Luminaires should be mounted at least one-third of the indicated mounting distance away from any ceiling-high partition.

If more than one type of luminaire (excluding exit signs) is to be located within one space enclosed with ceiling-high partitions, the spacing between different luminaires must be the larger of the required spacing for the two luminaries.

The lamp/ballast combination and luminaire-type need to be carefully considered for visual comfort, glare control, efficacy (lumen/watt output), and total system efficiency to meet task and ambient lighting requirements for a particular space type. The proper specification of lighting equipment is necessary to optimize lighting quality and minimize energy use.

None of the following luminaires should be employed:

- luminaires employing Edison (standard screw-in) baseline voltage sockets or halogen lamps using any sockets rated over 150 W
- luminaires designed for incandescent or halogen low-voltage lamps exceeding 75 W
- track lighting systems of any kind or voltage of operation
- line-voltage monopoints permitting the installation of track luminaires.

However, for every 20 luminaires meeting these requirements, a single hard-wired luminaire of any type (except track), rated not more than 150 lamp W may be placed as desired. This permits architects, interior designers, and lighting designers the ability to add lighting for aesthetic effects or décor without an unreasonable energy burden. Note that if more than one such luminaire is permitted, any number of them may be located in any of the project's spaces. In other words, in a project with 100 types of luminaires from Tables 13-1, 13-2, or 13-3, five decorative luminaires would be permitted, and they could all be installed over a receptionist's desk.

These lists are not intended to be comprehensive but rather straightforward and instructive. There are certainly other satisfactory (and efficient) designs that are not listed. Professional lighting design assistance may be needed to reach optimum performance in complex spaces and for specific conditions.

In all cases, be certain to review the subsequent sections on other aspects of lighting for detailed information on product specifications and additional energy-saving ideas.

When/Where Applicable

The above systems are generally good for most conventional space types with ordinary ceiling systems. These include the following:

- typical private offices
- typical open office areas
- office area corridors
- conference rooms and classrooms
- meeting and seminar rooms
- most laboratories
- equipment, server, and cable rooms
- building lobbies
- elevator lobbies
- building core and circulation areas
- industrial areas, shops, and docks
- big box and grocery stores

For commercial buildings, these recommendations assume standard acoustical tile ceilings (with a reflectance of 80%). For industrial buildings, open bar joist construction is assumed. Ceiling heights and wall and floor finishes are assumed to be standard as well.

Efficient Lamps and Ballasts

The lighting industry has made significant improvements in lamp and ballast technology over the last 25 years. Recent improvements, while not as widely publicized, continue to permit good lighting at decreasing power levels. Proper specification of lamps and ballasts are an important part of actualizing these results.

Specifications. The following specifications are recommended to ensure the latest technology is being employed.

Ballasts for all fluorescent lamps and for high-intensity discharge (HID) lamps rated 150 W and less should be electronic. Harmonic distortion should be less than 20%.

- *T-8 System Ballasts.* Four foot (1.2 m) T-8 fluorescent lighting systems should employ high-efficiency electronic ballasts. Because instant-start ballasts are the most efficient and least costly, they should be used in all longer duty cycle applications where the lights are turned on and off infrequently. Fluorescent systems controlled by motion sensors in spaces where the lights will be turned on and off frequently should employ programmed-start ballasts. Designers are strongly encouraged to use ballasts with low-ballast-factors (BF < 0.80) wherever possible. T-8 low-ballast-factor and normal-ballast-factor ballasts should be high-efficiency electronic, not exceeding 28 input W/4 ft (1.2 m) lamp at BF > 0.85 and not exceeding 24 input W for BF > 0.70 (American National Standards Institute free air rating). In lieu of the above, electronic dimming ballasts may be used as needed.
- *Metal Halide Ballasts.* Metal halide ballasts 150 W and less should be electronic. Metal halide systems greater than 150 W should use linear-reactor, pulse-start type ballasts wherever 277 volt power is available. For other voltages, pulse-start lamps and ballasts should be used.

The lamps listed in Table 13-4 represent the best common lamp types to employ. Note that this list is not comprehensive and a better choice for a particular project may not be listed. However, for the majority of applications, this list is a good guide.

The lamps recommended for primary lighting systems are both energy-efficient and have long lives, representing excellent cost benefits. Lamps for other applications are generally less efficient, have shorter lives, or both. Also, designers should use the minimum number of different types of lamps on a project to reduce maintenance costs and improve the efficiency of inventory management.

Table 13-4: Common Lamp Types

Generic Lamp Types	Applications	Requirements
4 ft (1.2 m) T-8 lamps F32T-8	Primary lighting systems in commercial, institutional, and low bay industrial spaces	TCLP compliant (low-mercury) lamps with barrier coat and high lumen phosphor (minimum 3100 initial lumens) Premium long-life-rated lamp
Fluorescent T-5 and T-5HO lamps F14T-5, F21T-5, and F28T-5; F24T-5HO, F39T-5HO, and F54T-5HO	Primary lighting systems in commercial, institutional, and low and high bay industrial spaces	Standard T-5 and T-5HO lamps
Metal halide pulse-start lamps over 250 W	Primary lighting systems in large spaces with very high ceilings and/or special lighting requirements	Pulse-start lamps only— be certain to specify pulse-start ballasts Use linear reactor ballasts on 277 volt systems
Fluorescent T-8 lamps F17T-8, F25T-8	Secondary and specialized applications in commercial, institutional, and low bay industrial spaces	TCLP compliant (low-mercury) lamps with barrier coat and 800 series phosphor Premium long-life-rated lamps
Compact fluorescent long lamps F40TT-5, F50TT-5, and F55TT-5	Specialized applications in commercial, institutional, and low bay industrial spaces	Standard long twin-tube lamps

Table 13-4: Common Lamp Types (Continued)

Generic Lamp Types	Applications	Requirements
Compact fluorescent 4-pin lamps CF13, CF18, CF26, CF32, CF42, CF57, and CF70	Downlighting, wallwashing, sconces, and other common space and secondary lighting systems in commercial, institutional, and low-bay industrial spaces	Standard twin-, quad-, triple-tube, and four-tube lamps.
Halogen MR16 lamps	Accent lighting for art and displays only; do not use for general lighting	Halogen IR 12 volt compact reflector lamps
Ceramic PAR and T HID Lamps PAR20, PAR30, PAR38, ED17, and T-6	Downlighting, accent lighting, and other special, limited applications in commercial, institutional, and low bay industrial spaces, retail display lighting	39, 70, 100, and 150 W ceramic lamps
Halogen infrared reflecting PAR30 and PAR38 lamps	Applications requiring full-range dimming, retail display lighting	Halogen IR 50, 60, 80, and 100 W reflector lamps

Lighting Power Density Criteria

For efficiency, a complete, hardwired lighting system should be installed with the following lighting power density (LPD) requirements:

- Private offices shall not exceed a connected LPD of 0.9 W/ft^2 (10 W/ m^2).
- Open office areas shall not exceed a connected LPD of 0.8 W/ft^2 (9 W/m^2).
- Conference rooms and similar spaces shall not exceed a connected LPD of 1.2 W/ft^2 (13 W/m^2).
- Core areas (e.g., lobbies, elevator lobbies, mailrooms, lunchrooms, restrooms, copy rooms, locker rooms, and similar spaces) shall not exceed a connected LPD of 0.8 W/ft^2 (9 W/m^2).

- Hallways, corridors, storage rooms, mechanical and electrical rooms, and similar spaces shall not exceed a connected LPD of 0.7 W/ft^2 (8 W/m^2).
- Any other space not listed shall not exceed a connected LPD of 0.6 W/ft^2 (6 W/m^2).

Additional lighting, such as lighting within furniture systems, should not be installed in a space unless a more complete analysis and design are undertaken. These systems need to be carefully coordinated with the permanent lighting systems of the building. An exception is portable plug-in lamps and under-cabinet luminaires that are attached to the underside of modular furniture, overhead cabinets, bins, or shelves, which should be used where needed.

There are a few space types (e.g., video teleconferencing rooms, showrooms, retail space, and food service spaces) that usually require more lighting power than provided above. For these uncommon space types, an appropriate LPD requirement should be determined using from *ANSI/ASHRAE/IES Standard 90.1-2010, Energy Standard for Buildings Except Low-Rise Residential Buildings* (ASHRAE 2010).

Application Notes

Open Offices. For general illumination in spaces with ceilings that are 9 ft (2.7 m) or higher, consider suspended linear fluorescent indirect, direct/indirect, or semi-indirect lighting systems, supplemented by task lights. General layouts should be between 0.6 and 0.8 W/ft^2 (6 and 9 W/m^2) and should use high-performance luminaires and T-8, T-5, or T-5HO lamps. Task lights can be used where needed. If troffers are preferred, consider using T-8 lamps as specified with low-ballast-factor ballasts. This will ensure appropriate energy use while maintaining recommended light levels. Task lighting should be added underneath shelves and bins where required.

Private Offices. Suspended linear fluorescent lighting should be a first consideration for private offices, although recessed troffers can also be used. Luminaires should use T-8 or T-5 lamps. LPD should be around 0.8 to 0.9 W/ft^2 (9 to 10 W/m^2). Task lights can be used where needed.

Executive Offices, Board, and Conference Rooms. Executive offices can be designed similarly to private offices. If desired, a premium approach using compact fluorescent downlights, wallwashers, and/or halogen accent lights can be used, but the overall design should not exceed 1.2 W/ft^2 (13 W/m^2). If the number of executive offices is high, lighting power levels should be reduced to match the recommendations for private offices.

Classrooms. Classrooms should be lighted using direct/indirect classroom lighting systems, with about 0.9 W/ft^2 (10 W/m^2) of connected power using T-8 super lamps and efficient electronic ballasts.

Corridors. In general, corridors should be lighted using compact fluorescent sconces, downlights, ceiling-mounted or close-to-ceiling decorative diffuse fixtures, or similar equipment. Power density should be about 0.5 to 0.6 W/ft^2 (5 to 6 W/m^2)

overall. Note that these luminaires may be equipped with emergency battery backup when needed as an alternative to less attractive "bug eye" type emergency lighting.

High Bay Spaces. Industrial, grocery, and retail space without ceilings or with very high ceilings (usually 15 ft [4.6 m] and above) need special lighting fixtures. For mounting heights up to 20 to 25 ft (6.1 to 7.6 m), first try to use fluorescent industrial luminaires that employ T-8 lamps, keeping in mind that two super 4 ft (1.2 m) T-8 lamps and a high light output overdrive ballast at 77 W produces as much light (mean lumens) as a 100 W metal halide lamp that, with ballast, consumes 120 W. Four super T-8 lamps with overdrive ballasts at 154 W produce as much light as a 175 W pulse-start metal halide (195 to 205 W) or a standard 250 W metal halide lamp (286 to 295 W with ballast).

For mounting heights above 25 ft (7.6 m), consider T-5HO high bay luminaires. Similar savings relative to metal halide are possible. High-wattage metal halide should be reserved for very high mounting (above 50 ft [15.2 m]) and for special applications (e.g., sports lighting).

Other Applications. The following luminaire types are generally recommended for these areas:

- Artwork, bulletin/display surfaces, etc., use compact fluorescent wallwashers or low-voltage monopoint lights.
- Utility spaces (e.g., cable and equipment rooms) use two-lamp strip lights, industrials, or surface luminaires.
- Lobby spaces, cafeterias, and other public spaces, as much as possible, use appropriate selections from among these luminaires.

DAYLIGHT HARVESTING

General Description

Most buildings have some type of natural light that is transmitted into the building through windows and/or skylights. The majority of commercial, industrial, and institutional buildings have windows and, in some cases, skylights, clerestories, and more extensive fenestration systems.

From an energy perspective, the optimal use of daylight is to reduce the load of the electric lighting system by dimming or switching off luminaires when natural light provides ample illuminance for the tasks performed in the space. It is important to note that the incoming light is only useable if it is controlled to reduce glare and lights a space in a way that is comfortable to the occupant (including thermal comfort). This process of reducing electric lighting in the presence of daylight, which is known as *daylight harvesting* (see Figure 13-1), is discussed in this section because of its significant energy saving potential. The prediction of daylight harvesting savings is a complicated process that

Image courtesy of Cannon Design

Figure 13-1 Example of daylight harvesting rendering.

involves a comprehensive understanding of site, building orientation, weather conditions, materials, and system integration. There are added capital costs for daylight harvesting elements such as dimming ballasts and photoelectric controls. It is important to justify these costs by accurately predicting the potential energy savings of daylight harvesting techniques. However, when the challenges of daylighting are appropriately addressed, significant energy savings are possible.

From a lighting design perspective, daylight can be treated similarly to any other light source, so it can be used to compose lighting design solutions that take illuminance, luminance, contrast, color, and other lighting design elements into consideration. However, the lighting designer is challenged to deal with the fact that the light source location is given, and that, in most cases, the only means available to change its characteristics is through blinds, shades, lightshelves, light conveyors, and other mechanical forms of attenuation and shielding.

It is possible to simulate the performance of natural lighting to determine the amount, and to a certain extent, the quality of available daylight under varying conditions of season, time of day, and weather. However, this is exhaustive analytical work of a highly specialized nature, and it is recommended that appropriate experts perform such studies. In the meantime, some buildings can benefit tremendously from some simple daylight harvesting considerations.

Basic Toplighting

Basic toplighting typically involves using simple skylights in the roof. (This is not to say that other toplighting configurations [e.g., the clerestory, roof monitor, or sawtooth roof] are not workable; indeed, they often have advantages over horizontal skylights.) Needless to say, there are many architectural elements, including structure, waterproofing, and other details, that should be considered when exploring the appropriateness of skylights. When used in a manner similar to light fixtures and laid out to provide uniform illumination, toplights are an acceptable way to illuminate single-story, large spaces that use (primarily) daylight.

Toplighting is best when a number of smaller skylights are used, much the way effective lighting systems utilize many light fixtures rather than one larger light source in the middle of the room. Skylights should be diffuse or prismatic rather than clear to avoid harsh glare from direct sunlight. Skylights generally do not have to incorporate mechanical or electronic light control louvers, since the optimum size of the skylight is chosen for passive skylighting (i.e., there are no active or moving elements needed to regulate the amount of interior light).

To determine the optimum size of skylights, one can download a program called SkyCalc from www.energydesignresources.com/resource/129/. This program, which is optimized for California and the northwestern region of the United States, can be applied with some care anywhere in North America. It takes into account location, utility rates, and other basic data, and yields recommended skylight area.

Note that the ideal amount of fenestrated roof is generally about 5%. Most architects design skylights that are too big. An HVAC&R designer's input here, especially when backed up by calculations, can help ensure that energy is not wasted.

When/Where It's Applicable

Daylight harvesting is most likely to be suitable for large-volume, single-story or top-story space types with ordinary structures. These include the following:

- Gyms
- Industrial workspaces
- Big box retail stores
- Grocery stores
- Exhibition halls
- Storage
- Warehousing

In each case, automatic lighting controls that dim or extinguish electric lights when there is adequate daylight are essential. Without them, the energy savings will not be realized. (See the section on "Lighting Controls.")

Pros of Daylighting

- Daylight harvesting offers significantly reduced energy costs (can be more than 60%) and reduced HVAC load (as long as solar gains don't outweigh electric lighting reductions).
- It extends the electric lighting maintenance cycle (lamps last two to three times as long in calendar years).
- It ensures low power use.
- It has been shown to lead to improved human factors and increased enjoyment of space.

Cons of Daylighting

- Daylight harvesting requires intensive architectural, structural, and lighting design coordination.
- There is no assurance that the design will meet exact project lighting requirements.
- There is increased building cost.
- There is a risk of poor design or installation workmanship, which can result in roof leaks.
- Daylighting may not be suitable for uncommon room shapes, sizes, and/or finishes.
- There is net decreased roof insulation.

THE LIGHT CONVEYOR

The light conveyor is a specialized technique whereby light from a source is transmitted some distance from the source to light spaces, either along its length or some distance away. The source can be either natural light or an artificial source. It is described in GreenTip #30.

LIGHTING CONTROLS

General

While all modern energy codes require automatic shutoff controls for commercial buildings, implementing automatic controls in all building projects is a sound money- and energy-saving idea. There are two ways to reduce lighting energy use through controls:

- Turn lights off when not needed (which reduces hours).
- Reduce lighting power to minimum need (which reduces kW).

By code, each interior space enclosed by ceiling-high partitions must have separate local switching or dimming and some form of automated "off" control.

(e.g., occupancy-sensing, time-based scheduling, or other). In addition, wherever possible, providing separate switching/dimming for lights in daylighted zones can further reduce energy usage, or contrarily, provide occupant control in situations where more light is required. In order to comply with code requirements and ensure maximum energy savings, specify the most appropriate lighting control option(s) as described below and outlined in Table 13-5.

Table 13-5: Recommended and Optional Lighting Controls

Type of Space	Minimum Recommended Control	Optional Control(s)				
Private office, exam room	1	2	2 + 4	1 + 8	2 + 4 + 8	2 + 8
Open office	3		3 + 4	3 + 8	3 + 4 + 8	
Conference rooms, teleconference rooms, boardrooms, classrooms	2		1	2 + 8	1 + 8	
Server rooms, computer rooms, other clean work areas	5					
Toilet rooms, copy rooms, mail rooms, coffee rooms	5 or 6					
Individual toilets, janitor closets, electrical rooms, and other small spaces	6					
Public corridors	3					

330 | Chapter 13: Lighting Systems

Table 13-5: Recommended and Optional Lighting Controls *(Continued)*

Type of Space	Minimum Recommended Control	Optional Control(s)
Corridors, hallways, lobbies (private spaces only)	3	3 + 8
Public lobbies	7	7 + 8
Industrial work areas	7	7 + 8
Warehousing and storage	9 (high-intensity discharge [HID] systems) 3 or 5 (fluorescent systems)	3 or 5 + 8 (fluorescent)
Stores, newsstands, food service	7	
Mechanical rooms	Manual switching only	
Stairs	None	Motion sensors can be used to reduce light levels to minimum egress lighting levels only

Control Options

Below are some considerations for useful lighting control system components:

- *Ceiling-Mounted Motion Sensor with Transformer/Relay, Auxiliary Relay, and Series Switch.* The sensor should be located to look down upon the work area, so as to detect anything from a small hand motion to major movements. The sensor may be mounted to the upper wall if a ceiling location is not workable. More than one sensor can be used for a large room or a room with obstructions (e.g., a library or server room). In such situations, sensor coverage zones should be slightly over-lapped to ensure comprehensive coverage. The main transformer relay should con-trol the overhead lighting system (usually 277 volt) and the auxiliary relay should control at least one-half of a receptacle to switch task lights and other applicably controlled plug loads. Note that the light switch is in series so that it can only turn lights off in an occupied room; it cannot override the motion sensor's "off" control.

- *Ceiling-Mounted Motion Sensors Connected to Programmable Time Controller.* During programmed "on" times, the lights remain on. During programmed "off" times, motion within the space initiates lights on for a time out period. The con-troller should be programmable according to the day of the week and should have an electronic calendar to permit programming holidays.

- *Workstation Motion Sensor Connected to a Plug Strip or Task Light with Auxil-iary Receptacle.*

- *One or More Ceiling-Mounted Motion Sensors with Transformer/Relay (Mini-mum of Two Luminaires Controlled.)*

- *Switchbox Motion Sensor (One or More Luminaires Controlled).*

- *Programmable Time Controller with Manual Override Switch(es) Located in a Protected or Concealed Location.* There are separate zones for retail and similar applications where displays can be controlled separately from general lighting. This may also control dimmers.

- *Automatic Daylighting Sensor Connected to Dimming Ballast(s) in Each Lumi-naire in the Daylighted Zone (In Addition to Any of the Above).*

- *Motion Sensor Connected to a High-Low Lighting System.*

When using controls such as motion sensors or daylight sensors, be very thor-ough and carefully read the manufacturer's literature. Different sensors work for different applications, and their sensing systems are optimized. For instance, avoid wallbox motion sensors except in spaces where their sensing field is appropriate (e.g., small private offices, individual toilets, etc). For spaces with small-motion work, a lookdown sensor (situated on the ceiling) generally works much better than a lookout sensor (situated on a wallbox). Consider the sensing technology when specifying sensors—infrared, ultrasonic, and microphonic sensor technologies present opportunities to fine-tune lighting control system design and can enhance the overall effectiveness of the lighting system.

Applicability

The controls mentioned in the previous section are applicable to most commer-cial, institutional, and industrial buildings. Use common sense in special spaces, keeping in mind safety and security. Never switch path-of-egress lighting systems except with properly designed emergency transfer controls.

Pros

- There is low to moderate cost for most space types.
- There is virtually no maintenance.
- These controls will generally lower energy use.

Cons

- If controls are not properly commissioned, unacceptable results may occur until they are fixed.
- There is no assurance that the controls meet exact project lighting requirements.
- Substitutions and value engineering can cause bad results.

COST CONSIDERATIONS

Lighting Systems

The systems that we described are generally low-to-moderate cost lighting systems. On average, they also use low-maintenance lamps and ballasts. The combination of low first cost, low maintenance, and low energy use leads to lighting choices that are among the most economical available.

Lamps and Ballasts

The costs of premium lamps and ballasts over conventional lamps and ballasts can be as much as 100% of the cost of the materials. This can increase the cost of a lighting system by 20% to 30%.

However, premium lamps, especially the T-8 4 ft (1.2 m) lamps shown, offer the following specific benefits:

- *Increased lamp life by as much as 50%.* In a T-8 application, this can be 5000 to 10,000 h. The cost of replacing a lamp is about 75% labor and 25% material. Relamping cost savings alone pay the difference.
- *Reduced lamp energy use when used with the correct ballast.* In a typical T-8 application, this means achieving energy savings of around 6 W/lamp. At 3000 annual hours and $0.085/kWh, the combination saves more than $1.50/yr in energy costs per lamp. The premium for a two-lamp ballast and lamps is about $12.00. The energy savings pay for the added costs in about four years. (Costs are as of year 2003.)

Daylight Harvesting

Daylight harvesting is a potentially complex undertaking in which the first cost of lighting remains the same, the cost of lighting controls increases, and the added cost of skylights and/or structural changes/complications are incurred as well. To be cost-effective, this needs to be offset by a combination of HVAC energy savings, lighting energy savings, HVAC system first-cost reduction, and perhaps savings from utility incentives or tax credits. Expect daylight harvesting systems to yield a 4 to 5 yr simple payback with a utility incentive, 6 to 8 yr or more without.

Controls

The lighting control systems described previously are generally of low to moderate cost. However, using better quality sensors and separate transformer/relay packs with remote sensors costs much more than wallbox devices. Savings can range from modest to considerable, depending on the building and occupants.

ASHRAE
GreenTip #30

Light Conveyors

GENERAL DESCRIPTION

A light conveyor is large pipe or duct with reflective sides that transmits artificial or natural light along its length. There are two types of such light-directing devices. The first is a square duct or round pipe made of plastic. Based on how the inside of the duct or pipe is cut and treated, light entering one end of the pipe is reflected off these configurations (similar to the way light is refracted through a prism) and transmitted through. The reflected light continues to travel down the pipe, but the relatively small amount of light transmitted through the pipe provides continuous lighting along the length of the pipe. Because some light is absorbed and escapes along the length of the pipe (i.e., it is lost), the maximum distance that light can be piped into a building is generally about 90 ft (27.4 m).

There are a few installations where sun-tracking mirrors concentrate and direct natural light into a light pipe. In most applications, however, a high-intensity electric light is used as the light source. Having the electric light separate from the space where the light is delivered isolates the heat, noise, and electromagnetic field of the light source from building occupants. In addition, the placement of the light source in a maintenance room separate from building occupants simplifies replacement of the light source.

A second light-directing device is a straight tube with a highly reflective interior coating. The device is mounted on a building roof and has a clear plastic dome at the top end of the tube and a translucent plastic diffusing dome at the bottom end. The tube is typically 12 to 16 in. (300 to 400 mm) in diameter. Natural light enters the top dome, is reflected down the tube, and is then diffused throughout the building interior. The light output is limited by the amount of daylight falling on the exterior dome.

WHEN/WHERE IT'S APPLICABLE

The aforementioned light conveyor system is best suited to building applications where there is a need to isolate electric lights from the interior space (e.g., operating rooms or theaters) or where electric light replacement is difficult (for example, above swimming pools or in roadway tunnels). For the latter reflective tube system, each device can light only a small area (10 ft^2 [1 m^2]) and is best suited to small interior spaces with access to the roof, such as interior bathrooms and hallways.

PROS

- A light conveyor transports natural light into building interiors.
- The first type of light conveyor isolates the electric light source from the lighted space.
- The first type of light conveyor reduces lighting glare.
- It lowers lighting maintenance costs.

CONS

- A light conveyor may have greater capital costs than traditional electric lighting.
- The tube type may increase roof heat loss.
- The tube type runs the risk of poor installation, resulting in leaks.
- The effectiveness may not be worth the additional cost.

KEY ELEMENTS OF COST

Because of the specialized nature of these techniques, it is difficult to address specific cost elements. As an alternative to conventional electric lighting techniques, it could add to or reduce the overall cost of a lighting system—and the energy costs required—depending on specific project conditions. A designer should not incorporate any such system without thoroughly investigating its benefits and applicability, and should preferably observe such a system in actual use.

SOURCES OF FURTHER INFORMATION

McKurdy, G., S.J. Harrison, and R. Cooke. Preliminary evaluation of cylindrical skylights. 23rd Annual Conference of the Solar Energy Society of Canada Inc., Vancouver, British Columbia.

REFERENCES AND RESOURCES

Published

ASHRAE. 2010. *ANSI/ASHRAE/IES Standard 90.1-2010, Energy Standard for Buildings Except Low-Rise Residential Buildings.* Atlanta: American Society of Heating, Refrigerating and Air-Conditioning Engineers, Inc.

IESNA. 2000. *Lighting Handbook.* New York: Illuminating Engineering Society of North America.

NBI. 2001. *Advanced Lighting Guidelines.* Fair Oaks, CA: New Buildings Institute. www.newbuildings.org/lighting.htm.

Online

Architectural Energy Corporation
www.archenergy.com

BetterBricks
www.betterbricks.com

California Energy Commission
www.energy.ca.gov

Collaborative for High Performance Schools
www.chps.net

Energy Trust of Oregon
www.energytrust.org

Heschong Mahone Group
www.h-m-g.com

New Buildings Institute
www.newbuildings.org

RealWinWin, Inc.
www.realwinwin.com

Rising Sun Enterprises
www.rselight.com

Savings by Design
www.savingsbydesign.com

SkyCalc
www.energydesignresources.com/resource/129/

CHAPTER FOURTEEN

WATER
EFFICIENCY

Water efficiency and conservation continues to become a critical factor in green building design. Buildings consume 20% of the world's available water, a resource that becomes more scarce each year, according to the United Nations Environmental Program (Epoch Times 2009). Efficient practices and products provide opportunities to save significant amounts of water. The reduction of energy use and operating costs, and the expectation of increased government regulation will continue to drive faster adoption of water-efficient products and methods.

In a typical office building, HVAC systems account for approximately one third of water consumption. Therefore, minimizing the water needed to operate HVAC systems while not significantly increasing energy usage should be a major consideration in green building design.

Plumbing and fire protection systems are normally not considered within the purview of the HVAC&R designer's expertise. Nevertheless, both subsets of designers, in practice, must work closely in putting together a functional building mechanical system. Indeed, frequently the designer of the HVAC systems and plumbing systems are one and the same. For detailed design guidelines and information refer to the National Fire Protection Association and the American Society for Plumbing Engineers.

Recently, ASHRAE has partnered with the American Water Works Association (AWWA), the U.S. Green Building Council (USGBC), and the American Society for Plumbing Engineers (ASPE) to develop a new standard titled *Standard 191, Standard for the Efficient Use of Water in Building, Site and Mechanical Systems.* The target date for the final standard to be published is early 2012. You can follow the progress of this proposed standard at http://spc191.ashraepcs.org/.

In green building desing, it is important for the practitioners of each design discipline to be familiar with what the other disciplines may bring to an effective green design. This is especially so with plumbing design. The editors of this Guide have chosen to include discussion of some key aspects of plumbing design that can have an impact on green design—including several significant ASHRAE GreenTips. Several of these GreenTips may have an impact in other areas as well. For instance, point-of-use hot-water heaters would not only save heating energy and distribution energy, but they could also result in the use of less water.

THE ENERGY-WATER BALANCE

The continued security and economic health of the population depends on a sustainable supply of both energy and water. These two critical resources are inextricably and reciprocally linked. A nation's ability to continue providing both clean and affordable energy and water is being seriously challenged by a number of emerging issues.

Energy production requires a reliable, abundant, and predictable source of water, a resource that is already in short supply throughout much of the United States and the world. The electricity industry is second only to agriculture as the largest user of water in the United States. Electricity production from fossil fuels and nuclear energy requires 190,000 million gal of water/day, accounting for 39% of all freshwater withdrawals in the nation, with 71% of that going to fossil fuel electricity generation alone.

According to the World Health Organization (www.who.int/ water_sanitation_health/hygiene/en/), approximately 1.1 billion people do not have access to improved water supply sources. Two primary solutions—shipping in water over long distances or cleaning nearby, but dirty, supplies—both require large amounts of energy. Therefore, there is a significant amount of embodied energy in the water we use to drink, cook, flush toilets, and bathe.

In areas where water supply is not plentiful, a design engineer should consider taking into account the total energy required to operate a cooling plant, including the embodied energy of the water. For example, if a life-cycle analysis is performed to compare an air-cooled, chilled-water plant to a water-cooled, chilled-water plant, the total energy of the air-cooled plant may end up being approximately the same as the total energy that would be used by a water-cooled plant if, for example, the water-cooled plant was evaporating desalinated water that was delivered to the site.

Therefore, when evaluating predicted energy (and carbon) loads for alternative building system design options, it is important to look at the embodied energy of the water in areas where water is not a plentiful resource.

WATER SUPPLY

This basic resource is obviously essential at every building site, but what has changed over the last several decades is the realization that it is fast becoming a precious resource. While the total amount of water in its various forms on the planet is finite, the amount of fresh water, of a quality suitable for the purposes for which it may be used, is not uniformly distributed (e.g., 20% of the world's fresh

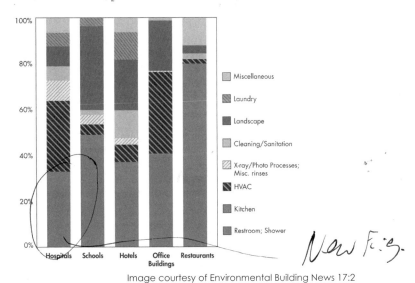

Image courtesy of Environmental Building News 17:2

Figure 14-1 Water use in buildings.

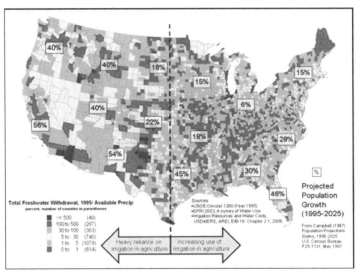

Image courtesy of Universities Council on Water Resources
Journal of Contemporary Water Research and Ed/Sandia National Laboratories

Figure 14-2 United States water availability map.

water is in the U.S. Great Lakes and elsewhere it is often nonexistent or in very meager supply). Nevertheless, water must be allocated somehow to the world's populated lands, many of which are undergoing rapid development. In short, it is becoming more and more difficult to provide for the adequate and equitable distribution of the world's water supply to those who need it.

This trend has implications for not only how prudently we use the water we have, but what we do to avoid contaminating water supplies. While many of the measures to protect and preserve the world's freshwater supplies are beyond ASHRAE's purview, there are a number of simple things related to building sites that can be done as part of a green design effort.

COOLING TOWER SYSTEMS

Cooling towers are efficient devices for removing heat from water through evaporation. Cooling towers remove heat by evaporation and can cool close to the ambient wet-bulb temperature. The wet-bulb temperature is always lower than the dry-bulb; thus, water cooling allows more efficient condenser operation (as much as a 50% energy savings) than air cooling. However, cooling towers use a significant amount of water. A typical tower operation will evaporate 3 gpm of water/100 tons of cooling capacity. In addition to evaporation, some recirculated water must be bled from the system to prevent soluble and semisoluble minerals from reaching too high a concentration. This bleed or blowdown is usually drained to the sanitary plumbing system and ends up being treated at a sewage waste treatment plant. By treating the water with chemical free systems, by appropriately addressing splash-out and spill issues, and by using filtration systems with low water usage for the blowdown requirement, it is possible to maximize both the energy and the water efficiency of the cooling tower system.

It is important, from a sustainability perspective, that a proper tower design is selected. The tower that it is selected must be energy efficient as defined in the following section, and designed to minimize splashout, spills, drift, and algae growth. For more information consult Chapter 39 in the 2008 *ASHRAE Handbook—HVAC Systems* (ASHRAE 2008).

Energy Efficiency

The energy consumed by a tower can vary with the tower fan design. Regardless of the tower selected, if one wants to maximize efficiency, it is recommended that the tower chosen should, at a minimum, meet the performance requirements of Table 6.8.1G in *ANSI/ASHRAE/IES Standard 90.1-2010, Energy Standard for Buildings Except Low-Rise Residential Buildings* (ASHRAE 2010). However, for a high-performance building, Table C-8 in *ANSI/ASHRAE/USGBC/IES Standard 189.1-2009, Standard for the Design of High-Performance Green Buildings* (ASHRAE 2009) will supersede Table 6.8.1G. It will be a good reference document for energy-saving criteria, such as improved energy efficiency of cooling towers.

There are two types of fans used in cooling towers: axial and centrifugal. Axial (or propeller-type) fans have blades mounted perpendicular to the axis of the shaft. All induced-draft cooling towers and some forced-draft designs use axial fans. With centrifugal (i.e., blower-type) fans, the blades are mounted parallel to the axis. Centrifugal fans are only used in forced-draft towers, and typically require twice the energy to achieve the same volume of airflow as an axial fan. Centrifugal fans are ideally suited to handle large amounts of static pressure, and as such, are best suited for indoor tower installations that require ducting or louvers external to the tower. Centrifugal fans may also have lower sound levels than standard propeller fans and may be considered for sound-sensitive projects. However, their relatively high energy consumption makes them much less desirable for typical outdoor applications where their high static capability and reduced sound levels are not needed.

Water Treatment

The water in the evaporative cooling loop must be treated to minimize biological growth, scaling, and corrosion. Typically, a combination of biocides, corrosion inhibitors, and scale inhibitors are added to the system.

Corrosion inhibitors are usually phosphate- or nitrogen-based (e.g., fertilizers) or molybdenum- or zinc-based (e.g., heavy metals). These inhibitors are more effective when added in combinations. These materials have low vapor pressure and are not used by the system. The inhibitors simply need to remain in the solution at the proper concentration to maintain a protective film on the metal components. Their only loss is through bleed and drift.

Most scaling inhibition is done by polymer-based chemicals, organic phosphorous compounds (e.g., phosphonates), or by acid addition. The acid reacts with the alkalinity in the water to release CO_2 and is used up. The polymer and phosphonate scale inhibitors remain in the solution to delay scaling; their major loss is through bleed and drift. Some polymers are designed to be biodegradable (i.e., easily broken down by bacteria in the environment) while others are not.

There are very wide assortments of biocides. A typical system will maintain an oxidizing biocide (e.g., bromine or chlorine) at a constant level and slug feed a nonoxidizing biocide once a week. Chlorine and bromine have a high vapor pressure in water. Much of the chlorine and bromine added to the tower is stripped from the water into the air; a small quantity actually reacts with organics in the tower. Drift and bleed will contain all of the nonoxidizing biocides and a small quantity of oxidizing biocides and the reaction products of the biocides.

Drift

To promote efficient evaporation, cooling towers force intimate contact between outdoor air and warm water. Besides removing heat by evaporation, dust, pollen, and gas, components of the air will become entrained in the water, while some high-vapor components of the water (e.g., bromine or chlorine), as well as entrained water drops, will migrate to the air. Airborne dust and pollen that are captured by the water can promote biological growth in the tower.

Small water droplets entrained and carried out with the air passing through the tower are called *drift*. Drift is always present when operating a cooling tower. Since drift is generated by small droplets of the cooling tower water, it contains all of the dissolved minerals, microbes, and water treatment chemicals in the tower water. Drift is a source of PM_{10} emission (i.e., particulate matter that is less than 10 μ in diameter) and is a suspected vector in Legionella transmission.

Drift is usually reported as a percentage of the recirculating water, though it is more accurately described in terms of the parts per million (ppm) of the air passing through the tower. Tower designs use drift eliminators to capture some of this entrained water. A typical value for drift from cooling towers is 0.005% of the recirculating water; many tower designs have drift values as low as 0.001%.

To put these values in perspective, an example of a 400 ton (1407 kWR) cooling system with a particular treatment program is useful. A 400 ton (1407 kWR) system would circulate approximately 1200 gpm (4542 L/min) through the tower and chiller. At nominal rates, 12 gpm (45.4 L/min) would be lost to evaporation, 0.06 gpm (0.23 L/min) would be lost to drift (0.005%), and, at four cycles of concentration, 4 gpm (15.1 L/min) would be intentionally bled from the system. Chlorine addition would be 0.09 gal/h (0.34 L/h) of 12.5% liquid bleach (0.06 lb/h or 0.027 kg/h Cl_2). This chlorine addition should maintain about 0.2 ppm free chlorine and 0.2 ppm combined chlorine. The combined chlorine is from the reaction of chlorine with organic molecules and may include some hazardous by-products (e.g., chloroform). For corrosion and scale protection, the water would be maintained with 2 ppm zinc, 3 ppm triazole, and 20 ppm polyphosphate. Once a week, 4 lb of a 1.5% solution of isothiazoline, a nonoxidizing biocide, would be fed to the system for biofilm control. The drift and bleed would contain the same quantity of minerals and chemicals as were maintained in the recirculated water.

Table 14-1 shows monthly results for operating this tower at an assumed 75 h/ week (300 h/month). The data in the table shows that most of the chlorine used in this tower is unaccounted for. Some of this loss is due to oxidation of organic and inorganic material in the cooling system, resulting in nonhazardous chloride ions. Much of the chlorine is released into the atmosphere as chlorine gas. While it is hard to be quantitative, over the course of one year, this tower could release more than 100 lb (45.4 kg) of chlorine gas into the immediate building environment. If less effective drift eliminators were used, 12,000 gal (45.4 kL) of contaminated tower water would also be released every year and 800,000 gal (3028 kL) of water containing heavy metals, phosphates, and biocides would be sent to a publicly owned treatment works (POTW) system. Most POTW systems are designed to handle only organic waste; much of these cooling tower chemicals will pass

Table 14-1: Material Release
from Example Cooling Tower Operation

	Release Rate	Total/Month
Evaporation	12 gpm (45.4 L/min)	216,000 gal (817,560 L)
Bleed at four cycles	4 gpm (15.1 L/min)	72,000 gal (272,520 L)
Drift	0.060 gpm (0.23 L/min) (0.005%) 0.012 gpm (0.05 L/min) (0.001%)	1080 gal (4088 L) 216 gal (818 L)
Chlorine addition	0.06 lb/h (0.027 kg/h)	18.0 pounds Cl_2 (8.2 kg)
Chlorine in bleed	free about 0.2 ppm combined about 0.2 ppm	0.12 lb free (0.055 kg) 0.12 lb combined
Unaccounted chlorine		17.7 lb Cl_2 (8.0 kg)

through the system untreated or will be released later as gaseous emissions at the POTW.

Over the lifetime of the building, these releases could be among the most significant impacts on the local environment that the building will cause. This example highlights the magnitude of what can happen if this issue is not addressed.

Green Choices—Water Treatment

The water treatment plan illustrated above is not the only choice. There are many ways to treat the system that will have a less negative impact on the environment. Besides being rapidly stripped into the air, chlorine and bromine may react with organic molecules to produce very hazardous daughter products. However, other oxidizing biocides (e.g., hydrogen peroxide) do not have this issue. With continuous monitoring of the cooling system, chemical additions can be added only when needed. This technique can yield equivalent performance with less-added chemicals. Also, the U.S. Environmental Protection Agency (EPA) maintains a Web site on green chemistry, www.epa.gov//greenchemistry/, which contains criteria on how to evaluate the life-cycle environmental impact of a particular chemical.

Nonchemical water treatment has the potential to be a powerful method for water treatment. However, its successful use depends on the water chemistry, operating procedures, and degree of pollution of the specific system. There are several different nonchemical technologies available including those based on pulsed electric fields, mechanical agitation, and ultrasound. Each of these technologies has developed a widespread following. ASHRAE has investigated the scale prevention effectiveness of some of these nonchemical technologies and has published the results from ASHRAE's Research Project RP-1155 (Cho et al. 2003). These technologies offer the promise of eliminating the storage and handling of toxic chemicals at the site, eliminating the risk caused by any spills or leaks of cooling tower water, eliminating the issues of the bleed water at the POTW, and eliminating much of the concern with drift. Bleed water, instead of being sent to the POTW, could be used on site for irrigation or other nonpotable needs.

Green Choices—Tower Selection + Design

All cooling tower designs are efficient at removing heat from water through evaporation. However, not all designs perform as well environmentally. Some tower designs are more prone to splashout, spills, drift, and algae growth than others. Splashout involves tower water splashing from the tower. This happens most often in no-fan conditions (i.e., when circulating tower water with the fans off) when there are strong winds. Cross-flow towers are more prone to this issue since, in no-fan condition, some water will fall outside of the fill.

Spills can happen from the cold-water basin from overflowing at shutdown when all of the water in the piping drains into the basin. Proper water levels will prevent this. Some tower designs use hot-water basins to distribute water at the top of the tower, while other designs use a spray header pipe. The hot-water basin design can overflow if the nozzles clog; a spray header pipe never overflows.

Algae are a nuisance in basins and can contribute to microbial growth. Algae control requires harsher chemical treatment than typical biological control. Since algae are plants, they need sunlight to grow. Some tower designs are light-tight, which completely eliminates algae as an issue in cooling towers, while other designs are more open and algae growth can be an issue.

The amount of drift varies extensively in tower design. Some tower designs have very little drift, and the less the drift from a tower, the lower the amount of water containing minerals, water treatment chemicals, and microbes that will be released into the surrounding environment.

Fan-power draw also varies between designs. There are two general types of fans: axial and centrifugal. With axial fans, the fan blades are mounted perpendicular to the axis like propellers on a plane or boat. All induced-draft cooling towers and some forced-draft designs use axial fans. With centrifugal fans, the fan blades are mounted parallel to the axis. Centrifugal fans are only used in forced-draft towers and typically use twice the energy to achieve the same amount of airflow as an axial fan.

Maintenance

An often overlooked method to minimize environmental impact is maintenance. Cooling towers operate outdoors under changing conditions. Wind damage to inlet air louvers, excessive airborne contamination, clogging of water distribution nozzles, and mechanical problems can best be prevented and quickly corrected with periodic inspections and maintenance. Continuous filtration of the circulating water and basin sweeping systems should be considered to keep the basins free from all visible dirt.

Green Choices –Filtration for Water Cooled Systems

A critical consideration with respect to green operation of water-cooled systems is to choose to design, install, and maintain a filtration system capable of continually removing visible solids (40 micron and larger) from the water-cooled system. Filtration of water-cooled systems is essential for sustainable operation. Keeping the system free from dirt, corrosion by-products, and scale maintains optimal heat transfer efficiency, reduces under-deposit corrosion, and minimizes the risk of Legionnaires disease. Filtration systems that utilize centrifugal action and require no media or moving parts have the advantage of reduced maintenance, no disposal of used media, better water efficiency, and offer minimal or zero liquid loss that reduces chemical usage and disposal.

The filtration system and sweeper piping should be able to provide adequate pressure and flow (constant 20 PSI at the nozzles, 1 gpm/ft^2 [138 kPa at the nozzles, 40.8 L/min per m^2]) to remove visible solids from the water and provide for efficient handling of the solids. It is not necessary to remove particles that are less than 40 microns (drinking water is filtered to 5 microns), and the extra energy and water loss to achieve this level of filtration for a water-cooled system is wasteful.

While it is obvious that water purity must meet the health and safety standards prescribed by the authorities, there are other techniques that can contribute not only to using lesser quantities of the highest-quality water needed at a site, but to requiring less energy to process that water (i.e., distribute it, heat it, and dispose of it once used).

Regarding the quality of the water provided for a given building/building site, the design team should do the following:

- Supply local or municipal water that exceeds the EPA's requirements or more stringent local requirements for potable and heated water.

- Meet the EPA's national primary drinking water regulations, including maximum contaminant level, by testing or by installing appropriate treatment systems. The quality of the municipal water supply shall be evaluated at applicable points (e.g., restrooms/showers, kitchen/pantry areas, drinking fountains, architectural fountains, and/or indoor water features).
- Exceed national primary drinking water regulation maximum contaminant level goals and secondary standards by testing or by installing appropriate treatment systems. The quality of the municipal water supply shall be evaluated at applicable points (e.g., restrooms/showers, kitchen/pantry areas, drinking fountains, architectural fountains, and/or indoor water features).

Some of the techniques for reducing the demand for domestic water in a building are well known and in fairly widespread use. These include water restrictors (e.g., flow-control shower heads) and spring-closing or timed lavatory faucets, especially in public or semipublic washrooms. GreenTip #31 addresses other water-conserving fixtures that can be used.

GreenTip #32 would also impact the amount of pure fresh water used at a site by making use of used water (known as *graywater*) for purposes where potability is not a requirement.

DOMESTIC WATER HEATING

One of the earliest techniques used for lowering the energy required for domestic water heating, going back to the mid-1970s, was reducing the temperature of the water supplied. The pre-Arab-oil-crisis norm for domestic hot water was 140°F (60°C), and the energy-saving recommendation thereafter was 105°F to 110°F (40°C to 43°C). While this can save heating energy, where hot/cold mixing valves are used (as with some shower controls), it may also cause more hot water to be used. In addition, because of the dangers of legionellosis, which thrives at the lower-heated water ranges, the prudent recommendation for the hot-water supply temperature has been revised to be 105°F to 120°F (40°C to 49°C). Protection against possible legionellosis can be achieved by generating 140°F (60°C) centrally (in a well-insulated heater/storage tank) and then mixing to the lower temperature through a mixing valve.

One energy-reducing technique is point-of-use water heating, which can also reduce the water quantity used. (This is covered in GreenTip #33.) Another technique to reduce water-heating costs is to combine the function of domestic and space water heating, where allowed by codes. (See Chapter 11 for GreenTip #17 on combination space and water-heating systems). Yet another water-heating technique, with more limited and specialized application, is covered in GreenTip #34.

Solar heating with PVs is often used for preheating or full heating of domestic hot-water systems.

Strategies should be considered to preheat and/or fully heat domestic hot water using waste heat (i.e., flash steam, etc.) from the main building heating system.

SANITARY WASTE

See GreenTip #32, which deals with sanitary waste water and a strategy to conserve potable water.

STORM DRAINAGE

GreenTip #35 also deals with a strategy for conserving potable water, though the water source differs.

FIRE SUPPRESSION SYSTEMS

These systems are designed for life safety of the occupants. However, there may be times when there is an opportunity to utilize the water source, or the water in the sprinkler and standpipe piping, as a heat sink for heat pump systems.

WATER RECOVERY AND REUSE

For HVAC&R engineers looking for water recovery and reuse opportunities, condensate collection should be considered on most projects. Factors that determine whether condensate collection should be considered include location (i.e., climate), building type (particularly relating to amount of outdoor air required), the size, number, and accessibility of air handlers that condition outdoor air, location of potential uses for the condensate, etc. Location determines both the potential to collect a significant amount of condensate as well as the value of the water to the local community. As water demand continues to grow, even regions that might have been considered water-rich will experience tight supplies of fresh, clean water.

Building or space occupancy type determines the amount of outdoor air required, and thus, the amount of moisture in the incoming air. As the air passes across cold cooling coils, if the coil surface temperature is less than the dew point of the airstream passing by, then the potential exists for water condensation on the coils. (See Digging Deeper sidebar titled "How Much Water Will Collect at Design Conditions?") Water that condenses on the coils will collect and drop to the drain pan below. The actual amount of water collected depends on parameters such as the absolute humidity level, total airflow, and coil bypass ratio. A major source of the moisture being condensed is from outdoor air brought in through outdoor air intakes or through infiltration exchange with the outdoors. A building or space that requires a lot of outdoor air on an ongoing basis (e.g., a laboratory) is an ideal candidate for condensate collection. Other obvious candidates include spaces with indoor water features, natatoriums, gymnasiums, and shower rooms, although these may face special challenges. Dedicated outdoor air systems, or DOAS units, are also prime candidates for consideration.

Move to after Greentip

Digging Deeper

HOW MUCH WATER WILL COLLECT AT DESIGN CONDITIONS?

For simplicity, consider the process of a unit conditioning 100% outdoor air (where the unit is a dedicated outdoor air system). The psychrometric chart represents a path of outdoor air as it passes across the cooling coil for the 0.4% cooling design condition in Athens, Georgia. Assuming a supply air condition of 55°F (12.8°C) and 85% relative humidity (wet-bulb temperature = 52.5°F [11.4°C]), the humidity ratio changes across the coil from 0.0141 to 0.0078 lb/lb$_{air}$ (kg/kg$_{air}$). The difference in absolute humidity (ω) between the incoming outdoor air and supply air leaving the unit represents the amount of condensation that occurs. Thus, for every lb (kg) of air supplied by the unit, 0.0141 – 0.0078 or 0.0063 lb (0.00286 kg) of water are condensed.

The total amount of condensate expected is determined by the equation below:

$$\text{Condensate} = \text{Airflow} \times \text{Density} \times 60\frac{\text{min}}{\text{h}} \text{ (I-P) or } 3600\frac{\text{s}}{\text{h}} \text{ (SI)} \times \Delta\omega$$

Assuming 1000 cfm (472 L/s) of outdoor air is being conditioned, the total amount of condensate expected would be the following:

$$\text{Condensate} = 1000\frac{\text{ft}^3}{\text{min}} \times \frac{\text{lb}}{13.133 \text{ ft}^3} \times 60\frac{\text{min}}{\text{h}} \times (0.0141 - 0.0078)\frac{\text{lb}_{water}}{\text{lb}_{dry\ air}} \quad \text{(I-P)}$$

$$= 28.8\frac{\text{lb}}{\text{h}}$$

$$\text{Condensate} = 0.472\frac{\text{m}^3}{\text{s}} \times \frac{\text{kg}}{0.820 \text{ m}^3} \times 3600\frac{\text{s}}{\text{h}} \times (0.0141 - 0.0078)\frac{\text{kg}_{water}}{\text{kg}_{dry\ air}} \quad \text{(SI)}$$

$$= 13.05\frac{\text{kg}}{\text{h}}$$

This is approximately 3.5 gal (13.1 L)/h at the cooling design condition. Similar calculations can be run for any locality, and the result can vary widely depending on the climate. For example, when the calculation is run for other representative cities the condensate yields are:

- Boston, Massachusetts (90.8°F [32.6°C] dry-bulb/73.3°F [22.8°C] mean coincident wet bulb [MCWB] temperature)
  = 3.2 gal (12.1 L)/h

- Sacramento, California (100.4°F [37.9°C] dry-bulb/70.7°F [21.4°C] MCWB)
  = 0.8 gal (3.1 L)/h
- Denver, Colorado (94.3°F [34.5°C] dry-bulb/60.3°F [15.6°C] MCWB)
  = no condensate collected

Interestingly, the total annual rainfall is only a partial indicator of how much condensate might be collected, as shown in Table 14-2. The two comparative eastern and western U.S. cities have similar rainfall totals, but they vary significantly in terms of the total amount of condensate collection potential.

What to do with Collected Water

The best end use for the collected water will depend on the particular circumstances of the location. In many locations the primary use of city water is for makeup water in cooling towers. Therefore, it may be the most logical choice to collected condensate to its cooling tower sump. In most cases, peak condensate production will occur at the same times as peak makeup water demands, creating an elegant feedback loop.

Table 14-2: Annual Condensate Collection Compared to Total Annual Rainfall

	Annual Condensate for Continuous Outdoor Air, gal/cfm (Liter per L/s)	Average Annual Rainfall, in. (mm)
Athens, Georgia	12.5 (100.4)	47.8 (1.21)
Boston, Massachusetts	4.5 (36.1)	42.5 (1.08)
Sacramento, California	1.3 (10.4)	17.9 (0.45)
Denver, Colorado	0.5 (4)	15.4 (0.39)

Digging Deeper

This is also the simplest retrofit, involving reasonably inexpensive equipment and piping; water can be routed directly to the tower with no need for treatment.

Complications arise when dealing with district cooling systems with satellite chillers, because it is possible to produce condensate in an air-handling unit while the chiller and cooling tower for that particular building are idle. While it is no tragedy that condensate sent to the cooling tower will simply overflow to the sewer (where it would have gone prior to retrofit), there is the risk that treatment chemicals in the sump will be diluted and needlessly washed away. In this scenario, care should be taken to prioritize condensate retrofits in buildings with baseline chiller plants.

Condensate collection can also be integrated into a rainwater collection system, a scheme often referred to as *rainwater plus*. This will usually involve a storage tank or cistern and can require considerably more expense and engineering than using the condensate in a cooling tower. Depending on the intended use (e.g., for irrigation, fountains, toilet flushing, or potable water), different amounts of further treatment will be required. In all cases, local building codes must be followed.

Add Water Sense!

ASHRAE
GreenTip #31

Water-Conserving Plumbing Fixtures

GENERAL DESCRIPTION

Water conservation strategies save building owners money when it comes to both consumption and demand charges. Further, municipal water and wastewater treatment plants save on operating and capital costs for new facilities. As a general rule, water conservation strategies are very cost-effective when properly applied.

The Energy Policy Act of 1992 set reasonable standards for the technologies then available. Now, there are plumbing fixtures and equipment capable of significant reduction in water usage. For example, a rest stop in Minnesota that was equipped with ultralow-flow toilets and waterless urinals has recorded a 62% reduction in water usage.

Tables 14-3, 14-4, and 14-5 list the maximum water usage standards established by the Energy Policy Act of 1992 for typical fixture types. Also listed is water usage for flush-type and flow-type fixtures. Listing of conventional fixture usage allows comparison to the low-flow and ultralow-flow fixture usage.

Table 14-3: Energy Policy and Conservation Act (EPCA) Maximum Flows

Fixture Type	Energy Policy Act of 1992 Maximum Water Usage
Water closets, gpf (L/f)	1.6 (6.1)
Urinals, gpf (L/f)	1.0 (3.8)
Shower heads, gpm (L/s)	2.5 (0.16)
Faucets, gpm (L/s)	2.5 (0.16)
Replacement aerators, gpm (L/s)	2.5 (0.16)
Metering facets, gal/cycle (L/cycle)	0.25 (0.95)

Note: gpf = gallons per fixture (L/f = liters per fixture); gpm = gallons per minute (L/s = liters per second). The gpm (L/s) value is at flowing water pressure of 80 psi (552 kPa).

These values would be used for tasks in for example LEED calculation. However std. 189.1 requires Water Sense or equivalent fixture efficacy. The correspondingly correspond to the WaterSense values listed in the RHS column of Tables 14-3 thru 14-5

Table 14-4: Flush-Fixture Flows

Flush-Fixture Type	Water Use, gpf (L/f)
Conventional water closet	1.6 (6.1)
Low-flow water closet	1.1 (4.2)
Ultralow-flow water closet	0.8 (3.0)
Composting toilet	0.0
Conventional urinal	1.0 (3.8)
Waterless urinal	0.0

Note: gpf = gallons per fixture (L/f = liters per fixture)

Table 14-5: Flow-Fixture Flows

Flow-Fixture Type	Water Use, gpm (L/s)
Conventional lavatory	2.5 (0.16)
Low-flow lavatory	1.8 (0.11)
Kitchen sink	2.5 (0.16)
Low-flow kitchen sink	1.8 (0.11)
Shower	2.5 (0.16)
Low-flow shower	1.8 (0.11)
Janitor sink	2.5 (0.16)

Note: gpm = gallons per minute (L/s = liters per second)

WHEN/WHERE IT'S APPLICABLE

Applicable state and local codes should be checked prior to design as some of them have approved fixture lists; some code officials have not approved the waterless urinal and low-flush toilet technologies. Waterless urinals and low-flow lavatory fixtures usually pay back immediately. Toilet technology continues to evolve rapidly, so be sure to obtain test data and references before specifying. Some units work very well, while others perform marginally.

Options that should be considered in the design of water-conserving systems include the following:

- Infrared faucet sensors
- Delayed-action shutoff or automatic mechanical shutoff valves (metering faucets at 0.25 gal/cycle [0.95 L/cycle])
- Low-flow or ultralow-flow toilets
- Lavatory faucets with flow restrictors
- Low-flow kitchen faucets
- Domestic dishwashers that use 10 gal (38 L)/cycle or less
- Commercial dishwashers (conveyor type) that use 120 gal (455 L)/h
- Waterless urinals
- Closed cooling towers (to eliminate drift) and filters for cleaning the water

A comparison of a typical ( ) building computing baseline (EPAct) and more efficient (W.S.) is given in the Diggs Deeper note that follows

PROS

- Water conservation reduces a building's potable water use, which reduces demand on the municipal water supply and lowers costs and energy use associated with water.
- It reduces a building's overall waste generation, thus putting fewer burdens on the existing sewage system.
- It may save capital costs since some fixtures (e.g., waterless urinals and low-flow lavatories) may be less expensive to install initially.

CONS

- Some states and municipalities have approved fixture lists that may not include certain newer and more efficient fixtures. However, the design engineer would likely have the option to go to a review process in order to get new fixture technologies put on the approved fixture list.

- Maintenance of these fixtures is different and requires special training of staff.

KEY ELEMENTS OF COST

The following provides a possible breakdown of the various cost elements that might differentiate a building using water-conserving plumbing fixtures from one that does not and an indication of whether the net cost is likely to be lower (L), higher (H), or the same (S). This assessment is only a perception of what might be likely, but it obviously may not be correct in all situations. There is no substitute for a detailed cost analysis as part of the design process. The listing below may also provide some assistance in identifying the cost elements involved.

First Cost

- Low-flow and ultralow-flow flush water closets   S/H
- Waterless urinals   S/L
- Low-flow shower heads   S
- Metering faucets   S
- Electronic faucets   M
- Dual-flush water closets   S/H
- Water-conserving dishwashers   S/H

Recurring Costs

- Potable water   L
- Sewer discharge   L
- Maintenance   L/S
- Training of building operators   S/H
- Orientation of building occupants   S
- Commissioning   S

SOURCES OF FURTHER INFORMATION

American Society of Plumbing Engineers
    www.aspe.org
Del Porto, D., and C. Steinfeld. 1999. *The Composting Toilet System Book*. New Bedford, MA: The Center for Ecological Pollution Prevention.

EPA. 2010. *How to Conserve Water and Use It Effectively*. U.S. Environmental Protection Agency, Washington, DC. www.epa.gov/owow/nps/chap3.html.

U.S. Green Building Council
www.usgbc.org

Water Sense

Insert "Digging Deeper" on water use calculations after here

ASHRAE
GreenTip #32

Graywater Systems

GENERAL DESCRIPTION

Graywater is generally wastewater from lavatories, showers, bathtubs, and sinks that is not used for food preparation. Graywater is further distinguished from blackwater, which is wastewater from toilets and sinks that contains organic or toxic matter. Local health code departments have regulations that specifically define the two kinds of waste streams in their respective jurisdictions.

Where allowed by local code, separate blackwater and graywater waste collection systems can be installed. The blackwater system would be treated as a typical waste stream and piped to the water treatment system or local sewer district. However, the graywater would be recycled by collecting, storing (optional), and then distributing it via a dedicated piping system to toilets, landscape irrigation, or any other function that does not require potable water.

Typically, for a commercial graywater system (e.g., for toilet flushing in a hotel), a means of short-term on-site storage, or, more appropriately, a surge tank, is required. Graywater can only be held for a short period of time before it naturally becomes blackwater. The surge tank would be provided with an overflow to the blackwater waste system and a potable makeup line for when the end-use need exceeds stored capacity.

Distribution would be accomplished via a pressurized piping system requiring pumps and some low level of filtration. Usually, there is a requirement for the graywater system to be a supplemental system. Therefore, systems will still need to be connected to the municipal or localized well service.

WHEN/WHERE IT'S APPLICABLE

Careful consideration should be given before pursuing a graywater system. While a graywater system can be applied in any facility that has a nonpotable water demand and a usable waste stream, the additional piping and energy required to provide and operate such a system may outweigh any benefits. Such a system is best applied where the ratio of demand for nonpotable water to potable water is relatively high and consistent, as in restaurants, laundries, and hotels.

Some facilities have a more reliable graywater volume than others. For example, a school would have substantially less graywater in the summer months. This may not be a problem if the graywater was being used for flushing, since it can be assumed that toilet use would vary with occupancy. However, it would be detrimental if graywater were being used for landscape irrigation.

PROS

- A graywater system reduces a building's potable water use, in turn reducing demand on the municipal water supply and lowering costs associated with water.
- It reduces a building's overall wastewater generation, thus putting less tax on the existing sewage systems.

CONS

- There is an added first cost associated with the additional piping, pumping, filtration, and surge tank required.
- There are additional materials and their associated embodied energy costs.
- There is negative public perception of graywater and health concerns regarding ingestion of nonpotable water.
- Costs include maintenance of the system, including the pumps, filters, and surge tank.
- Local health code authority has jurisdiction, potentially making a particular site infeasible due to that authority's definition of blackwater versus graywater.

KEY ELEMENTS OF COST

The following provides a possible breakdown of the various cost elements that might differentiate a building utilizing a graywater system from one that does not and an indication of whether the net incremental cost is likely to be lower (L), higher (H), or the same (S). This assessment is only a perception of what might be likely, but it obviously may not be correct in all situations. There is no substitute for a detailed cost analysis as part of the design process. The listings below may also provide some assistance in identifying the cost elements involved.

First Cost

- Collection systems   H
- Surge tank   H
- Water treatment   H
- Distribution system   H
- Design fees   H

Recurring Costs

- Cost of potable water   L
- Cost related to sewer discharge   L
- Maintenance of system   H
- Training of building operators   H
- Orientation of building occupants   S
- Commissioning cost   H

SOURCES OF FURTHER INFORMATION

Advanced Buildings Technologies and Practices
    www.advancedbuildings.org
American Society of Plumbing Engineers
    www.aspe.org
Del Porto, D., and C. Steinfeld. 1999. *The Composting Toilet System Book*. New Bedford, MA: The Center for Ecological Pollution Prevention.
Ludwig, A. 1997. *Builder's Greywater Guide and Create an Oasis with Greywater*. Oasis Design.
USGBC. 2009. *LEED 2009 Green Building Design and Construction Reference Guide*. Washington, DC: U.S. Green Building Council.

ASHRAE
GreenTip #33

Point-of-Use
Domestic Hot-Water Heaters

GENERAL DESCRIPTION

As implied by the title, point-of-use domestic hot-water heaters provide small quantities of hot water at the point of use, without tie-in to a central hot water source. A cold-water line from a central source must still be connected (as well as electricity) for heating the water.

There is some variation in types. Typically, the device may be truly instantaneous (e.g., lavatories), or it may have a small amount of storage capacity. With the instantaneous type, the heating coil is sized such that it can heat a normal-use flow of water up to the desired hot-water temperature (e.g., 120°F [49°C]). When a small tank (usually 3 to 10 gal) is incorporated in the device, the electric heating coil is built into the tank and can be sized somewhat smaller because of the small amount of stored water available. The device is usually installed under the counter of the sink or bank of sinks.

A similar type of device boosts the water supply (which is cold water) up to near boiling temperature (about 190°F [88°C]). This is typically used, for example, to make a cup of coffee or tea without having to brew it separately in a coffeepot or teapot.

WHEN/WHERE IT'S APPLICABLE

These devices are applicable wherever there is a need for a hot-water supply that is low in quantity and relatively infrequently used and is excessively inconvenient or costly to run a hot-water line (with perhaps a recirculation line as well) from a central hot-water source. Typically, these are installed in lavatories or washrooms that are isolated or remote, or both. However, they can be used in any situation where there is a hot-water need but where it would be too inconvenient and costly to tie in to a central source. (There must, of course, be a source of incoming water and a source of electricity.)

PROS

- A point-of-use device is a simple and direct way to provide small amounts of domestic hot water per use.

- Long pipe runs—and, in some cases, a central hot-water heating source—can be avoided.
- Energy is saved by avoiding heat loss from hot-water pipes and, if not needed, from a central water heater.
- In most cases, where applicable, it has a lower first cost.
- It is convenient—especially as a source of 190°F to 210°F (88°C to 99°C) water supply.
- When installed in multiple locations, central equipment failure does not knock out all user locations.
- It may save floor space in the central equipment room if no central heater is required.
- Water is saved by not having to run the faucet until the water warms up.

CONS

- This is a more expensive source of heating energy (though cost may be trivial if usage is low and may be exceeded by heat losses saved from a central heating method).
- Water impurities can cause caking and premature failure of electrical heating coils.
- It cannot handle changed demand for large hot-water quantities or too-frequent use.
- Maintenance is less convenient (when required), since it is not centralized.
- A temperature and pressure relief valve and floor drain may be required by some code jurisdictions.

KEY ELEMENTS OF COST

The following provides a possible breakdown of the various cost elements that might differentiate a point-of-use domestic hot-water heater from a conventional one and an indication of whether the net incremental cost for the system is likely to be lower (L), higher (H), or the same (S). This assessment is only a perception of what might be likely, but it obviously may not be correct in all situations. There is no substitute for a detailed cost analysis as part of the design process. The listings below may also provide some assistance in identifying the cost elements involved.

First Cost

- Point-of-use water-heater equipment   H
- Domestic hot-water piping to central source
  (including insulation thereof)   L
- Central water heater (if not required) and associated fuel
  and flue gas connections   L
- Electrical connection   H
- Temperature and pressure relief valve and floor drain
  (when required by code jurisdiction)   H

Recurring Costs

- Energy to heat water to appropriate temperatures   H
- Energy lost from piping not installed   L
- Maintenance/repairs, including replacement   H

SOURCES OF FURTHER INFORMATION

American Society of Plumbing Engineers
    www.aspe.org
ASPE. 1998. *Domestic Water Heating Design Manual*. Chicago:
    American Society of Plumbing Engineers.
Fagan, D. 2001. A comparison of storage-type and instantaneous
    heaters for commercial use. *Heating/Piping/Air Conditioning
    Engineering*, April.

ASHRAE
GreenTip #34

Direct-Contact Water Heaters

GENERAL DESCRIPTION

A direct-contact water heater consists of a heat exchanger in which flue gases are in direct contact with the water. It can heat large quantities of water for washing and/or industrial process purposes. Cold supply water enters the top of a heat exchanger column and flows down through stainless steel rings or other devices. Natural gas is burned in a combustion chamber, and the flue gases are directed up the heat exchanger column. As the gases move upward through the column, they transfer their sensible and latent heat to the water. A heat exchanger or water jacket on the combustion chamber captures any heat loss from the chamber. The gases exit only a few degrees warmer than the inlet water temperature. The heated water may be stored in a storage tank for on-demand use. Direct-contact water heaters can be 99% efficient when the inlet water temperature is below 59°F (15°C).

The low-temperature combustion process results in low emissions of NO_x and CO; thus, the system is, in effect, a low-NO_x burner. It is also a low-pressure process, since heat transfer occurs at atmospheric pressure.

Although there is direct contact between the flue gases and the water, there is very little contamination of the water. Direct-contact systems are suitable for all water-heating applications, including food processing and dairy applications; the water used in these systems is considered bacteriologically safe for human consumption.

WHEN/WHERE IT'S APPLICABLE

The high cost of direct-contact water heaters (due to stainless steel construction) restricts their use to where there is a large, almost continuous, demand for hot water. Appropriate applications include laundries, food processing, washing, and industrial processes. The system can also be used for closed-loop (or recirculating) applications (e.g., space heating). However, efficiency—the primary benefit of direct-contact water heating—will be reduced because of the higher inlet water temperature resulting from recirculation.

PROS

- Increases part-load and instantaneous efficiency.
- Reduces NO_x and CO emissions.
- Increases safety.
- Increases system response time.

CONS

- High cost.
- Less effective in higher-pressure or closed-loop applications or where inlet water temperatures must be relatively high.
- Due to high evaporation rates, results in considerable water usage beyond that required for the process.

KEY ELEMENTS OF COST

The following provides a possible breakdown of the various cost elements that might differentiate a direct-contact water heater from a conventional one and an indication of whether the net cost for the alternative option is likely to be lower (L), higher (H), or the same (S). This assessment is only a perception of what might be likely, but it obviously may not be correct in all situations. There is no substitute for a detailed cost analysis as part of the design process. The listings below may also provide some assistance in identifying the cost elements involved.

First Cost

- Water heater   H
- Operator training (unfamiliarity)   H

Recurring Costs

- Water heating energy   L

Direct-contact boilers are two to three times the price of indirect or conventional boilers, primarily because of the stainless steel construction. In high and continuous water use applications, however, the payback period can be less than two years.

SOURCES OF FURTHER INFORMATION

NSF. 2000. *NSF/ANSI 5-2000e: Water Heaters, Hot Water Supply Boilers, and Heat Recovery Equipment.* Ann Arbor, MI: National Sanitation Foundation and American National Standards Institute.

QuikWater, High Efficiency Direct Contact Water Heaters www.quikwater.com

ASHRAE
GreenTip #35

Rainwater Harvesting

GENERAL DESCRIPTION

Rainwater harvesting has been around for thousands of years. Rainwater harvesting is a simple technology that can stand alone or augment other water sources. Systems can be as basic as a rain barrel under a downspout or as complex as a pumped and filtered graywater system providing landscape irrigation, cooling tower makeup, and/or building waste conveyance.

Systems are generally composed of five or fewer basic components: a catchment area, a means of conveyance from the catchment, storage (optional), water treatment (optional), and a conveyance system to the end use.

The catchment area can be any impermeable area from which water can be harvested. Typically this is the roof, but paved areas (e.g., patios, entries, and parking lots) may also be considered. Roofing materials that are metal, clay, or concrete-based are preferable to asphalt or roofs with lead-containing materials. Similarly, care should be given when considering a parking lot for catchment due to oils and residues that can be present.

Conveyance to the storage will be gravity-fed, like any stormwater piping system. The only difference is that now the rainwater is being diverted for useful purposes instead of literally going down the drain.

Commercial systems will require a means of storage. Cisterns can be located outside the building (e.g., above-grade or buried) or placed on the lower levels of the building. The storage tank should have an overflow device piped to the storm system and a potable water makeup if the end-use need is ever greater than the harvested volume.

Depending on the catchment source and the end use, the level of treatment will vary. For simple site irrigation, filtration can be achieved through a series of graded screens and paper filters. If the water is to be used for waste conveyance, then an additional sand filter may be appropriate. Parking lot catchments may require an oil separator. The local code authority will likely decide acceptable water standards, and, in turn, filtration and chemical polishing will be a dictated parameter, not a design choice.

Distribution can be via gravity or pump depending on the proximity of the storage tank and the end use.

WHEN/WHERE IT'S APPLICABLE

If the building design is to include a graywater system or landscape irrigation—and space for storage can be found—rainwater harvesting is a simple addition to those systems.

When a desire exists to limit potable water demand and use, depending on the end-use requirement and the anticipated annual rainfall in a region, harvesting can be provided as a stand-alone system or to augment a conventional makeup water system.

Sites with significant precipitation volumes may determine that reuse of these volumes is more cost-effective than creating stormwater systems or on-site treatment facilities.

Rainwater harvesting is most attractive where municipal water supply is either nonexistent or unreliable, hence its popularity in rural regions and developing countries. *But rain collection growing everywhere*

PROS

- Rainwater harvesting reduces a building's potable water use, and reduces demand on the municipal water supply, lowering costs associated with water.
- Rainwater is soft and does not cause scale buildup in piping, equipment, and appliances. It could extend the life of systems.
- It can reduce or eliminate the need for stormwater treatment or conveyance systems.

CONS

- There is added first cost associated with the cisterns and the treatment system.
- There are additional materials and their associated embodied energy costs.
- The storage vessels must be accommodated. Small sites or projects with limited space allocated for utilities would be bad candidates.
- Costs include maintenance of the system (e.g., maintaining the catchments, conveyance, cisterns, and treatment systems).
- There is no U.S. guideline on rainwater harvesting. The local health code authority has jurisdiction, potentially making a particular site infeasible due to backflow prevention requirements, special separators, or additional treatment.

KEY ELEMENTS OF COST

The following provides a possible breakdown of the various cost elements that might differentiate a building utilizing rainwater harvesting from one that does not and an indication of whether the net cost is likely to be lower (L), higher (H), or the same (S). This assessment is only a perception of what might be likely, but it obviously may not be correct in all situations. There is no substitute for a detailed cost analysis as part of the design process. The listings below may also provide some assistance in identifying the cost elements involved.

First Cost

- Catchment area   S
- Conveyance systems   S
- Storage tank   H
- Water treatment   S/H
- Distribution system   S/H
- Design fees   H

Recurring Costs

- Cost of potable water   L
- Maintenance of system   H
- Training of building operators   H
- Orientation of building occupants   S
- Commissioning cost   H

SOURCES OF FURTHER INFORMATION

American Society of Plumbing Engineers
    www.aspe.org
Irrigation Association
    www.irrigation.org
Texas Manual on Rainwater Harvesting
    www.twdb.state.tx.us/publications/reports
    rainwaterharvestingmanual_3rdedition.pdf
USGBC. 2001. *LEED Reference Guide, Version 2.0.* Washington, D.C.: U.S. Green Building Council.

Waterfall, P.H. 1998. *Harvesting Rainwater for Landscape Use.* http://ag.arizona.edu/pubs/water/az1052/.

Environmental Protection Agency, Water Sense Program http://epa.gov/watersense/

ASHRAE
GreenTip #36

Air-Handling Unit (AHU) Condensate Capture and Reuse

GENERAL DESCRIPTION

As air passes across cold cooling coils in an AHU, if the coil surface temperature is less than the dew point of the airstream passing by, then the potential exists for water condensation on the coils. Water that condenses on the coils will collect and drop to the drain pan below. In conventional building systems, this water typically drains, unused, to the sewer system or elsewhere, but in some situations it can be worthwhile to capture and reuse it.

Condensate collection can either be designed into new construction or retrofitted into existing buildings. While the former is preferable (due to lower costs and fewer complications), the latter presents the highest potential, since existing buildings comprise about 98% of the building stock (the other 2% being new construction).

The best end use for the collected water will depend on the particular circumstances of the location. In a building with its own chiller and cooling tower, the most logical choice is to route collected condensate to the cooling tower sump to reduce the need to use fresh water for makeup. In most cases, peak condensate production will occur at the same times as peak makeup water demands, creating an elegant synergy. This is also the simplest retrofit, involving reasonably inexpensive equipment and piping; water can be routed directly to the tower with no need for treatment.

Condensate collection can also be integrated with a rainwater collection system, a scheme often referred to as *rainwater plus*. This will usually involve a storage tank or cistern and can require considerably more expense and engineering than using the condensate in a cooling tower. Depending on the intended use (e.g., irrigation, ornamental fountains, or other internal uses including toilet flushing), different amounts of further treatment will be required. In all cases, local building codes must be followed.

WHEN/WHERE IT'S APPLICABLE

Factors that determine whether condensate collection should be considered include location (e.g., climate), building type (particularly relating to amount of outdoor air required), the size, number, and accessibility of air handlers that condition outdoor air, location of potential uses for the condensate, etc. Location determines both the potential to collect a significant amount of condensate and the value of the water to the local community. In periods of drought, the actual value of a unit of water to the local society and economy may be worth much more than the rate currently paid to the local utility.

A building or space that requires a lot of outdoor air on an ongoing basis (e.g., laboratories) is an ideal candidate for condensate collection. Other obvious candidates include spaces with indoor water features, natatoriums, gymnasiums, or locker rooms. DOAS units are also prime candidates for consideration, since they are typically designed for optimal latent load removal.

Using typical meteorological year data, assumptions about the air-handling system, and the following equation, it is possible to estimate the amount of condensate that can be collected annually in a particular location.

LESSONS LEARNED

Attention must be paid to the cleanliness of the water and the system components. For example, any external condensate collection pan should be covered to prevent foreign particles from getting into the system. The potential is also there for biological growth and contamination. Also, there may be an increase in corrosion potential in the cooling tower loop, if that is where the condensate is sent.

Sweating on the outside of the condensate piping can be an issue, particularly in semiconditioned mechanical rooms, so all lines (as well as perhaps the collection basin itself) should be insulated. If the condensate line is tied into rain downspouts, you may want to consider running a smaller pipe or tube inside of the downspout for the condensate to avoid moisture buildup on the outside downspout surface.

The dimensions of the U-trap in the existing condensate drain pipe between the AHU and the floor drain should be maintained when connecting the drain pipe to the external collection pan. It is also highly recommended that a condensate flow meter be installed and that it be located to facilitate easy reading. The additional cost of the meter is worthwhile because of the good feedback on functionality and the education potential it provides. It's also a good way to verify water and cost savings.

PROS

- If condensate is routed to a cooling tower, demand for makeup water will reduce and so will the need for treatment chemicals. Blowdown frequency should decrease, and sewer costs could be reduced with appropriate metering.
- Cool condensate routed to a cooling tower will provide residual free cooling for condenser water.
- Incorporating condensate collection into a rainwater collection and storage system can reduce the cistern size requirement by providing a supplemental water source during long periods between rain events.

CONS

- Complications arise when dealing with district cooling systems with satellite chillers, because it is possible to produce condensate in an AHU while the chiller and cooling tower (for that particular building) are idle. This leads to the risk that treatment chemicals in the sump will be diluted and needlessly washed away via the overflow drain.
- In general, less-efficient systems have higher condensate production potential. Enthalpy wheels, for example, will greatly improve system efficiency but will dramatically reduce condensate production. A building with 100% outdoor air supply that is overpressurized will produce more condensate but will waste energy. Energy efficiency should always take precedence over water production.

KEY ELEMENTS OF COST

The following capital cost issues list the various cost elements associated with either building condensate collection into new construction or retrofitting an existing building. This assessment is only a perception of what might be likely, but it obviously may not be correct in all situations. There is no substitute for a detailed cost analysis as part of the design process.

Pipe. Depending on the distance between the AHU and the end use, and whether a storage tank is involved, the material and labor costs of the pipe installation are likely to be the most expensive part of the system. For new construction the additional cost should be minimal, since a condensate drain pipe would need to be furnished, regardless of the end use.

Storage. If condensate is to be stored for later use, a cistern or storage tank can represent a considerable part of the system cost. Additional costs will be incurred for system design (i.e., tank sizing) and tank site selection and installation. Finally, treatment of stored water prior to end use, if necessary, will add equipment, design, and maintenance costs.

Metering. A totalizing meter is a relatively inexpensive but important component of a condensate collection system. Once in place, a condensate meter will help verify payback on the investment in the system.

SOURCES OF FURTHER INFORMATION

Guz, K. 2005. Condensate water recovery. *ASHRAE Journal* 47(6):54–56.

Lawrence, T., J. Perry, and P. Dempsey. 2010. Making every drop count: retrofitting condensate collection on HVAC air handling units. *ASHRAE Journal* 52(1).

REFERENCES AND RESOURCES

[handwritten: ~~2010~~ 2011]

Published

ASHRAE. 2008. *ASHRAE Handbook—HVAC Systems and Equipment*, Ch. 6. Atlanta: American Society of Heating, Refrigerating and Air-Conditioning Engineers, Inc.

ASHRAE. 2009. *ANSI/ASHRAE/USGBC/IES Standard 189.1-2009, Standard for the Design of High-Performance Green Buildings.* Atlanta: American Society of Heating, Refrigerating and Air-Conditioning Engineers, Inc.

ASHRAE. 2010. *ANSI/ASHRAE/IES Standard 90.1-2010, Energy Standard for Buildings Except Low-Rise Residential Buildings.* Atlanta: American Society of Heating, Refrigerating and Air-Conditioning Engineers, Inc.

Cho, Y.I., S. Lee, and W. Kim. 2003. Physical water treatment for the mitigation of mineral fouling in cooling-tower water applications. *ASHRAE Transactions* 109(1):346–57.

Epoch Times. 2009. Water efficiency a priority for green buildings. www.theepochtimes.com/n2/content/view/17751.

Webber, M.E. 2008. *Energy versus Water: Solving Both Crises Together.* Scientific American Special Editions. www.sehn.org/tccenergyversuswater.html

Online

ASHRAE Standard Project Committee 191
http://spc191.ashraepcs.org/
U.S. Environmental Protection Agency, Green Chemistry
www.epa.gov/greenchemistry/

[handwritten: World Health Org.   From page 338]

CHAPTER FIFTEEN

BUILDING AUTOMATION SYSTEMS

Or represent a local control function such as t.stat for single zone RTU

Building control systems play an important part in the operation of a building and determine whether many of the green design aspects included in the original plan actually function as intended. Controls for HVAC and related systems have evolved over the years, but in general, they can be described as either distributed (local) or centralized. Local controls are generally packaged devices that are provided with the equipment. A building automation system (BAS), on the other hand, is a form of central control capable of coordinating local control operation and controlling HVAC and other systems (e.g., life-safety, lighting, water distribution, and security from a central location).

Control systems are at the core of building performance. When they work well, the indoor environment promotes productivity with the lighting, comfort, and ventilation people need to carry out their tasks effectively and efficiently. When they break down, the results are higher utility bills, loss of productivity, and discomfort. In modern buildings, direct digital control systems operate lights, chilled- or hot-water plants, ventilation, space temperature and humidity control, plumbing systems, electrical systems, life-safety systems, and other building systems. These control systems can assist in conserving resources through the scheduling, staging, modulation, and optimization of equipment to meet the needs of the occupants and systems that they are designed to serve. The control system can assist with operation and maintenance through the accumulation of equipment runtimes, display of trend logs, use of part-load performance modeling equations, and automated alarms. Finally, the control system can interface with a central repository for building maintenance information where operation and maintenance manuals or equipment ratings, such as pump curves, are stored as electronic documents available through a hyperlink on the control system graphic for the appropriate system. This chapter presents the key issues to designing, commissioning, and maintaining control systems for optimal performance.

In addition using a bldg control sys can provide expanded functions necessary for new user such as m&v, demand response programs and the interaction of bldg with the coming smart grid

This chapter is divided into seven sections as follows:

- *Control System Role in Delivering Energy Efficiency.* Through scheduling, optimal loading and unloading, optimal setpoint determination, and fault detection, controls have the capability of reducing building energy usage by up to 20% (or sometimes even more) in a typical commercial building.
- *Control System Role in Delivering Water Efficiency.* Used primarily in landscape irrigation and leak detection, controls can significantly reduce water usage compared to systems with simplistic control (such as time clock-based irrigation controllers). Building controls can also provide trending and alarming for potable and nonpotable water usage.
- *Control System Role in Delivering Indoor Environmental Quality (IEQ).* In most commercial buildings, controls play a crucial role in providing IEQ. Controls can regulate the quantities of outdoor air brought into the building based on occupancy levels, zone ventilation, zone temperature, and relative humidity, and can monitor the loading of air filters.
- *Control System Commissioning Process.* Of all the building systems, controls are the most susceptible to problems in installation. These can be addressed by a thorough process of commissioning and postcommissioning performance verification.
- *Control System Role in Attaining Leadership in Energy and Environmental Design (LEED®) Certification.* This section describes the elements of LEED certification that can be addressed by control system design and implementation.
- *Designing for Sustained Efficiency.* Control systems help ensure continued efficient building operation by enabling measurement and verification (M&V) of building performance and serving as a repository of maintenance procedures.

CONTROL SYSTEM ROLE IN DELIVERING ENERGY EFFICIENCY

A U.S. Department of Energy report (DOE 2005) featured the following information:

- Seventeen quad/yr (17.9 EJ/yr) of energy are used in commercial buildings.
- Only 10% of commercial buildings (33% of the floor space) have a building management system
- Less than 10% of the commercial building space has automated lighting control.
- A potential for nearly 1 quad/yr of energy savings (11% of total building energy) exists through installing automation systems in all buildings and fully commissioning them.

Thus, the potential for energy savings by installing building automation systems is huge. The study indicated that commercial building energy usage could be reduced by 2% to 11% (0.34 to 1.8 quad/yr [0.36 to 1.9 EJ/yr]) with proper management and control.

Building automation can save energy through a variety of methods, including the following:

- *Reduction of Equipment Runtime.* Examples include scheduled control of lighting and air-conditioning systems inside buildings and photoelectric controls for site (exterior) lighting.
- *Efficient Unloading of Equipment.* Examples include daylight control with dimming or stepped lighting in spaces with access to natural light. This also would include resetting setpoints for chilled, condenser water supply, hot-water temperature, coil discharge air temperature, or variable-air-volume (VAV) fan static pressure. Variable-speed control of pumps, fans, and compressors is another common method employed for cooling systems. Also, consider methods for optimization among building HVAC systems, such as in static pressure reset from VAV direct digital controllers with variable-frequency drives (VFDs), which often end up saving more energy than a VFD by itself.
- *Automated Fault Detection and Diagnostic Systems.* Examples include controls that report when dampers or valves are stuck open or closed.

The GreenTips included in this chapter give two detailed examples of how controls can be used to deliver energy efficiency in building air distribution systems.

CONTROL SYSTEM ROLE IN DELIVERING WATER EFFICIENCY

Control systems can deliver building water efficiency in two main areas: landscape irrigation and leak detection. Additionally, controls can be used to regulate and monitor on-site wastewater treatment plants where those systems are in place.

While the most obvious contribution to a sustainable design solution is to not include irrigated landscaping, when landscape irrigation is done, smart irrigation controllers using embedded sensors in the ground can make a significant contribution to reducing the annual water use of a building. (Note that this is a requirement for landscaping irrigation in *ANSI/ASHRAE/USGBC/IES Standard 189.1-2009, Standard for the Design of High-Performance Green Buildings* [ASHRAE 2009].) The level of contribution depends on the amount and type of landscaping, as well as on geographical location. The simplest irrigation controls are based on time clocks that open valves for a set duration, for a set number of periods per week. Unless the duration and frequency of watering is adjusted throughout the irrigation season, the use of time clock controllers often results in excessive water use. In order to automatically address seasonally varying irrigation requirements, some time clock controllers allow for 365 day programming.

An improvement on the time clock controller is to add moisture sensors, which can enable the system to bypass a watering period (if ground moisture levels are above a setpoint). Still more sophisticated controllers can gather data about local weather conditions—either directly via sensors, indirectly via a remote weather station, or by direct input from a remote weather station—and use that data to adjust the amount of water delivered to the landscape.

Integrating landscape irrigation controls into the building automation system (BAS) provides a number of advantages. Among these are the ability to adjust schedules and setpoints from a single location, the ability to perform remote diagnostics, and the ability to track system performance and water use. Integrating water meters into the BAS enables continuous measurement of water consumption. Water consumption data can be analyzed during unoccupied periods to determine whether leaks are present in the water distribution system. The judicious placement of submeters can allow building maintenance staff to find the system or location in which the leak or leaks are present. Continuous water meter data can also be used to identify processes and areas of high water use and guide postconstruction water conservation efforts.

Finally, some advanced green buildings feature on-site wastewater treatment plants. Such plants generally include pumps, fans, and sensors to monitor characteristics of the treated water (e.g., dissolved oxygen levels and total suspended solids). Depending on the goals and complexity of the wastewater treatment plant, an industrial supervisory control and data acquisition system may be necessary to ensure maximization of throughput, efficient energy use, and code compliance. The supervisory control and data acquisition system may be stand-alone or it may be integrated into the BAS.

CONTROL SYSTEM ROLE IN DELIVERING IEQ

Factors regulated by building control systems that impact IEQ include operative temperature, relative humidity, outdoor airflow rates, and light levels. The first two factors are addressed in the latest edition of *ANSI/ASHRAE Standard 55, Thermal Environmental Conditions for Human Occupancy* (ASHRAE 2010), the third factor is addressed in the latest edition of *ANSI/ASHRAE Standard 62.1, Ventilation for Acceptable Indoor Air Quality* (ASHRAE 2010), and the fourth factor is addressed in Chapter 10 of the IES *Lighting Handbook* (IES).

Thermal Comfort

The operative temperature is approximately equal to the average of the room air temperature and the mean radiant temperature (MRT) for most building interior environments. Radiant heating systems raise the MRT, and thus, lower the room air temperature required to provide a comfortable operative temperature. Radiant cooling systems lower the MRT, and thus, raise the room air temperature required to provide a comfortable operative temperature. Stand-alone thermostats and BASs typically measure and control room air temperature. When designing radiant systems, it is important to keep the distinction between operative temperature and air temperature in mind, as well as the impact of building thermal mass. The current level of control technology is generally not sophisticated enough to optimize energy consumption with MRT, but this is one area for future control system development. For a discussion of these two quantities, see Chapter 53 of the 2007 *ASHRAE Handbook—HVAC Applications* (ASHRAE 2007). ASHRAE Standard 55 describes methods for determining acceptable operative temperatures that depend on occupant clothing insulation levels and metabolic rates.

While they are less common than thermostats and temperature sensors, stand-alone humidistats and humidity sensors can be used to control room humidity levels. Standard 55 specifies a maximum humidity ratio of 0.012. The standard does not specify a minimum humidity ratio for thermal comfort but notes that nonthermal comfort factors (e.g., skin drying) may be used to establish such a minimum.

Air Quality and Ventilation

Procedures for determining minimum outdoor airflow rates are described in ASHRAE Standard 62.1 (ASHRAE 2010). Building controls play a critical role in ensuring that minimum outdoor airflow rates are achieved in three areas: VAV system control, mixed-mode ventilation systems, and dynamic reset of outdoor air intake flows.

It is difficult to ensure that minimum outdoor airflow rates are met by VAV systems over the entire range of operating conditions in the absence of controls designed, installed, and maintained specifically for that purpose. One means of achieving such control is to measure the supply airflow rate and CO_2 concentrations in the occupied zones, and outdoor air intake on a continuous basis. Another potential method is by measuring the outdoor air intake flow. Control systems based on CO_2 levels, as well as those that measure outdoor air intake flow, all have their potential errors and design difficulties. The BAS can determine if the outdoor airflow rate is sufficient based on this information and can adjust the mixed-air dampers accordingly. The preferred method of controlling outside air intake is to control the mixing plenum pressure based on a measured, mixing plenum, static pressure sensor. This will indirectly control the needed variations in outside air flow. If airflows are also measured at each VAV box, this control routine can be further improved upon. As described in Standard 62.1, zone air distribution effectiveness can change when the temperature of the supply air changes. Therefore, it may be necessary for the control system to reset the minimum outdoor airflow after a seasonal switchover of supply air temperature.

Mixed-mode ventilation refers to the combination of mechanical ventilation and operable windows that provide natural ventilation. During some times of the year, if the windows are sized, located, and operated (by automatic control) properly, it is not necessary to provide mechanical ventilation when the windows are open. Sizing must include factors such as, for example, location of the window with respect to prevailing wind patterns and solar loads. Perhaps the most straightforward way to control mixed-mode ventilation systems is to use the output of a window switch to shut down the terminal unit (e.g., the VAV box) when the window is open. This is most applicable for single-occupant zones or areas with a relatively small number of occupants. When the occupants decide that it is preferable to shut the window, the mechanical HVAC system is brought back online. It may be necessary to install an alarm or override based on space temperature, wind annoyance, wet weather, or in order to provide freeze protection.

It may be desirable to reset the minimum outdoor airflow based on changes in occupancy or changes in zone air distribution effectiveness. For example, occupancy can be estimated directly by a card reader system, providing there are card checks as the person enters and leaves the zone. Occupancy can be estimated indirectly by measuring the CO_2 concentration in the occupied space. If CO_2 levels are used to estimate occupancy, it is important to keep in mind the interaction of the various spaces in multizone systems. This is a topic of current research projects.

Lighting Levels

The BAS can maintain desired light levels by either adjusting electric light output or controlling the amount of daylight entering the building. One or more photocells may be used to measure the light level in the occupied space and the output used to brighten or dim electric lights. Alternatively, photocell output may be used to switch between multiple light levels. Photocell output may also be used to raise or lower window blinds, or adjust louvers to keep daylighting at comfortable levels and eliminate glare. Alternately, equations that calculate the sun position angle for various wall or roof orientations can be input into the BAS and used to vary the tilt angle of window blinds, in order to minimize glare and maximize daylighting. Of course, human perceptions of thermal and visual comfort vary considerably among individuals. For this reason, a good design principle to keep in mind is that building occupants should be given as much control over their thermal and visual environments as practical. Room thermostats, operable windows, dimming switches, and adjustable blinds are all means of giving people this control. Integrating these manually operable controls into the BAS can contribute significantly toward optimizing both IEQ and energy efficiency.

CONTROL SYSTEM COMMISSIONING PROCESS

The commissioning process is defined in *ASHRAE Guideline 0-2005, The Commissioning Process* (ASHRAE 2005), as:

> A quality focused process for enhancing the delivery of a project. The process focuses upon verifying and documenting that the facility and all of its systems and assemblies are planned, designed, installed, tested, operated, and maintained to meet the Owner's Project Requirements.

The full process from project planning through occupancy and operations is explained in ASHRAE Guideline 0 (ASHRAE 2005) and in Chapter 42 of the 2007 *ASHRAE Handbook—HVAC Applications* (ASHRAE 2007). Guidelines for applying the commissioning process to green buildings in general are found in Chapter 6 of this Guide. Additional information relative to design reviews and commissioning for designers and commissioning providers can be found on the Energy Design Resources Web site at www.energydesignresources.com/paublication/gd/.

This section will cover salient elements of applying the commissioning process to controls in new-construction green buildings and will focus on what the design engineer and commissioning provider can do during the design phase to facilitate a successful commissioning program. For commissioning of existing buildings, the reader is referred to sources of information, such as the U.S. Green Building Council's (USGBC) LEED program for Existing Buildings (see "References and Resources" section at the end of the chapter for Web site).

Include Commissioning Engagement in Design Fees

In estimating the fees for the design process, owners and the design team should include sufficient allowance to be fully engaged in the commissioning process during design. This includes responding to design review comments and incorporating commissioning requirements into the project specifications.

Conduct and Participate in Design Reviews

During the design reviews, the commissioning provider should see that the following control-related elements are included in the contract documents. This list of items is not comprehensive, but it provides an idea of the type of issues that should be addressed.

Provide Detailed Control Descriptions. One of the most prevalent reasons why control systems fail to perform as intended is that insufficient forethought is given to the sequence of operation prior to the contractor programming setup. The designers, and later, the control contractor's programmer often do not think the sequence out and consider how it will (or will not) function during all possible modes and scenarios of weather, loads, staging, and interactions. This issue can be mitigated by the following:

• Ensure that the designer provides flow diagrams of the major controlled systems, showing interfaces and control authorities between local and central control.
• Ensure that the designer includes detailed sequences of operation that include brief system narrative, points list, alarms, what initially starts equipment, staging, failure and standby functions, power outage response and reset requirements, interlocks to other systems, control authorities with local (packaged) controls, trending requirements, and energy efficiency strategies with given setpoints.

- Develop a graphical test simulation of the control program(s) to ensure that the mechanical equipment sequences on and off as load increases and decreases, according to the sequences of operation.

Match Control Strategies to Operator Capabilities. If the operators do not understand the features or sequences sufficiently and there is not a qualified controls technician maintaining the system, the advanced features or sequences that have problems will likely be overridden or disabled. Designers and design reviewers should make sure the complexity of control schemes matches the expected level of technical expertise of the operators. (It is a known fact that the operators will reduce the complexity of the control system to the operator's level of understanding.) It is critical that operator training be conducted in a timely manner, including some follow-up sessions as needed.

Strategies Relying on Drift-Prone Sensors. Control sensor and loop recalibrations are a necessary function for maintaining high-performing systems. The Owner's Project Requirements document should define the operator training and skill sets needed to maintain the system functioning at design efficiency. Major control strategies that depend on sensors that are known to drift should be avoided or, if called for, the necessary training and recalibration programs must be institutionalized into the building maintenance culture. For example, consider the case of a chiller staging sequence utilizing supply and return temperatures and a flowmeter(s). The sensors may well drift over time, and typical accepted errors in these types of sensors will yield load calculations that may disrupt proper staging. This strategy can result in high overall efficiency, but it requires a regular calibration and maintenance check.

Requirements for System Architecture Rationale. Ensure that in the requirements for the controls submittal, the controls contractor is required to provide calculations and rationale for the number and layout of the primary (peer-to-peer) and local (application-specific) controllers in relation to the total number of points and other network traffic. Require that the contractor describe how many points can be reasonably trended without appreciably affecting point value refresh rates, and describe the impacts on network speed that alternative layouts would have.

The BAS performance requirements should be defined in the contract documents (i.e., specifications such as those set forth in *ASHRAE Guideline 13-2007, Specifying Direct Digital Control Systems* [ASHRAE 2007]). The performance requirements are defined during the predesign phase and should be contained in the Owner's Project Requirements document in accordance with ASHRAE Guideline 0 (ASHRAE 2005).

Requirements for Clear Control Sequences. Ensure that the requirements for the control drawing submittals in the specifications include statements requiring the following:

- A brief overview narrative of the system, generally describing its purpose, components, and function (i.e., a design intent for the controls).
- All interactions and interlocks with other systems.
- Detailed delineation of interaction between any localized controls and the BAS, listing what points only the BAS monitors and what BAS points are control points and are adjustable.
- Start-up, warm-up, cooldown, occupied and unoccupied operating modes, plus power failure recovery and alarm sequences.
- Capacity control sequences and equipment staging.
- Initial and recommended values for all adjustable settings, setpoints, and parameters that are typically set or adjusted by operating staff and any other control settings or fixed values, delays, etc., that will be useful during testing and operating the equipment.
- Rogue zone analysis requirements to assure reset strategies are effective.
- Energy mapping requirements to help operators see the building efficiency at a glance.
- System override abilities and requirements.
- Description of building isolation areas for off-hours operation.
- Front-end graphics requirements including summary screens by system type, zone, and plant.
- To facilitate review and referencing in testing procedures, all sequences shall be written in short statements, each with a number for easy reference.

Requirements for Clear Control Drawings. The specifications must ensure that the control drawing submittal requirements include at least the following:

- The control drawings shall contain graphic schematic depictions of all systems showing each component (e.g., valves, dampers, actuators, coils, filters, fans, pumps, speed controllers, piping, ducting, etc.), each monitored or control point and sensor, and all interlocks to other equipment. Drawings may include fan and pump flow rates as well as horsepower.
- The schematics will include the system and component layout of any equipment that the control system monitors, enables, or controls, even if the equipment is primarily controlled by packaged controls.
- Provide a full points list, including point abbreviation key, point type, system point with which it is associated, point description, units, panel ID, and field device.
- Network architecture drawing showing all controllers, workstations, printers, and other devices in a riser format and including protocols and speeds for all trunks. Include the network buses with the bus speeds.
- Sketches of all graphics screens for review and approval.

Specify a Systems Manual

Ensure that the commissioning scope for the commissioning provider, contractor, and designer includes a systems manual that, among other things, includes narratives explaining all energy-efficiency features and strategies, a setpoint and parameter table that indicates the impacts of changing the values, a recalibration and retesting frequency table, suggested smart alerts in the control system to send alerts on malfunctioning sensors and actuators, and a list of standard trend logs to view to verify proper performance. The building operators need to be trained on the systems manual and its contents in order to properly operate and maintain the system.

CONTROL SYSTEM ROLE IN ATTAINING LEED CERTIFICATION

In Chapter 7, the LEED® and other green building rating programs are discussed. This section explicitly discusses how controls can be used in various sections of the *LEED 2009 Green Building Operations and Maintenance* (USGBC 2009) (for existing buildings) and the *LEED 2009 for New Construction and Major Renovations* (USGBC 2009). (These are the latest versions in effect as of this writing.) A BAS or building control system can be of great assistance with the certification and maintaining certification for existing buildings under the LEED-Existing Building program, but the impact is dependent on the type of control system available within the building. This section on LEED and controls will connect control methods discussed earlier in this chapter with either of the two LEED rating systems cited above. The credit areas that can be affected include the following:

- Water efficiency (WE)
- Energy and atmosphere (EA)
- Indoor environmental quality (IEQ)

The remainder of this section discusses the impact of controls in meeting LEED prerequisites or obtaining credit points. If the control option was covered earlier in this chapter, the reader will be referred to that section.

Water-Efficient Landscaping: WE Credit 1

Controls allow soil moisture levels to be sensed and watering to take place on a required basis. This reduces the water consumption for landscaping to that needed to maintain the landscaping health for the specific site, weather, and vegetation requirements based on soil moisture levels, types of plants, etc. The BAS can also monitor and trend the actual water usage. So, as the building moves to the existing building operations and maintenance phase, data will be available for submission. See the "Control System Role in Delivering Water Efficiency" section in this chapter for more detail.

Water-Efficient Landscaping Via Rainwater Collection

A rainwater harvesting system is commonly used for landscape irrigation or for toilet flushing. A BAS can be used, for example, to sense the amount of water collection in a cistern, and this data can be used to quantify the percentage of potable water reduction, which can help a building owner obtain LEED credits. Efforts to increase rainwater harvesting, increase graywater use, and reduce demand on local water aquifers may support the following LEED 2009 Green Building Operations and Maintenance credits:

Sustainable Sites Credit 6: Stormwater Quantify Control

Water-Efficiency Credit 3: Water-Efficient Landscaping

Energy and Atmosphere

Fundamental Commissioning—EA Prerequisite 1 and Enhanced Commissioning: EA Credit 3. Both fundamental and enhanced commissioning can be aided by the control system—especially if the equipment calibration has been verified. The BAS can also help in verifying proper calibration from the factory.

Along with verifying feature and system sequences of operation, calibration, and functionality, the commisioning authority is responsible for applying appropriate sampling techniques to verify equipment start-up and operation. Although commissioning is a process and not a technology, it seems logical that the facility BAS can assist in this sampling process. For example, a typical rooftop VAV system might be set up to display the system operating conditions in a manner similar to that shown in Figure 15-1. Such a control display might include the following:

- Supply air conditions that include fan control pressures
- Space conditions
- Fan speed
- Other load conditions

Using the control system, it is pretty easy to see that the mixed-air temperature sensor is not working properly.

For a commissioning example, according to *ANSI/ASHRAE/IES Standard 90.1-2010, Energy Standard for Buildings Except Low-Rise Residential Buildings* (ASHRAE 2010), in a direct digital control VAV system, fan static pressure setpoint optimization is required. Even for simple VAV fan static pressure reset programs, fulfilling this requirement requires, at a minimum, having VAV damper positions available. More sophisticated, model-based control programs that are based on the duct system static pressure model for the system require additional data such as VAV box flows or flow setpoints, VAV box damper commands, and fan discharge static pressure. Even on what most people consider a fairly simple system, there are quite a few control points that must be calibrated and in working order. With equipment-manufacturer engineered and installed controls, many of the

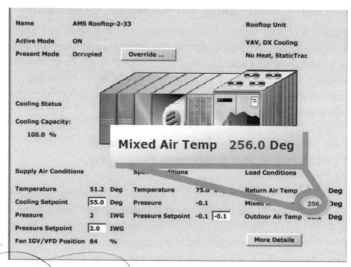

Image courtesy of Trane, A Business of Ingersoll Rand

Figure 15-1 Example of daylight harvesting rendering.

Title error

points would be factory-commissioned. The BAS can easily be used to sample and determine if any points are not working properly.

For enhanced commissioning, the commissioning authority is required to write an operations manual. The BAS can be used to enhance the building operator's use of this manual. See "Control System Commissioning Process" section in this chapter for additional details.

Energy Performance—EA Prerequisite 2 (Minimum) and Optimized: EA Credit 1. *Minimum energy performance* is defined as meeting Standard 90.1-2007 (ASHRAE 2007). For example, some of the Standard 90.1 requirements that require controls include the following:

- Zone thermostatic controls that respond to temperature variations within the zone, and when the zone controls include both heating and cooling, a deadband of at least 5°F (2.8 K) must be used to separate heating and cooling activation. Within the deadband, heating or cooling energy to the zone is shut off or reduced to a minimum.
- Automatic shutdown of HVAC systems during unoccupied periods of 30 min or more. (This conflicts with ASHRAE Standard 62.1 [ASHRAE 2010], which always requires a specified minimum ventilation rate to remove building effluents during unoccupied periods.)

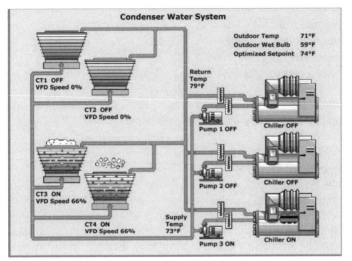

Image courtesy of Trane, A Business of Ingersoll Rand

Figure 15-2 Sample cooling tower fan control display.

- Unoccupied period (night) heating setback and cooling setup controls
- VAV fan static pressure reset
- Optimum start controls
- High-occupancy ventilation control
- Air- and/or water-side economizer controls
- Exhaust air energy recovery
- Chilled- and hot-water temperature reset
- Automated lighting shutoff based on time of day or occupancy

Credit points are accrued by reducing energy costs below Standard 90.1-2007. System strategies often require controls to optimize the energy performance. These strategies include the following:

- Supply temperature reset (air and hydronic)
- Demand shed controls
- Optimization of central plants
- Chiller staging
- Pump control and staging
- Cooling tower fan control (see Figure 15-2)
- Variable-condenser water flow

- Variable chilled-water flow
- Dual minimums for VAV boxes
- Demand-controlled ventilation
- Economizer isolation zone control
- Occupancy-sensed HVAC and lighting

In addition, there are many mechanical systems that require well-operated controls for optimization. They include the following:

- Water-side heat recovery
- Variable primary-flow systems
- Low-flow systems
- Geothermal heat-pump systems

In addition to HVAC control, the BAS or other stand-alone controls can be used to automatically open and close blinds, or vary their tilt angle, to reduce system load. There are many ways that automated controls can help reduce energy consumption and costs.

Measurement and Verification: EA Credit 5. M&V of the building systems is developed according to the International Measurement and Verification Protocol. While a BAS cannot perform all the requirements to gain the M&V credit, it can greatly simplify tracking and trending the data, especially in the isolation of systems for verification (International Performance Measurement and Verification Protocol [IPMVP] Options A or B). Examples of data that can be gathered include the following:

- Economizer cycles
- Heat exchanger cycles
- Air distribution
  - Pressures
  - Volume flow rates
- Process loads
- Water usage
- Lighting systems and control
- Motor loads
- VFD operation
- Chiller efficiency
- Boiler efficiency
- Cooling load

The data may also be presented using trend logs available from many control providers (see Figure 15-3).

Existing Building Commissioning—Investigation and Analysis: EA Credit 2.1. Option 1 under this credit requires the development of a retrocommissioning, recommissioning, or ongoing commissioning plan for the building's major energy-using systems, listing the operating problems that affect the occupant's comfort and energy use, and identifying the capital improvements that will provide cost-effective energy savings. (Retrocommissioning is the commissioning of the building operation systems [e.g., the HVAC system, lighting, and domestic hot-water systems], after occupancy has begun, that was never performed when the building was new. Recommissioning applies to buildings that were previously commissioned as part of new construction or buildings covered by existing building commissioning. Ongoing commissioning is a continuous process that methodically identifies and corrects system problems to maintain optimal building performance; it includes regular measurement and comparative analysis of building energy data over time.) This option also requires the documentation of the breakdown of the energy use within the building. The BAS is the tool of choice to fulfill this requirement. Energy use within the building should, at minimum, include the following systems:

• Lighting system energy

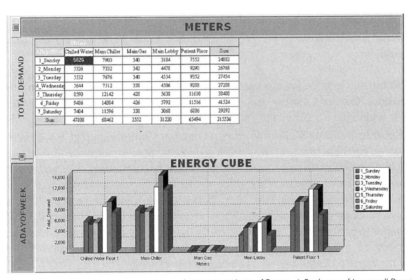

Image courtesy of Trane, A Business of Ingersoll Rand

Figure 15-3 Sample rooftop unit control display.

- Cooling system energy, including chiller, primary, and distribution system pumping, condenser-water system pumping, and cooling tower fan energy.
- Heating system energy, including boiler, hot-water converter, primary and distribution system pumping, and domestic hot-water system energy
- Ventilation system energy

Existing Building Commissioning—Implementation: EA Credit 2.2. In addition to updating the building operation plan to reflect any changes to occupancy and equipment runtime schedules, setpoints, and training in sustainable building operational practices, this credit requires the implementation of no- or low-cost operational improvements and the creation of a capital plan for major upgrades and improvements. Simple control system repairs and a BAS can greatly assist in the implementation of the following no- or low-cost building mechanical system control improvements:

- If necessary, repair the motorized damper for any outside air intake.
- Repair duct leaks where found.
- Repair or replace any malfunctioning space temperature, humidity, or CO_2 sensors.
- Install space temperature sensors and terminal equipment controllers to schedule space temperature conditioning, according to occupancy patterns.
- Optimize the start and stop time for all air-handling units (AHUs).
- Optimize the sequencing of multiple chillers.
- Reprogram controls to prevent simultaneous heating and cooling in identified areas.

Significant energy savings can often be obtained by recalibrating, repairing, or replacing defective sensors and controlled devices. These changes can often be made within the established maintenance budget.

Existing Building Commissioning—Ongoing Commissioning: EA Credit 2.3. Ongoing commissioning is an unending, dynamic process intended to facilitate the efficient operation of a previously retrocommissioned building. The ongoing commissioning process repeats many of the elements of the standard retrocommissioning over a long time period, and the intervals between operation and equipment reviews should be frequent. Ongoing commissioning incorporates the monitoring and analysis of building performance data generated by the BAS, or other permanently installed metering equipment, to verify high-level building performance, occupant satisfaction, and the expected financial outcome of capital investments.

This credit requires the creation of a written plan that summarizes the commissioning cycle for the building by equipment or building system group. The ongoing commissioning cycle must not exceed 24 months. This plan must include a building equipment list, performance measurement frequency for each equipment item, and steps to respond to deviation from expected performance.

The building control system can assist with this area for existing buildings in a similar manner as outlined for the new construction EA Credit 3 (Enhanced Commissioning) mentioned earlier in the chapter.

IEQ

Indoor Environmental Quality—Outdoor Air Delivery Monitoring: EQ Credit 1. This credit requires the installation of a permanent, continuous monitoring system to ensure that ventilation systems maintain minimum outdoor airflow rates under all operating conditions. A BAS is ideally suited to perform this function. For systems that are mechanically ventilated (Case 1), it depends on whether the space is densely occupied or not. For densely occupied spaces, a CO_2 sensor is required to be installed in each space to measure CO_2 concentration. For mechanical ventilation systems, 20% or more of the design supply flow serves nondensely occupied spaces, so the design should provide an outdoor airflow measurement device capable of measuring the outside air within 15% of the design minimum outdoor airflow rate, as defined in ASHRAE Standard 62.1-2007 (ASHRAE 2007). Similarly, CO_2 monitoring would be done with all naturally ventilated spaces (Case 2). BAS controls can be used to monitor CO_2 and any direct airflow measurement devices required to achieve this credit (see Figure 15-4).

Indoor Environmental Quality—Increased Ventilation: EQ Credit 2. For mechanically ventilated spaces (Case 1), this credit requires the ventilation airflow to be at least 30% above the ASHRAE Standard 62.1-2007 ventilation requirements in each breathing zone. For naturally ventilated spaces, the requirements are different, but in either case, and for many systems, there are calculations that must be dynamically performed in response to system loads and ambient conditions. The BAS can monitor, perform the required calculations, and reset damper positions to maintain the ventilation required.

Indoor Environmental Quality—Construction Indoor Air Quality (IAQ) Management Plan — Before Occupancy: EQ Credit 3.2. Option 1 for this credit requires flushing the building either prior to occupancy or while the building is occupied. In either case the amount of ventilation air, as well as proper humidity control, are required if Option 1 of this credit is used. The BAS can monitor, trend, and sum the amount of outdoor air delivered to the space, as well as ensure that the mechanical system is controlled (in order to maintain the required humidity levels).

Indoor Environmental Quality—Indoor Chemical and Pollutant Source Control: EQ Credit 5. The HVAC system must be operated to properly pressurize the space while exhausting sufficient air to provide pollutant removal. The BAS can monitor exhaust air measurements, sense various space pressures, and perform control algorithms to maintain proper space pressure relationships.

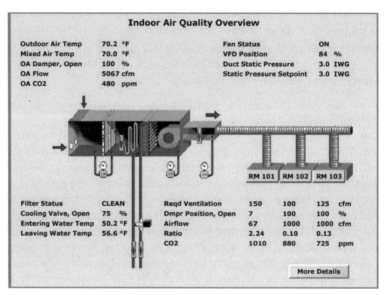

Indoor Air Quality Overview					
Outdoor Air Temp	70.2 °F		Fan Status	ON	
Mixed Air Temp	70.0 °F		VFD Position	84 %	
OA Damper, Open	100 %		Duct Static Pressure	3.0 IWG	
OA Flow	5067 cfm		Static Pressure Setpoint	3.0 IWG	
OA CO2	480 ppm				

				RM 101	RM 102	RM 103
Filter Status	CLEAN		Reqd Ventilation	150	100	125 cfm
Cooling Valve, Open	75 %		Dmpr Position, Open	7	100	100 %
Entering Water Temp	50.2 °F		Airflow	67	1000	1000 cfm
Leaving Water Temp	56.6 °F		Ratio	2.24	0.10	0.13
			CO2	1010	880	725 ppm

More Details

Image courtesy of Trane, A Business of Ingersoll Rand

Figure 15-4 Sample IAQ control display.

Controllability of Systems—Lighting: EQ Credit 6.1. This credit requires lighting controls that enable adjustments to suit the task needs and preferences of individuals for at least 50% of the building occupants. The BAS can provide lighting controls that meet this requirement, as well as the mandatory provisions of Standard 90.1-2007 (e.g., automated lighting shutoff and independent control within the space). Alternatively, occupancy sensor control of lighting may be more suitable for some situations.

Controllability of Systems—Thermal Comfort: EQ Credit 6.2. If the HVAC system is properly designed, the BAS can provide individualized controls and maintain thermal comfort conditions, as described in ASHRAE Standard 55 (ASHRAE 2004) and illustrated in Figure 15-5. The primary factors for such a system will be

- Air temperature
- Radiant temperature
- Air speed
- Relative humidity

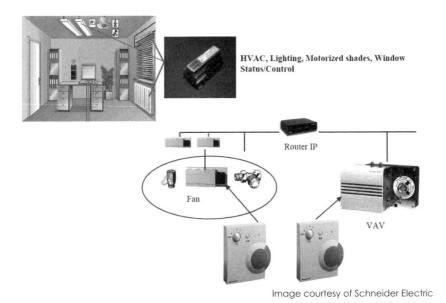

Image courtesy of Schneider Electric

Figure 15-5 Sample IAQ control arrangement.

Daylight and Views, Daylight 75% of Spaces: EQ Credit 8.1. While not directly responsible for earning points under this credit, a BAS or other open-protocol control systems can change lighting levels in response to photocell-based sensors and reduce artificial lighting while still maintaining proper space illumination.

See the "Control System Role in Delivering IEQ" section of this chapter for additional details concerning the EQ credits discussed above.

LEED 2009 Green Building Design and Construction

Controls impact the following LEED prerequisites and credits, which are taken from the *LEED 2009 Green Building Design and Construction Reference Guide* (USGBC 2009). The LEED Guide includes the design, construction, and major renovations of commercial and institutional buildings, including core and shell renovations and K–12 schools.

Fundamental Commissioning of Building Energy Systems: EA Prerequisite 1

This prerequisite requires commissioning for the following energy-related systems:

- HVAC systems and associated controls
- Lighting and daylighting controls
- Domestic hot-water systems
- Renewable energy systems

Each of these systems can be tied into a BAS to provide monitoring and control capabilities.

Innovation in Design

BAS can aid in achieving exceptional performance in water reduction, energy efficiency, etc., and can help attain innovation in design credit points.

DESIGNING FOR SUSTAINED EFFICIENCY

This chapter contains a number of recommendations on how building and system controls can be used to obtain a good, green design. Getting a good design up front is important but is only the beginning. Sustainability also includes continued efficient building operation over its entire lifetime. Three factors that are critical to sustaining the efficiency level of a new building are (1) a well-designed M&V process, (2) implementing an ongoing commissioning program, and (3) good operator training on the control system functions. The first two factors allow building operators to monitor performance on a regular basis and to intervene when problems are detected. As discussed in this chapter, the control system is essential in implementing a good M&V process. Good training can help ensure that all of the capabilities of the control system, including those related to M&V, are used to their full potential over the lifetime of the building.

Expand & enhance
- M &V , Std 189.1
- Smart grid
- Add reference to EI here
and Article in Energy of Bldgs.

(Add Green Tip on submetering, monitoring)

ASHRAE
GreenTip #37

Mixed-Air Temperature (MAT) Reset

GENERAL DESCRIPTION

MAT, in this case, refers to the temperature of the mix of outdoor and return (recirculated) air that exists on an operating supply air-handling unit (AHU) before any new thermal energy is added to the airstream. In the days when constant-air-volume (CAV) systems were prevalent, it was customary to set the MAT controls to maintain a constant 55°F (13°C) nominally. (The controls would adjust the relative positions of outdoor and return air dampers to apportion the relative quantities of each airstream to satisfy the MAT setpoint, but would never allow less than the code-required minimum outdoor air by limiting the closure position of the outdoor air damper.) In the winter—or heating season—when the outdoor air temperature was generally below 55°F (13°C), the MAT would be the cooling airstream or cold-deck—the lowest-temperature air available for zones that needed cooling in this season. As heating was required, heat would be added at some point, either through a hot-deck airstream within the AHU or through reheat by downstream coils.

The reset technique is based on the premise that the MAT from a supply air-handling system is colder than any one zone requires to maintain the setpoint conditions of that zone. To the extent that this condition prevails, it means that the mixed (or cold) airstream must be mixed with some warm (hot-deck) air to yield the proper supply air temperature to satisfy even the zone requiring the lowest temperature air supply. Since warmer air would need to be mixed in to do this, that would require new energy, which is somewhat wasteful of heating energy (a form of simultaneous heating and cooling). In the heating season, cooling—being derived from outdoor air—is free.

The idea is to reset the MAT to a temperature that just satisfies the space with the lowest cold-air demand. Reset controls involve raising the setpoint of the MAT controls, based on input that indicates the demand of the zone needing the coldest air, limited still by the need to main the minimum quantity of outdoor air. This, in turn, requires sensors that can monitor that condition and other zone demands continuously; this input could come from hot-deck/cold-deck mixing dampers, mixing box damper positions, or thermostat output signals that indicate zone temperature demands.

The goal would be to raise the MAT just enough so the zone with the lowest supply air temperature demand is satisfied on a continuing basis. (As conditions change over time, that zone may change.) One idea to ensure that the mixing dampers are providing sufficient air to just meet the needs of the cold-plenum temperature setpoint, whether reset by demand or at a fixed temperature, is to control the mixing dampers by the cold-plenum sensor and to use the mixed-air temperature readout as a maintenance item. This prevents requiring mechanical cooling to remove the heat of the fan or to meet the setpoint of the cooling-plenum sensor when there is a difference in the readouts of the two sensors, which is typically caused by sensor error.

WHEN/WHERE IT'S APPLICABLE

As stated above, this technique, in most cases, should only be used on CAV systems. If it is used with VAV systems, it can often backfire, since other energy variables (e.g., fan energy, in the case of air systems) may change in the opposite direction from heating energy saved, possibly resulting in a net increase in energy use or cost. Thus, if it is applied to VAV systems, it should come into play when any other affected variable is already at its minimum (e.g., the fan is already at its minimum turndown rate [but note that this may conflict with recent changes to Standard 90.1 (ASHRAE 2010)]). As such, this GreenTip may be more applicable to the operation of existing buildings rather than new construction.

As the season becomes warmer and the outside temperature rises, this technique may become less and less effective, especially since the served zones may require more cooling and ever lower supply air temperatures.

Although there may not be a lot of CAV systems installed in new designs, there are still plenty operating in existing buildings (though it should not be applied to CAV systems converted to variable volume). This technique does lend itself well to retrofit, and since the controls are basically the same for large- or small-sized air-handling systems, the savings can be large for a relatively low capital cost.

PROS

- It saves heating energy and the associated operating cost.
- It can yield a fast payback, especially on larger air-handling systems.

- It is relatively low in capital cost in the full spectrum of energy retrofits.
- It is relatively easy to do as a retrofit on existing systems.

CONS

- It may require greater attention to periodic controls calibration.
- To be effective, there must be evidence that worst-zone demands will allow sufficient upward reset of temperature to realize savings worthy of the added effort.
- Sampling of zone demands may be difficult to do in remote or scattered locations. However, it may be cost effective in some cases to install BAS sensors throughout and retrofit the terminal controls to BAS-controlled units.

KEY ELEMENTS OF COST

The following provides a possible breakdown of the various cost elements that might differentiate a MAT reset system from a conventional one and an indication of whether the net cost for the alternative is likely to be lower (L), higher (H), or the same (S). This assessment is only a perception of what might be likely, but it obviously may not be totally accurate in all situations. There is no substitute for a detailed cost analysis as part of the design process. The listings below may also provide some assistance in identifying the cost elements involved.

First Cost

- Reset controls and installation   M
- Zone input sensors and connection to reset controls   H

Recurring Costs

- Heating energy (heating coil)   L
- Maintenance   M
- Operator training   H

SOURCE OF FURTHER INFORMATION

ASHRAE. 2007. *ASHRAE Handbook—HVAC Applications*. Atlanta: American Society of Heating, Refrigerating and Air-Conditioning Engineers, Inc.

ASHRAE
GreenTip #38

Cold-Deck Temperature Reset with Humidity Override

GENERAL DESCRIPTION

Cold-deck temperature (CDT) reset is very similar to MAT reset, but it applies to the air temperature leaving a cooling coil—or CDT of a CAV AHU during the summer, or the season when mechanical cooling is required. In this situation, the object is to save cooling energy supplied at the cooling coil by allowing the setpoint CDT to ride up above a nominal design level (e.g., 55°F [13°C]) as long as all zone cooling needs are met.

The control needs and techniques are similar to MAT reset (reviewing GreenTip #37 is a prerequisite for this one) with one addition: a relative humidity override. When in the mechanical cooling mode in moderate-to-humid climates, mechanically cooled air serves the function of dehumidification (i.e., latent cooling), as well as sensible cooling. The degree of dehumidification achieved in the occupied zones served depends largely on the CDT being maintained. Thus, if the CDT is allowed to ride up for cooling purposes, it should not be allowed to rise beyond the temperature needed to maintain comfortable humidity conditions. Thus, the occupied zone humidity parameter sets an upper limit for the reset function.

Zone relative humidity input can be sensed from a sampling of served zones. One could sense the return airstream at the AHU, but this is not preferred, as this would yield an average relative humidity of all spaces served rather than the highest humidity of any one space. However, given that return air relative humidity would probably be a lot easier and less expensive to sense than that of several remote zones, it may be good enough to serve the desired purpose.

The upper limit of humidity chosen as the limiting factor for this reset technique would depend on what the building operator thinks will be comfortable to occupants. While a nominal relative humidity level of 50% is often the goal for cooling season comfort, higher levels can be tolerated, and sometimes an upperlimit of 55% to 60% may be selected. (For most typical zone temperatures, these values correspond to an absolute humidity ratio in the range of 0.01 to 0.011.) Whatever is chosen, however, is easily adjustable. High-quality humidity-sensing equipment is recommended.

Reducing the CDT off the cooling coil can also result in savings at other upstream components of the building's cooling system, such as requiring a not-as-cold temperature off a central chiller or reduced chilled-water flow in a variable-flow pumping system. (In fact, this is where the cost savings would actually be realized.) If considering this technique, the designer should ensure that the piping, valves, and control configurations are such that up-the-line energy and cost savings are indeed achievable.

WHEN/WHERE IT'S APPLICABLE

The same constraints apply here as with MAT reset. Again, before doing this, the designer should be sure that there are likely to be opportunities for significant upward reset to take place. If it is found that there is just one space that is likely to need the design CDT during the cooling season, regardless of weather or other changing conditions, then this technique is probably not the best. In that case, the team may determine that a dedicated cooling unit would be best for achieving the minimum energy consumption.

PROS

- CDT reset saves cooling energy and associated operating costs.
- It can yield a good payback when the situation is right, although not as low as MAT reset.
- Capital cost is still relatively low (though more controls are required than with MAT reset).

CONS

- There are the same drawbacks as with MAT reset.
- There could be added problems with excessive space humidity if the humidity sensing is not accurate.

KEY ELEMENTS OF COST

The following provides a possible breakdown of the various cost elements that might differentiate a CDT reset system from a conventional one and an indication of whether the net incremental cost for the alternative option is likely to be lower (L), higher (H), or the same (S). This assessment is only a perception of what might be likely. There is no substitute for a detailed cost analysis as part of the design process. The listings below may also provide some assistance in identifying the cost elements involved.

First Cost

- Same elements as for MAT reset   M
- Humidity sensor(s) and connection reset controls   H

Recurring Costs

- Cooling energy   L
- Maintenance   H
- Operator Training   M

SOURCE OF FURTHER INFORMATION

ASHRAE. 2007. *ASHRAE Handbook—HVAC Applications.* Atlanta: American Society of Heating, Refrigerating and Air-Conditioning Engineers, Inc.

REFERENCES AND RESOURCES

Published

ASHRAE. 1996. *ASHRAE Guideline 1-1996, The HVAC Commissioning Process.* Atlanta: American Society of Heating, Refrigerating and Air-Conditioning Engineers, Inc.

ASHRAE. 2002. *ASHRAE Guideline 14-2002, Measurement of Energy and Demand Savings.* Atlanta: American Society of Heating, Refrigerating and Air-Conditioning Engineers, Inc.

ASHRAE. 2004. *ANSI/ASHRAE Standard 55-2004, Thermal Environmental Conditions for Human Occupancy.* Atlanta: American Society of Heating, Refrigerating and Air-Conditioning Engineers, Inc.

ASHRAE. 2005. *ASHRAE Guideline 0-2005, The Commissioning Process.* Atlanta: American Society of Heating, Refrigerating and Air-Conditioning Engineers, Inc.

ASHRAE. 2007. *ANSI/ASHRAE Standard 62.1-2007, Ventilation for Acceptable Indoor Air Quality.* Atlanta: American Society of Heating, Refrigerating and Air-Conditioning Engineers, Inc.

ASHRAE. 2007. *ANSI/ASHRAE/IES Standard 90.1-2007, Energy Standard for Buildings Except Low-Rise Residential Buildings.* Atlanta: American Society of Heating, Refrigerating and Air-Conditioning Engineers, Inc.

ASHRAE. 2007. *ASHRAE Handbook—HVAC Applications.* Atlanta: American Society of Heating, Refrigerating and Air-Conditioning Engineers, Inc.

ASHRAE. 2007. *ASHRAE Guideline 13-2007, Specifying Direct Digital Control Systems.* Atlanta: American Society of Heating, Refrigerating and Air-Conditioning Engineers, Inc.

ASHRAE. 2009. *ANSI/ASHRAE/USGBC/IES Standard 189.1-2009, Standard for the Design of High-Performance Green Buildings.* Atlanta: American Society of Heating, Refrigerating and Air-Conditioning Engineers, Inc.

ASHRAE. 2010. *ANSI/ASHRAE Standard 55-2010, Thermal Environmental Conditions for Human Occupancy.* Atlanta: American Society of Heating, Refrigerating and Air-Conditioning Engineers, Inc.

ASHRAE. 2010. *ANSI/ASHRAE Standard 62.1-2010, Ventilation for Acceptable Indoor Air Quality.* Atlanta: American Society of Heating, Refrigerating and Air-Conditioning Engineers, Inc.

ASHRAE. 2010. *ANSI/ASHRAE/IES Standard 90.1-2010, Energy Standard for Buildings Except Low-Rise Residential Buildings.* Atlanta: American Society of Heating, Refrigerating and Air-Conditioning Engineers, Inc.

CBE. 2007. *Summary report: Control strategies for mixed-mode buildings.* Center for Built Environment. www.cbe.berkeley.edu/research/pdf_files/SR_MixedModeControls2007.pdf.

DOE. 2005. Energy impact of commercial building controls and performance diagnostics: Market characterization, energy impact of building faults and energy savings potential. U.S. Department of Energy, Washington, D.C.

IESNA. 2000. *Lighting Handbook*. New York: Illuminating Engineering Society of North America.

USGBC. 2009. *LEED® 2009 Green Building Operations and Maintenance*. Washington, D.C.: U.S. Green Building Council.

USGBC. 2009. *LEED® 2009 for New Construction and Major Renovations*. Washington, D.C.: U.S. Green Building Council.

Online

DDC Online
    www.ddc-online.org

Energy Design Resources
    www.energydesignresources.com/publication/gd/

International Performance Measurement and Verification Protocol
    www.evo-world.org

National Building Controls Information Program
    www.buildingcontrols.org

U.S. Green Building Council
    www.usgbc.org

CHAPTER SIXTEEN

COMPLETING DESIGN AND DOCUMENTATION FOR CONSTRUCTION

DRAWINGS/DOCUMENTS STAGE

Once the project has reached the working drawing/construction document stage, the green design concepts and resulting configurations should be well set, and the task of incorporating them into the documents that contractors will use to build the project should be relatively routine. However, quality control at this stage is especially important in green design projects.

Many firms have a routine procedure to review the documents for quality before they are released to contractors (to ensure that concepts are adequately depicted and described and to catch errors and omissions). This process should also include a green design concept review, preferably by one or more design team members that were in on the early stages of the project. This is particularly true if those preparing the construction documents were not part of that process. This is not the time to allow an excellent green design to become diluted or slip away.

SPECIFYING MATERIALS/EQUIPMENT

Green Building Materials

Sources for guidance on selecting and specifying materials for a green project are:

- Athena Institute, www.athenasmi.ca
- BuildingGreen, www.buildinggreen.com

Also see the DiggingDeeper sidebar titled "One Design Firm's Materials Specification Checklist."

Controlling Construction Quality

It is far easier to control construction quality in the design and specification stage of a project than during its construction. During preparation of the final construction drawings and specifications, it is critical to be diligent in spelling out the quality expected in the field to carry through the green design concepts developed throughout the early design stages. Some further thoughts on this subject, many applicable to the design phase, are covered in Chapter 17 of this Guide.

COST ESTIMATING AND BUDGET RECONCILIATION

It is very important to have the cost estimator involved right from the start of the project to ensure that the project budget reflects the decisions made by the rest of the project team throughout the integrated design process.

The chapters, case studies, resources, and cost data included in the latest edition of the RS Means' publication *Green Building: Project Planning & Cost Estimating, Second Edition* (Adler et al. 2002) are good resources that include information on the following:

- Green building approaches, materials, systems, and standards.
- Evaluating the cost vs. value of green products over their life cycle.
- Specifying green building projects—complete with a list of often-specified products/materials and a sample spec.
- Low-cost green strategies—and special economic incentives and funding.
- Deconstruction—featured in a new chapter on this key element of sustainable building.

This publication has been completely updated with the latest in green building technologies, design concepts, standards, and costs.

BIDDING

The following is an excerpt from the Harvard University Office for Sustainability, Green Building Resource, Design Phase Guide Web site (www.green.harvard.edu/theresource/new-construction/design-phase/bidding-construction/):

"The expectations of general and subcontractors on Leadership in Energy and Environmental Design (LEED®) and other green projects are different than those associated with conventional projects. Practices such as recycling, erosion, and sedimentation control, indoor air quality (IAQ), and filling out LEED (and other rating system) submittals require special attention, and should be communicated to the team early in the construction process.

Include sustainability language in the Request for Proposals and Owner's Project Requirements document. Consider green building expertise and LEED (or other green rating system) project experience as key criteria in the selection process. Ask to see evidence of experience with LEED, material tracking, construction and demolition waste management, and plans for IAQ during construction."

According to the same Web site, the contractor is responsible for conveying the following to subcontractors: workplace practice expectations for recycling and erosion and sedimentation control, and construction IAQ practices. The Owner's Sustainability Representative (OSR) is responsible for coordinating regular LEED meetings to track the LEED documentation process and to collect submittal and audit requirements from contractors. Also, a submittal review process should be established among the commissioning authority, the architect, and OSR.

MANAGING RISK

Green Design Documentation Issues

Reviewing green design work done by others allows engineers to see how built projects have created new opportunities and can guide efforts to sell and provide green engineering services. Performing sustainable design can yield important benefits to design engineers individually and to their firms. Improved client service, more repeat work, improved market position, enhanced public relations, and better employee satisfaction and retention are among the many benefits that numerous architectural firms and several pioneering engineering firms have derived from informing their practices with sustainable design expertise.

On the other hand, failure to address client concerns about green design can harm reputation. Disproportionate start-up costs, risk, or other perceived obstacles (e.g., the educational investment and commitment required to change engineering thinking and culture) may be perceived as being associated with undertaking sustainable design. Managing each of these issues, communicating frankly, and crafting creative solutions, as required, can reduce exposure to these potentially negative issues.

However, when documenting the project requirements for bidding by contractors and subcontractors, it is important that the engineer not guarantee that the results predicted by building simulation modeling will actually be achieved. It is important that the engineer not take more than his or her fair share of the risk in incorporating newer technologies into a building design project. Sustaining fair and practical business practices is critical to being a successful green engineer.

Contract Provisions

The following is an excerpt from the online essay, "Green Buildings and Risk," by Tim Corbett (www.aepronet.org/ge/no43.html):

> A good contract is the best line of defense when it comes to mitigating your risk. The contract is an excellent method for defining your scope of services (e.g., what will be provided, when, and what will not). Contracts are also an excellent method for qualifying clients and managing and establishing expectations. Contracts should address the following:
>
> - New and innovative products and technology may be used; they may lack proven history of successful application. Owner understands and agrees that project objectives may not be realized.

- Ordinary skill and care will be used to achieve project objectives; however there is no warranty or guarantee the project will achieve LEED certification.

- Verify the level of investigation and analysis that will be performed for new material and technologies, with no expressed or implied warranty or guarantees of results.

- Client agrees to measure the potential risks related to incorporating the innovation product and/or systems and accepts the risks.

- Limit your exposure to consequential damages by including appropriate language in your contract.

ONE DESIGN FIRM'S MATERIALS SPECIFICATION CHECKLIST

Choose at least one portion of materials/products that are:

- Local and/or indigenous, reducing the environmental impacts resulting from transportation and supporting the local economy.
- Extracted, harvested, recovered, manufactured regionally within a radius of 500 miles (805 km).
- Low-embodied energy.
- Reused, recycled, and/or recyclable, reducing the impacts resulting from extraction of new resources.
- Salvaged building materials (e.g., lumber, millwork, plumbing fixtures, hardware, etc.)
- Post-consumer recycled content material and/or post-industrial recycled content (recovered) material.
- Nonhazardous to recycle, compost, or dispose of.
- Renewable and sustainably harvested (no old-growth timber), preferably with minimal associated environmental burdens (reducing the use and depletion of finite raw and long-cycle renewable materials).
- Rapidly renewable building materials, including any nonwood materials that are typically harvested within a 10 yr or shorter cycle.
- Nontoxic/nonpolluting in manufacture, use, and disposal.

Use finished materials, products, and furnishings that are free of known, probable, and suspected carcinogens, mutagens, teratogens, persistent toxic organic pollutants, and toxic heavy metals pursuant to the U.S. Environmental Protection Agency's (EPA) Toxicity Characteristic Leaching Procedure Test, 40 CFR Part 260. (Based on the EPA's Universal Waste Rule and Part 260, building owners and their contractors must use the toxicity characteristic leaching procedure to determine if they are generators of hazardous waste and

Digging Deeper

subject to EPA and state hazardous waste regulations when disposing of mercury lamps and other waste products.)

Specify lead-free solder for copper water supply tubing; do not use plastic for supply water

Avoid plastic foam insulation.

Specify natural, nontoxic, low-volatic organic compoud–emitting, non-solvent-based finishes, paints, stains, and adhesives.

When specifying painting:

- Consider surfaces that don't require painting.
- Choose paints that have been independently certified (e.g., Green Seal).
- Choose latex over oil-based paint.
- Increase direct-to-outdoors ventilation when painting.
- Dispose of oil-based paints like hazardous waste.
- Recycle latex paint or save for touch-ups.

Avoid the use of materials containing or produced with ozone-depleting chlorofluorocarbons (CFCs) or hydrochlorofluorocarbons (HCFCs) (often embedded in foam insulation and refrigeration/cooling systems).

Avoid CFC-based refrigerants in new base-building HVAC systems. When reusing existing base-building HVAC equipment, complete a comprehensive CFC phaseout conversion.

Commit to working with manufacturing teams who provide performance/service contracts of integrated systems for service delivery, product longevity, adaptability, and/or recycling.

Favor suppliers who will minimize packaging and will take back excess packaging (e.g., pallets, crates, cardboard, and excess building materials).

Maximize the use of materials that retain a high value in future life cycles

Specify products or systems that extend manufacturer responsibility through a lease or take-back program that ensures future reuse or recycling into a product of similar or higher value.

To guide material selection choices during the design process, educate designers and elicit life-cycle information from manufacturers to encourage selection of building materials and furnishings with favorable life-cycle performance. Select materials from manufacturers that are committed to improving their overall environmental performance at their manufacturing facilities and their suppliers' facilities.

Digging Deeper

REFERENCES AND RESOURCES

Published

Adler, A., J.E.Armstrong, S.K. Fuller, G.B. Guy, M. Kalin, A. Karolides, M. Lelek, B.C. Lippiatt, J. Macaluso, G. Spencer, H.A. Walker, and P. Waier. 2002. *Green Building: Project Planning & Cost Estimating,* 2d ed. Kingston, MA: RS Means.

Corbett, T. *Green Buildings and Risk.* www.aepronet.org/ge/no43.html.

EPA. Toxicity Characteristic Leaching Procedure (TCLP) Test, 40 CFR Part 260. U.S. Environmental Protection Agency, Washington, D.C.

EPA. Universal Waste Rule, 40 CFR Part 260. U.S. Environmental Protection Agency, Washington, D.C.

Online

Athena Institute
www.athenasmi.ca
BuildingGreen
www.buildinggreen.com
Harvard University Office for Sustainability, Green Building Resource, Design Phase Guide
www.green.harvard.edu/theresource/new-construction/design-phase/bidding-construction/www.aepronet.org/ge/no43.html

Section 3: Postdesign— Construction and Beyond

CHAPTER SEVENTEEN

CONSTRUCTION

To minimize gaps between design intent and what is actually built, the green-conscious engineer should provide a level of construction administration that is beyond the norm. That engineer (or an independent agent) may also provide mechanical/electrical system commissioning. (See Chapter 6 and Chapter 18, as well as a related section in Chapter 4 on project delivery methods and contractor selection.)

CONSTRUCTION PRACTICES AND METHODS

In design, the specifications should prescribe that certain construction methods and procedures must be followed to ensure a fully realized green project. This would include topics such as reduced site disturbance, handling of construction waste, control of rainwater runoff, and indoor air quality (IAQ) management during construction.

It is recommended that the engineer and architect work with the construction manager or general contractor and associated subcontractors to develop a IAQ Construction Management plan that the contractor would be required to follow. The Sheet Metal and Air Conditioning National Association's *IAQ Guideline for Occupied Buildings Under Construction* (SMACNA) is cited by the U.S. Green Building Council as a source document. The contractor should particularly protect installed or stored absorptive materials (e.g., insulation or sheetrock) from water damage or other contamination. Water damage is especially insidious if materials get wet, are installed wet, and are then covered up. If air-handling units (AHUs) run during construction, the construction manager and associated subcontractor should be required to protect AHU components and the duct distribution system from dirt and debris, clean any components and ductwork that are damaged, and replace filters before occupancy. (*ANSI/ASHRAE Standard 52.2-2007, Method of Testing General Ventilation Air-Cleaning Devices for Removal Efficiency by Particle Size* [ASHRAE 2007] deals with this subject.)

THE ENGINEER'S ROLE IN CONSTRUCTION QUALITY

In construction, the engineer's key roles encompass shop drawing review, review of equipment substitutions, handling of change order and value engineering requests, and site visits and inspections. Leadership in Energy and Environmental Design (LEED®) or other green design process documentation coordination and processing are sometimes required when the project team has decided to achieve LEED certification (or some other green design process recognition) for the building.

Shop Drawing Review

There should be a thorough review of shop drawing submittals. The specifications should require their timely submission to allow time for proper review without delaying the project. The purpose of the review is to ensure that the contractor is correctly interpreting the specifications and drawings and is not missing any important details. Areas for emphasis include checking motor horsepower and efficiency ratings, checking air filter details, checking for proper clearances around equipment for servicing, and checking anything else relevant on the project concerning green design elements. Thorough review of all control sequences submitted by the building automation system subcontractor is critical.

Alternative Equipment Substitutions and or Equivalent

Specifications may be written with several named manufacturers (often three) of a given product, or it may name one and say "or equivalent." In both cases, the system designed is usually based on a single manufacturer's product. If others are named, it usually means they are acceptable, as long as they meet the specified conditions and fit in the space provided on the project, including all required service and maintenance access clearances. The shop drawing reviewer must determine whether alternative equipment is truly equal to the base design, including meeting the green design aspects of the equipment and systems.

If "or equivalent" language is used to specify equipment, determining equivalence can be more difficult. It is advisable to be certain that what the contractor proposes is truly equivalent, if not superior, to the specified components or systems. Contractors may have legitimate reasons for proposing alternative products, such as better delivery times or negative experiences with the products or manufacturers specified. Such equivalent, or outright substitution, proposals from the contractor should be treated seriously and examined carefully to ascertain that they will not adversely impact the project goals. If they do not meet the requirements, the objections should first be discussed with the construction manager, owner's representative, and subcontractor. Only if no satisfactory alternative can be agreed on should they then be rejected. It is very important to clearly identify the substitution process requirements when specifying the equipment during the design phase of the project.

Change Order Requests

Many change orders are legitimate, such as an owner changing the scope, expansion or reduction of project scope, or the construction manager and/or subcontractors encountering unforeseen conditions. However, any change order that only cheapens the project or lowers the project's green design standards without counteracting benefits should be regarded with skepticism. Likewise, any value engineering (VE) offers should be carefully studied for their impact on the project's green design goals. (VE is often offered under the assumption that first-cost savings are paramount to the owner and project team.) The need for careful study remains true even in the case of genuine VE done by trained professionals who perform real trade-off analyses to arrive at the best value for a project. Before beginning such a VE exercise, the VE facilitator should clearly understand the green design objectives to ensure that his/her suggestions and recommendations are consistent with the project goals, as well as the priority those goals have with respect to first cost or life-cycle cost. Each VE item must include the first-cost impact to properly evaluate the suggestion.

Site Visits/Observations

Site visits should be planned for key times and should involve the engineer's best personnel. HVAC work should be viewed before it is covered up by ceiling, floor, and wall installations. Check that equipment nameplates are correct. For example, if high-efficiency motors were specified, check in the field to be certain that is what is being installed. Look up the manufacturer's data on motor efficiency and see that it matches the specification. Check that absorptive construction materials (e.g., insulation) are being stored in accord with the IAQ Construction Management Plan and that no contamination has occurred. Check for air filters in any operating air-handling units. Ensure that air-handling equipment has been stored properly, cleaned (internals), and that filters were installed before start-up. If air-handling units were used for construction activities, check that return air paths have proper temporary filtration at the inlets to the ductwork.

Work with the commissioning authority to review their site observations and address any design-based questions that arise during the final commissioning process. More information on this is provided in the following chapter.

Final punch list preparation, follow-up, and the final sign-off observation are particularly important. If the earlier site visits and observations were done thoroughly and at appropriate intervals, and if the construction manager and subcontractors have been part of the team and in accord with the green design goals, the final punch list should be minimal and the final observation should go smoothly.

CONSTRUCTION FACTORS TO CONSIDER IN A GREEN DESIGN

- Determine locations for construction vehicle parking, temporary piling of topsoil, and building material storage in order to minimize soil compaction and other site impacts.
- Control erosion to reduce negative impacts on water and air quality.
- Design a site sediment and erosion control plan that conforms to best management practices specified in the U.S. Environmental Protection Agency's *Storm Water Management for Construction Activities* (EPA) or local erosion and sedimentation control standards and codes, whichever is more stringent.
- Conserve existing natural areas and restore damaged areas to provide habitat and promote biodiversity.
- Schedule construction carefully to minimize impacts.
- Avoid leaving disturbed soil exposed for extended periods.
- Fill trenches quickly to minimize damage to severed tree roots.
- Avoid building when the ground is saturated and easily damaged.
- Estimate the amount of material needed to avoid excess.
- Design to accommodate standard lumber and drywall sizes.
- Assess the construction site waste stream to determine which materials can be reduced, reused, and recycled.
- Conduct a waste audit, quantifying material diversion by weight.
- Recycle and/or salvage construction and demolition debris.
- Specify materials that minimize waste and reduce shipping impacts through bulk packaging, dry-mix shipping, reused bulk packaging, recycled-content packaging, or elimination of packaging.
- Develop and implement a waste management plan, quantifying material diversion by weight.
- Research markets in area for salvaged materials.
- Establish on-site construction material recycling areas and recycle and/or salvage construction, demolition, and land clearing waste.
- Contract with licensed haulers and processors of recyclables.
- Require subcontractors to be responsible for their waste (including lunch wastes); create incentives for minimizing waste.
- Educate employees and subcontractors.
- Monitor and evaluate waste/recycling program.
- Review the IAQ Construction Management Plan to ensure that all subcontractors understand the process and goals desired.

REFERENCES AND RESOURCES

Published

ASHRAE. 2007. *ANSI/ASHRAE Standard 52.2-2007, Method of Testing General Ventilation Air-Cleaning Devices for Removal Efficiency by Particle Size.* Atlanta: American Society of Heating, Refrigerating and Air-Conditioning Engineers, Inc.

EPA. Storm water management for construction activities. EPA document No. EPA-8320R-92-005. U.S. Environmental Protection Agency, Washington, D.C.

SMACNA. 2007. *IAQ Guidelines for Occupied Buildings Under Construction.* Chantilly, VA: Sheet Metal and Air Conditioning Contractors' National Association, Inc.

CHAPTER EIGHTEEN

OPERATION/MAINTENANCE/ PERFORMANCE EVALUATION

COMMISSIONING FOR BUILDING OCCUPANCY

A proper commissioning process (covered in Chapter 6 and *ASHRAE Guideline 0-2005, The Commissioning Process* [ASHRAE 2005]) is critical to meeting sustainable/green goals and is an essential component for success. The commissioning process includes the education of the operators and putting into place tools that monitor ongoing commissioning and the facility and operator's performance.

Before operator training, the commissioning authority (CxA) reviews the operation and maintenance (O&M) documentation to verify that the information provided by the contractors and vendors matches the actual model of equipment and assembly types installed, verify warranty and preventive maintenance requirements are defined, trouble shoot guidance, and ensure that emergency shutdown instructions are in the documentation. Training of the building occupants, O&M staff, and emergency responders is critical to protecting the owner's investment and maintaining the facility's performance. Verification that the correct level of training and content are provided, along with the documentation of who was trained, and a plan for training new individuals is essential to efficient lifetime operation. At building turnover, the designers should provide an overview of their design intent and how they expect the building to be operated to achieve desired performance. The CxA verifies the specific training defined in the Owner's Project Requirements (OPR) document has been provided and reviews the final modifications and reasoning for modifications during commissioning with the operators. This is essential to ensuring that a building designed to be sustainable/green can be operated correctly, minimize environmental impact, and ensure maximum benefit to society and the owner.

Educating operators to understand building operation can reduce operation errors, but does not eliminate them. Operators typically respond to complaints and often override systems to eliminate complaints. Often, the operators forget or are busy "fighting fires" and never determine the root cause of the complaint such that it can be permanently resolved. The resolution of these complaints frequently results in changes that negatively impact facility performance. The CxA working with the owner evaluates the facility's O&M staff to determine level of experience with systems being proposed, level of training contractors and vendors are to provide, and the amount of training time needed for both the operators and occupants. Based on the information gathered, the CxA provides specific training requirements and specifications to the designers for inclusion in the project's contract documents. During the construction phase training, agendas that include the specific training topics and level of training for O&M staff and occupants are provided to the contractors and vendors for their use in developing the training to satisfy the OPR. Monitoring-based, ongoing commissioning to verify the operator's understanding of building operation (and to identify operational errors and degradation of system performance) provides great value to the designers, owner, and society. The commissioning process, if implemented during the warranty phase, requires the CxA to monitor building performance during the warranty period, conduct seasonal testing, if necessary, and identify systems that are not performing to specification to help ensure that peak performance is achieved by the end of the warranty period. Modifications implemented during the warranty period that vary from the construction documents are reviewed with the designers and owner for approval and implementation. The CxA, assisted by the operations staff, implements and documents the changes and the associated reasoning for them in the facility's system manual.

Use of monitoring-based commissioning provides operators and owners a benchmark for continually assessing building performance under dynamic conditions. It also notifies operators and owners when building performance has drifted from peak performance, signaling that action is need. Warranty phase commissioning focuses on facility optimization and identifying warranty performance issues causing a reduction in performance and development of a plan to correct performance deficiencies through repair/replacement during the warranty phase.

Competent and well-trained O&M staff is essential to sustainable/green buildings as is monitoring performance. Both help owners make the important connection between the building performance and the competence of the building operations staff. Building personnel can do much good—or inadvertent great harm—depending on whether they understand the impact of their actions on the building's operating efficiency. Obtaining the maximum benefit and performance from the design team's vision and the owner's goals requires not only that the systems operate as intended at the end of commissioning but that they continue to operate that way throughout the life of the building. This requires trained operators and using tools such as monitoring-based commissioning. Systems with efficiencies that wane are identified, repaired, and recommissioned, providing greater assurance that a building designed to be sustainable will realize its full green potential over time.

Monitoring performance is critical to maintaining performance and is typically beyond the owner's capacity to perform. Operational staff can input utility information, but engineering knowledge is required to evaluate performance. Monitoring-based commissioning is beyond the scope of most new construction projects but is becoming a common service owners are employing to manage costs, maintain occupant satisfaction, and minimize environmental impact. The building industry needs this type of follow-up data to verify that new design techniques are working and that change is occurring in how buildings are designed. In short, the industry needs to know that green design is working. It is certainly worth the effort by the designer and/or CxA to convince the owner that this could be a worthwhile extra service.

ENERGY EFFICIENCY IN EXISTING BUILDINGS

New construction each year adds roughly 1% to the U.S. building stock. Considering that an average commercial building in the United States has an estimated life of 40 years, even governmental regulations requiring that all new buildings be constructed to green specifications would not transform the commercial building stock to cleaner and greener until well past 2048. Because energy and operations account for approximately 75% of a building's costs over its lifetime, whereas design and construction costs are 11% and financing is approximately 14%, it's clear that existing buildings are perfect candidates for green retrofit (von Paumgartten).

Engineers can help building owners and managers of existing buildings understand the economic benefits of improving systems and operations. "Energy Efficiency in Existing Buildings, Our Greatest Opportunity for a Sustainable Future" was ASHRAE President, Gordon Holness', theme during his 2009–2010 term. A summary of his address can be viewed at www.ashrae.org/aboutus/page/2372.

The guidelines for making existing buildings more energy efficient include:

- Benchmarking the current energy utilization index (EUI) (kBtu/ft^2·yr [MJ/m^2·yr]).
- Establishing a target energy utilization index and an initial budget estimate for achieving this goal.
- Conducting an internal energy audit or having the facility retro-commissioned by a certified retrocommissioning firm. This activity may result in a modification to the estimated budget amount.
- Identifying energy efficiency measures with attractive rates of return on energy retrofit or renovation investments.
- Implementing the recommended energy conservation measures that will get the facility to the desired goal within the stipulated budget.
- Commissioning the energy conservation measures by a certified commissioning firm. This process should include training of facility personnel on properly operating and maintaining equipment and systems.

RETROFIT STRATEGIES FOR EXISTING BUILDINGS

Buildings that are more than five years old are often good candidates for retrofit projects that make them more energy- and water-efficient and improve their indoor environmental quality (IEQ). Many retrofit projects can be justified by the attendant cost savings. Common retrofit strategies that offer good savings to investment ratios include HVAC and control system retrocommissioning, energy recovery, air- and water-side free cooling, variable speed control of fans and pumps, lighting system improvements, and plumbing fixture upgrades.

HVAC and control system retrocommissioning is addressed in detail in the next section of this chapter. Energy recovery includes such diverse strategies as glycol run-around loops and entropy wheels to transfer energy between exhaust and outdoor airstreams, preheaters to transfer energy from boiler stack gases to combustion air, and heat pipes to reheat air using energy from upstream air entering the cooling coil. Air- and water-side free cooling refers to the use of outdoor air to cool interior spaces, either via air-handling unit economizer controls or a plate-and-frame heat exchanger piped between the chilled-water system and a cooling tower. And installing variable-speed drives (together with ancillary equipment and controls) makes it possible to match air and water flows to heating and cooling demands more effectively than was the case in the past.

Moving beyond the realm of HVAC, lighting systems can be upgraded by applying relatively new technologies (e.g., electronic ballasts, T5 and T8 lamps, compact fluorescent lamps, light-emitting diode (LED) signage, and occupancy sensors). In addition to saving energy, lighting retrofits often improve light quality significantly, by improving color rendering and eliminating flicker. Finally, new low-flow plumbing fixtures, including water closets, urinals, lavatory faucets, and shower heads, can reduce both water and energy use without compromising performance or comfort.

When major mechanical equipment (e.g., chillers and boilers) reach the end of their service lives, they should of course be replaced with more efficient equipment. Such retrofits generally cannot be justified in terms of energy cost savings alone. Replacing a standard efficiency motor with a premium efficiency motor is another retrofit strategy that usually cannot be cost-justified unless the motor is close to failure and needs to be replaced or rewound.

Renewable energy technologies should not be overlooked during a building retrofit project. In areas with high fossil fuel costs, solar service water and pool heating are likely to have the most attractive savings to investment ratios of these technologies.

RETROCOMMISSIONING (SM)

Commissioning of existing buildings (i.e., retrocommissioning) focuses on identifying current facility requirements needed by owners and occupants to efficiently and effectively deliver their daily mission. Opportunities to improve performance through optimizing HVAC system operation and control, lighting modifications, and identification and control of phantom vampire loads are brought to the owner's attention, along with cost-benefit analysis, to assist the owner with selection of an improvement strategy. Commissioning of existing buildings has proved to be very cost-effective and has the greatest promise for substantially reducing energy consumption in the country and reducing dependency on foreign oil. Most existing buildings could immediately reduce energy consumption by 10% to 50% and could realize a return on investment in as little as six months to two years. The retrocommissioning process also identifies improvements that can further reduce energy usage and carbon emissions that are directly related to the greenhouse effect so that owners can include these improvements in their capital improvement plans.

After being commissioned, building performance generally declines after two to five years. As a result, commissioning of existing buildings can return the building to its peak performance. It is important that designers have a deeper understanding of why performance wanes and how design decisions affect building operation efficiencies. Information on commissioning of existing buildings is available through various organizations, including the federal government.

MEASUREMENT AND VERIFICATION (M&V)

Several guidelines have been published on M&V energy savings. Each of the guidelines listed in this section are unique, albeit similar, and are intended for use in different instances. All of these documents provide standard M&V methods that are proven and accepted strategies.

INTERNATIONAL PERFORMANCE MEASUREMENT AND VERIFICATION PROTOCOL

The International Performance Measurement and Verification Protocol (IPMVP) is a document that discusses procedures that, when implemented, allow building owners, energy service companies, and financiers of building energy efficiency projects to quantify energy conservation measure performance and energy savings. The IPMVP provides an overview of current best-practice techniques available for verifying savings from both traditional- and third-party-financed energy- and water- efficiency projects.

The IPMVP is now in three volumes, available at the Efficiency Valuation Organization's Web site, www.evo-world.org:

- Volume I—Concepts and Options for Determining Savings
- Volume II—Concepts and Practices for Improving Indoor Environmental Quality
- Volume III—Applications Cover Renewable Energy, New Construction, Emissions Trading, and Demand Reduction Baseline Calculation Methods)

FEDERAL ENERGY MANAGEMENT PROGRAM (FEMP) GUIDELINES VERSION 2.2

The FEMP Guidelines provide procedures and guidelines for quantifying the savings resulting from the installation of energy conservation measures. The FEMP Guidelines are fully compatible and consistent with the IPMVP. Intended for use in Energy Savings Performance Contracting and utility program projects, the guideline provides the methodology for establishing energy cost savings called for in the Energy Savings Performance Contracting rule. These guidelines are available at www1.eere.energy.gov/femp/pdfs/mv_guidelines.pdf.

FEMP M&V OPTION A DETAILED GUIDELINES

FEMP has developed the *M&V Option A Detailed Guidelines* (FEMP 2008), which provides recommended practices for using the Option A methods described in FEMP's *M&V Guidelines for Federal Energy Projects, Version 3.0.* http://mnv.lbl.gov/keyMnVDocs/femp.

ASHRAE GUIDELINE 14-2002

ASHRAE Guideline 14-2002, Measurement of Energy and Demand Savings (ASHRAE 2002) was developed by ASHRAE to provide guidance on the minimum acceptable level of performance in the measurement of energy and demand savings for the purpose of a commercial transaction based on that measurement. It only deals with the measurement of energy and demand savings.

BUILDING LABELING

A program for labeling buildings based on predicted and actual energy usage was introduced by ASHRAE in 2009, and a pilot program was initiated in early 2010. The Building Energy Quotient program, known as ASHRAE Building eQ, includes both "As Designed" (asset) and "In Operation" (as operated) ratings for all building types, except residential. A sample label is shown in Figure 18-1. It also provides a detailed certificate with data on actual energy use, energy demand profiles, indoor air quality and other information that will enable building owners to evaluate and reduce their building's energy use.

This program is similar to a program initiated in 2002 by European member countries called the Energy Performance of Buildings Directive (EPBD). A web portal has been created to help facilitate the exchange of information on building energy efficiency, which can be accessed at www.buildup.eu.

Information on a building's energy use is the critical first step in making the necessary changes and choices that reduce energy use and costs. The ASHRAE Building eQ program provides an easily understood scale to convey a building's energy use in comparison to similar buildings, occupancy types, and climate zone, while also providing building owners with building-specific information that can be used to improve building energy performance.

OCCUPANT SURVEYS

Occupant surveys can alert owners to specific problems with IEQ, which could potentially have implications for occupant health and productivity. Occupants are an important and often underutilized source of information about IEQ and its effect on comfort, satisfaction, and productivity. Poor thermal comfort is a common occupant complaint in buildings. Relying on complaint logs only provides an indication of local, personal, or sporadic dissatisfaction. Surveys are much more effective, as they provide a systematic mechanism for occupants to provide feedback about a broader range of aspects of the indoor environment. They are an important tool for identifying the specific nature and location of any problems, guiding postoccupancy retrocommissioning and corrective actions, and helping owners decide how to prioritize their investments in building improvements. Everyone in the building process benefits from learning how a building actually performs in practice. Occupant surveys are an informative and critical link in closing the feedback loop and allowing building owners, facility managers, and the design team to understand more completely how the building design and operation is affecting occupant productivity and well-being.

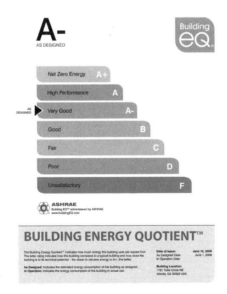

Figure 18-1 ASHRAE Building eQ rating scale.

A survey should be designed so that participation is voluntary, occupants' responses remain anonymous, and results are reported only in aggregate. The survey should ask occupants for general location information only, so one can identify if problems are occurring in particular zones of the building. After asking about basic demographics and workstation characteristics, a survey should then ideally address a wide variety of IEQ features, including thermal comfort, air quality, lighting, acoustics, office layout and furnishings, and building cleanliness and maintenance. A common form of satisfaction question asks occupants to respond on a seven-point satisfaction scale ranging from very dissatisfied, to neutral, to very satisfied. Ideally, occupants who are dissatisfied with a particular aspect of their environment are presented with follow-up questions that allow them to more specifically identify the nature and potential source of their dissatisfaction. This is important for providing diagnostic information, and helping the building operators become more informed about how to respond.

Surveys can be administered in a variety of ways, but once the method is selected it should be consistently applied and available for all normal occupants of the building. Surveys can be administered directly, either by phone or in person, although this is very time-intensive and raises potential issues about privacy and accuracy of results. Web-based surveys are becoming a more common alternative to the traditional paper-based surveys and offer many advantages. They can be far less expensive to administer to a large number of people or to multiple buildings. The the cost and potential errors of manually entering data from a paper survey are not present. They allow for more interactive branching features that provide diagnostic information, while keeping the survey to a reasonable length. Lastly, they offer the potential for automated reporting so that building owners and professionals can get quick access to the survey results.

Sources of sample surveys include, but are not limited to (see "References and Resources" section at the end of the chapter for more information):

• Center for the Built Environment (CBE) Occupant IEQ Survey
• Usable Buildings Trust

ONE DESIGN FIRM'S OPERATIONS, MAINTENANCE, AND PERFORMANCE EVALUATION CHECKLIST

Provide for the ongoing accountability and optimization of building energy and water consumption performance over time.

Design and specify equipment to be installed in base building systems to allow for comparison, management, and optimization of actual vs. estimated energy and water performance.

Provide for the ongoing accountability and optimization of building energy and water consumption performance over time.

Comply with the installed equipment requirements for continuous metering as stated in *Option B: Methods by Technology* of the U.S. Department of Energy's (DOE) IPMVP (www.energyautomation.com/pdfs/ipmvp-vol2.pdf) for the following:

- Lighting systems and controls
- Constant and variable motor loads
- Variable-frequency drive operation
- Chiller efficiency at variable loads (kW/ton)
- Cooling load
- Air and water economizer and heat recovery cycles
- Air distribution static pressures and ventilation air volumes
- Boiler efficiencies
- Building-specific process energy efficiency systems and equipment
- Indoor water risers and outdoor irrigation systems.

Allocate an appropriate percentage of building funds for ongoing monitoring of environmental performance, product purchasing, maintenance, and improvements.

Provide for the ongoing accountability of waste streams, including hazardous pollutants.

Use environmentally safe cleaning materials.

Educate operation and maintenance workers.

Facilitate the reduction of waste generated by building occupants.

Provide an easily accessible dedicated area for the collection and storage of materials for recycling of paper, glass, plastics, metals, and hazardous substances.

After six months, evaluate existing ecosystems to determine if they have remained undisturbed.

- Assess building energy use to ensure it is at predicted levels.

Digging Deeper

Digging Deeper

Determine if indoor air quality levels are at predicted levels (particularly CO_2 and airborne particulates).

Measure water consumption and evaluate against target usage in original plan.

Monitor water levels and determine if recycling and reuse of materials meet expectations.

Monitor and evaluate additional sustainability goals for project including the following:

- Building specific process, energy-efficient systems, and equipment.
- Indoor water risers and outdoor irrigation systems.

REFERENCES AND RESOURCES

Published

ASHRAE. 2002. *ASHRAE Guideline 14-2002, Measurement of Energy and Demand Savings*. Atlanta: American Society of Heating, Refrigerating and Air-Conditioning Engineers, Inc.

ASHRAE. 2005. *ASHRAE Guideline 0-2005, The Commissioning Process*. Atlanta: American Society of Heating, Refrigerating and Air-Conditioning Engineers, Inc.

FEMP. 2008. *M&V Option A Detailed Guidelines*. Washington, DC: U.S. Department of Energy, Federal Energy Management Program.

Leaman, A., B. and Bordass. 1993. Building design, complexity and manageability. *Facilities*, Vol. 11.

Zagreus, L., C. Huizenga, E. Arens, and D. Lehrer. 2004. Listening to the occupants: A Web-based indoor environmental quality survey. *Indoor Air 2004* 14(suppl 8):65–74.

Online

ASHRAE Building eQ
    www.buildingeq.com

Center for the Built Environment, Occupant Indoor Environmental Quality Survey
    www.cbe.berkeley.edu/RESEARCH/survey.htm

Euporean Commission, BUILD UP program
    www.buildup.eu/

von Paumgartten, P. *Existing Buildings Hold the Key*. Alliance for Sustainable Built Environments.www.awarenessintoaction.com/whitepapers/how-existing-buildings-high-performing-green-leed-certified.html (28 Sep. 2010).

The Federal Energy Management Program Continuous Commissioning (SM) Guidebook
www1.eere.energy.gov/femp/program/om_guidebook.html
International Performance Measurement and Verification Protocol
www.evo-world.org
M&V Guidelines for Federal Energy Projects, Version 3.0
http://mnv.lbl.gov/keyMnVDocs/femp
Option B: Methods by Technology
www.energyautomation.com/pdfs/ipmvp-vol2.pdf
Usable Buildings Trust
www.usablebuildings.co.uk
U.S. Department of Energy, Federal Energy Management Program Guidelines
www1.eere.energy.gov/femp/pdfs/mv_guidelines.pdf

REFERENCES
AND RESOURCES

These listings do not necessarily imply endorsement or agreement by ASHRAE or the authors with the information contained in the documents.

BOOKS AND SOFTWARE PROGRAMS

ACGIH. 1999. *Bioaerosols: Assessment and Control.* J. Nacher, ed. Cincinnati, Ohio: American Conference of Governmental Industrial Hygienists. www.acgih.org.

AGCC. 1994. *Applications Engineering Manual for Direct-Fired Absorption.* Washington, DC: American Gas Cooling Center.

Adler, A., J.E.Armstrong, S.K. Fuller, G.B. Guy, M. Kalin, A. Karolides, M. Lelek, B.C. Lippiatt, J. Macaluso, G. Spencer, H.A. Walker, and P. Waier. 2002. *Green Building: Project Planning & Cost Estimating,* 2d ed. Kingston, MA: RS Means.

AIA. 1996. *Environmental Resource Guide.* J. Demkin, ed. American Institute of Architects. New York: John Wiley & Sons, Inc.

AIA. 2006. *Guidelines for Design and Construction of Health Care Facilities.* Washington, DC: American Institute of Architects.

Alvarez, S., E. Dascalaki, G. Guarracino, E. Maldonado, S. Sciuto, and L. Vandaele. 1998. *Natural Ventilation of Buildings—A Design Handbook.* F. Allard, ed. London: James & James Science Publishers Ltd.

Argiriou, A., A. Dimoudi, C.A. Balaras, D. Mantas, E. Dascalaki, and I. Tselepidaki. 1996. Passive Cooling of Buildings. M. Santamouris and A. Asimakopoulos, eds. London: James & James Science Publishers Ltd.

ARI. 1997. *ARI STANDARD 275-97, Standard for Application of Sound Rating Levels of Outdoor Unitary Equipment.* Arlington, VA: Air-Conditioning and Refrigeration Institute.

Arthus-Bertrand, Y. 2001. *Earth from Above: 365 Days.* New York: Harry N. Abrams.

Arthus-Bertrand, Y. 2002. *Earth From Above.* New York: Harry N. Abrams.

ASHRAE. 1975. *ASHRAE Standard 90-75, Energy Conservation in New Building Design.* Atlanta: American Society of Heating, Refrigerating and Air-Conditioning Engineers, Inc.

ASHRAE. 1988. *Active Solar Heating Systems Design Manual.* Atlanta: American Society of Heating, Refrigerating and Air-Conditioning Engineers, Inc.

ASHRAE. 1995. *Commercial/Institutional Ground-Source Heat Pump Engineering Manual.* Atlanta: American Society of Heating, Refrigerating and Air-Conditioning Engineers, Inc.

ASHRAE. 1996. *ASHRAE Guideline 1-1996, The HVAC Commissioning Process.* Atlanta: American Society of Heating, Refrigerating and Air-Conditioning Engineers, Inc.

ASHRAE. 1998. *Fundamentals of Water System Design.* Atlanta: American Society of Heating, Refrigerating and Air-Conditioning Engineers, Inc.

ASHRAE. 1999. *ANSI/ASHRAE/IESNA Standard 90.1-1999, Energy Standard for Buildings Except Low-Rise Residential Buildings.* Atlanta: American Society of Heating, Refrigerating and Air-Conditioning Engineers, Inc.

ASHRAE. 2000. *ANSI/ASHRAE Standard 52.2-1999, Method of Testing General Ventilation Air-Cleaning Devices for Removal Efficiency by Particle Size.* Atlanta: American Society of Heating, Refrigerating and Air-Conditioning Engineers, Inc.

ASHRAE. 2000. Interpretation IC-62-1999-30 (August) of *ANSI/ASHRAE Standard 62-1999, Ventilation for Acceptable Indoor Air Quality.* Atlanta: American Society of Heating, Refrigerating and Air-Conditioning Engineers, Inc.

ASHRAE. 2002. *ASHRAE Guideline 14-2002, Measurement of Energy and Demand Savings.* Atlanta: American Society of Heating, Refrigerating and Air-Conditioning Engineers, Inc.

ASHRAE. 2003. *HVAC Design Manual for Hospitals and Clinics.* Atlanta: American Society of Heating, Refrigerating and Air-Conditioning Engineers, Inc.

ASHRAE. 2004. *Advanced Energy Design Guide for Small Office Buildings.* Atlanta: American Society of Heating, Refrigerating and Air-Conditioning Engineers, Inc.

ASHRAE. 2004. *ANSI/ASHRAE Standard 55-2004, Thermal Environmental Conditions for Human Occupancy.* Atlanta: American Society of Heating, Refrigerating and Air-Conditioning Engineers, Inc.

ASHRAE. 2004. *ANSI/ASHRAE/IESNA Standard 90.1-2004, Energy Standard for Buildings Except Low-Rise Residential Buildings.* Atlanta: American Society of Heating, Refrigerating and Air-Conditioning Engineers, Inc.

ASHRAE. 2005. *ASHRAE Handbook—Fundamentals.* Atlanta: American Society of Heating, Refrigerating and Air-Conditioning Engineers, Inc.

ASHRAE. 2005. *ASHRAE Guideline 0-2005, The Commissioning Process.* Atlanta: American Society of Heating, Refrigerating and Air-Conditioning Engineers, Inc.

ASHRAE. 2006. *ANSI/ASHRAE/IESNA Standard 100-2006, Energy Conservation in Existing Buildings*. Atlanta: American Society of Heating, Refrigerating and Air-Conditioning Engineers, Inc.

ASHRAE. 2006. *Advanced Energy Design Guide for Small Retail Buildings*. Atlanta: American Society of Heating, Refrigerating and Air-Conditioning Engineers, Inc.

ASHRAE. 2007. *ASHRAE Handbook—HVAC Applications*. Atlanta: American Society of Heating, Refrigerating and Air-Conditioning Engineers, Inc.

ASHRAE. 2007. *ASHRAE Guideline 1.1-2007, HVAC&R Technical Requirements for the Commissioning Process*. Atlanta: American Society of Heating, Refrigerating and Air-Conditioning Engineers, Inc.

ASHRAE. 2007. *ASHRAE Guideline 13-2007, Specifying Direct Digital Control Systems*. Atlanta: American Society of Heating, Refrigerating and Air-Conditioning Engineers, Inc.

ASHRAE. 2007. *ANSI/ASHRAE Standard 62.1-2007, Ventilation for Acceptable Indoor Air Quality*. Atlanta: American Society of Heating, Refrigerating and Air-Conditioning Engineers, Inc.

ASHRAE. 2007. *ANSI/ASHRAE/IESNA Standard 90.1-2007, Energy Standard for Buildings Except Low-Rise Residential Buildings*. Atlanta: American Society of Heating, Refrigerating and Air-Conditioning Engineers, Inc.

ASHRAE. 2007. *ANSI/ASHRAE Standard 90.2-2007, Energy Efficient Design of Low-Rise Residential Buildings*. Atlanta: American Society of Heating, Refrigerating and Air-Conditioning Engineers, Inc.

ASHRAE. 2008. *ASHRAE Handbook—HVAC Systems and Equipment*. Atlanta: American Society of Heating, Refrigerating and Air-Conditioning Engineers, Inc.

ASHRAE. 2009. *ASHRAE Handbook—Fundamentals*. Atlanta: American Society of Heating, Refrigerating and Air-Conditioning Engineers, Inc.

ASHRAE. 2009. *ANSI/ASHRAE/USGBC/IES Standard 189.1-2009, Standard for the Design of High-Performance Green Buildings*. Atlanta: American Society of Heating, Refrigerating and Air-Conditioning Engineers, Inc.

ASHRAE. 2009. *The ASHRAE Guide for Buildings in Hot and Humid Climates*. Atlanta: American Society of Heating, Refrigerating and Air-Conditioning Engineers, Inc.

ASHRAE. 2009. *Indoor Air Quality Guide: Best Practices for Design, Construction and Commissioning*. Atlanta: American Society of Heating, Refrigerating and Air-Conditioning Engineers, Inc.

ASHRAE. 2010. *ASHRAE Handbook—Refrigeration*. Atlanta: American Society of Heating, Refrigerating and Air-Conditioning Engineers, Inc.

ASHRAE. 2010. *ANSI/ASHRAE Standard 62.1-2010, Ventilation for Acceptable Indoor Air Quality*. Atlanta: American Society of Heating, Refrigerating and Air-Conditioning Engineers, Inc.

ASHRAE. 2010. *ANSI/ASHRAE Standard 62.2-2010, Ventilation and Acceptable Indoor Air Quality in Low-Rise Residential Buildings*. Atlanta: American Society of Heating, Refrigerating and Air-Conditioning Engineers, Inc.

ASHRAE. 2010. *ANSI/ASHRAE/IES Standard 90.1-2010, Energy Standard for Buildings Except Low-Rise Residential Buildings*. Atlanta: American Society of Heating, Refrigerating and Air-Conditioning Engineers, Inc.

ASPE. 1998. *Domestic Water Heating Design Manual*. Chicago: American Society of Plumbing Engineers.

ASTM. 1998. *ASTM D 6245-1998: Standard Guide for Using Indoor Carbon Dioxide Concentrations to Evaluate Indoor Air Quality and Ventilation*. Philadelphia: American Society for Testing and Materials.

Baker, N. 1995. *Light and Shade: Optimising Daylight Design*. European Directory of sustainable and energy efficient building. London: James & James Science Publishers Ltd.

Balcomb, J.D. 1984. *Passive Solar Heating Analysis: A Design Manual*. Atlanta: American Society of Heating, Refrigerating and Air-Conditioning Engineers, Inc.

Bauman, F.S., and A. Daly. 2003. *Underfloor Air Distribution Design Guide*. Atlanta: American Society of Heating, Refrigerating and Air-Conditioning Engineers, Inc.

Beckman, W., S.A. Klein, and J.A. Duffie. 1977. *Solar Heating Design*. New York: John Wiley & Sons, Inc.

BRESCU, BRE. 1999. *Natural Ventilation for Offices Guide and CD-ROM*. ÓBRE on behalf of the NatVent Consortium, Garston, Watford, UK, March.

CEC. 2001. *Nonresidential Alternative Calculations Methods Manual*. Sacramento, CA: California Energy Commission.

CEC. 2002. *Part II: Measure Analysis and Life-Cycle Cost 2005, California Building Energy Standards*, P400-02-012. Sacramento, CA: California Energy Commission.

Crosbie, M.J., ed. 1998. *The Passive Solar Design and Construction Handbook*. Steven Winter Associates. New York: John Wiley & Sons, Inc.

Del Porto, D., and C. Steinfeld. 1999. *The Composting Toilet System Book*. New Bedford, MA: The Center for Ecological Pollution Prevention.

Dorgan, C., and J.S. Elleson. 1993. *Design Guide for Cool Thermal Storage*. Atlanta: American Society of Heating, Refrigerating and Air-Conditioning Engineers, Inc.

Elleson, J.S. 1996. *Successful Cool Storage Projects: From Planning to Operation*. Atlanta: American Society of Heating, Refrigerating and Air-Conditioning Engineers, Inc.

EPA. 2010. *Guide to Purchasing Green Power*. Washington, DC: U.S. Environmental Protection Agency. www.epa.gov/grnpower/buygreenpower/guide.htm.

Esty, D.C., and A.S. Winston. 2006. *Green to Gold: How Smart Companies Use Environmental Strategy to Innovate, Create Value, and Build Competitive Advantage*. New Haven, CT: Yale University Press.

Evans, B. 1997. Daylighting design. *In Time-Saver Standards for Architectural Design Data.* New York: McGraw-Hill.

FEMP. 2008. *M&V Option A Detailed Guidelines.* Washington, DC: U.S. Department of Energy, Federal Energy Management Program.

Givoni, B. 1994. *Passive and Low Energy Cooling of Buildings.* New York: Van Nostrand Reinhold.

Gottfried, D. (Continuous updating). *Sustainable Building Technical Manual, Green Building Design, Construction, and Operations.* Washington, DC: U.S. Green Building Council. www.usgbc.org.

Hawkin, P., A. Lovins, and L.H. Lovins. 1999. *Natural Capitalism.* Little Brown.

Henning, H-M., ed. 2004. *Solar Assisted Air-Conditioning in Buildings—A Handbook For Planners.* Wien: Springer-Verlag.

Heubach, J.G., J.C. Montgomery, W.C. Weimer, and J.H. Heerwagen. 1995. Pacific Northwest Laboratory. *Assessing the Human and Organizational Impacts of Green Buildings.*

Houghton, J.T., G.J. Jenkins, and J.J. Ephraums, eds. 1990. *Climate Change: The IPCC Scientific Assessment.* Intergovernmental Panel on Climate Change. New York: Cambridge UP.

Howell, J., R. Bannerot, and G. Vliet. 1982. *Solar-Thermal Energy Systems: Analysis and Design.* New York: McGraw-Hill.

IECC. 2006. *International Energy Conservation Code.* Available from www.icc-safe.org.

IESNA. 2000. *Lighting Handbook.* New York: Illuminating Engineering Society of North America.

IESNA. 1998. *RP-33-99, Lighting for Exterior Environments; RP-20-98, Lighting for Parking Facilities.* New York: Illuminating Engineering Society of North America. www.iesna.org.

IESNA. 2002. Proposed revisions to ASHRAE/IESNA Standard 90.1-2001. Illuminating Engineering Society of North America, Energy Management Committee.

Kavanaugh, S.P., and K. Rafferty. 1997. *Ground-Source Heat Pumps: Design of Geothermal Systems for Commercial and Institutional Buildings.* Atlanta: American Society of Heating, Refrigerating and Air-Conditioning Engineers, Inc.

Kinsley, M. 1997. *Economic Renewal Guide.* Colorado: Rocky Mountain Institute.

Klein, S., and W. Beckman. 2001. *F-Chart Software.* The F-Chart Software Company., Madison, WI. www.fchart.com.

Kowalski, W.J. 2006. *Aerobiological Engineering Handbook: Airborne Disease and Control Technologies.* New York: McGraw-Hill.

Kreith, F., and J. Kreider. 1989. *Principles of Solar Engineering*, 2d ed. Wasington, DC: Hemisphere Pub.

Ludwig, A. 1997. *Builder's Greywater Guide and Create an Oasis with Greywater.* Oasis Design.

Macher, J., ed. 1999. *Bioaerosols: Assessment and Control.* Cincinatti, Ohio: American Conference of Governmental Industrial Hygenists.

McIntosh, I.B.D., C.B. Dorgan, and C.E. Dorgan. 2002. *ASHRAE Laboratory Design Guide*. Atlanta: American Society of Heating, Refrigerating and Air-Conditioning Engineers, Inc.

Mendler, S.F., and W. Odell. 2000. *HOK Guidebook to Sustainable Design*. New York: John Wiley & Sons, Inc.

NADCA. *General Specifications for the Cleaning of Commercial Heating, Ventilating and Air Conditioning Systems*. Washington, DC: National Air Duct Cleaners Association.

Nattrass, B., and M. Altomare. *The Natural Step for Business; Wealth, Ecology and the Evolutionary Corporation*. Gabriola Island, British Columbia: New Society Publishers.

NBI. 1998. *Gas Engine Driven Chillers Guideline*. Fair Oaks, CA: New Buildings Institute and Southern California Gas Company. www.newbuildings.org/downloads/guidelines/GasEngine.pdf.

NBI. 2001. *Advanced Lighting Guidelines*. Fair Oaks, CA: New Buildings Institute. www.newbuildings.org/lighting.htm.

NFPA. 2004. *NFPA 45, Standard on Fire Protection for Laboratories using Chemicals*. Quincy, MA: National Fire Protection Association.

NFPA. 2005. *NFPA 99, Standard for Health Care Facilities*. Quincy, MA: National Fire Protection Agency.

NRC. *Photovoltaic Systems Design Manual*. Ottawa, Ontario, Canada: Natural Resources Canada, Office of Coordination and Technical Information.

NRC. RETScreen (Renewable Energy Analysis Software). Natural Resources Canada, Energy Diversification Research Laboratory, Ottawa, Ontario, Canada. www.retscreen.net.

NSF. 2000. *NSF/ANSI 5-2000e: Water Heaters, Hot Water Supply Boilers, and Heat Recovery Equipment*. Ann Arbor, MI: National Sanitation Foundation.

PG&E. 2002. *Codes and Standards Enhancement Report, Code Change Proposal for Cooling Towers*. California: Pacific Gas & Electric.

Savitz, A.W., and K. Weber. 2006. *The Triple Bottom Line*. San Fransisco: John Wiley & Sons, Inc.

Schaffer, M. 2005. *Practical Guide to Noise and Vibration Control for HVAC Systems, Second Edition*. Atlanta: American Society of Heating, Refrigerating and Air-Conditioning Engineers, Inc.

SMACNA. 2005. *HVAC Duct Construction Standards,* 3d ed., Chapter 1. Chantilly, VA: Sheet Metal and Air Conditioning Contractors National Association, Inc.

SMACNA. 2007. *IAQ Guidelines for Occupied Buildings Under Construction*. Chantilly, VA: Sheet Metal and Air Conditioning National Association, Inc.

Spitler, J. 2009. *Load Calculation Applications Manual*. Atlanta: American Society of Heating, Refrigerating and Air-Conditioning Engineers, Inc.

Taylor, S., P. Dupont, M. Hydeman, B. Jones, and T. Hartman. 1999. *The CoolTools Chilled Water Plant Design and Performance Specification Guide*. San Francisco, CA: PG&E Pacific Energy Center.

Trane. 1994. *Water-Source Heat Pump System Design*. Trane Applications Engineering Manual, SYS-AM-7. Lacrosse, WI: Trane Company.

Trane Co. 1999. *Trane Applications Engineering Manual, Absorption Chiller System Design*, SYS-AM-13. Lacrosse, WI: Trane Company.

Trane. 2000. *Multiple-Chiller-System Design and Control Manual*. Lacrosse, WI: Trane Company.

Trane. 2005. *Trane Installation, Operation, and Maintenance Manual: Series R$^{®}$ Air-Cooled Rotary Liquid Chillers*, RTAA-SVX01A-EN. Lacrosse, WI: Trane Company. www.trane.com/Commercial/Uploads/Pdf/1060/RTAA-SVX01A-EN_09012005.pdf.

UG. 2010. *Wise Energy Guide*. Chatham, ON: Union Gas. www.uniongas.com/residential/energyconservation/education/wiseEnergyGuide/WEG_Booklet_Web_Final.pdf/.

USGBC. 2001. *LEED Reference Guide, Version 2.0*. Washington, DC: U.S. Green Building Council.

USGBC. 2005. *LEED Reference Guide, Version 2.2*. Washington, DC: U.S. Green Building Council.

USGBC. 2009. *LEED 2009 for New Construction and Major Renovations*. Washington, D.C.: U.S. Green Building Council.

USGBC. 2009. *LEED 2009 Green Building Operations and Maintenance*. Washington, DC: U.S. Green Building Council.

Watson, D., and G. Buchanan. 1993. *Designing Healthy Buildings*. Washington, DC: American Institute of Architects.

Watson, R.D., and K.S. Chapman. 2002. *Radiant Heating and Cooling Handbook*. New York: McGraw-Hill.

Watsun. 1999. *WATSUN-PV—A computer program for simulation of solar photovoltaic systems, User's Manual and Program Documentation*, Version 6.1. Watsun Simulation Laboratory, University of Waterloo, Ontario, Canada.

Wolverton, B.C. 1996. *How to Grow Fresh Air: 50 Plants That Purify Your Home of Office*. Baltimore, MD: Penguin Books.

PERIODICALS AND REPORTS

Adamson, R. 2002. Mariah Heat Plus Power$^{™}$ Packaged CHP, applications and economics. Second Annual DOE/CETC/CANDRA Workshop on Microturbine Applications, January 17–18, University of Maryland, College Park, MD.

Afify, R. 2008. Designing VRF systems. *ASHRAE Journal* 50(6):52–55.

Alliance for Sustainable Built Environments. Existing buildings hold the key. www.awarenessintoaction.com/whitepapers/how-existing-buildings-high-performing-green-leed-certified.html.

Andersson, L.O., K.G. Bernander, E. Isfält, and A.H. Rosenfeld. 1979. Storage of heat and coolth in hollow-core concrete slabs. Swedish experience and application to large, American style buildings. Second International Conference on

Energy Use and Management, Lawrence Berkeley National Laboratory, LBL-8913.

ASHE. 2002. Green healthcare design guidance statement. American Society of Healthcare Engineering, Chicago.

Aynur, T., Y. Hwang, and R. Radermacher. 2008. Experimental evaluation of the ventilation effect on the performance of a VRV system in cooling mode—Part I: Experimental evaluation. *HVAC&R Research* 14(4):615–30.

Aynur, T., Y. Hwang, and R. Radermacher. 2008. Simulation evaluation of the ventilation effect on the performance of a VRV system in cooling mode—Part II: Simulation evaluation. *HVAC&R Research* 14(5):783–95.

Bahnfleth, W.P., and W.S. Joyce. 1994. Energy use in a district cooling system with stratified chilled water storage. *ASHRAE Transactions* 100(1):1767–78.

Balaras, C.A. 1995. The role of thermal mass on the cooling load of buildings. An overview of computational methods. *Energy and Buildings* 24(1):1–10.

Balaras, C.A., E. Dascalaki, P. Tsekouras, and A. Aidonis. 2010. High solar combi systems in Europe. *ASHRAE Transactions* 116(1).

Balaras, C.A., H.-M. Henning, E. Wiemken, G. Grossman, E. Podesser, and C.A. Infante Ferreira. 2006. Solar cooling—An overview of european applications and design guidelines. *ASHRAE Journal* 48(6):14–22.

Bauman, F., and T. Webster. 2001. Outlook for underfloor air distribution. *ASHRAE Journal* 43(6):18–25.

Beebe, J.M. 1959. Stability of disseminated aerosols of *Pastuerella tularensis* subjected to simulated solar radiations at various humidities. *Journal of Bacteriology* 78:18–24.

Bisbee, D. 2003. Pulse-power water treatment systems for cooling towers. Energy Efficiency & Customer Research & Development, Sacramento Municipal Utility District.

Braun, J.E. 1990. Reducing energy costs and peak electrical demand through optimal control of building thermal storage. *ASHRAE Transactions* 96(2):876–88.

CBE. 2007. Summary report: Control strategies for mixed-mode buildings. Center for Built Environment, Berkeley, California. www.cbe.berkeley.edu/research/pdf_files/SR_MixedModeControls2007.pdf.

CEC. 1996. Source energy and environmental impacts of thermal energy storage. Completed by Tabors, Caramanis & Assoc. for the California Energy Commission.

CEC. 2004. Monitoring the energy-use effects of cool roofs on California commercial buildings, CEC PIER study report. California Energy Commission.

CEC. 2005. Title 24 2005 Reports and Proceedings. California Energy Commission. www.energy.ca.gov.

Cendón, S.F. 2009. *New and Cool: Variable Refrigerant Flow Systems*. AIArchitect.

CETC. 1996a. Technical report on Bentall Corporation Crestwood 8 C-2000 Building. CANMET Energy Technology Centre, Natural Resources Canada, Ottawa, Ontario, Canada.

CETC. 1996b. Technical report on Green on the Grand C-2000 Building. CAN-MET Energy Technology Centre, Natural Resources Canada, Ottawa, Ontario, Canada.

CFR. 1995. Energy conservation voluntary performance standards for commercial and multi-family high rise residential buildings; mandatory for new federal buildings. Code of Federal Regulations 10 CFR 435, Office of the Federal Register, National Archives and Records Administration, Washington, DC.

Chapman, K.S. ASHRAE RP-907, Final report, Development of design factors for the combination of radiant and convective in-space heating and cooling systems. American Society of Heating, Refrigerating and Air-Conditioning Engineers, Inc., Atlanta.

Chapman, K.S. 2002. Development of radiation transfer equation that encompasses shading and obstacles. *ASHRAE Transactions* 108(2):997–1004.

Chapman, K.S., J.M. DeGreef, and R.D. Watson. 1997. Thermal comfort analysis using BCAP for retrofitting a radiantly heated residence. *ASHRAE Transactions* 103(1):959–65.

Chapman, K.S., J.E. Howell, and R.D. Watson. 2001. Radiant panel surface temperature over a range of ambient temperatures. *ASHRAE Transactions* 107(1):383–89.

Chapman, K.S., J. Rutler, and R.D. Watson. 2000. Impact of heating systems and wall surface temperatures on room operative temperature fields. *ASHRAE Transactions* 106(1):506–14.

Cho, Y.I., S. Lee, and W. Kim. 2003. Physical water treatment for the mitigation of mineral fouling in cooling-tower water applications. *ASHRAE Transactions* 109(1):346–57.

Coad, W.J. 1999. Conditioning ventilation air for improved performance and air quality. *Heating/Piping/Air Conditioning*, September.

Corbett, T. *Green Buildings and Risk*. www.aepronet.org/ge/no43.html.

Darlington, A., M. Chan, D. Malloch, C. Pilger, and M.A. Dixon. 2000. The biofiltration of indoor air: Implications for air quality. *Indoor Air 2000* 10(1):39–46.

Darlington, A.B., J.F. Dat, and M.A. Dixon. 2001. The biofiltration of indoor air: Air flux and temperature influences the removal of toluene, ethylbenzene, and xylene. *Environ Sci Technol* 35(1):240–46.

Darlington, A., M.A. Dixon, and C. Pilger. 1998. The use of biofilters to improve indoor air quality: The removal of toluene, TCE, and formaldehyde. *Life Support Biosph Sci* 5(1):63–69.

DeGreef, J.M., and K.S. Chapman. 1998. Simplified thermal comfort evaluation of MRT gradients and power consumption predicted with the BCAP methodology. *ASHRAE Transactions* 104(1):1090–97.

Deru, M., and P. Torcellini. 2007. *Source Energy and Emissions Factors for Energy Use in Buidlings.* Technical Report NREL/TP_550-38617, National Renewable Energy Laboratory, Golden, CO.

DOE. *The International Performance Measurement and Performance Protocol* (IPMPP). U.S. Department of Energy, Office of Energy Efficiency and Renewable Energy, Washington, DC.

DOE. 2002. *Energy Tip Sheet #1*, May. U.S. Department of Energy, Office of Industrial Technologies, Energy Efficiency, and Renewable Energy, Washington, DC.

DOE. 2005. Energy impact of commercial building controls and performance diagnostics: Market characterization, energy impact of building faults and energy savings potential. U.S. Department of Energy, Washington, DC.

DOE. 2006. Solar buildings. Transpired air collectors ventilation preheating. DOE/GO-102001-1288, U.S. Department of Energy, Washington, DC.

Duffy, G. 1992. Thermal storage shifts to saving energy. *Eng. Sys.* July/August: 32–38.

EDR. 2009. *Chilled Water Plant Design Guide*. Energy Design Resources. www.energydesignresources.com/Resources/Publications/DesignGuidelines/tabid/73/articleType/ArticleView/articleId/422/Default.aspx.

Ehrt, D., M. Carl, T. Kittel, M. Muller, and W. Seeber. 1994. High performance glass for the deep ultraviolet range. *Journal of Non-Crystalline Solids* 177:405–19.

EIA. Table 10.8, Photovoltaic cell and module shipments by type, trade, and prices, 1982–2008. U.S. Energy Information Administration. www.eia.doe.gov/aer/txt/stb1008.xls.

El-Adhami, W., S. Daly, and P.R. Stewart. 1994. Biochemical studies on the lethal effects of solar and artificial ultraviolet radiation on *Staphylococcus aureus*. *Arch Microbiol* 161:82–87.

Ellis, M.W., and M.B. Gunes. 2002. Status of fuel cell systems for combined heat and power applications in buildings. *ASHRAE Transactions* 108(1):1032–44.

EPA. Storm water management for construction activities. EPA document No. EPA-8320R-92-005. U.S. Environmental Protection Agency, Washington, DC.

EPA. Toxicity Characteristic Leaching Procedure (TCLP) Test, 40 CFR Part 260. U.S. Environmental Protection Agency, Washington, DC.

EPA. Universal Waste Rule, 40 CFR Part 260. U.S. Environmental Protection Agency, Washington, DC.

EPA. 2010. *How to Conserve Water and Use It Effectively*. U.S. Environmental Protection Agency, Washington, DC. www.epa.gov/owow/nps/chap3.html.

EPIA. 2010. 2014 global market outlook for photovoltaics until 2014. European Photovoltaic Industry Association. www.epia.org/fileadmin/EPIA_docs/public/Global_Market_Outlook_for_Photovoltaics_until_2014.pdf.

Epoch Times. 2009. Water efficiency a priority for green buildings. www.theepochtimes.com/n2/content/view/17751.

Erickson, D.C., and M. Rane. 1994. Advanced absorption cycle: Vapor exchange GAX. ASME International Absorption Heat Pump Conference, January 19–21, New Orleans, LA.

ESTIF. 2010 Solar thermal markets in Europe—Trends and market statistics 2009. www.estif.org/fileadmin/estif/content/market_data/downloads/2009%20solar_thermal_markets.pdf.

EU. 2008. Climate change: Commission welcomes final adoption of Europe's climate and energy package. Europa press release IP/08/1998, European Union, Brussels.

European Comission. 2002. Energy Performance of Buildings, Directive 2002/91/EC of the European Parliament and of the Council. Official Journal of the European Communities, Brussels.

Fagan, D. 2001. A comparison of storage-type and instantaneous heaters for commercial use. *Heating/Piping/Air Conditioning Engineering*, April.

Fernandez, R.O. 1996. Lethal effect induced in *Pseudomonas aeruginosa* exposed to ultraviolet-A radiation. *Photochem & Photobiol* 64(2):334–39.

Fiorino, D.P. 1994. Energy conservation with stratified chilled water storage. *ASHRAE Transactions* 100(1):1754–66.

Fiorino, D.P. 2000. Six conservation and efficiency measures reducing steam costs. *ASHRAE Journal* 42(2):31–39.

Galuska, E.J. 1994. Thermal storage system reduces costs of manufacturing facility (Technology Award case study). *ASHRAE Journal*, March.

Gansler, R.A., D.T. Teindil, and T.B. Jekel. 2001. Simulation of source energy utilization and emissions for HVAC systems. *ASHRAE Transactions* 107(1):39–51.

Goetzler, W. 2007. Variable refrigerant flow systems. *ASHRAE Journal* 46(4): 24–31.

Goss, J.O., L. Hyman, and J. Corbett. 1996. Integrated heating, cooling and thermal energy storage with heat pump provides economic and environmental solutions at California State University, Fullerton. *Proceedings of the EPRI International Conference on Sustainable Thermal Energy Storage, Minneapolis, MN,* pp. 163–67.

Grondzik, W.T. 2001. The (mechanical) engineer's role in sustainable design: Indoor environmental quality issues in sustainable design. HTML presentation available at www.polaris.net/~gzik/ieq/ieq.htm.

Guz, K. 2005. Condensate water recovery. *ASHRAE Journal* 47(6):54–56.

GWEC. 2010. Global wind 2009 report. Global Wind Energy Council, Brussels, Belgium. www.gwec.net/index.php?id=167.

Hayter, S., P. Torcellini, and R. Judkoff. 1999. Optimizing building and HVAC systems. *ASHRAE Journal* 41(12):46–49.

Heerwagen, J. 2001. Do green buildings enhance the well being of workers? www.edcmag.com.

Hilten, R.N. 2005. An analysis of the energetics and stormwater mediation potential of greenroofs. Master's thesis, University of Georgia, Athens, GA.

HPAC. 2004. Innovative grocery store seeks LEED certification. *HPAC Engineering* 27:31.

ICC. 2010. International green construction code™, Public version 1.0. International Code Council, Washington, DC.

IUVA. 2005. General guideline for UVGI air and surface disinfection systems. IUVA-G01A-2005 International Ultraviolet Association, Ayr, Ontario, Canada, www.iuva.org.

Jarnagin, R.E., R.M. Colker, D. Nail, and H. Davies. 2009. ASHRAE Building eQ. *ASHRAE Journal* 51(12):18–21.

Jones, B., and K.S. Chapman. ASHRAE RP-657, Final report, Simplified method to factor mean radiant temperature (MRT) into building and HVAC system design. American Society of Heating, Refrigerating and Air-Conditioning Engineers, Inc., Atlanta.

Kainlauri, E.O., and M.P. Vilmain. 1993. Atrium design criteria resulting from comparative studies of atriums with different orientation and complex interfacing of environmental systems. *ASHRAE Transactions* 99(1):1061–69.

Keeney, K.R., and J.E. Braun. 1997. Application of building precooling to reduce peak cooling requirements. *ASHRAE Transactions* 103(1):463–69.

Kintner-Meyer, M., and A.F. Emery. 1995. Optimal control of an HVAC system using cold storage and building thermal capacitance. *Energy and Buildings* 23:19–31.

Kosik, W.J. 2001. Design strategies for hybrid ventilation. *ASHRAE Journal* 43(10):18–19, 22–24.

Larsson, N., ed. 1996. *C-2000 Program Requirements*. Natural Resources Canada, Ottawa, Ontario, Canada.

Lawrence, T.M. 2004. Demand-controlled ventilation and sustainability. *ASHRAE Journal* 46(12):117–21.

Lawrence, T. 2008. Selecting CO_2 criteria for space monitoring. *ASHRAE Journal* 50(12):18–27.

Lawrence, T., J. Perry, and P. Dempsey. 2010. Capturing condensate by retrofitting AHUs. *ASHRAE Journal* 52(1):48–54.

Lawson, 1988. Computer facility keeps cool with ice storage. *HPAC*, August.

Leaman, A., and B. Bordass. 1993. Building design, complexity and manageability. *Facilities*, Vol. 11.

LeMar, P. 2002. Integrated energy systems (IES) for buildings: A market assessment. Final report by Resource Dynamics Corporation for Oak Ridge National Laboratory, Contract No. DE-AC05-00OR22725.

Mathaudhu, S.S. 1999. Energy conservation showcase. *ASHRAE Journal* 41(4):44–46.

McDonough, W. 1992. The Hannover principles: Design for sustainability. Presentation, Earth Summit, Brazil.

McKurdy, G., S.J. Harrison, and R. Cooke. Preliminary evaluation of cylindrical sky-lights. 23rd Annual Conference of the Solar Energy Society of Canada Inc., Vancouver, British Columbia.

Morris, W. 2003. The ABCs of DOAS. *ASHRAE Journal* 45(5).

Mumma, S.A. 2001. Designing dedicated outdoor air systems. *ASHRAE Journal* 43(5):28–31.

NREL. 2010. NREL highlights utility green power leaders. NREL press release NR-1910, National Renewable Energy Laboratory, Golden, CO.

O'Neal, E.J. 1996. Thermal storage system achieves operating and first-cost savings (Technology Award case study). *ASHRAE Journal* 38(4).

Palmer, J.M., and K.S. Chapman. 2000. Direct calculation of mean radiant temperature using radiant intensities. *ASHRAE Transactions* 106(1):477–86.

Patnaik, V. 2004. Experimental verification of an absorption chiller for BCHP applications. *ASHRAE Transactions* 110(1):503–507.

Pearson, F. 2003. ICR 06 Plenary Washington. *ASHRAE Journal* 45(10).

Rautiala, S., S. Haatainen, H. Kallunki, L. Kujanpaa, S. Laitinen, A. Miihkinen, M. Reiman, and M. Seuri. 1999. Do plants in office have any effect on indoor air microorganisms? *Indoor Air 99: Proceedings of the 8th International Conference on Indoor Air Quality and Climate, Edinburgh, Scotland*, pp. 704–709.

Reindl, D.T., R.A. Gansler, and T.B. Jekel. 2001. Simulation of source energy utilization and emissions for HVAC systems. *ASHRAE Transactions* 107(1):39–51.

Reindl, D.T., D.E. Knebel, and R.A. Gansler. 1995. Characterising the marginal basis source energy and emissions associated with comfort cooling systems. *ASHRAE Transactions* 101(1):1353–63.

Rosenbaum, M. 2002. A green building on campus. *ASHRAE Journal* 44(1):41–44.

Rosfjord, T., T. Wagner, and B. Knight. 2004. UTC microturbine CHP product development and launch. Presented at the 2004 DOE/CETC Annual Workshop on Microturbine Applications, January 20–22, Marina del Rey, CA.

Ruud, M.D., J.W. Mitchell, and S.A. Klein. 1990. Use of building thermal mass to offset cooling loads. *ASHRAE Transactions* 96(2):820–29.

Ryan, W.A. 2003. CHP: The concept. Midwest CHP Application Center, Energy Resources Center, University of Illinois, Chicago. www.chpcentermw.org/presentations/WI-Focus-on-Energy-Presentation-05212003.pdf

Scheatzle, David. ASHRAE RP-1140 Final report, Establishing a base-line data set for the evaluation of hybrid HVAC systems. American Society of Heating, Refrigerating and Air-Conditioning Engineers, Inc., Atlanta.

Schell, M., and D. Int-Hout. 2001. Demand control ventilation using CO_2. *ASHRAE Journal* 43(2):18–24.

Stack, A., J. Goulding, and J.O. Lewis. Shading systems: Solar shading for the European climates. DG TREN, Brussels, Belgium. http://erg.ucd.ie/down_thermie.html.

Svensson C., and S.A. Aggerholm. 1998. Design tool for natural ventilation. ASHRAE IAQ 1998 Conference, October 24–27, New Orleans, LA.

Taylor, S. 2002. Primary-only vs. primary-secondary variable flow chilled water systems. *ASHRAE Journal* 44(2):25–29.

Taylor, S.T. 2005. LEED and Standard 62.1. *ASHRAE Journal Sustainability Supplement*, September.

Taylor, S., and J. Stein. 2002. Balancing variable flow hydronic systems. *ASHRAE Journal* 44(10):17–24.

Torcellini, P.A., N. Long, and R. Judkoff. 2004. Consumptive water use for U.S. power production. *ASHRAE Transactions* 110(1):96–100.

Torcellini, P., S. Pless, M. Deru, B. Griffith, N. Long, and R. Judkoff. 2006. Lessons learned from case studies of six high-performance buildings. Technical report, NREL/TP-550-37542. National Renewable Energy Laboratory, Golden, CO.

Torcellini, P., N. Long, S. Pless, and R. Judkoff. 2005. Evaluation of the low-energy design and energy performance of the Zion National Park Visitor Center, NREL Report No. TP-550-34607. National Renewable Energy Laboratory, Golden, CO. www.eere.energy.gov/buildings/highperformance/research_reports.html.

Trane. 2000. Energy conscious design ideas—Air-to-air energy recovery. *Engineers Newsletter* 29(5).

Trane. *A Guide to Understanding ASHRAE Standard 62-2001*. Publication IAQ-TS-1, July. Trane Company, Lacrosse, WI. http://trane.com/commercial/issues/iaq/ashrae2001.asp.

USGBC. LEED-NC v 2.2 Rating System. U.S. Green Building Council, Washington, DC.

USGBC. 2009. LEED Version 3. U.S. Green Building Council, Washington, DC.

von Kempski, D. 2003. Air and well being—A way to more profitability. *Proceedings of Healthy Buildings 2003, Singapore*, pp. 248–354.

von Kempski, D. 2009. Going beyond green—green perception A paradigm change in IAQ for the well-being and health of the occupants. *Proceedings of Healthy Buildings 2009, Syracuse, New York*, paper 138.

von Paumgartten, P. *Existing Buildings Hold the Key*. Alliance for Sustainable Built Environments.www.awarenessintoaction.com/whitepapers/how-existing-buildings-high-performing-green-leed-certified.html (28 Sep. 2010).

Waterfall, P.H. 1998. *Harvesting Rainwater for Landscape Use*. http://ag.arizona.edu/pubs/water/az1052/.

Watson, R.D., K.S. Chapman, and L. Wiggington. 2001. Impact of dual utility selection on 305 m^2 (1000 ft^2) residences. *ASHRAE Transactions* 107(1):365–70.

Watson, R.D., K.S. Chapman, and J.M. DeGreef. 1998. Case study: Seven-system analysis of thermal comfort and energy use for a fast-acting radiant heating system. *ASHRAE Transactions* 104(1).

Waye, K.P., J. Bengtsson, R. Rylander, F. Hucklebridge, P. Evans, and A. Clow. 2002. Low frequency noise enhances cortisol among noise sensitive subjects during work performance. *Life Science* 70(7):745–58.

Webber, M.E. 2008. *Energy versus Water: Solving Both Crises Together*. Scientific American Special Editions. www.sehn.org/tccenergyversuswater.html.

Weiss, W., I. Bergmann, and G. Faninger. 2008. *Solar Heat Worldwide*. Solar Heat & Cooling Programme, International Energy Agency, Paris. www.iea-shc.org/publications/statistics/IEA-SHC_Solar_Heat_Worldwide-2008.pdf.

Weiss, W., and F. Mauthner. 2010. Solar heat worldwide—Markets and contribution to the energy supply 2008. www.iea-shc.org/publications/statistics/IEA-SHC_Solar_Heat_Worldwide-2010.pdf.

Zagreus, L., C. Huizenga, E. Arens, and D. Lehrer. 2004. Listening to the occupants: A Web-based indoor environmental quality survey. *Indoor Air 2004* 14(suppl 8):65–74.

WEB SITES

Advanced Buildings Technologies and Practices
www.advancedbuildings.org

AGORES—A Global Overview of Renewable Energy Sources (the official European Commission renewable energy information centre and knowledge gateway, with a global overview of RES)
www.agores.org

Air-Conditioning, Heating and Refrigeration Institute
www.ahrinet.org/

Alliance for Sustainable Built Environments
www.awarenessintoaction.com/whitepapers/how-existing-buildings-high-performing-green-leed-certified.html

Alliance to Save Energy
http://ase.org

American Council for an Energy-Efficient Economy
www.aceee.org

American Gas Association
www.aga.org

The American Institute of Architects
www.aia.org

American Society of Healthcare Engineering
www.ashe.org

American Society of Healthcare Engineering, *Green Guide for Health Care*
www.gghc.org

American Society of Plumbing Engineers
http://aspe.org

American Solar Energy Society
www.ases.org

American Wind Energy Association
www.awea.org
Architecture 2030 Challenge
www.architecture2030.org/
Architectural Energy Corporation
www.archenergy.com
Armstrong Intelligent Systems Solutions
www.armstrong-intl.com
ASHRAE
www.ashrae.org
ASHRAE Building eQ
www.buildingeq.com
ASHRAE Engineering for Sustainability
www.engineeringforsustainability.org/
ASHRAE Standard Project Committee 191
http://spc191.ashraepcs.org/
ASHRAE's Sustainability Roadmap
http://images.ashrae.biz/renovation/documents/sust_roadmap.pdf
ASHRAE TC 8.3, recently sponsored programs and presentations
http://tc83.ashraetcs.org/programs.html
Athena Institute
www.athenasmi.ca
BetterBricks
www.betterbricks.com
Building Energy Efficiency Research Project at the Department of Architecture, The University of Hong Kong
www.arch.hku.hk/research/beer/
Building for Environmental and Economic Sustainability (BEES)
www.bfrl.nist.gov/oae/software/bees.html
BuildingGreen
www.greenbuildingadvisor.com
Building Research Establishment Environmental Assessment Method (BREEAM®) rating program
www.breeam.org
California Debt & Investment Advisory Commission document
www.treasurer.ca.gov/cdiac/publications/p3.pdf
California Energy Commission
www.energy.ca.gov
California Energy Commission, Renewable Energy Program
www.energy.ca.gov/renewables/
The Canadian Renewable Energy Network
www.canren.gc.ca/

The Center for Health Design
   www.healthdesign.org
Center for the Built Environment, Occupant Indoor Environmental Quality Survey
   www.cbesurvey.org
Center of Excellence for Sustainable Development
   www.sustainable.doe.gov
Center of Excellence for Sustainable Development, Smart Communities Network
   www.smartcommunities.ncat.org
Centre for Analysis and Dissemination of Demonstrated Energy Technologies
   www.caddet-re.org
Collaborative for High Performance Schools
   www.chps.net
Cool Roof Rating Council
   www.coolroofs.org
DDC Online
   www.ddc-online.org
Dena
   www.dena.de/en/
Earth Energy Society of Canada
   www.earthenergy.ca/
ecoENERGY for Renewable Power
   www.ecoaction.gc.ca/ecoenergy-ecoenergie/power-electricite/index-eng.cfm
EN4M Energy in Commercial Buildings (software tool)
   www.eere.energy.gov/buildings/tools_directory/software.cfm/ID=299/
Energy Design Resources
   www.energydesignresources.com/publication/gd/
ENERGY STAR®
   www.energystar.gov
Energy Trust of Oregon
   www.energytrust.org
Europe's Energy Portal
   www.energy.eu/#renewable
European Biomass Association
   www.aebiom.org
European Biomass Industry Association
   www.eubia.org/about_biomass.0.html
Euporean Commission, BUILD UP program
   www.buildup.eu/
European Commission, Concerted Action Energy Performance of Buildings Directive
   www.epbd-ca.org
European Commission (DG TREN), SARA Project
   www.sara-project.net

European Photovoltaic Industry Association
www.epia.org
European Renewable Energy Centres Agency
www.eurec.be
European Solar Thermal Industry Federation
www.estif.org
European Wind Energy Association
www.ewea.org
EUROSOLAR—The European Association for Renewable Energies e.V.
www.eurosolar.org
F-Chart Software
www.fchart.com
The Federal Energy Management Program Continuous Commissioning (SM)
Guidebook
www1.eere.energy.gov/femp/program/om_guidebook.html
Geoexchange
www.geoexchange.org
Global Wind Energy Council
www.gwec.net
Green Building Advisor
www.greenbuildingadvisor.com
Green Energy In Europe
www.ecofys.com/
Green Globes
www.greenglobes.com
Green Roof Industry Information Clearinghouse and Database
www.greenroofs.com
GreenSpec® Product Guide
www.buildinggreen.com/menus/index.cfm
Green Venture
www.greenventure.on.ca
Hannover Principles
www.mindfully.org/Sustainability/Hannover-Principles.htm
Harvard University Office for Sustainability, Green Building Resource,
Design Phase Guide
www.green.harvard.edu/theresource/new-construction/design-phase/bidding-
construction/www.aepronet.org/ge/no43.html
Heat Pump Centre
www.heatpumpcentre.org
Heschong Mahone Group
www.h-m-g.com/projects/daylighting/projects-PIER.htm

Illuminating Engineering Society of North America
www.iesna.org
Intergovernmental Panel on Climate Change
www.ipcc.ch
International Code Council
www.iccsafe.org
International Energy Agency, Bioenergy
www.ieabioenergy.com
International Energy Agency, Photovoltaic Power Systems Programme
www.iea-pvps.org
International Energy Agency, Solar Heating And Cooling Programme
www.iea-shc.org
International Energy Agency, Task 38
www.iea-shc.org/task38
International Hydropower Association
www.hydropower.org
International Hydropower Association Fact Sheet
www.hydropower.org/downloads/F1_the_contribution_of_hydropower.pdf
International Living Building Institute, The Living Building Challenge V2.0
http://ilbi.org/the-standard/version-2-0
International Organization for Standardization family of 14000 standards,
www.iso.org/iso/en/iso9000-14000/index.html
International Performance Measurement and Verification Protocol
www.evo-world.org
International Solar Energy Society
www.ises.org
Irrigation Association
www.irrigation.org
Labs 21, Environmental Performance Criteria
www.labs21century.gov
Lawrence Berkeley National Laboratories
www.lbl.gov/
Lawrence Berkeley National Laboratories,
Environmental Energy Technologies Division
http://eetd.lbl.gov/
Lawrence Berkeley National Laboratory, Radiance
http://radsite.lbl.gov/radiance/HOME.html
Massachusetts State Building Code
www.mass.gov/bbrs/code.htm
Minnesota Sustainable Design Guide
www.sustainabledesignguide.umn.edu

Mondaq
    www.mondaq.com/canada/article.asp?articleid=23737
M&V Guidelines for Federal Energy Projects, Version 3.0.
    http://mnv.lbl.gov/keyMnVDocs/femp
National Building Controls Information Program
    www.buildingcontrols.org
National Hydropower Association
    www.hydro.org
National Oceanic and Atmospheric Administration
    www.noaa.gov
National Renewable Energy Laboratory
    www.nrel.gov
National Renewable Energy Laboratory, Building-Integrated PV
    www.nrel.gov/pv/building_integrated_pv.html
National Renewable Energy Laboratory, Buildings Research
    www.nrel.gov/buildings/
National Renewable Energy Laboratory, Solar Energy Research Facility
    www.nrel.gov/pv/facilities_serf.html
Natural Resources Canada, Commercial Buildings Incentive Program
    http://nrcan.gc.ca/evaluation/reprap/2001/cbip-pebc-eng.php
Natural Resources Canada, EE4 Commercial Buildings Incentive Program
    http://canmetenergy-canmetenergie.nrcan-rncan.gc.ca/eng/software_
    tools/ee4.html
Natural Resources Canada, Office of Energy Efficiency
    http://oee.nrcan.gc.ca/commercial/newbuildings.cfm?attr=20
Natural Resources Canada, RETScreen
    (software for renewable energy analysis)
    www.retscreen.net.
The Natural Step
    www.naturalstep.org
New Buildings Institute
    www.newbuildings.org
New York's Battery Park City Authority
    www.batteryparkcity.org/page/index_battery.html
New York City Department of Design and Construction, Sustainable Design
    www.nyc.gov/html/ddc/html/design/sustainable_home.shtml
National Oceanic and Atmospheric Administration
    www.noaa.gov
North Carolina Cooperative Extension Service, Water Quality and Waste Management
    www.bae.ncsu.edu/programs/extension/publicat/wqwm
North Carolina Solar Center, DSIRE
    www.dsireusa.org/

Oak Ridge National Laboratory, Bioenergy Feedstock Information Network
    http://bioenergy.ornl.gov/

Oikos: Green Building Source
    www.oikos.com

Option B: Methods by Technology
    www.energyautomation.com/pdfs/ipmvp-vol2.pdf

Photovoltaic Resource Site
    www.pvpower.com

QuikWater, High Efficiency Direct Contact Water Heaters
    www.quikwater.com

RealWinWin, Inc.
    www.realwinwin.com

Regional Climate Data
    www.wrcc.dri.edu/rcc.html

Renewable Energy Deployment Initiative
    www.nrcan.gc.ca/redi

Rising Sun Enterprises
    www.rselight.com

Rocky Mountain Institute
    www.rmi.org

Savings by Design
    www.savingsbydesign.com

School of Photovoltaic and Renewable Energy Engineering,
    University of New South Wales
    www.pv.unsw.edu.au

Sheet Metal and Air Conditioning Contractors' National Association
    www.smacna.org

SkyCalc
    www.energydesignresources.com/resource/129/

Solar Energy Industries Association
    www.seia.org

Spirx Sarco Design of Fluid Systems, Steam Learning Module
    www.spiraxsarco.com/learn/modules.asp

Sustainable Building Challenge
    www.iisbe.org/

Sustainable Building Guidelines
    www.ciwmb.ca.gov/GreenBuilding/Design/Guidelines.htm

Sustainable Buildings Industry Council
    www.sbicouncil.org

Sustainable Communities Network
    www.sustainable.org

Sustainable Sources
www.greenbuilder.com
Sustainable Sources Bookstore
bookstore.greenbuilder.com/index.books
Texas Manual on Rainwater Harvesting
www.twdb.state.tx.us/publications/reports/
rainwaterharvestingmanual_3rdedition.pdf
"Tips for Daylighting with Windows"
http://windows.lbl.gov/pub/designguide/designguide.html
Tool for the Reduction and Assessment of Chemical and Other Environmental Impacts (TRACI)
www.epa.gov/nrmrl/std/sab/traci/
Trane Company
www.trane.com
Tri-State Generation and Transmission Association, Inc.
http://www.tristategt.org/
Usable Buildings Trust
www.usablebuildings.co.uk
U.S. Department of Energy, Energy Efficiency and Renewable Energy
www.eere.energy.gov/
U.S. Department of Energy, Energy Efficiency and Renewable Energy, Biomass program
www1.eere.energy.gov/biomass
U.S. Department of Energy, Energy Efficiency and Renewable Energy, Biomass program, Resources for Consumers Web page
www1.eere.energy.gov/biomass/for_consumers.html
U.S. Department of Energy, Energy Efficiency and Renewable Energy, Energy Savers
www.energysavers.gov/
U.S. Department of Energy, Energy Efficiency and Renewable Energy, Zero Energy Buildings
http://zeb.buildinggreen.com
U.S. Department of Energy, Federal Energy Management Program
www.eere.energy.gov/femp
U.S. Department of Energy, Federal Energy Management Program Guidelines
www1.eere.energy.gov/femp/pdfs/mv_guidelines.pdf
U.S. Department of Energy, High Performance Buildings Institute
www1.eere.energy.gov/buildings/commercial_initiative/
U.S. Energy Information Administration, Commercial Building Energy Consumption Survey
www.eia.doe.gov/emeu/cbecs/

U.S. Environmental Protection Agency
   www.epa.gov
U.S. Environmental Protection Agency, Building Energy Analysis Tool, eQuest
   www.energydesignresources.com/resource/130/
U.S. Environmental Protection Agency, Green Chemistry
   www.epa.gov/greenchemistry/
U.S. Environmental Protection Agency, Water Sense Program
   http://epa.gov/watersense/
U.S. Green Building Council
   www.usgbc.org
U.S. Green Building Council, Leadership in Energy and Environmental Design, Gold building, Hewlett Foundation
   www.usgbc.org/Docs/Certified_Projects/Cert_Reg67.pdf
U.S. Green Building Council, Leadership in Energy and Environmental Design, Green Building Rating System™
   www.usgbc.org/DisplayPage.aspx?CategoryID=19
U.S. Green Building Council, Regional Priority Credit Listing
   www.usgbc.org/DisplayPage.aspx?CMSPageID=1984
The Whole Building Design Guide
   www.wbdg.org
World Meteorological Organization, World Radiation Data Centre
   http://wrdc-mgo.nrel.gov/
The World's Water
   www.worldwater.org

Terms, Definitions, and Acronyms

Δ	=	change or change in
ΔT	=	change or change in temperature
A/C	=	air-conditioning
ACGIH	=	American Conference of Governmental Industrial Hygienists
AHU	=	air-handling unit
AIA	=	American Institute of Architects
ANSI	=	American National Standards Institute
ASHRAE	=	American Society of Heating, Refrigerating and Air-Conditioning Engineers
BAS	=	building automation system
BEES	=	Building for Environmental and Economic Sustainability
BF	=	ballast factor
BIM	=	building information modeling
BOMA	=	Building Owners and Managers Association
BREEAM®	=	Building Research Establishment Environmental Assessment Method
brownfield	=	real estate property that is, or potentially is, contaminated
Btu	=	British thermal unit
C	=	centigrade (temperature scale)
C-2000	=	Canadian Integrated Design Process program
CAN	=	Canada
CAV	=	constant air volume
CBE	=	Center for the Built Environment
CBIP	=	Commercial Buildings Incentive Program
CCHP	=	combined cooling, heating, and power
CDT	=	cold deck temperature
CFC	=	chlorofluorocarbon
cfm	=	cubic feet per minute
CFR	=	current facility requirements
charette	=	intense effort to solve a design problem within a limited time
CHP	=	combined heating and power
CHW	=	chilled water
condenser	=	device to dissipate (get rid of) excess energy in A/C systems
COP	=	coefficient of performance
CRAC	=	computer room air conditioners

CxA	=	commissioning authority
daylighting	=	lighting (of a building) using daylight directly or indirectly from the sun
D/B	=	design/build
dB(A)	=	A-weighting
D/B/B	=	design/bid/build
DDC	=	direct digital control
DE	=	district energy
DG	=	distributed generation
DHW	=	domestic hot water
DOAS	=	dedicated outdoor air system
DOE	=	U.S. Department of Energy
DX	=	direct expansion
E	=	ventilation effectiveness
EA	=	energy and atmosphere
ECM	=	electronically commutated motor
EDC	=	environmental design consultant
EDG	=	engine-driven generator
ENERGY STAR®	=	a government-backed program/rating system that helps consumers achieve superior energy efficiency
energy source	=	on-site energy in the form in which it arrives at or occurs on a site (e.g., electricty, gas, oil, or coal)
energy resource	=	raw energy that (1) is extracted from the earth (wellhead or mine mouth), (2) is used in the generation of the energy source delivered to a building site (e.g., coal used to generate electricty), or (3) occurs naturally and is available at a site (e.g., solar, wind, or geothermal energy)
enthalpy	=	the thermodynamic property of a system resulting from the combination of observable properties (per unit mass) thereof: namely, the sum of internal energy and flow work; flow work is the product of volume and specific mass (i.e., energy transmitted into or out of a system or transmitted across a system boundary)
entropy	=	a measure of the molecular disorder of a system, such that the more mixed a system is, the greater its entropy, and the more orderly or unmixed a system is, the lower its entropy
E&O	=	errors and omissions
EPA	=	U.S. Environmental Protection Agency
EPBD	=	Directive on the Energy Performance of Buildings
EPC	=	energy performance certificate
EU	=	European Union
F	=	fahrenheit (temperature scale)
F-chart	=	method of calculating solar fraction
fenestration	=	window treatment
GBC	=	Green Building Challenge
GHG	=	greenhouse gas
gpf	=	gallons per fixture
gpm	=	gallons per minute
GSHP	=	ground-source heat pump
Guideline	=	within ASHRAE, a document similiar to a Standard but less strict on consensus
HCFC	=	hydrochlorofluorocarbons
HEPA	=	high-efficiency particulate air

HID	=	high-intensity discharge
HVAC&R	=	heating, ventilating, air-conditioning, and refrigerating
hybrid ventilation	=	combination of natural and mechanical outdoor air ventilation
hydronic	=	pertaining to liquid flow
IAQ	=	indoor air quality
IDP	=	integrated design process
IEA	=	International Energy Agency
IEC	=	indirect evaporative cooling
IEQ	=	indoor environmental quality
IES	=	Illuminating Engineering Society of North America
insolation	=	entry into a building of solar energy
IPCC	=	Intergovernmental Panel on Climate Change
IPMVP	=	International Performance Measurement and Verification Protocol
K	=	Kelvin or absolute (temperature scale)
kW	=	kilowatt
kWh	=	kilowatt-hour
kWR	=	refrigeration cooling capacity in kW
latent load	=	thermal load due strictly to effects of moisture
LCA	=	life-cycle assessment
LCCA	=	life-cycle cost analysis
LCEA	=	life-cycle environmental assessment
LD	=	liquid desiccant
LED	=	light-emitting diode
LEED	=	Leadership in Energy and Environmental Design
leeward	=	the downwind side—or side the wind blows away from
L/f	=	liters per fixture
low-E	=	low emissivity
LPD	=	lighting power density
LP	=	liquefied petroleum
L/s	=	liters per second (airflow and water flow)
MAT	=	mixed air temperature
media	=	energy forms distributed within a building, usually air, water, or electricity
MEP	=	minimum energy performance
MERV	=	minimum efficiency reporting value
mhp	=	motor horsepower
MNEBC	=	Model National Energy Code for Buildings
MRT	=	mean radiant temperature
M&V	=	measurement and verification
NADCA	=	National Air Duct Cleaning Association
NC	=	noise criteria
NO_x	=	oxides of nitrogen
NOAA	=	National Oceanic Atmospheric Administration
NR	=	natural refrigeration
NREL	=	National Renewable Energy Laboratory
NZEB	=	net zero energy building
OC	=	on center
O&M	=	operations and maintenance
OPR	=	Owner's Project Requirements
OSHA	=	Occupational Safety and Health Administration
P3	=	public-private partnership
parametric analysis	=	in situations where multiple parameters affect an outcome, an

		analysis that determines the magnitude of one or more parameter's impact alone on that outcome
plug loads	=	loads (electrical or thermal) from equipment plugged into electrical outlets
POTW	–	publicly owned treatment works
precooling	=	cooling done prior to the time major cooling loads are anticipated
PV	=	photovoltaic
R (as in R-100)	=	resistivity to thermal heat transfer
RC	=	room criteria
renewables	=	energy resources that have definite, although sometimes unknown, quantity limitations
RES	=	renewable energy source
RFP	=	request-for-proposal
ROI	=	return on investment
sensible load	=	thermal load due to temperature but not moisture effects
sg	=	specific gravity
SHW	=	space hot water
skin	=	building envelope
SMACNA	=	Sheet Metal and Air Conditioning Contractors National Association
SR	=	synthetic refrigeration
SS	=	sustainable sites
Standard	=	within ASHRAE, a document that defines properties, processes, dimensions, materials, relationships, concepts, nomenclature, or test methods for rating purposes
sustainability	=	providing for the needs of the present without detracting from the ability to fulfill the needs of the future
TC	=	technical committee (an ASHRAE group with a common interest in a particular technical subject)
TCLP	=	toxicity characteristic leaching procedure
TES	=	thermal energy storage
Title 24	=	slang for California's Building Energy Efficiency Standards (Title 24, Part 6 of the California State Building Code)
ton	=	cooling capacity, equal to 12,000 Btu/h
TRACI	=	Tool for the Reduction and Assessment of Chemical and Other Environmental Impacts
USGBC	=	U.S. Green Building Council
VAV	=	variable-air-volume
VE	=	value engineering
VFD	=	variable-frequency drive
VOC	=	volatile organic compound
VRF	=	variable refrigeration flow
WE	=	water efficiency
windward	=	the upwind side, or side the wind blows toward

INDEX

N

national primary drinking water regulations (NPDWR) 346
night precooling 172–74
nonrenewable energy 4, 8–9, 279–80, 302

O

Owner's Project Requirements 47–48, 60–61, 64–66, 68, 76–77, 84–85, 89, 102, 121–29, 133, 135, 380, 382, 404, 417, 456

P

parametric analysis 83, 163, 456
phase
    warranty 123, 418
photovoltaic (PV) 53, 102, 118, 144, 234, 280, 289, 438, 456
plug loads 79, 83, 165, 177–78, 331, 455
precooling 171–76, 275, 440, 455
publicly owned treatment works (POTW) 224, 342, 456

R

rainwater harvesting 102, 365–67, 385
rating methods
    BREEAM® (Building Research Establishment Environmental Assessment Method) 23, 43, 444, 453
    Leadership in Energy and Environmental Design (LEED) 9, 23–24, 62, 93, 102, 124–25, 129, 131–32, 134, 137–40, 142–47, 149–51, 153–54, 190,–91, 194, 238, 240, 376, 381, 384–85, 393, 402, 404, 406, 412, 439, 455
recommissioning 56, 136
renewable energy 4, 9, 21, 51, 53–54, 58, 61, 64, 83, 90, 92, 102, 118–19, 143–44, 152–53, 165, 192, 249, 251, 279–82, 289, 290, 294, 296, 299, 302–303, 394, 420–21, 434, 456

renewable energy sources 51, 279, 281, 294, 296, 299, 310
request-for-proposal (RFP) 404
retrocommissioning 123, 389–90, 419–21, 423
room air temperature 378

S

sensible load 30, 37, 39, 205
skin (see also *building envelope*) 163–64, 168, 379, 456
space
    heating 161, 215, 231, 235, 243, 247, 250–52, 281–83, 286, 295, 299
    humidity 399
    pressure 391
    temperature 39, 215, 375, 380, 390
space/water heating 254
stormwater 4, 55, 69, 94, 98–99, 100, 120, 137, 139, 140, 142, 365–66, 385, 439
supervisory control and data acquisition (SCADA) 378
sustainability 4–6, 14, 17, 19, 23, 43, 68, 80, 84–85, 89, 91, 100, 107, 125, 130, 143, 145, 157, 181, 340, 394, 404, 408, 426, 440, 453, 456

T

temperature and pressure (T&P) 360–61
thermal
    ANSI/ASHRAE Standard 55, Thermal Environmental Conditions for Human Occupancy 19, 29, 39, 42, 118–119, 150, 156, 183, 195, 378
    breaks 29
    comfort 19, 56–57, 62, 65, 90, 146, 149–50, 170, 175, 182–84, 305, 325, 378–79, 392, 423–24
    efficiency 32, 197, 222, 235, 241, 249, 295, 298
    energy 27, 31, 72, 104, 173, 174, 188, 222, 224, 228–29, 231–33, 248, 264–65, 269, 282, 285, 395, 457
    energy storage (TES) 72, 104, 173–74,